When Justice Meets Politics

STUDIES IN POLITICAL TRANSITION

Edited by Klaus Bachmann

Vol. 2

PETER LANG
EDITION

Klaus Bachmann
Thomas Sparrow-Botero
Peter Lambertz

When Justice Meets Politics

Independence and Autonomy of *Ad Hoc* International Criminal Tribunals

PETER LANG
EDITION

Bibliographic Information published by the Deutsche Nationalbibliothek
The Deutsche Nationalbibliothek lists this publication in the Deutsche Nationalbibliografie; detailed bibliographic data is available in the internet at http://dnb.d-nb.de.

The publication was financially supported by the Polish National Research Council (Narodowe Centrum Nauki) and the University of Social Sciences and Humanities, Warsaw, Poland.

Cover Design:
© Olaf Gloeckler, Atelier Platen, Friedberg

ISSN 2191-3307
ISBN 978-3-631-63356-4

Peter Lang Edition is an imprint of Peter Lang GmbH

www.peterlang.de

Table of Contents

Introduction

International criminal tribunals are very specific institutions. They are courts and as such their main task is to administer justice and to judge the perpetrators of the most horrendous crimes of our times, mostly war crimes, crimes against humanity, and genocide. In this respect, they are instruments of justice, like any other criminal court.

But at the same time, international criminal tribunals are international institutions, created by states, alliances of states, or international organisations. They are therefore subject to power politics, political influences and international bargaining; their final institutional design and the content of their rules is the result of compromises between states. By creating specific tribunals, states try to anticipate possible outcomes of the prosecutors' actions and the judges' verdicts; they introduce institutional, financial and legal safeguards in order to prevent the tribunal from infringing their interests.

International criminal tribunals are special. In contrast to municipal courts, they are not embedded in a stable, traditional and commonly known legal system; they cannot resort to coercion without seeking the assistance of a state, and they do not have efficient means to compel hesitant governments and state agencies to comply with their orders. Much of their actual power comes from the prestige and the support of the public, which they often enjoy.

In the past international criminal tribunals have often been instruments of victor's justice, but this, surprisingly, did not always prevent them from gaining acceptance within the society they were established for. The International Military Tribunal in Nuremberg, which judged the leadership of the Third Reich between 1945 and 1946, was established by the Allied Powers, which had defeated and conquered Germany, and was uniquely staffed with prosecutors and judges from Britain, France, the United States, and the Soviet Union. Its jurisdiction restricted all investigations to the crimes committed by Germany. Any attempt to elucidate other crimes, like the fate of Polish officers killed at Katyń by death squads of the Soviet special services, was immediately curtailed. The Nuremberg Tribunal proceeded for less than a year and meted out an extraordinary high percentage of death penalties. Nevertheless, as long as it operated, it enjoyed the support and acclaim of an overwhelming majority of the German population.[1] Other examples

1 During the Nuremberg Tribunal's proceedings, German public opinion was very much in favor of the trials; an overwhelming majority of Germans regarded the trials as fair and the defendants as guilty. The harsh convictions were welcomed and seen as justified. This changed dramatically a few years later when polls revealed that a majority of Germans now deemed the Nuremberg trials biased and the accused innocent. For the first polls, conducted by US pollsters, see: Merritt, Anna and Richard (eds): Public Opinion in occupied Germany. The OMGUS surveys 1945-49. Urbana, Chicago, London 1970 and Merritt, Anna and Richard (eds): Public Opinion In semi-

of victor's justice were less successful. The Leipzig Tribunal and the attempts of the Entente powers after World War I to judge key politicians and generals of Germany and Turkey for war crimes (committed by Germany) and mass atrocities against the Armenian population (committed by Turkey) led to legal and political quagmires and are today mostly regarded as failures.[2]

The Cold War and the frequent blockade of the United Nations Security Council prevented any consensus for creating new international tribunals. Dictators, perpetrators of gross human rights violations, were usually protected by the super power to whose sphere of influence the country in question belonged, or they were judged according to the laws of their countries once they lost power. In many cases, they were able to retain enough power and influence to secure a negotiated transition and immunity for the post-transition period. Therefore, even the third wave of democratisation[3] saw only a few cases of retributive justice directed against fallen autocratic rulers. Many of the South American and African transitions were accompanied by examples of restorative rather than retributive justice, by "truth commissions", like the South African "Truth and Reconciliation Commission", and by numerous amnesties, which secured stability and peaceful transitions in exchange for the impunity of perpetrators.[4]

The end of the century brought a retributive turnaround to this current. Truth commissions and national amnesties, often supported by the international community, became the exception to the now increasingly retributive rule. When in the early 1990s the entities of the Socialist Federation of Yugoslavia broke away from the center, and cruel and bloody conflicts over territory and minorities followed, the United Nations Security Council decided to create the International Criminal Tribunal for the former Yugoslavia in The Hague, in order to "prosecute persons responsible for serious violations of international humanitarian law."[5] A year later, after the smoldering Rwandan civil war had

---

sovereign Germany. The HICOG surveys 1949-1955. Urbana, Chicago, London 1980. For the later polls, carried out by the Allensbach Institute for Public Opinion, see: Noelle, Elisabeth; Neumann, Erich Peter: Jahrbuch der öffentlichen Meinung 1947–1955. Allensbach 1956, 200-220.

2 Bass, Gary Jonathan: Stay the Hand of Vengeance. The Politics of War Crimes Tribunals. Princeton and Oxford 2002, 58-146.

3 We use the term according to Huntington, Samuel: The Third Wave of Democratisation in the late Twentieth Century. University of Oklahoma Press 1992.

4 On the South African TRC see, among others: Hayner, Priscilla: Unspeakable Truth: Confronting State Terror and Atrocity. New York: Routledge 2001 (and 2011 for the second edition)

5 United Nations Security Council Resolutions 955 (8.11.1994) and 827 (25.5.1993), establishing the ICTR and the ICTY. See: Repertoire of the Practice of the UN Security Council: www.un.org/en/sc/repertoire/subsidiary_organs/international_tribunals.shtml

escalated into large-scale massacres, the Security Council created the International Criminal Tribunal for Rwanda. Both tribunals are based on the same principles, have a similar legal basis, share the same appeals chamber, and, until 2003, also shared the same chief prosecutor.

Both tribunals differ considerably from their predecessor, the Nuremberg Tribunal. They comprise international prosecutors and judges from all over the world, except from countries which fall under the tribunals' jurisdictions. There are therefore no Serbian, Croatian, Bosnian or Slovenian judges at the ICTY, and the ICTR does not include a single judge from Rwanda.[6] Both tribunals are financially supported by the United Nations, but also, to a lesser degree, by direct contributions from governments and non-governmental organisations. Both tribunals, unlike the Nuremberg Tribunal, operate outside of their territory jurisdiction and far away from the theatre of the conflicts they have to deal with. Both tribunals are also formally far more independent than the Nuremberg Tribunal could ever pretend to be. Despite all these features, both tribunals have frequently been the subject of harsh criticism accusing them of meting out victor's justice rather than impartial verdicts, of being "instruments of the superpowers" and "manipulated by states".[7]

Trials were denounced as "travesties of justice", judges were accused of disdain for the victims, and court decisions were criticized as "biased". It is impossible to summarize the whole debate about the ICTY and the ICTR, which ranges from political science, law, and history to anthropology and philosophy. There is one crucial element of this debate which touches upon the core of this book: the issue of autonomy, independence, and impartiality of these tribunals. According to their statutory provisions, both tribunals are independent and the decision-making procedures reflect these legal guarantees. The Security Council appoints the chief prosecutor for a fixed term, during which she or he (two of the chief prosecutors were women) cannot be dismissed. Judges are appointed by a special procedure within the United Nations, either as *ad limitem* judges (with a three-year term, which then expires) or as permanent judges, with no possibility to sanction them for incommodious verdicts.[8]

---

6 However, there are Rwandan citizens working as prosecutors in the OTP of the ICTR, as Hassan Bubacar Jallow revealed to Klaus Bachmann in July 2012 during an interview at the ICTR in Arusha.

7 Laughland, John: Travesty. The Trial of Slobodan Milošević and the Corruption of International Justice. London, Ann Arbour: Pluto Press 2007.

8 In order to avoid any influence from the UN bureaucracy or member states on judges, the judges are directly paid from the general UN budget. Their income does not suffer from cuts of the tribunal budget. Klaus Bachmann's interviews with Anees Ahmed, chief of chambers at the ICTR and ICTR president Vagn Joensen in July 2012 in Arusha.

But claims concerning partiality of both tribunals are not so much rooted in statutory provisions or direct external influences on verdicts. Rather, they address the actual outcomes of the proceedings, which show a strong statistical imbalance to the detriment of specific groups. Due to the pressure from the Rwandan government, which time and again threatened to suspend cooperation with the ICTR, the subsequent chief prosecutors of the tribunal refrained from prosecuting crimes committed by soldiers of the Rwandan Patriotic Front, which in 1994 invaded the country from Uganda and terminated the ongoing genocide of the Tutsi population. Since all defendants at the ICTR were Hutu connected to the interim government installed after the coup d'état in 1994, the ICTR actually prosecutes only one side of the conflict. By restricting the temporal jurisdiction of the ICTR to 1994, the Security Council prevented it from investigating earlier and more recent violations of international humanitarian law.

In the case of the ICTY, the imbalance between former conflict parties is less striking, since the prosecution managed to indict suspects from all ethnic communities. But there is a strong dual imbalance concerning the percentage of suspects. More Serbs than members of any other ethnic community were indicted. This fact is undisputed, but is often justified by alleging a disproportionally high number of crimes committed by Serbs. Second, a simple statistical analysis of the indictment / verdict ratio reveals that the likelihood of an acquittal of a Serb defendant is dramatically lower than the chance of acquittal for members of any other ethnic community involved in the war. The ratio is particularly low for Albanian suspects from Kosovo, a fact that has been publicly admitted by Carla Del Ponte in her recently published memoirs.[9]

The question of international criminal tribunals' autonomy is much broader than the issues of bias and impartiality suggest. It can be approached from an institutionalist perspective – by assessing the place and role of an international tribunal in international relations. This involves the question of whether (and if at all, in how far) international criminal tribunals can be regarded as independent participants in international relations, which can shape and change states' preferences, act independently and – in extreme cases – against the interest of states. Are they norm-creators and norm-enforcers, whose influence is strong enough to constrain states' actions and change the balance of power in international relations, or should we rather regard them as agents following the orders of their state–principals, enabling them to lower transaction costs in

---

9 Del Ponte, Carla: Madame Prosecutor. Confrontations with Humanity's Worst Criminals and the Culture of Impunity. Milan: Feltrinelli 2008, 273-304.

international bargaining.[10] When tribunals become awkward players, are they sidelined by states, marginalized, and ignored? Or are they capable of launching their own political initiatives and of achieving outcomes which run opposite to state preferences? We answer these questions in the first part of our book by analyzing the decision-making process between the European Union and its member states on the one hand and the policy of the ICTY toward Croatia and Serbia on the other hand. In which situation can we attribute actorness to the ICTY, and when does the tribunal merely act as an instrument of the European Union and its member states? The emphasis of the analysis lies on the chief prosecutor, since he or she is the actual agenda setter of the tribunal's internal decision-making process. If he does not submit an indictment to a trial judge for confirmation, the tribunal remains passive. Neither judges nor trial chambers are entitled to substitute him. Hence, when it comes to the political initiative of a tribunal, the role of the chief prosecutor is crucial.

We designed a roadmap to answer these questions. As a first step, we delved into the documents of two key EU institutions: the Council of the European Union, which is the main decision-making and coordinating body in the EU; and the European Commission, the Union's executive body. A thorough search of these institutions' documents for the years 1997 to 2011 allowed us to see where and when changes occurred in the European Union's policy towards Croatia and Serbia's obligation to comply with the ICTY. For the purpose of this study, a policy change or policy shift refers to the moment when the EU applies, in writing or in practice, a new condition for EU accession, withdraws or ignores an old one, or when it specifies an existing one by adding new elements to it.

With the shifts clearly marked, the second step aimed at finding the reasons behind each policy change and the player (an EU body, the ICTY or Serbia or

10 In International Relations Theory, there has been a long discussion about the role international organisations play with respect to states. According to some theories, they are able to shape and alter states' preferences and influence policy outcomes, while according to others, they are merely forums which enable states to reduce the cost of negotiation processes. The concept of cost, which lies behind this notion, is not limited to money, but also includes efforts to be undertaken by states. The "cost reduction" argument is quite consensual among theorists. It means, for example, that states use the United Nations bodies because they make it easier to negotiate with many other states than individually organizing bi- or multinational negotiations. There is no consensus among theorists regarding the question of whether international organisations are more than just an instrument states use for negotiations; they could be fully fledged actors of international relations which can conduct their own policies and cause states to change their policies. Whether channeling negotiations through international organisations can create different outcomes compared to negotiations carried out between the same partners outside an international organisation is also unclear

Croatia) that triggered it in the first place. Both primary sources (interviews) and secondary sources (books, EU reports, academic books and essays) were used to shed light on the process.

The research material was complemented by academic essays and reports by think tanks such as the Institute for Security Studies, the European Council on Foreign Relations, the Institute for War and Peace Reporting and the International Crisis Group; with reports by influential NGOs, such as Human Rights Watch; and with information from the media, in particular The New York Times, The Guardian, the BBC, European Voice, The Economist, Time Magazine, CNN and El País, media from the region and reports in the Dutch and the Belgian press, which frequently followed events at the ICTY and the ICTR up close and often relied on inside information and leaks from anonymous informers. In order to double-check information from the secondary sources and get first-hand information about policy shifts, we backed our research with a series of interviews.

The novelty of this book lies not only in the application of approaches from political science and sociology to research material which has mostly been analyzed by lawyers. At the core of this book is additional research material which until now has not been used for such a purpose. For part I and II, and, to a lesser extent, for part III, we used a large number of interviews with actors and observers – prosecutors, judges, witnesses, observers, experts and expert-witnesses, many of which provided completely new insights into the relations between the tribunals and states, but also (especially in part II) into the internal mechanisms, customs and habits of the ICTR and the ICTY. These insights cannot be retrieved from public or even confidential documents.

In part I, these interviews shed light on the reasons behind the policy shifts and allow us to understand what triggered them or who the most influential player in the process was. In part II, they contribute to a better understanding of the interaction between external factors and the decision making process of the Prosecution and the trial chambers. In part II, they helped us to understand the way, judges conceive of their roles and duties when deliberating about judgments and sentences and how they understand the duty to contribute to stabilisation and reconciliation in Rwanda and the former Yugoslavia.

National courts enforce norms that are based on societal values and a social consensus of what is good and bad. Prosecutors and judges in municipal courts can easily apply these values in the interpretation of legal norms. They have grown up in their society, they know the legal system and local traditions, and they often intuitively feel what is acceptable in their society and what is not. They act in the framework of a legal system which has developed over years, decades, and centuries. The risk of mismatch between their verdicts and social expectations is relatively low and the possibility of referring to earlier case law, decisions of higher courts, and constitutional provisions reduces this risk even further.

Judges in international criminal tribunals, on the other hand, are deprived of this kind of social and historical embeddedness. The statutes and the rules of procedure and evidence of the ICTR and the ICTY are the results of bargaining between those UN member states with the strongest interest in the future actions of the tribunals, and as such they emanate from compromises. There is no embedding, everything is created for the first time, and when the judges work together in the trial chambers, they often realize how different the same standard, the same event, the same evidence may be interpreted by a fellow judge who comes from a different culture or legal system. Reaching a compromise between judges does not necessarily solve the problem, since the constituency of an international criminal tribunal consists at the same time of the international community and the countries affected by the tribunal's jurisdiction. This is where different concepts of justice, different standards of proof, and different notions of reconciliation clash. Judges from municipal courts behave like musicians who perform in front of a familiar and predictable audience. International judges do not have such a comfort – they often do not even know who their audience is, what it expects from them, and how it may react to their decisions. This opens international tribunals to external influence. The discretion every judge, no matter if municipal or international, enjoys, is constrained by the need to ensure legitimacy for his verdicts. It is the pursuit of legitimacy that makes judges vulnerable (and receptive) to external influences, whether political or social. We trace this influence in the second part of this book by applying the media-analytical concept of framing, well known and widely used in public opinion research. In this last part of the book, we test in how far judges accept, ignore or reject popular narratives about the conflict they are supposed to solve. We retrieve these narratives from government statements, human rights campaigns, influential international non-governmental organisations, and from prominent media outlets, and compare their frames to the ones used in indictments and judgments.

A tribunal may not enjoy autonomy with respect to states, it may not be able to undertake its own political initiatives, and it may be completely dependent on state cooperation and deprived of any impact on states' preferences, but it may still be able to safeguard its internal independence and the full integrity of its decision-making process. We can imagine a tribunal that is deprived of any attributes of actorness on the international level, but still capable of conducting fair and expeditious trials and issuing verdicts which meet the highest legal standards. This is to a large part dependent on the tasks a tribunal is given by its founders. Are prosecutors and judges expected to be concerned with justice and nothing but justice? Are there additional objectives that the tribunal is supposed to achieve, and do they belong to the legal, the juridical, or to the political realm? If there are additional objectives, are prosecutors and judges inclined to serve these aims, and do they internalize or reject them? How do these additional tasks affect indictments, verdicts, and the decision-making process within the tribunal? When addressing these issues, we focus on the notion of reconciliation, which is crucial for answering this question, since it has pushed the tribunals into the realm of politics by burdening them with non-legal tasks which are partly contradictory to the aims and objectives of justice in national (rather than international) settings and in municipal law. How can tribunals simultaneously fulfill the task of "doing justice and punishing perpetrators" and "contribute to the maintenance of peace" or "provide reconciliation", as several United Nations Security Council resolutions required, when the punishment of perpetrators outrages the communities that take sides with these perpetrators? How can acquittals lead to reconciliation when acquittals enrage the communities that identify with the victims? This is one of the dilemmas the ICTY was (and partly still is) confronted with. Can a distant tribunal, whose actions can hardly be followed by ordinary citizens, provide reconciliation to a society when its actions are restricted to one side of conflict? This was the dilemma of the ICTR. How do prosecutors and judges apply the notion of reconciliation, which content, which sense do they attribute to it and how does it, if at all, affect their decisions and verdicts? We answer these questions in part III of our book.

This book was written by three authors. Each of them followed a different approach and style, and each of them used the method relevant to the research question he tried to answer. Nevertheless, this is a joint endeavor and we embarked on it with the strong intention, to produce a joint and homogeneous result. That is why we did our best to unify style and references. The reader will notice some differences between the different chapters anyway, so it may only increase transparency to admit that each of the chapters was shaped to a different extent by one or two co-authors. Klaus Bachmann was responsible for the introduction, the second part (on framing) and the chapters dealing with reconciliation and the ICTY of part 3, and he also contributed to the theoretical introduction of part 1. He contributed to Thomas Sparrow-Botero's chapter by adding clarifications to the theoretical part about principal-agent approaches and by positioning the whole chapter within the debate about International Relations theory and international organisations. Peter Lambertz is the father of part 3, since the main part of the theoretical section on reconciliation and the analysis of the ICTR's use of reconciliation come from him. Thomas Sparrow–Botero wrote part 1 on the ICTY and its role in Croatia's and Serbia's EU accession. The entire book draft was revised and discussed among all three authors, and they wrote the final conclusion together.

This book would not have come into being without the help and contribution of many other people who were not directly involved in the process of writing and editing. First of all, the authors would like to thank the EMGS consortium and its coordinator, the University of Leipzig, who brought us together. We are grateful to Filip Reyntjens, who gave as access to the unpublished manuscript of his most recent book on Rwanda, and to Tim Waters, who allowed us to read and quote from his volume about the Milošević Trial.[11]

We also would like to thank numerous reviewers, who helped us to refine our arguments, correct factual errors, and address structural shortcomings. We are especially grateful to the members of the advisory board of the series "Studies in Political Transition", Gerhard Kemp, Aleksandar Fatić and Lavinia Stan. We would like to extend our gratitude to Mina Zirojević and the staff of the Review of International Affairs in Belgrade, who published an earlier and shorter version of the chapter about Račak, and to James Gow, who criticized it (and convinced us to amend the part about frame analysis and judicial behavior) during a panel at the Annual Convention of the Association for the Study of Nationalities at Columbia University, New York, in April 2012.

Next, we would like to thank all the people who helped us with our field research in Serbia, Croatia, Belgium, The Netherlands, Tanzania, Kenya, Rwanda, and in New York, among them Irena Ristić in Belgrade for her help with sources and literature from Serbia and Jovana Mihajlović Trbov, who is a junior research fellow at the Peace Institute (Mirovni inštitut) in Lubljana, for her material about the Bosnian government's reaction to the Srebrenica crisis, and Dominic Kennedy, head of the office of the Association of Defence Counsel Practising before the ICTY, for his help in establishing contacts with the defence lawyers associations at the ICTY and the ICTR and the counselors, who were ready to talk to us. In Arusha, Elisabeth Gachanja was a great help in organizing interviews with so many high-level interlocutors, and we extent our gratitude to the whole staff of the ICTR, especially in the library and the press office.

We are grateful for the Polish National Research Center's (Narodowe Centrum Nauki) grant to Klaus Bachmann, which allowed him to carry out field research in various countries, and the University of Social Sciences and

11 Reyntjens, Filip: Ruling Under a Volcano. Political Governance in Post-Genocide Rwanda. Timothy Waters (ed): The Milošević Trial. An Autopsy. Oxford University Press 2013. Since the precise pagination was not yet established at the time of reading, we quote from both books according to their chapters.

Humanities in Warsaw, Poland, which generously sponsored the printing and editing of this book. Of course, we thank all the people – judges, prosecutors, witnesses, victims, politicians, journalists and diplomats –, who agreed to be interviewed, many of them confidentially. We did our best to authorize their statements before the book went to press. All interviewees who agreed to be quoted by name obtained copies of the book and the opportunity to correct the quotes relating to them.[12] Finally, we are grateful to Barbara Kurowska, our proof reader and language editor, who meticulously went through the whole text, analyzing and correcting every sentence, bringing grammar and style as close as possible to the rules, and helping us to clarify our thoughts. We also thank Anna Bachmann, who put the text into the pagebreak and the makeup required by Peter Lang International and we extend our gratitude to Jens Bachmann, who prepared the electronic files containing ICTY judgments for our qualitative analysis.

The enormous amount of primary sources we used for this book, from interviews with key actors to think tank reports and the huge online-archives of international media, both tribunals, the UN, the EU, academic databases and governmental and parliamentary documents from about a dozen countries made it necessary to make some adaptations. In order to avoid inflating the footnotes with endless and incomprehensible hyperlinks, we decided to add internet links only when a source was referenced for the first time, or when a link seemed extraordinarily necessary (for example when it leads very precisely to very controversial information that would be difficult to retrieve otherwise). We refrained from giving information about the time of access to a link or internet resource, also because many documents were accessed at many times, often by two or all three authors. However, we were anxious to add all information which is necessary for the reader to find and exactly identify the sources we quoted.

At the end of this introduction, we would like to insert a moral and political disclaimer. This book touches upon many emotionally and politically difficult issues, and it does so by using a detached and distanced approach, inquiring whether academic theories and models can explain certain historical facts and mechanisms on the ground in a meaningful way. It is not the purpose of this book, and it is certainly not the intention of its authors, to pass judgment. In this book, we compare frames to judgments, we compare the behaviour of actors, and we analyze the indictments of prosecutors and the verdicts of judges and trial chambers. At no point do we intend to evaluate individual or collective actions of human beings in moral or legal terms. At no time do we intend to

12 Information about the interview method, the selection criteria, and other details about the interviews can be found in the annex.

impose our own interpretation of what happened in the Balkans throughout the conflicts during the last decade of the 20th century. Neither do we want to offer a judgment about what happened in Rwanda in 1994.

When we describe the events that followed the air crash in Kigali in April 1994, and we deconstruct the different interpretations which were created about those events, we do not side with or against an actor who put forward his own interpretations. It is not our intention to confirm or abolish a specific interpretation of the events in Rwanda in 1994: we neither say that they constituted genocide, nor do we want to imply that they did not. What we do say is that several international bodies, the UNSC and the ICTR, came to the conclusion that what happened should be regarded as genocide. It is of utmost interest to this book to establish how and why they came to this conclusion and how it affected further interpretations of other actors (judges, trial chambers, appeals chambers, prosecutors), but we are not dealing with the question of whether they were right in reaching this conclusion. In the same way, we are interested in analyzing media frames, political claims, and legal concepts about what took place on the Balkans. But whenever we quote political actors who make claims about Serb guilt, ancient hatred, and Bosnian victimhood, this should neither be regarded as support for nor as a rejection of such claims. It just means that we attribute these claims to their authors, no matter whether we see them as justified or not. These reservations should be kept in mind whenever the reader may have the impression that our quotes and references reveal our own judgment. Each of us may have his own convictions about the issues mentioned here, but it was never the purpose of this book to underpin them, prove them, test or challenge them. It is the aim of this book to evaluate the degree of autonomy and the actorness of *ad hoc* international criminal tribunals, but it is not the aim of the book to replace them as moral authorities.

Part I
The ICTY's Role in Serbia's and Croatia's EU Accession – an Agent or a Principal of Europeanisation?

Introduction

There were only a few days left in 2009 when Serbia decided to make a historic move. On December 22, President Boris Tadić officially handed in his country's application for European Union (EU) membership in Stockholm, Sweden.[13] Hailed as a "new beginning"[14] and as "a crossroads"[15], this move carried huge significance, as it signalled Serbia's official intention to join the ever-growing EU club and forget, once and for all, the international isolation it was subject to in the past.

Six years before, Serbia's neighbouring country and former enemy, Croatia, had also achieved the same benchmark when it applied for membership. Despite being regarded as one of the region's frontrunners in negotiations with the EU, Zagreb's path towards the EU has not been free of hurdles and postponements. Nevertheless, it was given the go-ahead by the European Commission in 2011, signed the Treaty of Accession in December 2011 and then, in January 2012, voted in a referendum to join the group of nations. If everything goes according to plan, the country on the Adriatic will be able to proudly boast about its EU membership status in 2013.[16]

Both in Serbia's case and in Croatia's situation, one key fact stands out: as the signatories of the Thessaloniki Summit in June 2003 emphatically asserted, "the future of the Balkans is within the European Union."[17] What is most striking about this statement is that not long ago, the future of this war-stricken region did not seem that clear-cut, and certainly, after being violently fragmented by armed conflict, nothing pointed towards a new integration into a bigger group of nations. In the process of transforming the Balkans from a scarred region to one aiming at EU membership, one organisation has played an important role: The International Criminal Tribunal for the Former Yugoslavia (ICTY). Its importance relies heavily on its capacity to link the past to the future,

---

13 Swedish Presidency of The European Union. Serbia applies for EU membership. 22.12.2009. www.se2009.eu/en/meetings_news/2009/12/22/serbia_applies_for_eu_membership.

14 Cendrowicz, Leo: "A Pariah No More: Serbia Bids to Join the EU". Time Magazine. 23.12.2009.

15 Op. cit.

16 The press release of the Council of the European Union announcing the signature of the Accession Treaty stipulates that Croatia could become the 28th member of the EU on 1 July 2013. The Council of the EU, Council conclusions on enlargement and stablisation and association process. 3132nd General Affairs Council meeting, 5.12.2011. www.consilium.europa.eu/uedocs/cms_data/docs/pressdata/EN/genaff/126577.pdf

17 European Commission. "EU-Western Balkans Summit – Declaration". Thessaloniki, 21.6.2003. http://ec.europa.eu/enlargement/enlargement_process/accession_process/how_does_a_country_join_the_eu/sap/thessaloniki_summit_en.htm.

because it attempts to perform its dual task of dealing with the atrocities of the wars in the 1990s and simultaneously serving as an actor that can be decisive to the European Union accession prospects of countries in the Western Balkans. At various moments in the past, "full cooperation" with the ICTY by Serbia and Croatia has been a publicly declared precondition for entering the EU.

This unique feature has put the ICTY in a special position vis-à-vis both the countries applying for EU membership and the EU as such. On the one hand, it has tried to fulfil its ideal of independence and equality in the midst of argumentative crossfire between the respective nations (and their sometimes hyper-nationalistic political parties and political movements) and the European Union. On the other, it has turned this position to its advantage and attempted to bring to justice some of the most wanted criminals in the region. The ICTY has therefore gotten involved in what Victor Peskin calls "trials of cooperation", i.e. the power struggles between the Tribunal, the states involved, and international actors.[18]

There is one specific feature of these power struggles that is worth pointing out. Because of their evident political nature, they ultimately show that the policies of the different players –Croatia and Serbia, the EU, and the ICTY– are hardly ever carved in stone, and are always case-sensitive and moulded by the particular political and historical contexts.

For instance, although both Croatia and Serbia have the obligation to cooperate with the Tribunal, they have used different strategies to delay, object to or avoid compliance with the ICTY's demands, for example through open obstruction of the Tribunal's work or counter-shaming campaigns. In turn, the ICTY has also resorted to a wide array of methods in order to get a positive reply from these states. These methods include negotiation, blaming states in international forums, and even using the promised EU accession as a tool for putting pressure on accession states to hand over suspects. The EU, despite its strict and lengthy accession conditions, has also been open to modifying its stance towards one country or another, or even towards the ICTY, when particular events have so warranted. For instance, when the Union wanted to exert pressure on one country concerning fulfilment of the accession rules, it used 'the ICTY card', reminding the respective government of the need to comply with the Tribunal, or it personalised its demands by asking for one particular suspect rather than compliance in general.

These power dynamics and the decisions they have triggered will be at the fore in the present section of this book, which sets out to shed new light on the

18 Peskin; Victor: International Justice in Rwanda and the Balkans. Virtual Trials and the Struggle for State Cooperation. Cambridge University Press 2008, 9-13.

enlargement policies of the European Union, considering that the prospective inclusion of Serbia and Croatia contains two distinctive elements in comparison to most countries that joined during the previous enlargement processes.

The first is the fact that one of the cornerstones of the negotiations with Zagreb and Belgrade consists of dealing with the remnants of a recent war on Europe's doorstep. For the Union, which was initially proposed as an avowed rejection of war,[19] including the Balkans into the group of nations is, ultimately, a matter of fundamental interest.

Intrinsically linked to this is a second element: in the cases being studied here, the negotiations include not only the respective states and the EU but also a third actor, the ICTY, which is similarly charged with the promotion of peace in the Balkans.[20] As a 2009 paper by the Institute for Security Studies in Paris highlighted, with the inclusion of the ICTY, "the Balkans have introduced a new and very important dimension to European conditionality".[21]

Understanding the power struggles between the EU and the ICTY will highlight how the EU relates to a United Nations body established by, and reporting to, the United Nations Security Council (UNSC), and will also provide elements for understanding the ICTY in a novel way: not from the perspective of key ICTY decision-makers like Carla Del Ponte; not from the analysis of its structures and internal dynamics, such as in John Hagan's *Justice in the Balkans*; and not from a comparison with other tribunals, as in Victor Peskin's *International Justice in Rwanda and the Balkans*. The main focus will instead stem from the European Union as such, and aspires to understand the politics of the Tribunal as it deals with the EU and the countries seeking accession.

---

19 The Schuman Declaration of 1950 states that "world peace cannot be safeguarded without the making of creative efforts proportionate to the dangers which threaten it. The contribution which an organized and living Europe can bring to civilisation is indispensable to the maintenance of peaceful relations". European Union. "The European Declaration of 9 May 1950". http://europa.eu/abc/symbols/9-may/decl_en.htm.

20 In her 2000 address to the Security Council, ICTY Prosecutor Carla Del Ponte stated that the Security Council created the ICTY "not as a quick fix to a political crisis, but as a serious and lasting contribution to creating a meaningful and durable peace in the Balkans". Address to the Security Council by Carla Del Ponte, Prosecutor of the International Criminal Tribunals for the former Yugoslavia and Rwanda, to the UN Security Council. www.icty.org/sid/7803. For a discussion of the UN Security Council resolutions establishing the ICTR, which also contain references to "peace", "justice" and reconcialition" see part III of this book.

21 De Vasconcelos, Àlvaro: Preface. In: Batt, Judy; Obradović-Wochnik, Jelena (eds): War Crimes, Conditionality and EU Integration in the Western Balkans. Paris: Institute for Security Studies, June 2009. www.iss.europa.eu.

With those elements in mind, the main research questions of this part are: To what extent is the Tribunal independent in its decision-making vis-à-vis the EU? How should it be seen: as a principal or as an agent of Europeanisation?

We regarded the ICTY as a principal whenever an initiative for policy change in the EU originated from or was decisively influenced by the ICTY or its Chief Prosecutor (as the agenda setter in the Tribunal) and was subsequently applied by the European Union in its policies towards Serbia or Croatia.

On the other hand, we considered the ICTY an agent when the ICTY followed, without significant influence, a policy initiative promoted by the EU that directly affected the work of the Tribunal. A third option was also valid: when the most influential reason for an EU policy change was a reaction to internal political dynamics in the countries themselves. These three options ultimately highlight a conclusive element of this part of the book, namely whether the ICTY is an important player in international relations or merely implements decisions made by other actors.

With the purpose of presenting the abovementioned structure, this chapter has been divided into two clearly identifiable sections. The first refers to the historical background and the theoretical approach. For the latter, two processes are defined: Europeanisation and the principal-agent dichotomy, both of which are mentioned in the research question and are therefore of utmost importance to the whole project. Using this as a base, the second part of this section examines EU policy shifts towards Serbia and Croatia in detail, bringing together the sources mentioned above so as to highlight the role played by the Tribunal in the accession process of both countries. The conclusions then give a concrete answer to the question of whether the ICTY is an agent or a principal of Europeanisation.

Europeanisation

Both Serbia and Croatia will become part of the European Union. What was not clear when the process began was exactly when that would happen. Tentative dates appeared every now and then in the media, but as one EU official in Brussels admitted in April 2011, "there are no probable dates" until negotiations are completed.[22] Ultimately, the accession of these countries to the European group of nations depends on how they transform their structures and institutions to comply with the accession criteria and, in general, how they cope with the tools of EU conditionality. Or, in plain language, how they react to a widely utilised concept called Europeanisation.

22 Interview by Thomas Sparrow-Botero with EU official who requested anonymity. Brussels, April 2011.

The concept of Europeanisation is frequently used in the media and in intellectual debates about European integration, but in these cases, it has a strong normative inclination – it refers either to the preferences and political concepts their authors consider desirable, or to a situation which has already come about and is regarded as positive. Europeanisation is also a popular approach in European Integration research and integration theory, but there it serves as a tool for explaining why and when certain outcomes come about, rather than how and why they should come about. At the origin of the scientific concept of Europeanisation was an observation about the increasing influence that central EU institutions exercise upon member states. This already suggests that most definitions consider a top-down procedure whereby "domestic policy areas become increasingly subject to European policy-making."[23]For the picture to be complete, however, three more aspects have to be clarified. The first refers to the need to specify which countries are included in Europeanisation dynamics. Most reviewed analyses refer to the concept as one mostly applicable to current European Union members, but there are also a handful of authors who have stressed the relevance of including other nation-states in the package,[24] such as those aspiring to become part of the EU.[25] This project, as is only natural, adheres to the latter, on the basis that "there is undoubtedly Europeanisation of policy in the countries applying for EU membership."[26]

Before and during the EU's biggest enlargement in 2004, when 10 new member states joined the organisation, the original view on Europeanisation broadened in order to also encompass the impact of EU decision-making, norms, values, and institutions on accession states and, subsequently, on countries and societies in the EU's neighbourhood. In the meantime, some authors also apply the concept to non-accession and non-neighbouring countries, which are subject to EU norm export, transborder governance,[27] and attempts by the EU to

23 Radaelli, Claudio M. (quoting Tanja Börzel): Whither Europeanisation? Concept Stretching and Substantive Change. *European Integration Online Papers.* Vol. 4, Nr. 8, (2000). http://eiop.or.at/eiop/texte/2000-008a.htm.

24 There are also authors who examine the influence of the EU on countries that are neither members nor candidates, and other scholars have approached Europeanisation from another perspective, namely by analysing why the EU does not or can not proliferate norms and values in certain areas of the world.

25 See Gwiazda, Anna: Europeanisation in Candidate Countries from Central and Eastern Europe. Paper prepared for the EPIC workshop in Florence, EUI, 19-22 September 2002. http://aei.pitt.edu/737/.

26 Radaelli, op. cit.

27 Bachmann, Klaus: Frontex and transborder governance in the EU. *The Review of International Affairs*, vol. LIX, No 1132, October – December 2008 Belgrade, 13-23.

influence internal developments and shape norms and values in these countries.[28] Europeanisation, seen as the process of spreading specific norms and values like liberal democracy, market economy, trade liberalisation, and human rights beyond the EU's external borders, has therefore become a widely used approach for analysing the EU's neighbourhood policy, another large field of Integration Studies, International Relations research and the study of regionalisation.[29]

The second issue refers to the reason behind Europeanisation. In other words, it aims to answer what conditions have to be met for a country to become Europeanized. The answer is not very difficult to find: there must be an initial incompatibility between the European model and the model in the respective countries for the EU to promote change and the countries to respond to the demands. This incompatibility has been referred to as misfit[30] and generates different degrees of pressure to which facilitating factors – such as institutions – respond.

One of the elements of that misfit – certainly present in the Europeanisation of the Balkans and the role of the ICTY – is, for example, different views on conflict and conflict resolution. That is why some authors have expanded the debate on

---

De Bardeleben, J. (ed): The Boundaries of EU Enlargement. Finding a place for neighbors, Houndsmill, Basingstoke: Palgrave MacMillan 2008.

28 For examples for such approaches see: Emerson M., Noutcheva G.: Europeanisation as a Gravity Model of Democratisation, *CEPS Working Document* N 214, November 2004. Howell K.: Developing Conceptualisations of Europeanisation: Synthesising Methodological Approaches, *Queen's Paper on Europeanisation*, nr 3/2004; Bauer, M.; Knill, C.; Pitschel, D.: "Differential Europeanisation in Eastern Europe: The Impact of Diverse EU Regulatory Governance Patterns". *Journal of European Integration* 29, 2007, 405-423; Dimitrova, A. and Dragneva, R.: "Constraining external governance: interdependence with Russia and the CIS as limits to the EU's rule transfer in the Ukraine". *Journal of European Public Policy,* 16(6) 2007 and Knill, C. and Tosun, J.: "Hierarchy, networks, or markets: how does the EU shape environmental policy adoptions within and beyond its borders?" *Journal of European Public Policy*, 16, 2009, 873-894.

29 For literature about European Neighborhood Policy (ENP) see: Gstöhl, S.: "A Neighbourhood Economic Community: Finalité Économique for the ENP?" *EU Diplomacy Papers* no. 3. 2008; Guild, E., Khasson, V. and Mir, M.: "State of the Art. The Nexus between European Neighbourhood Policy and Justice and Home Affairs" *CASE Reports* No. 73/2007. Haukkala, H.: "A Hole in the Wall? Dimensionalism and the EU's New Neighbourhood Policy". *UPI Working Papers*: 41, 2003. Kelley, J.G.: "New Wine in Old Wine Skins: Policy Adaptation in the European Neighbourhood Policy". *Journal of Common Market Studies, 44(1) 2006*,29-55.

30 Börzel, Tanja and Risse, Thomas: "When Europe Hits Home: Europeanisation and Domestic Change". *European Integration Online Papers*. Vol.4, Nr. 15. (2000). http://eiop.or.at/eiop/texte/2000-015a.htm.

Europeanisation to include the ways in which the EU can export its principles on conflict resolution. In that regard, Europeanisation can be seen as "a process which is activated and encouraged by European institutions, primarily the European Union, by linking the final outcome of the conflict to a certain degree of integration of the parties involved in it into European structures."[31]

Other authors have taken into account a perspective from below in order to discover to what extent there is a societal demand for Europeanisation, and to understand the preferences and attitudes of particular local actors in the process.[32] Both viewpoints are essential to a comprehensive understanding of Europeanisation dynamics, as the process involves both inter- and intra-state relationships. In this regard, Europeanisation might be defined both as a process by which the EU "downloads directives, regulations and institutional structures to the domestic level"[33], and also as a process of "uploading to the EU shared beliefs, informal and formal rules, discourse, identities and vertical and horizontal policy transfer."[34] Since the latter approach is almost uniquely applied to the study of member states' influence on the EU's policies and norm production, and since we intend here to undertake an analysis of the EU's impact (through the ICTY) on Serbia and Croatia, this study will concentrate on the way the EU proliferates norms, values and policies down to the two states. Even though the political and economic situation in the countries often influences the decision-making process in Brussels, it is ultimately the EU that establishes the conditions for enlargement and that puts (or releases) pressure on the countries to comply with conditionality tools.

But this double perspective on the issue of Europeanisation does highlight the fact that the focus is not exclusively set on the decisions stemming from the EU but also considers the role played by local actors, collective identities, and the foundational values of the respective states.[35] After all, "European policy is not a mysterious deus ex machina situated 'up there'."[36] On the contrary, "it

---

31 Coppieters, Bruno; Emerson, Michael; Huysseune, Michel; Kovziridze, Tamara; Noutcheva, Gergana; Tocci, Nathalie and Vahl, Marius: "Europeanisation and Conflict Resolution: Case Studies from the European Periphery." Special Issue of the *Journal of Ethnopolitics and Minority Issues in Europe* 1/2004. Retrieved from: http://www.ecmi.de/fileadmin/downloads/publications/JEMIE/2004/1-2004Chapter1.pdf

32 Jelena Subotić: "Explaining Difficult States. The Problems of Europeanisation in Serbia". *East European Politics and Societies*. May 11, vol. 4, 2010, 595-616.

33 Howell, Kerry: "Developing Conceptualisations of Europeanisation and European Integration: Mixing Methodologies". http://aei.pitt.edu/1720/.

34 Op. cit.

35 Subotić, Explaining Difficult States, op cit.

36 Radaelli, Wither Europeanisation, op. cit.

originates from processes of bargaining, imitation, and diffusion wherein domestic governments and national interest groups play an important role, together with European institutions."[37] That is why, with those two perspectives in mind, Europeanisation can be seen, in a somewhat broad manner, as "the evolution of the national and the Union policies and institutions, their interaction and mutual influence."[38]

The third key element of the broader picture concerns the way in which the concept is applied. Most authors agree that there are two mechanisms through which Europeanisation works. The first element is conditionality (or rational institutionalism), which focuses on rational, goal-oriented actors and explains that they "engage in strategic interactions using their resources to maximize their utilities on the basis of given, fixed and ordered preferences."[39] A second mechanism is norm diffusion and social learning (also called sociological institutionalism), which "suggests that Europeanisation leads to domestic change through a socialisation and collective learning process resulting in norm internalisation and the development of new identities."[40] These mechanisms are not exclusive and often occur simultaneously or successively.

But although both mechanisms explain how Europeanisation works, they do not suffice to explain in what areas Europeanisation materializes and to what extent. One of the authors explaining some of these issues is J.P. Olsen, who has identified phenomena that change with Europeanisation. Those events include changes in external territorial boundaries, the development of supranational governance institutions, and exporting EU governance and policy tools beyond EU borders.[41]

Other scholars have also delved into this topic and have found additional elements. According to Radaelli, areas affected by Europeanisation include domestic political structures (such as institutions, public administration, international relations, and the legal structure), as well as structures of representation (party systems in particular), cognitive and normative structures (values, norms, and discourses), and public policy (policy frames, narratives, and paradigms).[42]

---

37 Ibid.

38 Pantev, Plamen: "The 'Europeanisation' of National Foreign, Security and Defense Policy". *Institute for Security and International Studies Research Reports*. (Sofia, November 2005). http://www.isis-bg.org/Publications/research_reports/RR18.pdf.

39 Börzel, Risse, When Europe hits home, op. cit.

40 Op. cit.

41 Olsen, Johan P.: The many faces of Europeanisation. Journal of Common Market Studies Journal of Common Market Studies, december 2002, vol. 40, issue 5, 921–952. http://onlinelibrary.wiley.com/doi/10.1111/1468-5965.00403/pdf

42 Radaelli, Whither Europeanisation, op. cit.

How those areas change with Europeanisation or, more specifically, how the respective countries react to the proposed changes is another matter. Three degrees of domestic change resulting from Europeanisation have been spelled out: absorption, whereby states adapt European policies without substantially changing their pre-existing structures (domestic change is low); accommodation, whereby states leave the essentials of their own structures intact but modify certain elements (domestic change is moderate); and transformation, which implies a fundamental change of policy and a replacement of structures (domestic change is high).[43] A fourth degree, not explained by the authors but still present, is when there is no domestic change and when Europeanisation becomes unsuccessful. In a nutshell, the smaller the differences between the European policies and the policies in the respective governments, the smaller the pressure for Europeanizing and the lower the degree of change at the domestic level.[44]

The degree of Europeanisation depends, to a large extent, on domestic factors, as this part of the book sets out to show for the Serbian and Croatian cases. The European Union has the power to establish rules and put pressure on states to obey them, but the decision to internalize them relies to a large extent on local elements. Börzel and Risse refer to two mediating factors in the respective countries: change agents or norm entrepreneurs, and a political culture (including institutions) that might be conducive to consensus building.[45]

Jelena Subotić presents another view in her analysis of Europeanisation in Serbia (an issue which will be further developed in these chapters). In her work, Subotić sets out to present a theoretical framework to explain why countries like Serbia, one of the most reluctant Europeanizers, have refrained from Europeanizing at a constant pace, and why the EU has not been able to have a larger impact. To answer her research question, Subotić describes certain elements that determine the effect of the EU on "difficult"[46] candidate states. First, she presents a view from below, i.e. a look at the societal demands for Europeanisation and, in particular, whether there is a shared belief of a 'European idea' as a foundational element of state identity. Moreover, she sheds light on the role and the authority of political spoilers and of political elites that might act as agents of Europeanisation. Subotić stresses the question of where power is located in the state and in the hands of which actors: the "Euro resisters", the "instrumental promoters" or the "Euro enthusiasts".[47]

43 Börzel, Risse, When Europe hits home, op. cit.
44 Ibid.
45 Ibid.
46 Subotić, Explaining Difficult States, op. cit.
47 Ibid.

Subotić's perspective completes the picture of Europeanisation as the basic approach for this part of the book. All in all, it can be concluded that it is a process that basically stems from the European Union and is enforced through methods such as conditionality and norm diffusion. It is moulded by particular actors' interests and influenced by local contexts in the respective countries – both member states and candidate countries – and thus generates different degrees of domestic change. The cases of Serbia and Croatia will serve as practical examples in order to understand the abovementioned characteristics.

Principal-Agent Dichotomy

For many decades, scholars have been disputing the role that international organisations and institutions play in International Relations. Many of the great International Relations debates[48] have been dedicated to the question of whether, if at all, international organisations and their institutions can shape and alter states' preferences, trigger policy changes in states, and act as independent, autonomous actors in international relations, or whether they act solely as states' instruments and in accordance with states' preferences. Summarizing those debates here would be both misplaced and redundant. What is important for the purpose of this book is to place the international criminal tribunals into that debate. As Andrew Moravcsik has pointed out, states may agree to sign and ratify treaties and adhere to institutions without exactly knowing how these institutions will affect their preferences at a later stage.[49] Governments may sign human rights treaties and ratify court statutes, and in the long run, this can force them into compliance with these statutes' provisions. This can be perfectly rational, since it reduces the likelihood of "free-riding" by other contracting states and, by imposing legal regimes onto these governments, increases the credibility of these governments' human rights commitments toward their own constituencies. Even more: by signing and ratifying treaties that constrain government action, a government may seek to limit the scope for retaliation by a future government with respect to itself. The latter aspect is the more relevant,

48 More about the different "great debates" about International Relations: Wendt, Alexander: "On constitution and causation in International Relations." *Review of International Studies*, (1998), 24, 101-118; Lapid, Yosef: "The third debate. On the prospects of International Theory in a post-positivist era." *International Studies Quarterly* 1989, vol. 33, 235-254. Baldwin, David Allen: Neorealizm and neoliberalizm. The contemporary debate. Columbia University Press, 1993.

49 Moravcsik, Andrew: "The Origins of Human Rights Regimes: Democratic Delegation in Postwar Europe." *International Organization*, Vol. 54, No. 2 (Spring, 2000), 217-252.

the more likely violent regime change is in a country. By adopting binding and enforceable human rights provisions which involve independent external actors, governments may accept a trade-off between their autonomy (which will be restricted by these provisions) and their future security. From this perspective, binding and enforceable human rights regimes with supranational features provide a solution for overcoming the "hostage dilemma" in (actual or expected) transition settings.[50] Introducing "third party enforcement" as such is always a rational way of reducing transaction costs, irrespective of whether such an agreement involves commodities between traders or rights between political actors.

The basic requirement for third party enforcement is the independence of such an institution. This is true for human rights regimes and international courts, whose jurisdiction reaches out to the contracting states. The ICTY and the ICTR can only very partially be regarded as fitting into these criteria, since both were created by an international organisation (the United Nations' Security Council) and were accepted very reluctantly by the countries which were affected by their jurisdiction. Both tribunals can therefore not be put on an equal footing with the European Court of Human Rights in Strasbourg, which resolves conflicts between states and their citizens on behalf of these states. It can also not be compared to the International Court of Justice in The Hague, which decides on conflicts between states that have previously accepted its jurisdiction. The ICTY jurisdiction was accepted by the state parties to the Dayton Peace Treaty (and hence, what is important here, by the Federation of Yugoslavia and the Republic of Croatia), but as soon as the ICTY's actions started to interfere with Serbia's and Croatia's state preferences, both countries did their best to sideline the tribunal, circumvent or openly ignore its orders and prevent even "absorption" and any domestic change at all. The case of the ICTR is even more complicated, since its jurisdiction was extended to Rwanda by the Security Council, with the Rwandan (RPF) government, a non-permanent UNSC member, dissenting.[51] Whereas it would be possible to discuss the International Criminal Court, which was set up by an assembly of states, in terms of a supranational actor for third party enforcement, the ICTY and the ICTR escape from such classifications. Both tribunals may eventually lower transaction costs and help to solve coordination problems for the UN, but they certainly increase rather than lower transaction costs for Croatia and Serbia. As will be shown later in this book, by introducing the requirement of ICTY compliance into accession

50 Nalepa, Monika: Skeletons in the Closet. Transitional Justice in Post-Communist Europe. Cambridge University Press 2010, 42-44.

51 For the details see: Peskin, International Justice, 161-162.

negotiations, the EU actually managed to increase its bargaining power with respect to Serbia and Croatia and raised the stakes for both countries. This asymmetry is deeply contradictory to the logic of third party enforcement. Initially, the ICTY was not designed in order to further Europeanisation and increase EU leverage over specific countries seeking accession (both countries were far from entering the EU when the ICTY was founded), although it actually began to function this way after the EU had agreed to membership negotiations (and earlier to trade liberalisation). But this was a one-way mechanism, and the ICTY's jurisdiction and legal basis were not designed and did not work as a tool for Serbia and Croatia to coerce the EU into compliance with anything whatsoever. We may therefore view the ICTY as an instrument for overcoming coordination problems and lowering transaction costs among EU member countries, but not for Serbia and Croatia. Hence it would be a mistake to treat the ICTY as a classical "human rights regime" or international court. However, it still makes sense to scrutinize it as a potential tool for the EU. What makes this relationship so interesting from an institutionalist and International Relations perspective is the ICTY's total statutory independence from the EU. The tribunal was neither created nor run by the EU; the EU's organs have no formal say over ICTY activities, and neither member states nor central EU institutions (such as the European Commission, the European Parliament, the European Court of Justice or the Council of the EU) have any legally enshrined leverage over prosecutors and judges. Legally and institutionally, the ICTY is a separate, independent institution and there is nothing in European treaties or the ICTY's statute that would entitle an EU organ to issue any orders or even make recommendations to the ICTY. In 1993, the ICTY was created as a subsidiary of the Security Council (the legitimacy of which is strongly contested among international lawyers) rather than of the EU or, as some of its critics and defendants used to claim, of NATO. We cannot therefore regard the ICTY as a transnational actor or a typical human rights regime, but we may still analyze its relationship with the European Union with respect to the specific situation of accession negotiations with Serbia and Croatia. In order to do this in a meaningful way, we will adopt a concept from an area of studies that is not typical for international relations research, but which allows interactions between two or more actors in asymmetrical relationships to be described and analysed: the principal-agent dichotomy emanating from delegation theories.[52]

---

52 Bendor, Jonathan; Glazer, Andrew and Hammond, Theodore: "Theories of Delegation." *Annual Review of Political Science*. Vol. 4 (2001), 235-269.

Frequently used in political science, public administration, and economics, this concept generally refers to the contractual arrangements on which social life is based. It addresses the problems that arise when a person, a party, or an organisation (hereinafter called agent) acts on behalf of another person, party, or organisation (called principal).[53] The principal wants a specific task to be accomplished, but cannot easily perform its duties on his own. He therefore resorts to delegation and requires substantial assistance from the agent. That relationship between principal and agent is called an 'agency' and involves certain obligations and duties for both sides: the agent assumes an obligation of loyalty to the principal, whereas the principal reposes trust in the agent. In the process, particular problems may arise, for example if the principal hires the wrong agent, or if the agent does not perform his task properly. Those problems are called 'adverse selection' and 'moral hazard', respectively.[54] Common examples of these dynamics refer to the relationship between state and governed, employer and employee, or a provider of goods and services and a buyer. In this case, it will also refer to the relationship between an institution – the ICTY– and an international organisation. This is also the main reason why we have refrained from extending this concept to the analysis of the ICTR. In the latter case, it would be very difficult, if not impossible, to identify a distinct principal other than the UN and to disentangle the influences of different putative principals from one another.

The contractual arrangement between principal and agent establishes the rules of the game. Both sides have an initial desire or incentive to maximize their own benefits. Thus, the principal cannot be sure that the agent will work in the principal's best interest. From the principal's point of view, the contract should establish parameters aimed at blocking the agent's ability to work contrary to the principal's goals and, simultaneously, should increase to the greatest extent possible the tasks that are unique to the agent.[55] This dissimilarity generates, from the start, a process with two core assumptions: "that goal

---

53 Although the model has been built to explain the dynamics between agents and principals as unitary players, authors like Waterman and Meier explain that the model based on a dyadic relationship is unrealistic. They note the common existence of agents with multiple principals and point towards the role that externalities might play in the process. See Waterman, Richard and Meier, Kenneth: "Principal-Agent Models: An Expansion?" *Journal of Public Administration Research and Theory*. 8,2,1998, 173-202.

54 Michael Álvarez and Thad Hall. "Controlling Democracy: The Principal-Agent Problems in Election Administration". *The Policy Studies Journal*, Vol. 34, No. 4., (2006).

55 Waterman, Meier, Principal Agent Models, op. cit.

conflict exists between principals and agents and that agents have more information than their principals, which results in an information asymmetry between them".[56]

During the interaction process, which develops over time, agent and principals engage in particular dynamics. With that in mind, the general, simplified model can work in the following manner: The principal moves first and offers the agent a contract. The agent, considering the incentives and the particular utility function that determines his type,[57] considers whether to accept the principal's offer and how to act. If and when the task is fulfilled, the principal pays the agent, depending on the incentives, and himself receives a payoff.

It is assumed that the information asymmetry and the information flows that are generated are at the core of the whole process.[58] Informational problems are basic ingredients of the dynamics between principal and agent. They may occur when the principal delegates a task to an agent with private information, when the latter engages in hidden action, or if both agent and principal share the same information but this cannot be observed by a third party (the so-called case of non-verifiability). These problems often prevent society from achieving the best allocation of resources, something that would be possible if all information were common knowledge.

In the specific case of this chapter, the main question is to address whether the ICTY was an agent of the European Union. The inverse question, whether it acted as a principal, demonstrates the difficulties of this approach in this particular case. We cannot reasonably assume the ICTY to be a principal of the EU in general. Such a perspective could easily be ridiculed as an attempt to examine whether the tail can wag the dog. Nevertheless, since international tribunals are forced to rely on state cooperation, state institutions sometimes may act upon their delegation and thus become, for a limited time and under narrowly defined conditions, agents of tribunals. And certainly, tribunals may – successfully or not – try to delegate tasks to states, taking advantage of specific information deficits that states may have in such a game. A famous example is ICTY chief prosecutor Louise Arbour's secret indictment strategy. When confronted with the unwillingness of states to risk casualties when arresting indicted war crime suspects in Bosnia, she managed to convince judges at the

---

56 Op. cit.

57 Maskin, Eric; Tirole, Jean: "The Principal-Agent Relationship with an Informed Principal: The Case of Private Values". Econometrica, Vol. 58, No. 2 (Mar., 1990), 379-409.)

58 Waterman, Meier, Principal Agents models, op. cit.

ICTY to keep certain indictments secret, sending them confidentially to SFOR officers on the ground. They could arrest suspects with less effort than would have been necessary had the suspects known about the indictment. By lowering transaction costs for SFOR[59] (and the states involved), she provided incentives for her agent to comply with her delegation order. By bypassing government structures and cooperating directly and privately with SFOR officers, she took advantage of an information deficit on the side of these governments in order to get her suspects arrested and extradited. By resorting to the media and putting public pressure on reluctant governments, she actually forced some of the governments to make arrests in Bosnia and Serbia. Within the narrow framework of the ICTY's mandate and jurisdiction, we can thus assume that the ICTY acts as a principal and foreign states and international organisations as its agents.

Yet another issue needs to be defined in order to make this assumption meaningful. In the overwhelming majority of cases, it will be the chief prosecutor who will act as principal on behalf of the Tribunal, not the judges, trial chambers, appeal chambers, or the president of the Tribunal. This is due to the specific position of the chief prosecutor, who acts as an agenda setter[60] within the decision-making process at the Tribunal. In order to kick off the juridical machinery of the Tribunal, the chief prosecutor has to formulate an indictment, which needs the approval of a judge before it can be acted upon. In the whole procedure from investigation through to final judgment, the prosecutor acts as an agenda-setter, whereas the judges and the trial chamber act as veto players who can stop the decision-making process.[61] In this process, the chief prosecutor is the only *de jure* agenda-setter. If he does not indict a suspect, there is no legal way to force him. Once the process has started, the prosecution ceases to control it. Pre-trial, trial, and appeal fall under the auspices of the judges, trial chambers, and appeal chamber. *De jure*, it is the tribunal president who represents the Tribunal in its relations with states and non-state actors. Politically and de facto, it is the chief prosecutor. The strategy that he (or she, as two of the five ICTY chief prosecutors were women) follows can best be described as an "indictment policy". It is the choice of who to indict, when, and

59 SFOR: Stabilisation Force, NATO troops deployed in Bosnia-Herzegovina, charged with the implemention and supervision of the Dayton Peace Agreement.

60 As agenda setter we regard an actor who has the right and possibility to start a decision-making process. Agenda-setting should therefore be understood according to game-theoretical, not media-theoretical definitions.

61 A veto player is an actor whose approval is needed in order to continue the decision-making process. See: Tsebelis, George: Veto players. How Political Institutions Work. Princeton University Press, New Jersey 2002.

for what, and it is a choice which often involves politics and has a political meaning and political consequences for the Tribunal – much more than the rather non-political choices of the judges, trial chambers, and appeals chamber of who and when to sentence or acquit.[62]

It remains to be established how we are going to define which actor actually triggers a policy change and therefore has to be regarded as the principal during the transaction under scrutiny. Sequence and chronology play a crucial role in assessing this. Which player acted first, which player reacted and under what conditions, and how did the process unfold?[63] If the ICTY acted first or played a decisive role in the process, it will be considered a principal; otherwise, if it responded to the strategy of another player, it will be considered an agent. It is obvious that the EU is not the only principal whose initiatives the ICTY could respond to when acting as an agent. We also include other possibilities in our analysis. The ICTY may respond to initiatives of the UN (the Secretary General or other bodies), it may answer requests from the United States, some EU member states, or NATO. In terms of delegation theory, it is the peculiar character of the ICTY as a potential agent that it may serve several principals at the same time.

---

62 There is perhaps one outstanding example of judges making political decisions which had serious political consequences, but this example took place at the ICTR, when the appeals chamber decided to set a defendant free because of grave irregularities pertaining to his pre-trial arrest. The decision was strongly contested by the Rwandan government and later, under huge pressure, reversed. See: Peskin, International Justice, 177-178; Moghalu, Kingsley: Rwanda's genocide. The Politics of Global Justice, New York: Palgrave MacMillan 2005, 101-104; see also: *The prosecutor versus Barayagwiza et al.* ICTR-97-19.

63 It is important to mention that agents are institutions, not states (except for some very specific cases, which are not relevant here). Therefore, the ICTY might be an agent of the EU, but the EU will not be an agent of the ICTY or Serbia or Croatia.

Historical Background: The Policies of the EU and the ICTY toward Serbia and Croatia

At the time this book is being written, Croatia's and Serbia's compliance with the ICTY is no longer a problem. Radovan Karadžić has been arrested and is standing trial in The Hague, and even Ratko Mladić was finally apprehended in May 2011. When this book is published, his trial will already have begun. Also apprehended was Goran Hadžić, who is indicted for crimes committed in 1991 mostly against the Croatian population of Eastern Slavonia. Cooperation with the ICTY is no longer a stumbling block for Croatia and Serbia in the accession process. This was very different at the end of the last decade of the 20th century and after 2000. At different stages, the EU made compliance with the ICTY and even the extradition of specific suspects a precondition for further steps in mutual relations between the EU and Croatia and Serbia.

A key moment for that linkage was the turn of the century, when a series of fundamental processes came together. The ICTY completed its biggest achievement to date with the transfer of Slobodan Milošević to The Hague; the EU designed the first comprehensive, long-term framework for the accession of countries in the Western Balkans; and the countries themselves underwent deep internal change after their nationalistic presidents fell from power. Moreover, beginning in 2000-2001, the United States started reneging on the International Criminal Court (ICC), demanding a deadline for further indictments and proceedings. The EU became the main supporter of the Tribunal as time progressed, and since then it has been its most reliable and stable partner, one that the ICTY's chief prosecutor could count on for pressurizing Croatia and Serbia concerning the apprehension and extradition of suspects.

Serbia and Croatia in the 1990s: Key Events in Retrospect

Ante Gotovina, Croatia's most visible living war criminal, was sitting in the last row of the ICTY's Courtroom I in The Hague during his judgment, on April 15, 2011. He did not utter a word, his face did not show any emotions. He only stood when Dutch Judge Alphons Orie read the verdict aloud, dampened in the gallery by the wailing of the Croat's relatives: 24 years' imprisonment for his participation in a Joint Criminal Enterprise (JCE), the objective of which was the permanent removal of the Serbian population in the Croatian region of Krajina, between July and September 1995, during the so-called Operation Storm. The means: persecutions, deportation of at least 200,000 Serbs from the region, plundering of property, wanton destruction, murder, and cruel treatment.

Ten years after Gotovina's initial indictment and after a trial lasting 303 days, that verdict was an important moment for international criminal justice, and journalists from around 40 international media outlets were there to witness it.[64]

In the Balkans, the feeling that it was a decisive episode was also in the air, but the Trial Chamber judgment evoked opposing opinions in the region. In Croatia, where Gotovina is still seen by many groups as a national hero, they came as a complete shock; in Serbia, on the other hand, there was a certain feeling that justice had finally been done. These differing views on the topic not only epitomize the contrasts of historical interpretation in the Balkans, they also serve as a basis for this historical background, which will introduce the events that are central to an understanding of the relationship between both countries, the ICTY, and the EU. In a nutshell, the goal at this point is not to provide a chronological summary of the region's recent history, given the fact that in-depth accounts of the wars are plentiful and insightful, but to relate key incidents of the past to the ways in which they are interpreted in the present. After all, as Elizabeth Pond states, a cornerstone for understanding the Balkans today is to look "at the initial wars of the Yugoslav succession as they are perceived in retrospect."[65]

In Zagreb, the reasons for discontent regarding the verdict are not difficult to find. The whole case of Ante Gotovina in the ICTY touches sensitive fibres in Croatia's recent history. In particular, the Tribunal's assessment that Gotovina in Krajina participated in a JCE, of which the country's founding father Franjo Tudjman was also allegedly a member, directly questions Croatia's official view of Operation Storm and of the conflicts in the 1990s. For Croatia, its so-called Homeland War was a liberation struggle and a "counterterrorist operation" to retake "Croatian territory from Serb rebels".[66] In short, the war was seen as the cornerstone of the independent country and Operation Storm as one of its main pillars.[67]

The April 2011 verdict went against the idea, common in Croatia, that the country should not be seen as a victimiser, but mainly as a victim of the

64 Thomas Sparrow-Botero's coverage of the judgment, as one of the accredited journalists in The Hague. April 15, 2011. The number of journalists comes from the list of participants present at the trial.

65 Pond, Elisabeth: Endgame in the Balkans: Regime Change European Style. Washington, D. C.: Brookings Institution, 2006, ix.

66 Subotić, Jelena: Hijacked Justice. Dealing With the Past in the Balkans. Cornell University Press. 2009, 94.

67 As an example, see: Nenad Ivanković's pamphlet defending Gotovina: Što smo mu učinili. Zagreb 2011, 137-152.

expansionist desires of its neighbour, Serbia.[68] This is in line with the reaction by Croatian President Ivo Josipović and Prime Minister Jadranka Kosor after Gotovina's judgment.[69] A prominent example of that victimisation is the destruction of Vukovar and Dubrovnik in the early stages of the war. "The more Croatian towns were attacked, the more likely it became that international support for Croatia would grow,"[70] James Gow argued in this respect. This view of presenting Croatia as a victim by presenting Serbia as a victimizer was one of the core elements of Croatia's first stint as an independent nation, under historian Franjo Tudjman, who set out to redefine his country's identity as soon as he became President, in 1990.

Tudjman based his interpretation of Croatia's identity on historical and cultural grounds. In his book *Horrors of War*, for example, he argued that his country's role in World War II was manipulated by the Serbs to harm the reputation of Croatia.[71] In addition, he constantly portrayed Serbia and Croatia as completely different cultural entities, and exploited the differences: it is no surprise that Tudjman gave an increasing importance to religion and the Catholic Church, a distinct and evident element which differentiates Catholic Croatia from Orthodox Serbia and Muslim Bosnia. In short, the re-imagination of Croatia's past, to put it one way, rested on two premises: the premise of breaking from its recent Yugoslav, non-independent history, and the premise of defining exactly what 'being Croat' meant. And that was achieved, in part, by emphasising the contrasts with Serbia.

The ICTY found itself in the middle of that strategy as soon as it began digging into the region's troubles in the early 1990s. For instance, as the wars in the Balkans evolved, Tudjman continuously strove to point the finger at his Serb neighbours. This explains why Croatia was initially a fervent defender of the

---

68 Linguistic formulations by Croatian officials regarding the war point in the direction of presenting Croatia as a victim. It is not a coincidence that terms such as "liberating" or "defensive" are used. See, for more information, the special declaration by the Croatian Parliament, in December 2000, about Croatia's participation in the war. http://narodne-novine.nn.hr/clanci/sluzbeni/274008.html (in Croatian)

69 Kosor described the war as a military operation with the aim of "liberating Croatian territory", whereas Josipović highlighted the fact that Croatia managed to protect its "freedom from aggression and criminal politics of Slobodan Milošević". See Enis Zebić, Branka Mihajlović: "Gotovina Conviction Riles Croats, Mollifies Serbs". *Institute for War and Peace Reporting*, 22.4.2011. http://iwpr.net/report-news/gotovina-conviction-riles-croats-mollifies-serbs.

70 Gow, James: The Serbian Project and Its Adversaries. A Strategy of War Crimes. London: Hurst and Company 2003, 239.

71 See Bellamy, Alex J.: The Formation of Croatian National Identity. A Centuries Old Dream. Manchester University Press 2003.

ICTY as long as it tried Serbs for their crimes in the Peninsula. The support turned into open opposition when the ICTY also looked into Croatian atrocities during the Homeland War, especially in the Krajina region. Croatia's involvement in serious war crimes was a phenomenon that its leaders definitely wanted to sweep under the carpet. The ICTY, then, became a thorn in the side of the government.

What is telling about Tudjman's strategy is that his Serbian counterpart, Slobodan Milošević, resorted to a very similar strategy and defined his country eminently as a victim of international attacks. Portraying Serbia in that light was, in fact, one of the central aspects of his government and his entire political life. For instance, the speech that boosted his profile as Yugoslav leader, in front of a million people in Kosovo Polje in 1989, was based on the 600th anniversary of the Battle of Medieval Serbia against the Ottomans. "Although the Serbs were defeated at Kosovo Polje," writes James Gow, "the nobility found in having stood up against overwhelming Ottoman forces remained an important part of Serbia's self-image,"[72]

With the military campaigns he led during the 1990s, Milošević intended to spread a specific version of history. He wanted to make sure, even if that meant going to war, that Serbia would no longer be trodden on, as happened in 1389, and that Serbian pride would be restored. That explains why, for example, after NATO bombed Belgrade and Kosovo in 1999, Milošević defended his idea of Serbian victimhood by holding the West responsible. It also explains why, after being captured and transferred to the ICTY compounds in The Hague, in 2001, he argued that his trial was "an evil and hostile action aimed at justifying the crimes committed against my country"[73] and defined himself as a victim. Put bluntly, Milošević – just like Tudjman – raised the victim status of his country by always blaming outsiders – Croatia, Bosnia, the West, the ICTY.

This idea fits particularly well with Serbia's reaction to Gotovina's judgment. Aleksandar Fatić, Director of the Centre for Security Studies in Belgrade, argues in this regard that "especially after the verdict passed by ICTY to the three Croatian generals for crimes against the Serbs, in April 2011,[74] the perception of the Tribunal in Serbia has changed."[75] Fatić analyses why:

---

72 Gow, The Serbian Project, 41.

73 "Milošević, Calling Himself a Victim, Asks to Be Freed by Court", The New York Times, January 31, 2002. http://www.nytimes.com/2002/01/31/world/Milošević-calling-himself-a-victim-asks-to-be-freed-by-court.html.

74 Apart from Ante Gotovina, two other Croatian generals were receiving their sentences that day: Ivan Čermak, Assistant Minister of Defense in the Croatian government and commander of the Knin garrison, and Mladen Markač, Commander of the Special

> Most people in Serbia do understand that crimes were committed during the civil wars, and that the perpetrators of some of these crimes were Serbs. What was lacking for them to fully embrace the ICTY is a major decision that would state something that everybody in the region knew, and that concerned another nation.[76]

That other nation was Croatia, and what everyone knew was that Croatian nationals had been perpetrators of crimes against Serbs during the war. Thus, the fact that the ICTY recognised that issue officially by giving Gotovina a 24-year sentence was received in a positive way in Belgrade. In addition, the reaction highlights two important historical trends that are central to the present understanding of the countries vis-à-vis the EU and the ICTY.

The first concerns the fact that Serbia's relationship towards the ICTY has been strained since the initial stages of the Tribunal. There is a general feeling in Serbia that there is an anti-Serb bias in the ICTY, and this turned into open resistance over the years. It was particularly evident during the Milošević years and continued when Vojislav Koštunica was in power (he was President between 2000 and 2003 and Prime Minister between 2004 and 2008).

Related to that is a second argument: Despite the crimes perpetrated by other parties involved in the conflict, Serbian public opinion feels that Serbs are being demonized and unjustly portrayed as the main victimisers. It is nevertheless a fact that armed men of this ethnic background committed most of the tragically memorable atrocities during the 1990s. Those events include not only the long siege of Sarajevo and the mass and systematic targeting of civilians by snipers, but also two other events that have been particularly important for the ICTY and the EU, as the next section explains in detail. Those two events are the massacre in Srebrenica, in July 1995, and the war in Kosovo, three years later.

More than fifteen years after "Europe's worst atrocity since World War II", the issue of Srebrenica still divides Serbs as they try to come to terms with that shameful part of their past.[77] Briefly, the events unfolded as follows. Bosnian Serb forces under the command of Ratko Mladić and subordinated to the political leadership of Republika Srpska, the self-declared Serb entity in Bosnia, after a year-long siege, conquered the enclave in Eastern Bosnia in July 1995, then separated men and boys from the rest of the population, driving them to abandoned farms surrounding Srebrenica, where several thousands of them were executed and buried in mass graves. Women and girls were driven in buses into

---

Police of the Ministry of the Interior of Croatia. Čermak was found not guilty on all counts, whereas Markač was sentenced to 18 years' imprisonment.

75 Thomas Sparrow-Botero's e-mail interview with Aleksandar Fatić. April 2011.

76 Ibid.

77 "Serbia's MPs offer apology for Srebrenica massacre". BBC News, March 31, 2010. http://news.bbc.co.uk/2/hi/europe/8594625.stm.

territory held by Bosnian government forces. Together with other inhabitants of Srebrenica, who were hunted down, shot or died from exhaustion while trying to sneak out of the town through the mountains and forests to territory under the control of the government in Sarajevo, the death toll as established by international organisations amounts to more than 7,000, with a large number of victims still missing today.[78] Those events took place despite the presence of a contingent of Dutch peacekeepers in Srebrenica, a town that had previously been defined by the UNSC as a 'safe area'. Even at the time of writing, the presence of Dutch citizens during the Srebrenica massacre is a highly controversial issue in The Netherlands, and a reason why that country has been the most fervent EU member state supporting the ICTY and demanding the handover of the perpetrators of that massacre to The Hague as an inescapable condition for Serbia's EU accession. As Fatić argues, "the fact that a Dutch government fell over Srebrenica is telling enough about just how important the issue of cooperation with ICTY is for Dutch foreign policy."[79] In the Netherlands, the issue of the Srebrenica massacre is closely linked to the resignation of a whole cabinet in 2002. At that time, the Nederlands Instituut for Oorlogsdocumentatie (NIOD) published its final report (comprising several thousand pages) on the events in Srebrenica and the reaction of the Dutch political establishment, the military, and the government to the massacre back in 1995. The report mentioned a number of shortcomings, misrepresentations, and attempts to cover up the massacre and some details following the fall of the town, and led to the resignation of several ministers, who also had been cabinet members in 1995. This "Srebrenica crisis of 2002", as it is sometimes called by the media, led to the resignation of the whole cabinet of Prime Minister Wim Kok.[80] By 2001, the ICTY had established that the events in and around Srebrenica in 1995 amounted to genocide, in accordance with the statute of the ICTY. This was a trial chamber finding in *the pros. vs. Krstić*, the first European defendant an international tribunal sentenced for genocide after World War II.[81] Among the

---

78 *The pros. vs. Krstić*, IT-98-33. Judgment, 2.8.2011. http://www.icty.org/x/cases/Krstić/tjug/en/krs-tj010802e.pdf.

79 Telephone-Interview with Aleksandar Fatić. April 2011.

80 There were a number of other inquiries by different stakeholders (special rapporteurs and parliamentary commissions) in the Netherlands, which attempted to elucidate the events of July 1995 in and around Srebrenica. The largest was the NIOD report. For more information see the special dossier of NRC Handelsblad on http://vorige.nrc.nl/dossiers/srebrenica/niodrapport/ and the part dedicated to Srebrenica in the second part of this book.

81 Krstić had been chief of staff of the Bosnian Serb Army and commander of its Drina corps (responsible for the assault on Srebrenica). His sentence was slightly lowered (from 46 to

alleged perpetrators were two prominent and well-known figures, in particular because they have been a constant problem for Serbia's European aspirations: Radovan Karadžić, President of Republika Srpska, and Ratko Mladić, military commander of the Army of Republika Srpska (VRS).[82]

The second event happened three years after Srebrenica, and again put Serbia under intense international scrutiny. Formally part of Serbia at the time but with a majority of ethnic Albanians, the little province of Kosovo first became the centre of a civil conflict between the Kosovo Liberation Army (KLA or in Albanian UÇK)[83] and Serbian forces plus the Army of Yugoslavia (Vojske Jugoslavije, VJ) and the paramilitary group led by the infamous Željko Ražnatović, a.k.a Arkan, who was later indicted by the ICTY. Later, the situation evolved into an international war that included NATO. But what ensued was, in James Gow's words, "a new campaign of ethnic cleansing"[84] by Belgrade against the ethnic Albanian population. The final outcome was that 1.4 million Kosovar Albanians became either refugees or internally displaced persons (IDPs), 11,000 people were killed, there were massacres (the most controversial and disputed one in the town of Račak)[85], and landmines were scattered over the region which still today pose a threat for locals and tourists alike.[86]

Suddenly, the nightmares of Srebrenica came back to haunt the international community, which had been blamed for not reacting in a timely manner in 1995 to prevent the massacre in that Bosnian town. In Kosovo, the situation could not be the same. As the Rambouillet peace talks failed in 1999, NATO started a so-called humanitarian intervention in March 1999 and bombed the Federal Republic of Yugoslavia (FRY) by air, a military campaign that has been subject to controversy regarding its legitimacy and the number of civilian casualties.[87]

---

35 years' imprisonment) on appeal, and the verdict was changed from "committing genocide" to "aiding and abetting genocide". *The pros. vs. Krstić* IT-98-33.

82 See: *the pros. vs. Karadžić* IT-95-5/18-I and *the pros. vs. Mladić* T-09-92

83 In Albanian: Ushtria Çlirimtare e Kosovës, Army for the Liberation of Kosovo.

84 Gow, The Serbian Project, 201.

85 See the second part of this book and some chapters in this part for more details on how the massacre impacted the ICTY's work.

86 For more statistical information, see "World: Europe: Kosovo: The Conflict by Numbers". BBC News, June 11, 1999. http://news.bbc.co.uk/2/hi/europe/366981.stm.

87 Jović, Dejan: "Croatia after Tudjman: The ICTY and Issues of Transitional Justice". In: Batt and Obradović-Wochnik, 18. For the controversies about NATO intervention and Western support for the KLA see: Daalder, Ivo H.; O'Hanlon, Michael O.: Winning ugly. NATO's War to Save Kosovo. Washington D. C.: Brookings Institution 2000 and Joksimovich, Vojin: Kosovo Crisis. A Study in Foreign Policy Mismanagement. Los Angeles: Graphics Management Press 1999.

Milošević ordered the withdrawal of Serbian troops in June 1999 and agreed to the presence of peacekeepers, but the damage was already done. On May 24, 1999, Milošević was indicted for crimes against humanity and war crimes by the ICTY.[88]

And in that sense, Srebrenica and Kosovo become important points of reference even when the topic is not Serbia directly, but Croatia, its most important neighbour: just as high-profile Serbs were tried for those two pivotal events and thus considered perpetrators, so Serbia celebrated the fact that Croatia's highest-ranking general received a severe prison sentence by the ICTY. With that in mind, it does not seem far-fetched when author Dejan Jović states that "Croatia and Serbia were 'Siamese twins' of the conflict – the political and security situation in one of them inevitably influenced the other."[89]

The ICTY 1993-2001: Between Power Politics and "Rhetorical Action"

February 22, 1993, was hailed as a historic moment. In New York, the fifteen members of the United Nations Security Council ratified Resolution 808 and, in the process, established the basis for the first war crimes tribunal since Nuremberg and Tokyo. Conscious of the importance of the day, diplomats at UN Headquarters did not keep any words to themselves and expressed their satisfaction at the new institution. "There is an echo in this chamber today", U.S. Ambassador Madeleine Albright grandiloquently summed up. "The Nuremberg principles have been reaffirmed. The lesson that we are all accountable to international law may finally have taken hold in our collective memory."[90]

Behind the scenes, away from the cameras and journalists, the situation was radically different. Albright herself recalled nine years later that "it was easy enough to take the first vote in February to get the Tribunal created, but nobody really believed that it would work."[91] Important actors in the international community – i.e. the United States, seconded by its European allies – viewed the new experiment with open scepticism and even "shocking silence".[92] Elizabeth

---

88 *The pros. vs. Milošević* IT-02-54.

89 Jović, Croatia after Tudjman, op. cit.

90 Cerone, John (quoting Madeleine Albright): "Dynamic Equilibrium. The Evolution of US Attitudes Toward International Criminal Courts and Tribunals". *The European Journal of International Law*. Vol. 18, Nr. 2, (2007). http://ejil.oxfordjournals.org/content/18/2/277.full.pdf+html.

91 Pond, Endgame, 21.

92 Hazan, Pierre: Justice in a Time of War. The True Story Behind the International Criminal Tribunal for the Former Yugoslavia. Texas A&M University Press 2004, 11.

Pond goes further and adds that "it was an unwanted stepchild of both the European and the American governments, something forced on them by the 'CNN effect' as the brutality in the Yugoslav wars escalated and appalled Western TV viewers."[93]

The doubts in Europe and the United States resided not only in the sacredness of national sovereignty, which could be eroded by the ICTY, but also in the thought that indicting the figures responsible for the bloodshed in the Balkans could leave the region without authoritative interlocutors to eventually negotiate peace with. It was what Mahmoud Cherif Bassiouni, an Egyptian war crimes expert who chaired the commission in charge of creating the ICTY and was then controversially nominated to become its first Chief Prosecutor, called "the realpolitik exponents' resistance to justice"[94] or, in plain language, the eternal discussion between peace and justice that is at the heart of the creation of international criminal tribunals.

And even though Europe and the U.S. shared the initial reluctance to the existence of a new international tribunal, they also quickly understood the immense potential power the Tribunal could wield, and thus aimed to position themselves appropriately, so that they could exert influence. They were divided on the nature of such an international endeavour, and were embroiled in their own debates. One element of these debates was the very evident fact that the Americans were witnessing the conflict in the Balkans from afar and did not seem very interested in shedding the blood of a their soldiers to save foreign civilians, whereas Europe was experiencing the havoc on its own doorstep and was "sending thousands of Blue Helmets into the Balkans."[95] That might explain why, in Pierre Hazan's words, the Americans started to "speak of Justice to mask their unwillingness to deploy troops, while the French and the British, who dispatched soldiers, fear this justice even as they solemnly declare it to be of paramount importance."[96] The notion of the ICTY as a "cheap surrogate for intervention" and an "excuse for non-intervention" has become a popular argument in media debates and political quarrels about the role of international criminal justice in conflict resolution. But if the ICTY was created merely as a fig leaf to cover up the unwillingness of liberal democracies to stop the conflict by military means (and hence bear costs and sacrifices), how can we then explain that these states not only created and maintained it, but also were

93 Pond, Endgame, op. cit. 21. For CNN effect see: Robinson, Piers: The CNN effect. The Myth of News, Foreign Policy and Intervention. Routledge 2002.

94 Bassiouni, Cherif: "Foreword". In Hazan, Justice, xiii.

95 Hazan, Justice 24.

96 op. cit. 24.

confronted with a number of decisions and policy choices by subsequent chief prosecutors that were detrimental to some of these states' interests and brought forth harsh criticism from European capitals? How was it that the ICTY, despite the obstacles that built up during the Dayton peace negotiations, managed to indict, apprehend, and judge such high-ranking and initially unreachable suspects as Milošević, Karadžić, Mladić, and Gotovina? This can to a large extent be explained by referring to Schimmelpfennig's concept of "rhetorical action". When explaining why the EU had agreed to include Central and Eastern European countries instead of limiting itself to the conclusion of association agreements (which would have been restricted to trade liberalisation), Schimmelpfennig pointed to the "institutional environment" of the EU, where "political actors are concerned about their reputation as members and about the legitimacy of their preferences and behaviour. Actors who can justify their interests on the grounds of the community's standard of legitimacy are therefore able to shame their opponents into norm-conforming behaviour and to modify the collective outcome that would have resulted from constellations of interests and power alone."[97] In other words, the creation and functioning of the ICTY can only to a certain extent be explained in terms of rational behaviour and short–term cost avoidance and gain-seeking. Some of its features are easier to understand when referring to socialisation effects in an environment of shared values, norms and beliefs. Subsequent ICTY chief prosecutors managed to appeal quite well to these "shared values and beliefs" in order to increase their leverage over states whose cooperation the ICTY depended on so much. A large part of the public support that Louise Arbour and Carla Del Ponte enjoyed during their respective terms was the result of skilful appeals to values and norms. Since the ICTY had no monopoly over coercion and none of the coercive means that are at the disposal of municipal courts, resorting to "rhetorical action" was the only way left in order to increase its efficacy and to put pressure on reluctant states.[98]

Initially, and even before it formally started to work, the Tribunal was already stagnant: the Commission of Experts had no computers and no office to work in, the budget for the Tribunal's first year did not even reach 300,000 U.S. dollars, and the judges had to rent their robes from a theatrical provider.[99] Added to that was the fact that the Tribunal was short of adequate staffing and did not

97 Schimmelpfennig, Frank: "The Community Trap: Liberal Norms, Rhetorical Action, and the Eastern Enlargement of the European Union." *International Organization* 55, 1, 2001, 47–80.

98 It is striking that the current chief prosecutor Serge Brammertz almost totally refrains from using this method.

99 Pond, Endgame, 22.

have a military capability of its own, but relied heavily on cooperation and funds from the international community. It was therefore not hard to predict its initial results: the post of Chief Prosecutor was left vacant for fifteen months, after two years in existence only one person who had been accused was in custody, and the first trial only started after three and a half years. Egyptian judge Georges Abi-Saab bluntly recalled the situation:

> I would have never believed that the UN and in particular the states of the Security Council could be so irresponsible. They produced a big bang saying in nearly celestial terms 'Let there be a Tribunal' without conducting feasibility studies, without according a budget, without thinking of anything.[100]

Despite this initial mess, the ICTY slowly started to find a space in the geopolitical landscape of the Balkans and proved its value by convincingly reacting to two pivotal events in the region: the Dayton Peace Accords and the crisis in Kosovo, both of which served as important wake-up calls. It was during these two events that the ICTY – and especially its Chief Prosecutor – understood that the Tribunal could have a political impact and, after years of difficulties, could turn the balance in its favour.

In 1995, the ICTY's first Chief Prosecutor, Richard Goldstone from South Africa, signalled this change in various ways: first in July and then in November, he indicted Ratko Mladić and Radovan Karadžić, the two Bosnian Serb heads of the Srebrenica massacre, for genocide, war crimes, and crimes against humanity. This move not only prevented a possible amnesty deal for the two leaders and stopped them from appearing in Dayton as negotiators, which were ideas that were floating in the air, but also bolstered the profile of the Tribunal[101] and proved that the ICTY was capable of targeting the 'big fish', despite resistance by some countries in the international community that still believed in finding peace "at any price, even if it is a peace without justice."[102]

Goldstone also showed his intention of moving beyond Serb suspects and targeted a handful of Croat citizens, among them Tihomir Blaškić, a Bosnian Croat general who later became the first person accused to surrender voluntarily to the Tribunal. What is striking about these indictments, both the Serb and the Croat ones, is that they occurred in the months surrounding the Dayton Peace Talks (held between November 1 and 21), where peace was clearly winning the battle against justice. The indictments thus reveal the specific intention of Goldstone to put the ICTY on the international map as part of the solution to the Yugoslav wars. Moreover, as a result of the indictments roughly coinciding with

100 Hazan, Justice, 44.

101 Peskin, International Justice, 42-43.

102 Hazan, Justice, 67.

Dayton, where the Balkan countries committed themselves to cooperating with the ICTY, the ICTY profile was raised to a different level: at least on paper, the ICTY was giving initial signs of becoming an actor that had to be taken into consideration.[103]

But despite the improvements in Dayton, the situation of the ICTY still remained complicated. Except for the United States, none of the powerful nations in the world was sharing substantial information with the Tribunal and, on the contrary, most still continued to view the Court with suspicion. Moreover, the Scheveningen prison in the Netherlands remained basically empty, a powerful indictment of a Tribunal that had already been dubbed a 'paper tiger'. That situation, however, would start to change in the following years.

Soon after the peace deal, the tensions in Kosovo between the Kosovar Albanians and the Serb minority became more prominent, until they finally erupted on a dramatic scale in 1998. Here again, the international community was initially doubtful about pointing the finger directly at Slobodan Milošević and thus losing a possible interlocutor, but as the war unravelled, the situation changed. Victor Peskin explains in his comparison of international justice in Rwanda and the Balkans that the Tribunal started to be regarded as a player that could promote stability and put pressure on the Serb leadership to stop the atrocities. "For the United States and Europe," he argues, "calling on the ICTY to conduct investigations paid political dividends."[104] The dividends for the US and Europe came in two ways: "first by portraying themselves as standing up to brutality in Kosovo, and second by shifting some of the responsibility to the tribunal for confronting Milošević."[105]

The main change for the ICTY would come, just as with Dayton, by strategically timing a key indictment and making it public with the biggest exposure possible. In doing so, the Tribunal proved that it could be influential and successful by reacting to the current situation, by becoming what author John Hagan described as a "Real-Time Tribunal"[106] and not a "Virtual Tribunal", one without teeth. In the language of rational choice or International Relations theory, states realized that by bringing in the ICTY, they could

103 Among the agreed measures in Dayton, full cooperation with the ICTY was called as an "essential condition for a lasting peace". See US Department of State. "Agreed Measures on Dayton Accords Compliance". March 18, 1996. http://www1.umn.edu/humanrts/icty/dayton/daytoncompl.html.

104 Hazan, Justice, 55.

105 Ibid.

106 Hagan, John: Justice In the Balkans. Prosecuting War Crimes In The Hague Tribunal. University of Chicago Press. 2003, 93.

increase their bargaining power with respect to the post–Yugoslav republics that had emerged from the war, and tame their quest for violent solutions and faits accomplis. This, however, came at a price. It also increased the leverage of the ICTY and its capacity to use "rhetorical action." From this moment on, we can observe two parallel strategies: while the Tribunal would appeal to shared norms and values, invoke justice as a major good, and emphasize the obligation of cooperation, states would resort time and again to the Tribunal to raise the stakes for the other side. During the years that followed, key politicians involved in the conflict, their generals, and also minor figures like the leaders of paramilitary groups involved in atrocities, not only faced threats of defeat, political isolation, economic sanctions, or military retaliation, but were also – additionally – confronted with the danger of being indicted, apprehended, and extradited to The Hague, where not only their political or military position but also their personal freedom was at risk. The ICTY thus became the cornerstone of a mechanism that could be described as a mutually reinforcing "blame and power game," during which the EU, its member states, and the US (before the Bush administration's shift away from international criminal law) carried out the power part, while the ICTY seemed to be responsible for "blaming" reluctant actors into compliance and adding legitimacy to the power play between the international community and key actors in the conflict.

One striking example clearly demonstrates how this game actually worked on the ground. In early December 1995 – long after Louise Arbour's indictments of Ratko Mladić and Radovan Karadžić[107] – an agreement was reached between Mladić, Milośević, and French president Jacques Chirac which guaranteed Mladić that he would not be handed over to the ICTY in exchange for the release of French pilots who had been shot down over Serb-held territory in Bosnia and were then being held hostage by Mladić's units.[108] The deal demonstrates that the mere existence of the ICTY and the indictment of Mladić had raised the cost for Mladić

107 Both were indicted in July 1995. *The pros. vs. Karadžić* IT-05/18-I; *The pros. vs. Mladić* IT-09-92.

108 The whole event was revealed by former Yugoslav president Zoran Lelić when he gave evidence as prosecution witness at the trial of Slobodan Milošević. In this evidence, Lelić confirmed the authenticity of an intercept that the Prosecution had released to Milošević under rule 68 (disclosure of exculpatory evidence) of the ICTY's rules of procedure and evidence. The evidence was heard on July 9th 2003. The transcript of the testimony is available at www.un.org/icty/transe54/030709IT.htm (access August 2004). The following day, a spokesperson of the French president denied that "any negotiations" were held with Bosnian Serbs during the time in question. Actually, the intercept suggests that the deal was struck not directly between Mladić and Chirac but through Milošević. Hence, Chirac's denial was not a full one.

when negotiating with Chirac. Without the ICTY, Mladić would have been able to ask for a different concession, probably a more costly one for Chirac, whereas the latter would have been short of one possible concession that he could make to Mladić in order to achieve a settlement (the release of the pilots). By interposing the ICTY between France and the Bosnian Serbs, France had improved its bargaining position. As will be shown later, the EU did the same with respect to Croatia and Serbia while negotiating trade concessions and EU accession. The question remains as to how far the ICTY was able to take advantage of its position as an "interface" and increase its own leverage over suspects.

Louise Arbour was probably the first to use this game to any great extent. In 1998, during the initial phase of the Kosovo crisis, she tried to enter the region herself in order to ensure access to her investigations. She was denied entry in front of a group of journalists, but still managed to win a battle against Milošević. By using the media, she showed the world how Belgrade obstructed the Tribunal's work, and in the process, also presented the image of a Tribunal that was in tune with the times and no longer disconnected from reality.

Arbour also took advantage of the attention given to the NATO bombings in Yugoslavia (March to June 1999) to make a decision that was worth its weight in gold: on May 27, 1999, she made public the indictment of none other than Slobodan Milošević. She accused the Serb leader of crimes against humanity for planning a campaign of terror and violence against Albanian civilians living in Kosovo, and thus made the Serb leader the first sitting head of state to be wanted by an international court. The US – once again – showed its scepticism at this decision, because it believed that the indictment could trigger a more violent reaction by Milošević instead of fostering peace.

Irrespective of this, the decision by Arbour boosted the profile of the Tribunal to new levels: the impact was immediate, the Tribunal made headlines all over the world, and the decision reminded ICTY sceptics of the importance of justice in achieving peace. As Hazan mentions in his book: "his indictment, coming at the end of a chaotic process, escaping at the last minute from the supporters of realpolitik, marks the entry of justice into international relations."[109] Whether this was a bold move which won the ICTY a place among the players of high politics remains in dispute, though. On the one hand, the Milošević indictment bolstered the ICTY's public image, but on the other hand, to some, it also appeared as proof of the ICTY's pro-NATO bias, since the alliance had started to bomb Serbia weeks before the indictment was made public.[110]

---

109 Hazan, Justice, 112.

110 Laughland claims that the bombing and the indictment were "two sides of the same coin". Laughland, Travesty, 2.

It was during Carla Del Ponte's tenure as ICTY Chief Prosecutor that in the evening of June 28, 2001, the news the ICTY had been expecting for two years finally became official: the government of Serbia, under financial pressure by the United States, had handed Milošević over to The Hague. For the ICTY, Milošević's transfer represented a pivotal moment, both the end of one process and the beginning of a new one. Now the tribunal finally had a very high-ranking political suspect and the opportunity to conduct a highly publicized trial.

It also emphasized an aspect central to an understanding of the ICTY: since the Tribunal has no coercive power of its own, it must rely on international cooperation for the transfer of its most-wanted criminals. Some of the Tribunal's goals are thus very often not achieved single-handedly, and it has to keep the interests and priorities of other, more powerful actors in mind. In Milošević's case, that powerful actor was the United States. In the examples studied later in this book, it was the European Union. In this regard, Frederick Swinnen, Special Advisor to ICTY Prosecutor Serge Brammertz, acknowledged that "without this political support, which is very real, we would not be where we are today."[111] That is why, as soon as Milošević appeared for the first time before the Tribunal, for a mere twelve minutes, another benchmark became clear: never before the appearance of Milošević in The Hague had so many eyes been fixed on the ICTY. On that day alone, more than a thousand members of the press from dozens of media organisations[112] stood attentively at the entrance to the Tribunal headquarters to hear how the former President of Yugoslavia attacked the Tribunal as a "false" and "illegitimate"[113] one. Instead of harming the Tribunal, this only served to bolster its public profile even more. As Peskin claims, Milošević's arrival in the Netherlands became a "defining symbol of the power of an international court."[114] The ICTY would have to revalidate that power time and again during the following years.[115]

111 Interview with Frederick Swinnen. ICTY Headquarters, The Hague. April 14, 2011.

112 Hagan, International Justice, 2.

113 "Lawyer says Milošević to accept help". CNN, July 4, 2001. http://edition.cnn.com/2001/WORLD/europe/07/03/Milosevic.court/index.html.

114 Peskin, International Justice, op. cit.

115 It is beyond the scope of this book to assess the ICTY's (and OTP's) media strategy and public image. However, it should be mentioned that the Milošević trial became a watershed for the ICTY, as it damaged a huge part of the goodwill that the ICTY had managed to build up during the preceding years. For a broad discussion of these issues see: Waters, Timothy (ed): The Milošević Trial. An Autopsy. Oxford University Press 2013. We are grateful to Tim Waters for giving us the table of contents and insights into a part of its contents. While this book is being written, Tim Water's book is not yet released. Throughout this book, we are therefore going to quote from chapters of his book, but without reference to page numbers. Chapter 19 is the one relevant here: Bachmann, Klaus: Framing the Trial of the Century: Influences of, and on, International Media.

The European Union 1990-1999: Transitional Justice Conditionality and Enlargement

In October 2010, just before an official visit to four countries in the Western Balkans, the President of the European Council, Herman van Rompuy, referred to this region's "European destiny". "There is a place for the Western Balkans in the European house", he argued in the video message posted on the Council's website. "Europe is committed to a European perspective of the Western Balkans."[116]

What Van Rompuy calls a "European destiny" is the continuation, in the post-Lisbon-Treaty EU, of the Union's decade-long ideal of luring the troublesome countries of the Western Balkans into the European Union and to the values traditionally attached to it: "liberty and solidarity, tolerance and human rights, democracy and the rule of law."[117]

But the prospect of EU enlargement to the Balkan countries is a much greater endeavour than exporting the said values and presenting the countries with the coveted EU status. On the one hand, the relationship between the EU and the countries in the Western Balkans is pivotal for the Union domestically, not only because political events in that region have triggered novel approaches in the Union, but also because any larger conflict, political, social or military, will have an immediate impact on the EU. [118] This goes hand in hand with the idea that the EU has used its presence in the Balkans as a means of strengthening its considerable leverage on the world stage. As former Commissioner for Enlargement Olli Rehn stated in an article for The *Economist's* Brussels outlet *The European Voice*, "the EU's credibility as a global actor continues to rest on our ability to shape our own immediate neighbourhood. In south-eastern Europe we can make a real difference."[119]

---

116 Van Rompuy, Herman: "The Western Balkans: A European Destiny (Video Message)". Council of the European Union, the President's Videos. http://vloghvr.consilium.europa.eu/?p=2861.

117 Kavalski, Emilian: (quoting Olli Rehn): Extending the European Security Community. Constructing Peace in the Balkans. London: Tauris Academic Studies 2008, 118.

118 In this regard, Europol and the European Monitoring Centre for Drugs and Drug Addiction concluded, in reports published in the media in January 2011, that the Balkans are growing in importance as a cocaine trading route from Latin America. See "Los Balcanes: Nueva puerta de la cocaína latinoamericana a Europa". BBC Mundo, January 3, 2011. http://www.bbc.co.uk/mundo/noticias/2011/01/101230_europa_droga_balcanes_latinoamerica_vh.shtml.

119 Rehn, Oli: "The Balkans Remains the EU's Litmus Test". *European Voice* 12.11.2009 http://www.europeanvoice.com/article/imported/the-balkans-remains-the-eu-s-litmus-test/66395.aspx.

That goal was not so clear in the early 1990s, when the bloodshed first started in the Balkans. Back then, Europe took part in international efforts to bring peace to the region, but the crisis revealed Europe's shortcomings. The continent was, as Belgian Minister of State Mark Eijskens wittily put it, "an economic giant, a political mouse and a military worm."[120] In other words, it had developed a common market and was a powerful trading bloc, but it lacked an influential common foreign policy. Moreover, it could wield real influence in economic, but only to a far lesser extent in diplomatic or political terms.[121]

One effect of that situation was that the United States took centre stage during the 1990s in the efforts to stop the havoc in the Balkans. The European Parliament recognized these problems in 1998 when it argued that there was a "lack of ambition in defining an overall policy through a common position on the Balkans, which has meant that the political impact of the EU has been very limited, compared to that of the USA."[122]

The Srebrenica massacre in 1995 and the subsequent peace negotiations in Dayton, served as an initial wake-up call for the EU, to borrow the term used by Elizabeth Pond.[123] First, the Process for Stability and Good Neighbourliness in South-Eastern Europe (more commonly called the Royaumont Process) was presented in the aftermath of Dayton as a means to support implementation of the recently won peace and to encourage democratisation. Second, the EU planned its Regional Approach, which set out mainly to offer the countries in the Western Balkans financial assistance and trade preferences. It also attached political conditions to these contractual relations by demanding full compliance with the Dayton Accords (among them assisting the ICTY). It was hailed as the Union's "first step towards the formulation of its own strategy designed to favour a progressive process of stabilisation and association in the region."[124]

This was further developed after the Kosovo crisis, the second wake-up call and a clear breakthrough in comparison with the recent past. Elizabeth Pond argues that the conflict in Kosovo cemented the idea that "the Balkans could no

120 Quote according to: Steven Blockmans, Steven: Tough Love: the European Union's Relations to the Western Balkans. The Hague: Asser Press 2007, 1.

121 Ibid.

122 Kavalski, Extending, 24. As stated earlier, EU member countries provided almost all the peacekeepers spread across the conflict theatre, but it was the US that made the difference in terms of military capabilities and actual interventions. There is a wide consensus that neither the Dayton agreements nor the solution of the Kosovo crisis could have been militarily enforced by the Europeans only.

123 Pond, Endgame, 5.

124 Blockmans, Tough Love, 242.

longer be regarded as outside Europe and that, willy-nilly, the EU would have to assume responsibility for their decent governance."[125]

With that in mind, the EU began to change its policy towards the region. By the end of the century, the Royaumont process had revealed its weaknesses in trying to solve the problems in the Western Balkans, and in 1999 the Stability Pact for South Eastern Europe (today the Regional Cooperation Council, with its headquarters in Sarajevo) thus came into force. This international institution (it is strictly speaking not an EU device, although it was initiated by the EU) was formed as a long-term conflict prevention mechanism and a body to foster regional support.

Additionally, in 1999 the European Commission started the *Stabilisation and Association Process* (SAP) with its *Stabilisation and Association Agreements* (SAA), a tailor-made framework towards eventual European Union accession for countries in the Western Balkans.[126] Not only did the EU further elaborate the conditionality principle for the region and signal the clear intention of attracting the Balkans to Brussels, it also understood the influence it could wield in the region through its potentially persuasive power of attraction.[127] No wonder the SAA soon came to be seen "both by the countries in the region and by the European Union as the most important instruments to achieve lasting peace and stability in the Western Balkans, because they offer the prospect of EU membership."[128]

The SAP was modelled on the previous enlargement schemes for a series of Central European countries and added specific conditions for the Balkans. Amongst those particular rules, the SAP stresses the need to have good neighbourly relations (a key issue when it comes to Kosovo) and to cooperate with the ICTY. This was mentioned in the 2000 Declaration of the Zagreb Summit, where the SAP system was launched, and it was ratified in the subsequent Thessaloniki Agenda for the Western Balkans, which confirmed the conditionality introduced by the SAP.[129] Additionally, the need to cooperate with the Tribunal was also explicitly brought up in the SAA document with Serbia, but not in the SAA with Croatia. It is worth mentioning that the ICTY conditionality encompassed in the Agenda was a novel step for the EU. Never

125 Pond, Endgame, 105.

126 Blockmans, Tough Love, 251.

127 It is important to note that the need to cooperate with the ICTY was mentioned in broad terms in EU documents prior to the SAP. Nevertheless, only as a result of the SAP, which is the main framework towards EU accession for the Western Balkans, was the EU enlargement process specifically linked to the ICTY.

128 Blockmans, Tough Love, 306.

129 Op. cit., 252-253.

before had the EU directly interfered with a country's transitional justice policy. During earlier enlargement rounds, specific choices concerning how to deal with a repressive past had been left to the respective country, regardless of whether the country had overcome a military dictatorship (like Spain, Portugal, and Greece) or a communist single party system (like the Central and East European countries that had joined the EU in 2004).

With time, the term "full cooperation" with the ICTY became a symbol of the relationship between the EU, the Tribunal, and Serbia and Croatia. It was not spelled out in the first place, and the fact that it has been interpreted, adapted to the times, and politically used has turned it into a controversial aspect of the whole accession process. Most analyses agree that the flexibility has proven to be a sensible decision in order to react to changing political environments ("only fools don't change,"[130] was the reaction by one interviewee in Brussels when asked about this topic). That phenomenon is at the heart of the EU policy shifts.

Frederick Swinnen, Special Advisor to the ICTY Prosecutor, commented that full cooperation "is a term which was defined or used by EU officials, it is [mentioned] in EU texts, it is not something we came up with."[131] Swinnen added that "the whole ICTY conditionality is an EU invention. However, our view is that it is up to the Office of the Prosecutor to assess cooperation, and up to the EU to take political decisions based on our technical assessment."[132] On the other hand, one EU official in Brussels pointed out during the interview that "it is not for us to explain [what it means]. It is for the Prosecutor."[133] But, as Geraldine Mattioli-Zeltner of Human Rights Watch (HRW) explained, the ICTY has been particularly careful when using this expression in its reports. "Everybody has tried to play with this term and has had very different understandings of what full cooperation means,"[134] she concluded. In short, it is not always clear who should be responsible for making sure that countries comply with the rule which was established at the beginning of the accession process. It should also not go unnoticed that the Security Council Resolutions establishing the ICTY require all states to cooperate with the Tribunal. This requirement, however, was emphasized only with respect to Croatia, Serbia, Bosnia and Kosovo, and did not play any role in relation to states outside the former war theatre, which were obliged to disclose documents and provide witnesses required (or even subpoenaed) by the ICTY. In many cases,

130 Thomas Sparrow-Botero's interview with EU official. Brussels, April 2011.

131 Interview with Frederick Swinnen, The Hague, April 2011.

132 Ibid.

133 Thomas Sparrow-Botero's interview with EU official. Brussels, April 2011.

134 Telephone interview with Geraldine Mattioli-Zeltner, April 2011.

governments either denied the tribunal these sources, hiding behind the notion of "national security", or restricted access to them in a way that often made the statutory provisions for "fair" and "public" trials an illusion. [135] Chief prosecutor's spokeswoman Florence Hartmann explicitly stated on various occasions that the Office of the Tribunal Prosecutor (hereinafter OTP) regarded cooperation as a requirement for all states, but from Serbia, the OTP expected compliance in the first place. It goes without saying that such a differentiation can be found neither in the ICTY's statute nor in the Security Council resolutions pertaining to the ICTY. [136]

Nevertheless, the emphasis placed on the compliance issue in the EU's conditionality shows the weight given by the European Union to conflict resolution and sustainable peace in the region. Today, as Serbia and Croatia are getting closer to the goal of EU membership, the European Commission's subsequent progress reports remain the framework that is used for measuring their progress. The SAA, as such, is part of the EU pre-accession strategy. The procedure for the conclusion of an SAA is very specific: before the negotiations can even start, each country must have achieved a specific level of progress. The Commission evaluates progress in each country and assesses whether it has met the EU's political and economic criteria (such as the Council's Guidelines of April 29, 1997, and the so called Copenhagen Criteria from the 2004 enlargement). In the case of Serbia and Croatia, these criteria include cooperation with the ICTY. When sufficient progress has been made, the Commission carries out, with the approval of the Council, a feasibility study regarding the possibility of opening negotiations for an SAA. A formal proposal is submitted if the Council gives a positive assessment and the feasibility study is completed, and then negotiations begin. Before the agreement can come into

135 During the Milošević trial, several high ranking military and political witness, among them former Nato's Supreme Allied Commander Europe (SACEUR), Wesley Clark, were heard partly *in camera* hearings, assisted by lawyers and with limited permission to disclose sensitive information.

136 The relevant article 29 of the ICTY Statute reads as follows: "1. States shall co-operate with the International Tribunal in the investigation and prosecution of persons accused of committing serious violations of international humanitarian law.
2. States shall comply without undue delay with any request for assistance or an order issued by a Trial Chamber, including, but not limited to:
(a) the identification and location of persons;
(b) the taking of testimony and the production of evidence;
(c) the service of documents;
(d) the arrest or detention of persons;
(e) the surrender or the transfer of the accused to the International Tribunal." No distinction is made between states.

force, however, the Council, the European Parliament, and all EU Member States and the non-member states concerned must first ratify and accept the SAA.[137]

The SAA is normally followed by a series of steps that finally lead to the ratification of an accession treaty. After the SAA has been signed, a country has to apply for membership. Based on an opinion expressed by the European Commission, the application must then be accepted by the Council of the European Union. This leads to a process called screening, whereby the EU assesses the country's readiness to begin negotiations. Based on this, a series of so-called chapters of the accession negotiations (on a wide range of issues, from public procurement to transport policy and science and research) are first opened and subsequently closed when the country has progressed according to EU standards. The completion of negotiations leads to a treaty of accession with a specific date of entry into the EU. When ratified by all EU members, the country can officially join the club.

It is important to mention these rules because both Serbia and Croatia are going through the process, which has not always been smooth and has resulted in unforeseen and sharp changes of direction. These changes are at the forefront of this chapter. The following section will delve into specific policy shifts by the European Union regarding Croatia's and Serbia's international obligation to comply with the ICTY, and will shed light on the process to discover which player actually sparked off the shift: the ICTY, the EU, or Serbia or Croatia.

137 Blockmans, Tough Love, 252. The member states may agree that some or all of the provisions of an SAA may be applied provisionally during the time between the signing and the end of the ratification process. This mechanism will later gain importance in the case of Serbia.

Transitional Justice Policy Changes of the EU Towards Croatia

From Tudjman's Death to Gotovina's Indictment

It was two o'clock in the morning on December 11, 1999, when Croatian television abruptly interrupted its regular program to announce a tragic piece of news: one of the architects of that country's independence and incumbent President, Franjo Tudjman, had died after more than a month in hospital.[138] Three days later, twenty thousand Croats[139] gave the political leader a last farewell in Zagreb and, with that gesture, also signalled the end of Croatia's first period as an independent nation, a period marked by authoritarianism and international isolation. No wonder the liberal newspaper Jutarnji List, commenting on the absence of high-level representatives of Western countries at the funeral, remarked that "it is a testimony to the fact that Tudjman's Croatia didn't have any friends."[140]

That was to change fairly quickly, and Zagreb's international status steadily improved after the death of its president, especially as a result of the elections in 2000. These brought major transformations to the country's political landscape. Not only was Tudjman's party, the Croatian Democratic Union (HDZ), heavily defeated in the polls, but the new centre-left coalition of President Stjepan Mesić and Prime Minister Ivica Račan started to take the country in a new direction, a closer relationship with the EU. A 2004 communication from the Commission of the European Communities looked back at that period and acknowledged that:

> the parliamentary elections in January 2000 and the election of Stjepan Mesić as President of the Republic in February 2000 marked a turning point in relations between the EU and Croatia. The new Croatian leadership immediately showed determination to entrench democratic values and principles and made rapid and significant progress on the main political outstanding questions.[141]

---

138 "Muere en un hospital de Zagreb Franjo Tudjman, padre de la independencia croata". Diario El País, 11.12.1999.

139 Erlanger, Steven: "Though Grieving for Tudjman, Many Croats Want Change". The New York Times, 13.12.1999.

140 Quoted according to El Pais: "Miles de croatas despiden a Tudjman ante una ausencia llamativa de mandatarios extranjeros". Diario El País. 14.12.1999.

141 It must be said that among the questions, cooperation with the ICTY was mentioned. See Commission of The European Communities. "Communication from the Commission. Opinion on Croatia's Application for Membership of the European Union". (2004) http://eur-lex.europa.eu/LexUriServ/site/en/com/2004/com2004_0257en01.pdf.

Croatia suddenly saw only open doors. It entered NATO's Partnership for Peace and was admitted to the World Trade Organisation, it received financial aid from the European Union and the United States, and it signed the SAA with the EU on October 29, 2001, and became the subject of the European Commission's country strategy for 2002-2006.[142]

Most importantly, the shift marked the beginning of a new relationship between Croatia and the ICTY, whereby the new government pledged to cooperate with the Tribunal, helped the ICTY to set up a liaison office in Zagreb, authorized the transfer of the first Bosnian Croat suspect to The Hague (Mladen Naletilić),[143] and gave the Tribunal the green light to investigate Operations Flash and Storm.[144] The importance of these two operations stems from the fact that they were not only the centre of Croatia's interpretation of its Homeland War, they also formed the basis for the ICTY's accusations of war crimes committed by Zagreb. Taken together, the abovementioned changes pointed, as Elizabeth Pond put it, to "an astonishing turnaround."[145]

A closer look at that turnaround sheds light on the dynamics of Croatia's new government and reveals the political calculations that very soon came to the fore. After all, Zagreb's renewed cooperation with the ICTY was not intended to be a simple gesture of goodwill indicating a convinced respect for international law. More likely, it showed that the improved relationship with the ICTY was mainly set up and maintained for purely instrumental reasons. Victor Peskin described this phenomenon by stating that "increased compliance with the ICTY was the key to winning the much sought after invitation to join the European Union and achieve Croatia's fervent quest to shun its Balkan heritage."[146]

Thus, the Croatian government used the 'ICTY card' to suit its own interests. It delayed or blocked assistance to the Tribunal when it considered it necessary to pour oil on troubled waters at home – for instance with recalcitrant nationalistic groups and opponents of the Tribunal – or it made things easier for the ICTY when it sought to receive praise from key international actors on its way to the European Union. The Tribunal, through Chief Prosecutor Carla Del Ponte, fought back in its intent to gain full cooperation from Zagreb.

Coincidentally, it was again after a television broadcast that the Croats experienced the clearest example of the utilitarian use of international justice by the Croatian government. It was the summer of 2001 and thousands of people in

142 Subotić, Hijacked Justice, 87.

143 *The pros. vs. Naletilić & Martinović* IT-98-34.

144 See Pond, Endgame, 131 and Peskin, International Justice, 120.

145 Pond, Endgame, 131.

146 Peskin, International Justice, 120.

the country were glued to their television sets to see Goran Ivanišević lift the silver cup at Wimbledon, the world's most prestigious tennis tournament, when it was announced that Ante Gotovina, another of Croatia's heroes (at least as seen by part of the population), had just been indicted by the ICTY.[147] This would mark the beginning of the official quest for the high-ranking general accused of crimes against humanity and war crimes allegedly committed while commanding Croat forces during Operation Storm,[148] who became the main obstacle to Croatia's compliance with international obligations and consequently to Croatia's bid for EU accession. The fact that one of the heroes of Croatia's liberation war[149] had just been indicted for crimes against humanity triggered a wave of protest and criticism in Croatia. Many believed, as author Jelena Subotić put it, that "to criminalise Operation Storm was to criminalise the Croatian state itself."[150]

The government was facing a conundrum: if it assisted the ICTY in handing over the general, it would no doubt please international governments and clear the path towards EU accession, but it would simultaneously endanger lasting stability at home; if it didn't cooperate, it would be violating an international commitment which could seriously threaten Croatia's hopes of joining the coveted club of nations. Amidst the uncertainty, Prime Minister Ivica Račan decided to do both. He first acknowledged he would do everything in his power to capture the general, above all because not doing so would tarnish the country's possibilities of EU accession. This was viewed positively by the international community, and Javier Solana, the EU's foreign policy chief, described the decision as "courageous" and as "a very constructive step towards Europe."[151] As later events would show, Račan's statement contained empty

---

147 Pond, Endgame, 131. See also: *The pros. vs. Gotovina et al.* IT-06-90.

148 Operations Storm and Flash were a joint attack by military forces from Croatia, Croat forces from Bosnia and units under the command of the Bosnian government in order to drive the Serb authorities and their armed forces out of the self declared "Repubika Krajina" and to reinstate Croatian territory that had been lost during the breakdown of the Yugoslav Federation in 1991/92. During these operations, atrocities were committed against civilians, and Croat forces carried out a huge campaign of ethnic cleansing against the traditional Serb population in the borderland. Several hundred civilians died, and about 200 000 were expelled to Serb held territories in Bosnia, the Republic of Serbia and Montenegro. See: Silber, Laura; Little, Allen: The Death of Yugoslavia. London: BBC Books and Penguin 1996, 353-363 and Goldstein, Ivo: Hrvatska 1918-2008. Zagreb: Liber 2008, 246-251.

149 For more information on this issue, read the chapter: *Serbia and Croatia in the 1990s: Key Events in Retrospect* in this part of the book.

150 Subotić, Hijacked Justice, 94.

151 Peskin, International Justice, 128.

words: his real commitment to arrest Gotovina remained lacklustre, proof of which is the fact that the general would only be handed over to the ICTY in 2005. By doing so, Račan engaged in rhetorical action, admitting the prevalence of international criminal justice and the country's moral and legal obligation to actually apprehend Gotovina. Actually, as it turned out, even empty words are never totally empty – for two reasons: first, they reflect a choice made by the speaker, who can chose to utter or not to utter them, and may be aware of the consequences of such a choice, and second, they trigger the "civilizing power of hypocrisy" (Jon Elster),[152] which inclines a speaker to bring his actions closer to his declarations, thus reducing cognitive dissonance. Viewed from this perspective, the Croatian Prime Minister fell into the ICTY's "rhetorical action" trap. But Račan was also conscious of the crisis in Zagreb. Four ministers had recently resigned, there were protests from different political organisations, and even Ivanišević, still in the midst of one of his most glorious moments as a tennis player, put his name to an open letter by popular sportsmen who believed there had been efforts to "distort historical facts as to who was the victim and who the aggressor"[153] in the Homeland War. Croatia, the sportsmen added, "was the victim and its generals and soldiers were heroes. That is the only truth."[154] Against that background, the Prime Minister called for – and won – a vote of confidence for his government. President Stipe Mesić wrote a letter to Carla Del Ponte objecting to the indictment and arguing against the Tribunal's interpretation of the Homeland War.[155]

More than other situations, Croatia's period from the death of Tudjman to the indictment of Gotovina highlights how particular events in the country –such as the election results which followed the death of its emblematic leader– can influence policy changes in the European Union which are closely linked to its transitional justice strategy. The clearest policy change that comes to mind is the

152 Elster, Jon: Deliberative Democracy. New York: Cambridge University Press 1998, 109-112. The concept points to people's psychological need to bring behaviour as close as possible to declaration, and vice versa. It argues that people who publicly declare intentions or opinions that they do not actually internalize will try to bring their future deeds closer to these declarations, in order to reduce stress emanating from cognitive dissonance and to gain more credibility in the eyes of others. This mechanism is called "the civilizing power of hypocrisy".

153 "Ivanisevic backs Croat suspects". CNN, 12.7.2001. http://edition.cnn.com/2001/WORLD/europe/07/12/croatia.goran/

154 Jamie Wilson and Ian Black: "Goran calls indicted men war heroes". The Guardian, 13.7.2001. http://www.guardian.co.uk/world/2001/jul/13/warcrimes.ianblack.

155 Drago Hedl: "Gotovina Interview splits Croatian leaders." IWPR Trial Issue 317 (wrongly dated 1.5.2005)http://iwpr.net/report-news/regional-report-gotovina-interview-splits-croatian-leaders

decision to start the SAA negotiations in November 2000, i.e. not even a year after Tudjman's death and barely ten months after the Parliamentary elections.

But this period in 2000 also sheds light on the way in which the local government – in this case under Račan's leadership – manipulated a transitional justice process not to comply with international law standards as such, but to suit national interest and at the same time gain international recognition. In this regard, Subotić emphatically argues that "transitional justice was once again placed in the service of the Croatian state and its European strategy.[156]"

The Postponement of Croatia's Entry Negotiations

In the early stages of the EU negotiations with Croatia, cooperation with the ICTY frequently appears in a broad way in the documents of EU bodies such as the European Commission and the Council of the European Union. Compliance is mentioned as a "key issue",[157] it is acknowledged that "the level of co-operation by the state and the entities with the ICTY is insufficient"[158] and occasionally, specific requests are made. One example of this is the Conclusions of the General Affairs Council session on 29 April 1997, where the Council of the European Union established political and economic conditions that were to be met by countries in South-Eastern Europe seeking EU accession, and where there is a specific paragraph requesting "evidence that the government of Croatia is using its influence to bring Croat war criminals in Bosnia to the international Tribunal."[159]

But that concrete example is more the exception than the rule, as EU documents analysed in this chapter reveal that the obligation to cooperate with the ICTY is always explicit, but not what that cooperation really entails. One EU official interviewed in Brussels in April 2011 confirmed this: "it is true that it was never spelled out, and there was a good reason to be never spelled out, because it would be difficult to agree on a definition."[160] The interviewee went on to say, "there is a general principle in European integration policy called constructive ambiguity: you don't need to be too precise. It is good to leave a

156 Subotić, Hijacked Justice, 96.

157 European Commission. "Commission Staff Working Paper. EU Stabilisation and Association Process for Countries of South-Eastern Europe. Compliance with the Council Conclusions of 29 April 1997 and 21/22.6. 1999". (2000).

158 Ibid.

159 Council Of The European Union. "Conclusions of the General Affairs Council of 29 April 1997".

160 Thomas Sparrow-Botero's interview with EU official. Brussels, April 2011.

certain room for interpretation and this can do the trick."[161] It can do the trick, but it can also generate a problem, and as Croatia's case exemplifies, the government often openly exploited that lack of definition to pursue its own goals.[162]

Carla Del Ponte's indictment of high-level Croats, especially Ante Gotovina, would address that ambiguity. Progressively, Croatia's fulfilment of ICTY conditions became 'personalized', and no longer was the discourse only about cooperation with the Tribunal in a broad sense, but more importantly about ensuring "that the remaining indictee is located and transferred to ICTY", [163] as the 2004 European Commission's Opinion on Croatia's Application for Membership to the European Union highlights. Furthermore, the level of insufficiency in Croatian cooperation also shifted to include more specific details. For instance, in Croatia's 2005 Progress Report, produced by the European Commission, Croatia's deficiencies were measured in the sense that its "efforts to locate, arrest and transfer Gotovina to The Hague were not sufficiently robust to yield significant results."[164]

The personalisation of Croatia's compliance with the ICTY became particularly important from the second half of 2004 onwards. In her 30 June, 2004, address to the United Nations Security Council, Carla Del Ponte acknowledged that "the Croatian authorities are at this point in time fully co-operating with my office,"[165] but she reminded the government that Gotovina was still at large. Five months later, again before the Security Council, she reiterated that plea, but in a harsher tone.

On 23 November, Del Ponte indicated that both the European Union and the ICTY agreed that the latter's objectives would not be fulfilled until high-level suspects, such as Gotovina, appeared in The Hague. She accused Croatia of allowing Gotovina to benefit from a support network within state structures and raised doubts concerning the "efficiency" and "seriousness"[166] of the government's measures to locate the whereabouts of the general. Roughly at the same time, in its December 2004 conclusions, the Presidency of the Council of the European Union

161 Ibid.

162 Peskin, International Justice, 123.

163 Commission of The European Communities. "Communication from the Commission. Opinion on Croatia's Application for Membership of the European Union". Op. Cit. 31, 37, 120

164 European Commission. "Croatia 2005 Progress Report" (2005), 23.

165 "Address by Carla Del Ponte, Chief Prosecutor of the International Criminal Tribunal for the Former Yugoslavia, to the United Nations Security Council, June 30, 2004".

166 "Address by Carla Del Ponte, Chief Prosecutor of the International Criminal Tribunal for the Former Yugoslavia, to the United Nations Security Council. 23.11.2004".

deemed it wise to propose 17 March 2005, as the potential starting date for EU negotiations with Croatia, provided there was full cooperation with the Tribunal.[167]

The coincidence in time of these last two events meant that more than ever before, Croatia's prospects of accession to the European Union depended mostly on the capture of one particular figure: the fugitive general. Thus, Del Ponte's harsh remarks of the previous November were echoed in the EU, which asked her in March 2005 to give a new assessment of cooperation. Not satisfied with the results from Zagreb, the Prosecutor rated the relationship as negative,[168] which prompted the Council of the European Union to postpone the opening of accession negotiations. This happened one day before the 17 March deadline. The discussion would be reopened, according to the communiqué, when the Council could establish "that Croatia is cooperating fully with the ICTY."[169] This move was the result of Dutch pressure in the EU Council. A high-ranking officer of the Dutch Ministry of Foreign Affairs admitted frankly: "We linked full cooperation with the Tribunal to the accession of Croatia." According to several confidential sources inside and outside the ICTY, the Netherlands had the support of Finland, the United Kingdom and Belgium, which did not expose themselves as clearly as the Netherlands. The decision by the Council of the EU created a political tremor in Croatia and became a stumbling block for the government of Ivo Sanader. After dreaming for years of the ultimate goal of joining the EU, the country's lacklustre performance in trying to capture Gotovina and send him to The Hague had finally brought concrete results: the negotiations had stalled. The government's decision, with that in mind, was to increase cooperation, which meant adopting a newly created Action Plan[170] to ensure full cooperation, allowing Del Ponte's office to work hand in hand with the Croatian State Prosecutor and his team in order to locate Gotovina. The Chief Prosecutor reflected on this work in her 2005 address to the Security Council, weeks after Gotovina was captured in Spain as a result of the "undisputable evidence"[171] provided by the Croatian authorities that the general

167 Council of the European Union. "Presidency Conclusions of the Brussels European Council 16/17.12.2004".

168 United Nations Security Council. "Sixtieth General Assembly. Report of the International Tribunal for the Prosecution of Persons Responsible for Serious Violations of International Humanitarian Law Committed in the Territory of the Former Yugoslavia since 1991".

169 Council of The European Union. "Council Conclusions on Croatia, March 16, 2005"

170 European Commission. "Croatia 2005 Progress Report", 7.

171 "Address by Carla Del Ponte, Prosecutor of the International Criminal Tribunal for the Former Yugoslavia, to the Security Council. December 15, 2005". http://www.pbs.org/frontlineworld/stories/bosnia502/ponte2.html.

was in the Canary Islands. Del Ponte admitted that "a solid relation of trust, based on full transparency, was established"[172] between both entities, and added that the operation had received "strong backing from the political leadership"[173] in Zagreb.

All in all, the postponement of Croatia's entry negotiations in 2005 was a huge blow to the national government. It not only proved that the manipulation of transitional justice decisions would not bring benefits in the long run, but it also showed the growing importance of the ICTY and the fact that Zagreb needed to meet its demands.

Thus, from the perspective of the Tribunal, the postponement was a pivotal process. By insisting on the importance of bringing indicted suspects to The Hague and publicly criticising non-compliance on this issue, the ICTY exerted pressure on the EU to link the capture of high-level suspects, such as Gotovina, to accession to the European Union. In addition, the ICTY Chief Prosecutor elucidated on the concept of 'full cooperation with the Tribunal', which was previously muddled and difficult to understand, and made it more difficult for the local government to evade its responsibilities. That is why Geraldine Mattioli-Zeltner, international justice advocacy director at Human Rights Watch in Brussels, argues that "the key for the Tribunal to achieve most effectiveness is when there is some kind of definition of what exactly is wanted without too many nuances."[174]

Third, the postponement also proved that the ICTY had leverage in its demands vis-à-vis the European Union, which stalled the negotiations under the premise that compliance with the Tribunal was a necessary step to achieving EU status. In this particular chain of events, the ICTY proved it can work as a principal, acting on its own behalf and managing in that process to influence the decisions of others. This would not be the case, however, a few months later.

The Run-Up to Gotovina's Arrest

Ante Gotovina was eating dinner and drinking wine at the beach restaurant of a luxury hotel in southern Tenerife, Spain, when he was captured in December 2005, after four years on the run. For the Croatian government, the news was positive in two ways: first, it was a relief that Gotovina was found far away, in the Canary Islands, and not on native soil. Croatia had long been accused of protecting the runaway general, and even shortly before his arrest, Del Ponte set

172 Ibid.

173 Ibid.

174 Telephone interview with Geraldine Mattioli-Zeltner. April 19, 2011.

alarm bells ringing by arguing that she had information that the general was hiding in a Franciscan Monastery under the protection of the Catholic Church.[175] She had even travelled to the Vatican, where her attempt to exert pressure on Vatican diplomacy resulted in "consternation and a rather tense conversation," as one insider told us later. Gotovina was finally arrested on a Spanish Island in the Mediterreanean, which must have caused relief in the Vatican and in Croatia. "It is the final confirmation of the credibility of Croatia and its state institutions", Prime Minister Ivo Sanader stated after he received the news of the arrest in the Iberian Peninsula. "Those who believed us when we were saying that Gotovina was not in Croatia today received the final and complete confirmation."[176]

What is striking about Gotovina's arrest is that the EU doors were opened for Croatia in 2005 before Gotovina's arrest, and not as a result of it. Despite most EU and ICTY documents inextricably linking the general's transfer to the Netherlands with EU accession, the actual arrest in Spain only served to confirm what had already happened two months before.

On October 3, 2005, i.e. nearly seven months after negotiations stalled because of the lack of cooperation with the ICTY, the EU restarted them with the goal of compliance with transitional justice not yet accomplished. And just as Carla Del Ponte played a key role with her negative assessment of Croatia in March, she was also crucial in October, but with a positive outcome for the country. What triggered that sudden change of position?

Both Pond's and Peskin's analyses point to the fact that the decision was probably not entirely in her hands, and that she was more likely included (or

---

175 "War Crimes Chief Accuses Vatican". BBC News, 20.9.2005.
In 2008, the Croatian weekly Nacional claimed that the allegations about Gotovina hiding inside Croatia were the result of a leak by British Special Services, and this had been confirmed in an interview by a correspondent of the Westdeutsche Allgemeine Zeitung (WAZ) with EU Commissioner Günter Verheugen (who supported Croatian membership). Indeed, Verheugen admitted that accession negotiations with Croatia had stalled because of "false claims" that Croatia had hidden Gotovina, but he made no allegations about Britain's role in these rumours, and he did not confirm that special services were involved. See:
Maroje Mihovilović, Ivo Pukanić: "Four years to the truth. British deception proven." Nacional 15.09.2008 http://www.nacional.hr/en/clanak/48714/british-deception-proven; see also the original interview of Knut Priest with Verheugen: EU Kommissar Günter Verheugen verteidigt die Osterweiterung. Der Westen - WAZ Themenportal 9.9.2008. http://www.derwesten.de/nachrichten/politik/EU-Kommissar-Guenter-Verheugen-verteidigt-die-Osterweiterung-id1114240.html

176 Renwick McLean and Marlise Simons: "War Crimes Suspect from Croatia Arrested in Spain's Canary Islands", The New York Times, 8.12.2005.

"hastily recruited",[177] as Pond says) in the internal political dynamics of EU countries. In this particular case, Austria allegedly threatened to veto Turkey's opening of negotiation talks with the EU unless Britain, which was in favour of Ankara's membership but critical of Croatia's compliance with transitional justice, also allowed Zagreb's negotiation process to resume simultaneously.[178] The deadlock was broken with the assistance of a third player: the ICTY.

That same day, Carla Del Ponte issued a positive assessment of Croatia's cooperation, which might have calmed Austria down[179] and allowed both countries to resume talks. "Yes, it is the first time we are saying it's full cooperation,"[180] she said during the meeting with EU foreign ministers, although in reality it was not the first time she mentioned that.[181] But it still served its purpose. Croatia had received ICTY backing, despite the fact that the country's most-wanted suspect was still on the run. Peskin explains in this regard that "it is not difficult to imagine that Del Ponte might well have come under pressure to render a favourable evaluation of Zagreb's search for Gotovina in order not to take responsibility for upsetting a political deal with far-reaching consequences for the future of Europe."[182] One EU official who met with Del Ponte various times ventured an opinion by saying that "this was in the media the following day, but personally I don't buy it,"[183] whereas another EU official added during the interview, "I cannot confirm it. I hear this for the first time."[184] According to sources from within the ICTY which at that time were close to Carla Del Ponte, she actually knew the whereabouts of Gotovina before she issued her positive assessment about Croatia, and she was being informed about the operation the Croatian government had mounted in order to apprehend him. The crucial information came from a phone call to his wife, in which he mentioned Del Ponte. The Croatian authorities apparently had monitored his wife's mobile phone.[185]

---

177 Pond, Endgame, 137.

178 Peskin, International Justice, 146. We received confidential confirmation of this linkage from diplomatic sources as well as from ICTY insiders.

179 "EU and Turkey Agree Terms". The Guardian, 3.10.2005.

180 "UN Gives Croatia the Green Light". The New York Times, 3.10.2005.

181 In her June 30, 2004 Address to the UNSC, she stressed that Croatian authorities were, at that point in time, "fully co-operating with my office". ICTY. "Address by Carla Del Ponte, Chief Prosecutor of the International Criminal Tribunal for the Former Yugoslavia to the United Nations Security Council".

182 Peskin, International Justice, 146.

183 Thomas Sparrow-Botero's interview with EU official. Brussels, April 2011.

184 Ibid

185 Radio B92, 5.7.2007 (based on Balkan Investigative Research Network) http://www.b92.net/eng/news/globe-article.php?yyyy=2007&mm=07&dd=05&nav_category=123&nav_id=42252

The ICTY view, as is only natural, also differs considerably from the one pointing to member states' preferences. Del Ponte not only rejected any claims that she had been put under pressure to give a positive assessment of Croatia, she also stated that the full cooperation she mentioned was in terms of the search for Gotovina, and that if cooperation continued, the general would be arrested soon.[186] In other words, full cooperation with the ICTY meant, in this particular case, Croatia's assistance in all steps leading to the arrest, and not necessarily the arrest as such. "I remember very clearly what she explained that day," an EU official who was with Del Ponte during the meeting on October 3, 2005, recalled. "There were questions, and one of them was what she meant by full cooperation. She said, 'I am now having full access to every piece of information. For me, this is full cooperation'."[187] This is in line with what Del Ponte herself explained in her assessment.

In her memoirs, the Chief Prosecutor acknowledges that the Croatian government had informed her on September 30, 2005 about Gotovina's alleged hiding place in the Canary Islands, but that she had promised to remain silent until the issue could be resolved and the runaway general could be captured. Three days later, she gave the EU the surprising positive assessment of Croatia's cooperation. "I was unable to explain publicly why I was so satisfied, because this would have tipped off Gotovina," Del Ponte recalled. "In a way, the misinformation about political pressure had helped. Without this, Gotovina might have suspected something was amiss and run off in some unknown direction, and I would have lost my gamble."[188]

Irrespective of the reasons behind the positive assessment of Croatia's international obligations, Del Ponte's information hints at the fact that cooperation between ICTY and the Croatian government was producing positive results. She would describe that teamwork a couple of months after the negotiations had restarted, during her December 2005 address to the Security Council, when she argued that the key to success in Gotovina's arrest could be found in the "combination of international incentives, provided mainly by the European Union's consistent policy of conditioning EU accession to full co-operation with the ICTY, and an effective joint operational plan between Croatia and the ICTY."[189]

---

186 ICTY. "Assessment by the Prosecutor of the Cooperation Provided by Croatia. October 3, 2005".

187 Thomas Sparrow-Botero's interview with EU official in Brussels. April 2011.

188 Del Ponte, Madame Prosecutor, 271. See also: Marlise Simons: "War Crimes Case Revives Passions in a Divided Croatia". The New York Times 12.12.2005.

189 "Address by Carla Del Ponte, Prosecutor of the International Criminal Tribunal for the Former Yugoslavia, to the Security Council. December 15, 2005".

For Croatia, the year 2005 ended with the good news of the arrest of Croatia's main suspect and the green light to continue with the European Union entry negotiations. For the ICTY, 2005 also came to an end on a positive note, although the lead-up to that moment was not as transparent as it could have been. Del Ponte played her hand and won. Nevertheless, after years of stating, time and time again, that full cooperation with Croatia required the transfer of its main suspect to The Hague, the ICTY Chief Prosecutor circumvented her own rules by positively assessing Croatia before the arrest. Viewed through the lens of the 2005 events, her own quote from the previous year seems as if it was from a different world:

> "Until Gotovina is located, be it inside or outside of Croatia, and transferred, it will mean that the networks protecting war criminals are more powerful than this part of the Government that genuinely wants to co-operate fully with the Tribunal. Should international pressure recede in this case, this will be perceived as a signal that the international community may not be interested anymore in having the most senior leaders responsible for the most serious crimes (...) appearing in front of the ICTY."[190]

It is also doubtful whether the whole story about Gotovina can be seen as a victory by international justice over state sovereignty. Croatia had managed to capture the general, but it had avoided surrendering him. It then launched an ambitious support project, which included transferring funds for his defence. By doing this, the Croatian government was able to achieve two contradictory goals at the same time – satisfy its critics in the EU by formally complying and getting a positive opinion from the ICTY Prosecutor, and assuage its nationalist constituency in the country by pointing at its support for Gotovina. There were attempts from within the EU to counterbalance this, but they were ultimately unsuccessful. After Gotovina's arrest, the OTP attempted to obtain crucial evidence from Croatia for the trial. Investigators wanted Croatian Army military documents, which they suspected contained orders for the shelling of civilian settlements during Operation Storm. In order to ensure that these were handed over, the Netherlands used a bureaucratic mechanism employed in EU accession negotiations to pressurize Croatia. EU enlargement negotiations are usually divided into chapters. In the language of EU bureaucrats, chapters are "opened" in order to start discussions about when and how a country will adopt the so called "acquis communitaire" (the totality of EU law relevant for such a chapter) and to

190 Address by Carla Del Ponte, Chief Prosecutor of the International Criminal Tribunal for the Former Yugoslavia, to the United Nations Security Council 23.11.2004. Op. Cit. (Italic emphasis added in quote).

define possible transition periods. A new chapter is opened after the previous one is closed, which means that the EU is satisfied about the actions and commitments undertaken by the candidate. Every chapter can be reopened at the end in order to conclude package deals and to enable issue linkage across chapters. Blocking the opening or closure of a chapter (which needs the unanimous approval of the member states) delays negotiations, and, for accession states which are likely to become net beneficiaries of the EU budget after accession, also postpones the financial profits of EU membership. The Netherlands used this mechanism by blocking the opening of chapter 23, which dealt with the rule of law, human rights and the judiciary. They were gently supported by the United Kingdom, Finland, and Belgium. A senior official from the Dutch Ministry of Foreign Affairs said, "we waited five years until we agreed to open chapter 23, in order to get the Croatians to deliver the logbooks. In 2010, the chapter was finally opened, but we put a safeguard clause into the Council decision which stipulated that it could only be closed after the ICTY Prosecutor had confirmed 'full cooperation' with the ICTY."[191] However, they failed. In May 2011, Gotovina was sentenced to 24 years' imprisonment by a ICTY trial chamber without the logbooks. According to the Dutch government source, this made it clear that the main goal had been achieved and the books were no longer necessary. At the end of June the same year, the last chapter was closed. Serge Brammertz said, "we got some material, but not the logbooks we had wanted. They never reached the OTP."[192]

In contrast to the previous section, in which ICTY decisions clearly influenced the policies of the European Union and Croatia, the renewal of the negotiation talks and the capture of Ante Gotovina show that the ICTY was an agent in this case, because the initiative for policy change stemmed from

191 Interview with high-ranking official of the Dutch Ministry of Foreign Affairs in The Hague, May 2012.

192 Interview with Chief Prosecutor Serge Brammertz, The Hague, May 2012. The Dutch deadlock over the books was a major concern for US diplomats, who saw that it was their duty to bring Croatia into the EU and NATO, but also might have had some interest in covering up the US' own involvement in Operation Storm. This was revealed by documents published by the British newspaper The Guardian on 9.12.2010: http://www.guardian.co.uk/world/us-embassy-cables-documents/237167
It is worth mentioning, that a few days before this book went to print, the appeals chamber of the ICTY acquitted Gotovina of all charges and ordered his immediate release, quashing the trial chamber verdict as "arbitrary" and arguing, that the charges concerning a JCE had been without any evidentiary substance. The judgment summary revealed an extraordinary number of dissenting opinions among the five judges and caused outrage in Serbia and an explosion of enthusiasm in Croatia.

the European Union. With its positive assessment, the Tribunal (through its Chief Prosecutor as an agenda setter) served to fulfil that initiative, and in the process went against its own principles. When asked about the reasons for Croatia's relative success in resisting EU pressure, our sources usually pointed to the relatively large support that Croatia enjoyed within the EU. Countries which hid behind the Netherlands in their support for ICTY conditionality were in a minority, but there were several of them. In enlargement negotiations, where every member state can veto any decision, even one member state may be enough to double-cross the veto of another member state. It is also worth noting that Croatia had already become a NATO member by 2009, and between 2008 and 2009 had been a non-permanent member of the UN Security Council. It is important to keep these facts in mind when comparing the Croatian situation to the one of the Republic of Serbia towards the EU and the ICTY.

The EU's Transitional Justice Policy Changes Towards Serbia

Unlike in any other Balkan country, Serbia's troubled past still looms large. The country has officially signalled its intention to join the European Union and has slowly progressed towards that goal. On March 1, 2012, the European Council granted Serbia candidate status.[193]

This process has been marked by three elements. The first is Serbia's highly polarized internal politics, which have been crucial in blocking or passing decisions relating to the country's European hopes. The second element refers to European Union decisions, which have simultaneously been a reaction to those internal dynamics and a force capable of triggering change. The third element is the ICTY and its most influential tool, the reports by the Chief Prosecutor to the UNSC, in which it assesses Serbia's cooperation with the Tribunal. The interplay between these forces in Belgrade's EU project forms the core of this chapter.

From Milošević to Karadžić and Mladić

Carla Del Ponte's efforts to bring Slobodan Milošević to justice in the Scheveningen compounds received a startling blow on March 11, 2006, nearly five years after he was brought to The Hague. On that Saturday, the former President of Yugoslavia was found dead in his bed in his cell, only months before a verdict was due.[194] The ICTY was again in the spotlight, just as it had been with the news of the indictment in 1999 and the transfer to The Hague in 2001. After all, the Tribunal's work had been equated with the trial of Milošević in the mind of the public. But after his death, in contrast to the positive comments which had highlighted the power of the ICTY after his handover, many voices now stressed their concern.

On the one hand, doubts were expressed regarding the possibility that the medical assistance Milošević had received from the ICTY during his trial might not have been up to the adequate standards, a concern which was boosted by the fact that Milošević's death came only six days after the suicide of Croatian Serb prisoner Milan Babić, who had played an important role in the Milošević trial.[195]

---

193 European Council, conclusions, 2.3.2012, EUCO 4/12, CO EUR 2 CONCL 1 http://www.consilium.europa.eu/uedocs/cms_Data/docs/pressdata/en/ec/128520.pdf

194 "Milošević found dead in his cell". BBC News 11.3.2006.

195 *The pros. vs. Babić* IT-03-72. The case of Milan Babić, one of the Prime Ministers of the self-declared Autonomous Republic of Serbian Krajina in Croatia is dealt with more extensively in part III of this book.

On the other hand, it was argued that the whole work of the Tribunal could be at stake, since the most important ICTY trial had ended with no sentence. Many media commentators saw Milošević's death as a huge failure by the Tribunal and a blow to the idea of international criminal justice.[196]

It could also be viewed in a different light. Due to the death of Milošević and the subsequent criticism, the need to apprehend Radovan Karadžić and Ratko Mladić increased steadily.[197] Especially because of their key role in the Srebrenica massacre in Bosnia, they were, after the dead president, the highest-profile alleged war criminals. Capturing the two fugitives became a key issue for the Tribunal's stature, and also for the relationship between Serbia and the European Union. "Now that Milošević was savouring his cigarillos and cognac with Tudjman in the afterlife," Del Ponte mentioned with a sarcastic tone, "it was obvious that the Office of the Prosecutor would have to redouble its efforts to convince the European Union to maintain the pressure it was applying upon Serbia."[198] That pressure had to be linked to the capture of the main architects of the 1990s havoc.

Obviously, the Mladić and Karadžić issue had already been raised before Milošević's death. In April 2005, the European Commission confirmed sufficient progress in Belgrade to open negotiations on the SAA. One of the reasons behind that decision was the handover of a dozen suspects to The Hague in the first few months of that year. In a statement, Commissioner Olli Rehn mentioned that "the trend must continue" and that "the only way (...) to move forward towards the EU"[199] was by capturing Mladić and Karadžić.

But with Milošević dead, the two architects of the Srebrenica massacre took his place at the top of Carla Del Ponte's agenda. Proof of this is that the Prosecutor acknowledged, shortly after the former president's death, that "now more than ever, I expect Serbia to finally arrest and transfer Ratko Mladić and Radovan Karadžić (…) The death of Slobodan Milošević makes it even more urgent for them to face justice."[200]

196 For the detrimental impact of the trial and of Milošević's death on the ICTY's public image see: Bachmann, Klaus: Framing the Trial of the Century. In: Waters, Timothy (ed): The Milošević Trial. An Autopsy. Oxford University Press 2013, chapter 19.

197 Peskin, International Justice, 85.

198 Del Ponte, Madame Prosecutor, 333.

199 Delegation of the European Union to he Republic of Serbia. "Serbia and Montenegro: Commission confirms sufficient progress to open negotiations on a Stabilisation and Association Agreement".

200 "UN Tribunal investigating death of accused genocide mastermind Slobodan Milošević". UN News Centre, 12.3.2006.

As Del Ponte recalled in her autobiography, she was aware that Olli Rehn, the European Enlargement Commissioner, had to present the decision as to whether the negotiations talks with Serbia should continue to the European Parliament in the first few months of 2006, and a major part of that decision depended on what Del Ponte would tell him about cooperation with the ICTY.[201] Moreover, the Chief Prosecutor knew, after speaking to Prime Minister Vojislav Koštunica, that he wanted – and needed – her to give Rehn a positive assessment, especially since the government in Belgrade was conscious of the political risks implicit in the whole Mladić issue.[202] The ICTY suddenly found itself centre stage: both the European Union and Serbia now required Del Ponte to assess whether the Balkan country should continue on its path towards the group of nations. Del Ponte played the game.

In February 2006, she told the BBC that Mladić was in Serbia, within "immediate reach" of the authorities, and that they could apprehend him "today, if they want."[203] Del Ponte's confirmation that Mladić was indeed in Serbia prompted a reaction from the EU, which stepped up its demands.[204] At stake was nothing less than the continuation of the accession talks, scheduled for April 4 and 5, which depended on Belgrade's cooperation in the Mladić case. At the end of March, the Prosecutor travelled to Belgrade to have a word with Koštunica, who promised that Mladić would be captured soon: "the Serbian government is absolutely determined to successfully bring this issue to the end."[205] Tacitly, these words supported Del Ponte's previous comment that Mladić was hiding in Serbia,[206] a topic which added to the pressure on Koštunica's government.

April came and went, and Mladić remained at large. But after a conversation between Rehn and Del Ponte at the end of March, both the EU and the ICTY decided to believe Belgrade's promises. The Chief Prosecutor gave a favourable report based on the "plausible possibility"[207] that Belgrade could comply in the near future, and accordingly Rehn postponed the deadline for another month, not

---

201 Del Ponte, Madame Prosecutor, 337.

202 Ibid.

203 Blockmans, Tough Love, 260; "Mladić 'may be seeking surrender'". BBC News, 23.2.2006.

204 Blockmans, Tough Love, 260; Lucia Kubosova: "Reports on Mladić' capture spark confusion". EU Observer, 22.2.2006. http://euobserver.com/9/20962.

205 "Serbia Promises to Cooperate with Tribunal". The New York Times, 30.3.2006.

206 Peskin, International Justice, 86.

207 Jovanović, Igor: "Promising Mladić". *Center for South Eastern Studies Country Analyses*. 10.4.2006. http://www.csees.net/?page=country_analyses&country_id=9&ca_id=3078.

before opening the political round of the SAA talks as a sign of confidence. But Belgrade again failed: a report by the Office of the Prosecutor found the government's efforts unsatisfactory and Rehn had no other alternative but to stall the negotiations on May 5, 2006. "This is now about the credibility of the European Union policy"[208] were the words used by the Finnish Commissioner. Hours later, Miroljub Labus, Deputy Prime Minister of Serbia and leader of the SAA negotiating team, resigned in protest.[209]

The fact that the enlargement process ended up being so entangled with Belgrade's cooperation in capturing Mladić underscores the political importance of the Tribunal as a body capable of triggering the continuation or the blockage of negotiation talks. Moreover, it highlights the main difference between Del Ponte's way of proceeding in trying to get Milošević captured and sent to The Hague and achieving the same results with Mladić.

In Milošević's case, regardless of the constant pressure by the ICTY, the decision to bring Milošević to The Hague was out of the Tribunal's hands. Since the ICTY does not have coercive power of itself, apprehending Milošević depended on the decisiveness of sovereign governments. The ICTY, through its Chief Prosecutor, could only increase and lower the pressure in different arenas. In the Mladić case, the final aim was the same – to have Mladić apprehended – but Del Ponte's strategy differed: the success of the ICTY did not as such depend on the capture of the general, something that again was out of the Tribunal's hands, but on the leverage it could exert to influence the future of Serbia's negotiation talks with the EU. That was a goal which was definitely within the ICTY's reach, and explains why the halting of negotiations with the European Union can be seen as a good example of where the ICTY acted as principal and not as an agent.

The EU's and Serbia's Local Politics

The postponement of the accession talks with Serbia came as a huge blow to Belgrade, but it did not take long for the European Union to overturn its decision, in what Jelena Subotić called a "stunning reversal".[210] In June 2007, i.e. a year after it had halted the talks, the European Commission deemed Serbia's cooperation adequate and gave Belgrade a new green light. The process towards accession started again. What triggered that turnaround?

208 Del Ponte, Madame Prosecutor, 338.

209 Nicholas Wood: "EU Ends Talks as Belgrade Fails to Produce Mladić." The New York Times, 3.5.2006.

210 Subotić, Hijacked Justice, 79.

The first signs appeared soon after the European Commission stopped the talks on May 3, 2006. Only 18 days later, a referendum came out in favour of independence in Montenegro, which officially ended the last union in the former Yugoslavia. Most international actors, as well as Serbian leaders, accepted the results and welcomed the new state,[211] but the positive attitude after the successful referendum became complicated when the independence of Montenegro started to be linked to the prospect of a similar outcome in Kosovo, a topic which was looming larger by the minute, and which Serbia fiercely opposed.[212]

For the European Union, the prospect that the secession of Montenegro and the possible independence of Kosovo could trigger political instability in Belgrade was not the only worry. Serbia had planned parliamentary elections for January 2007, and there was the fear that the Radical Party, ultra-nationalist and far-right in the political spectrum, could benefit from the failed talks with the EU to gain a majority of votes. All of a sudden, the halt of the SAA started to trouble the EU, either because it could have been badly timed or because it could have been inadequate in general.

This became even clearer when the EU's electoral nightmares came close to being true. Based on a strong anti-Western campaign, the Radical Party and its leader, Tomislav Nikolić, finished first in the elections and beat the pro-European parties of both the Prime Minister and the President, who nevertheless won the majority of the votes combined.[213] The Radical Party was thus not able to form a new coalition government, a situation that was greeted with evident joy in the European Union. Olli Rehn commented that he hoped "that the leaders of Serbia's democratic forces now realise their responsibility and choose a European future for Serbia, instead of letting the country fall back to its nationalist past," and added a promise: "Serbia's path to the EU will be revitalised immediately".[214]

And he kept that promise: according to the Commission of the European Communities Serbia 2007 Progress Report, the Council of the EU decision to support the Commission in its process towards restarting the talks with Serbia followed the parliamentary elections.[215] Negotiations began in June, a month after Belgrade put an end to what the Commission called "a period of political uncertainty"[216] and formed a pro-European coalition government which "soon

211 "In quotes: Reaction to Montenegro Vote". BBC News, 22.5.2006.

212 Nick Hawton: "Separation focuses Serbian minds". BBC News, 24.5.2006.

213 "Serbian nationalists claim victory." BBC News 22.1.2007.

214 "Serbia forms pro-European government". Euractiv 14.5.2007.

215 Commission Of The European Communities. "Serbia 2007 Progress Report" (2007)

216 Ibid.

after met the conditions set by the [European] Council."[217] Koštunica and Tadić remained in power, to the detriment of the Radical Party. One EU official pointed out in this context that "it is of course much easier if we have partners which look in the same direction." He added, "it is like a marriage: if both partners agree that they want to have a car, a house or children, if you agree on the basics, it is much easier to move ahead."[218]

What is most striking about the European Union's decision to resume talks with Serbia is that the Union's transitional justice policy was pushed into the background, despite the fact that one year before it had been deemed to be the key obligation in Serbia's way to Brussels.[219] The Commission demanded that Serbia, as mentioned in the Progress Report, capture "four ICTY indictees" and take "concrete and effective action for full cooperation with the ICTY,"[220] but the term "full cooperation" again became blurred. What was not blurred but obvious was, in Subotić' words, "that the government was no longer obliged to arrest Mladić and Karadžić as a condition for SAA talks."[221]

The go-ahead to the SAA without the capture of the main suspects not only undermined the transitional justice policy of the European Union,[222] in this case clearly dependent on and adaptable to internal political circumstances, it also put a question mark on Carla Del Ponte, as she gave her positive assessment despite her unsuccessful bid to have the remaining fugitives brought to The Hague. The answers to the change in ICTY policy vary: for Peskin, Del Ponte agreed with the EU decision to restart the SAA talks without asking for Mladić, and believed that the best way to maintain her authority and eventually have the fugitives handed over was to continue her own meetings with politicians and diplomats.[223] On the other hand, Del Ponte, who was in her last months as Chief Prosecutor of the Tribunal, highlighted the increased progress in Serbia's cooperation with the ICTY and the officials' clear commitment to finding the fugitives.[224]

The facts are that in the run-up to the June SAA decision, the Chief Prosecutor's strategy of reminding politicians and diplomats of Serbia's obligation to comply with the ICTY was strengthened through a new, powerful element: the unprecedented decision by the International Court of Justice (ICJ),

217 Ibid.

218 Thomas Sparrow-Botero's interview with EU official. Brussels, April 2011.

219 Subotić, Hijacked Justice, 79; Peskin, International Justice, 89.

220 Commission Of The European Communities. "Serbia 2007 Progress Report". op. cit.

221 Subotić, Hijacked Justice, 79.

222 See, for example, "EU/Serbia: Don't compromise on Mladić". Human Rights Watch, 6.11.2007. http://www.hrw.org/legacy/english/docs/2007/11/06/serbia17261.htm.

223 Peskin, International Justice, 89.

224 "Prosecutor Del Ponte's Address Before the Security Council". ICTY, 18.6.2007.

in February 2007, that Serbia had violated the Genocide Convention of 1948 for not handing Mladić and Karadžić to the ICTY.

Del Ponte recalled the significance of the ruling: It "provided us with powerful arguments to bring before the European Union countries: do you really want to integrate a state that is in violation of the Genocide Convention?"[225] But instead of strengthening the Chief Prosecutor's demands, the ICJ decision became a symbol of her reduced leverage vis-à-vis the European Union, "as the West sought to placate Serbia and ensure that it did not move away from Europe and towards Russia."[226]

Del Ponte nevertheless continued exerting pressure, and in the process improved her relationship with the government. She was officially invited for the first time to Belgrade, and shortly before the June SAA deadline, the Serbian government arrested two high-ranking fugitives: the Bosnian Serb General Zdravko Tolimir, who reported to Mladić during the Srebrenica massacre, and former Police General Vlastimir Djordjević.[227] Although Belgrade's "sudden"[228] cooperation was understood as a sign to influence the approaching decision by the EU, it was also an important step for Del Ponte, who commented in her June 2007 address to the United Nations Security Council that "those arrests demonstrate Serbia's commitment to cooperate fully with my Office."[229] She therefore not only gave the green light, but also, in an unprecedented statement for a Chief Prosecutor, said she would be grateful if EU "negotiations can start as soon as possible."[230] They did, one week after, on June 13.

Considering the role played by the European Union and the ICTY in the renewal of the SAA, one fact stands out: the events that occurred in Serbia were central. The Montenegrin secession, the fear of an independent Kosovo, the 2007 parliamentary elections, the doubts regarding the Serbian Radical Party, the arrest of two important suspects, and the change in attitude of the government officials highlight the way in which local politics can transcend

225 Del Ponte, Madame Prosecutor, 358.

226 Peskin, International Justice, 88.

227 Vlastimir Djordjević had been a high-ranking official in the Ministry of the Interior of the Republic of Serbia during the Kosovo conflict and was indicted for war crimes and crimes against humanity. In February 2001, the trial chamber sentenced him to 27 years' imprisonment. *The pros. vs. Djordjević* IT-05-87/1. Zdravko Tolimir, whose trial started only in 2010, was assistant commander responsible for intelligence and security in the Bosnian Serb Army during the siege and fall of Srebrenica. He is currently accused of genocide and crimes against humanity. *The pros. vs. Tolimir* IT-05-99/2.

228 op. cit. 89

229 United Nations Security Council. 5697th Meeting. 18.6.2007.

230 "Del Ponte urges EU-Serbia talks". BBC News, 6.6.2007.

state boundaries and affect international policies. This was particularly evident in the turnaround of the European Union.

When the Commission cut short the SAA negotiations in 2006, the decision was intended to pressure Belgrade into stopping making empty statements and starting to hand over the most-wanted fugitives. When it reinstated the negotiations, one year later, the harsh tone was gone, in order to reduce the possibilities of local turmoil, offer the country a political incentive, and keep it tightly attached to the European sphere of influence. In that game, in which the EU refrained from applying its transitional justice requirements, the ICTY was only able to exert limited pressure: the Chief Prosecutor strengthened her demands, added two suspects to the Scheveningen compounds in The Hague, and used the new arrests as an argument which formed the basis of a positive assessment that the EU desperately required.

Karadžić's arrest and the quest for Mladić

Most fugitives prefer to vanish into thin air, but not Radovan Karadžić. For 12 years, one of the world's most wanted suspects, accused of the siege of Sarajevo, lived in Serbia like any other citizen: he went on holiday, ate in restaurants, frequented a bar where he used to order red wine, and had a girlfriend, a job and even his own website. The long, white beard he cultivated and his false identity as Dragan Dabić, an expert in alternative medicine, allowed him to lead that fabricated life and, in the process, escape any police controls.[231] This came to a sudden end when the new Serbian government decided to replace the head of State Security after the elections.[232] Not only did the new one order Karadzić's arrest, he was also anxious to keep the ICTY chief prosecutor informed while the operation was going on. Serge Brammertz said, "we had all the information about the operation, live and 4 hours long."[233]

Karadzić's arrest was greeted with joy: the EU presidency, then held by France, said it was "an important step on the path to the rapprochement of

231 BBC: The Secret Life of Radovan Karadžić 25.07.2008. http://news.bbc.co.uk/2/hi/7520661.stm
See also: Thomas Sparrow. "El Criminal de Bosnia". Revista Semana, 26.7.2008. http://www.semana.com/mundo/criminal-bosnia/113941-3.aspx.

232 The head of the Serb Security Information Agency (Bezbednosno Informativna Agencija), Rade Bulatović (in office since 2004) was replaced by Saša Vukadinović (who was 14 years younger) on July 18th 2008. See: http://www.bia.gov.rs/eng/istorijat/dosadasnji-rukovodioci.html

233 Interview with ICTY Chief Prosecutor Serge Brammertz in May 2012 in The Hague.

Serbia with the European Union,"[234] to which José Manuel Barroso, President of the European Commission at the time, added: "it proves the determination of the new Serbian government to achieve full cooperation with the ICTY."[235] The United States, Great Britain, and former diplomats publicly expressed their satisfaction, and the Tribunal's Chief Prosecutor Serge Brammertz also welcomed the news by describing it as a "milestone in cooperation with the ICTY."[236]

Mutual patting on the back aside, Karadžić's arrest highlights important political dynamics, in particular if two processes are analysed: the reasons behind his detention at that precise moment (after all, he had been at large for more than a decade) and the shockwaves it generated. Local politics in Serbia and a string of EU decisions regarding the country's prospective EU membership are elements that are central to understanding both processes.

In January and February 2008, Serbia held presidential elections; in February, Kosovo declared independence; and in May, a new Serbian parliament was elected. In all three key political events, European Union leaders showed signs of uneasiness and tried to keep Serbia looking towards the EU. Kosovo's declaration of independence created tensions in Serbia to the extent that the government coalition collapsed. In March, Serbia's nationalist Prime Minister Vojislav Koštunica resigned and called for early elections in May. Among the main reasons for the breakdown were political differences between Koštunica and his main coalition partner, President Boris Tadić, regarding the alleged incompatibility between Serbia's accession to the EU, the country's vehement opposition to an independent Kosovo, and the recognition of its independence by most EU member states.[237] In addition to that political crisis, there were violent street protests in Belgrade following Kosovo's declaration and complaints about the EU decision to deploy the non-military European Union Rule of Law Mission in Kosovo (EULEX), aimed at strengthening institutions and democracy in the newly created country.

---

234 "Radovan Karadžić arrest hailed by world leaders". The Independent, July 22, 2008. http://www.telegraph.co.uk/news/worldnews/europe/serbia/2443553/Radovan-Karadžić-arrest-hailed-by-world-leaders.html.

235 Elisa Vucheva: "Serbia arrests top war crimes suspect Karadžić." EU Observer, 22.7.2008. http://euobserver.com/9/26520.

236 "UN war crimes tribunal prosecutor welcomes arrest of Radovan Karadžić". UN News, July 21, 2008.

237 See, for more details, International Crisis Group. "Kosovo's First Month". (Europe Briefing No.47 March 18, 2008). http://www.crisisgroup.org/~/media/Files/europe/b47_kosovo_first_month.ashx.

In the EU, on the other hand, recognition of Kosovo's independence not only revealed fractures between member states' interests, it also led to questions about how to avert further political turmoil in Serbia and how to safeguard the entire accession negotiations. One of the options mentioned in the press referred to the possibility of easing Serbia's conditions for joining the EU and, in particular, reducing pressure to capture war criminals.[238]

The EU's concern with the situation in Serbia was also present in the run-up to both elections. The presidential one was even described in the press as a "referendum on Serbia's relations with the EU,"[239] while EU foreign ministers met in Luxembourg prior to the parliamentary elections to discuss the "Serbian conundrum,"[240] i.e. how to stop the Radical Party from winning a majority. A Serbian government source admitted this fact when stating that

> it is of utmost importance to point out that 'European questions', namely the prospect of visa liberalisation, positive signs from the side of the EU, were the decisive factor for the democratic forces to win the election in 2008.[241]

According to press reports at the time, one of the offers that EU officials had been discussing for months in order to keep a pro-European majority in power was nothing less than signing the SAA, a benchmark decision on Serbia's road to the EU.[242]

This indeed happened on April 29, 2008, two weeks before the parliamentary elections. One of the elements that made the deal possible was that the Netherlands, the most adamant defender of ICTY conditionality in the EU, was put under pressure to relax its position that full cooperation with the ICTY literally meant bringing the most-wanted criminals (in particular Mladić) to The Hague.[243] Spain's Minister of Foreign Affairs, Miguel Ángel Moratinos, was even quoted in March 2008 as publicly saying, "we want to persuade our Dutch friends to change their attitude."[244] The Netherlands (as well as Belgium) finally agreed to the SAA being signed on the condition that its implementation

---

238 See, for example, Eric Witte and Kurt Bassuener. "Holding the Reins of Balkan Justice". European Voice, 13.9.2007. Toby Vogel: "EU Member States Threaten to Delay Talks with Serbia". European Voice, 10.1.2008.

239 Toby Vogel: "Tadić Re-election keeps Serbia Facing Westwards". European Voice 7.2.2008.

240 Toby Vogel: "Foreign Ministers Face Serbia Conundrum". European Voice, 24.4.2008.

241 Thomas Sparrow-Botero's Interview with a source from the Serbian government who requested anonymity. May 2011.

242 In 2007, Serbia and the EU had technical talks on the possibility of signing the SAA.

243 Toby Vogel: "Foreign Ministers Face Serbia Conundrum" op. cit.

244 Ricardo Martínez de RituertoM "Kosovo lleva otra vez a los serbios a elegir entre el aislamiento o Europa". Diario El País, 11.3.2008.

had to be withheld until full cooperation with the ICTY was achieved. This decision on April 29 was followed, on May 7, by the European Commission's announcement of a roadmap for visa liberalisation with Serbia aimed at ending that country's "time of isolation"[245]; on May 11, by the Parliamentary elections; and, on July 21, by the capture of Karadžić in Belgrade.

The succession of events was no mere coincidence, but sheds light on a very specific element of EU conditionality. In most cases, non-compliance by a candidate state, including Serbia and Croatia, resulted in the EU imposing a penalty (for example, halting talks) until the situation could be reversed. Only when that occurred would the EU give the anticipated prize (for example, restarting the negotiations). In this case it was different: the EU managed to get a desired response from Serbia (handing over a war criminal) by giving the rewards first (the SAA and the roadmap for visa liberalisation).

One of the EU officials interviewed for this book, who was involved in the negotiations, explained this phenomenon in plain language:

> We had two choices. We could create a lose-lose situation, where we don't move with Serbia, we don't have an SAA, and we have a Koštunica-Nikolić government, which would be very difficult. Or we have an agreement, a contractual relation with Serbia and much better cooperation with the ICTY.[246]

It is important to note that the Serbian government views this issue differently. A government source argued during an interview in May 2011 that "this event [Karadžić's transfer] cannot be seen as pressure from the EU, as the intelligence from 27 countries was used, thus making it a common success." The source added that finding the war criminal was the result of "many years of intelligence work, both in European and Serbian HQs and in the field. It was a product of the close cooperation between these services, and it bore fruit after years of chase."[247]

With time, a striking contradiction about Karadžić's transfer to The Hague became clear. If his arrest in 2008 was generally hailed by the international community and especially by the champions of international criminal justice as a step in the right direction, its effects produced a different and unexpected reaction. That reaction, in short, was an enhancement of the perception that the EU and Serbia were willing to move forward in the accession process despite the remaining war criminals (especially Ratko Mladić) being at large. The EU

245 "Roadmap on Visa Free Travel Opens EU Doors to Serbia". European Union Press Release, May 7, 2008.

246 Thomas Sparrow-Botero's Interview with EU official. Brussels, April 2011.

247 Thomas Sparrow-Botero's interview with a Serbian government source who requested anonymity. May 2011.

was willing to let Serbia get closer to the club even if it did not meet the condition of full cooperation with the ICTY.

Immediately after Karadžić was captured, however, that was not the general opinion. Most analysts welcomed the news and, at the same time, pointed to the fact that his main ally, Ratko Mladić, was still at large. That was the first effect of Karadžić's reappearance in July 2008: the increased belief that with him in jail, Mladić could follow soon after. This was explained metaphorically by Zarko Korać, a Serbian parliamentary deputy, during a BBC interview: "There is a real momentum now – and who would not buy two cars, if they can, for the price of one?"[248]

The opinions on Serbia's alleged renewed interest in apprehending Mladić were based on various events. On the one hand, Boris Tadić was re-elected, which was seen as a sign that Serbia was more convinced than ever, at least officially, about getting closer to Europe. According to Vuk Jeremić, the country's foreign minister, "this is probably the most pro-European government in the history of Serbia." Since apprehending war criminals is a condition for coming closer to Europe, the presence of a Western-leaning government was seen in a positive light.

Apart from that, Karadžić's arrest revealed a shift in the way Serbia's past was analysed. In a 2009 report for the European Union Institute for Security Studies, Jelena Obradović-Wochnik described how the revelation that Karadžić had been hiding as a 'charlatan doctor' – instead of suffering his exile for the sake of the Serb nation – undermined the belief that he, and Mladić, were national heroes and brave soldiers. "The arrest signalled the faint beginnings of a cultural and political change in Serbia," she analysed. Karadžić "undermined his own myth –something that the ICTY, EU and other external parties had unsuccessfully attempted for years."[249]

This has gone hand in hand with the fact that the intensity of feelings dominating the turmoil of the 1990s is fading. In an interview, Obradović-Wochnik stressed that "after virtually two decades of war or talk of war, (...) people have simply had enough".[250] She added: "People are quite tired of everything that the ICTY represents, and even though Serbia's EU future relies heavily on Mladić, most people are quite apathetic to the whole issue."[251]

248 Nick Thorpe. "Dramatic Ironies of Karadžić Arrest". BBC News, 23.7.2008.

249 Obradović-Wochnik, Jelena: "Strategies of Denial. Resistance to ICTY Cooperation in Serbia". In: Batt, Obradović, War Crimes, Conditionality, 45-46.

250 Interview with Jelena Obradović-Wochnik. May 2011.

251 Ibid.

Additionally, support for the remaining war criminals seemed to be getting thinner. Mladić, for instance, was said to be protected only by "a handful of loyalists."[252] This was in marked contrast to previous years, when he was supposedly surrounded by a large network and received a military pension (he did so until 2002). Moreover, after denying for years that Mladić was in Serbia, local officials acknowledged in mid-2009 that he was "somewhere within reach."[253] What is curious about the idea that Serbia was getting closer to the remaining war criminal is that the more he was mentioned in the press and in diplomatic circles and the more it was stressed that he had to be put behind bars, the less likely was it that this was going to happen in the near future.

One of the reasons for that diverging situation concerned the interests of different EU member states. Whereas some countries preferred to move forward in the process with Belgrade as quickly as possible, perhaps as a way of strengthening the overtly pro-EU Serbian government, the Dutch were left alone in their commitment to having Mladić arrested as a precondition for EU accession. As The New York Times put it, the bloc was trying to carry out a "complex balancing act" in the Balkans: "Give Belgrade too much too fast and there may be no justice for victims of the Srebrenica massacre."[254] Or, in Geraldine Mattioli-Zeltner's words, it is all about "the interaction between sticks and carrots and how that played out."[255] That dichotomy between member states' interests was already visible before Karadžić's arrest, when EU diplomats put pressure on Belgium and the Netherlands to lift their veto on the signing of the SAA. The renewed attention on the search for Mladić after Karadžić's detention would only make it more visible.

The reduced interest in Mladić in EU internal dynamics revealed an additional element in the relationship between Serbia and the bloc: the condition of full cooperation with the ICTY became less important for most EU members, as other processes took priority. Mariko Peters, a Dutch parliamentarian who recognised her country's isolation, acknowledged this: "Many nations are weighing Mladić's capture as just one of many factors: stabilisation of the Balkans, the Kosovo issue, upcoming Serbian elections and the need to give

252 Dan Bilefsky and Doreen Carvajal: "Europe Tested as War Crimes Suspect Remains Free". The New York Times, 21.10.2010.

253 Craig Whitlock: "Serbian Officials Say Mladić 'Within Reach'". The Washington Post, 30.7.2009. http://www.washingtonpost.com/wp-dyn/content/article/2009/07/29/AR2009072903280.html.

254 Stephen Castle: "Serbia's EU aspirations face long road ahead". The New York Times, 28.10.2010.

255 Telephone interview with Geraldine Mattioli-Zeltner. April 2011.

rewards to democratic forces that are weak."[256] Aleksandar Fatić concurs: "The issue of membership is decided much more by a political balancing act that takes place regularly between Belgrade and Brussels, than by Mladić's arrest."[257]

The succession of events after Karadžić's arrest proved this opinion right. Serbia rapidly completed some of the necessary steps for being granted EU accession with Mladić still at large. A year after the SAA was signed, Serbia officially applied for membership in the European Union (December 22, 2009). On June 14, 2010, the European Commission decided to start the SAA ratification process. EU foreign ministers agreed to entrust the Commission with Serbia's membership application, the first step on the path to formal negotiations. The decision was taken despite strong reservations by the Netherlands, whose government insisted on a safeguard clause concerning Serbia's cooperation with the ICTY. The Council's conclusion therefore reiterates that "at each stage of Serbia's path towards EU accession (...) further steps will be taken when the Council unanimously decides that full co-operation with the ICTY exists or continues to exist."[258] On that occasion, the Netherlands were alone in their reservations. According to both the Nice and the Lisbon Treaties, association agreements and accession require unanimity in the Council and the approval of the European Parliament, but from the perspective of a single member state, it makes a significant difference whether its government remains isolated in its opposition to a policy initiative or whether it is backed by several other member states.[259]

---

256 Dan Bilefsky and Doreen Carvajal: "Europe Tested as War Crimes Suspect Remains Free". The New York Times, 21.10.2010.

257 Thomas Sparrow-Botero's e-mail interview with Aleksandar Fatić. April 2011.

258 Council of the EU, Foreign Affairs Council, Press Release. "Conclusions on Serbia." Luxembourg, 25.10.2010.

259 There are strong arguments indicating that the Dutch reservations over Serbia's SAA and membership bid were caused by a sharp shift to the eurosceptic right, which is hostile to further EU enlargement, rather than by considerations about international justice. In June 2010, elections to the Dutch Second Chamber (Tweede Kamer) brought a landslide victory for the traditional liberals (VVD) and a new, right wing populist, anti-islamic and anti-immigration party, Geert Wilders' "Liberty Party" (Partij voor de Vrijheid, PVV). Both parties were strongly eurosceptic. See: VVD winnaar verkiezingen; PVV stijgt vijftien zetels. Elsevier 10.06.2010 http://www.elsevier.nl/web/Nieuws/Politiek/267858/VVD-winnaar-verkiezingen-PVV-stijgt-vijftien-zetels.htm.
Even after Mladić's extradition to The Hague, Dutch MPs continued to obstruct the ratification process of Serbia's SAA. On June 25, 2011, a majority of the Tweede Kamer postponed a vote on its ratification, awaiting Brammertz' report to the UN Security Council on Serbia's cooperation with the ICTY. At that time, the only ICTY suspect still at large was Goran Hadžić, former president of the Republic of Serbian

No wonder Vuk Jeremić commented, when handing in his country's application for membership, that "Serbia has the capacity and determination to beat all records for fastest EU accession."[260]

This string of decisions is particularly revealing when it is contrasted with the reports by the ICTY Prosecutor to the UNSC, and with the constant reminders by international NGOs to not forget Mladić. In his various reports to the UNSC since 2008, Chief Prosecutor Serge Brammertz stressed, in more or less the same words every time, that "the arrest of the fugitives Mladić and Hadžić remains the highest priority for my Office."[261] In June 2009, Brammertz praised Belgrade for its "additional progress"[262] in cooperating with the ICTY, acknowledged "full briefing"[263] from Serbian services about the tracking of Mladić and expressed his desire that "this trend will continue."[264] A press release by the European Commission explains that, as a result of this, the Council of the European Union unblocked the interim agreement on the SAA, which had stalled when the SAA was signed in 2008,[265] and, by doing so, made Serbia –seriously affected by the global economic crisis – eligible for substantial financial assistance.[266] At that time, the EU was almost unanimously in favour of a rapid accession of Serbia into the bloc. The readiness to forget about the fugitives was strong enough to sideline even the ICTY. Some preliminary remarks are needed in order to explain how this happened. The ICTY's chief prosecutor delivers his report to the UNSC twice a year. During Brammertz' term, the report to the UNSC would also be discussed afterwards at the nearest EU Council meeting. But in summer 2010, Brammertz briefed ministers confidentially about his assessment before he flew to New York. The ministers knew that the report would usually be leaked to the press in New York as soon as it left the Security Council. They took advantage of that delay. Despite Brammertz' critical assessment in Brussels, they stated in the Council

---

Krajina and who was indicted for war crimes and crimes against humanity allegedly committed in Eastern Slavonia (Vukovar) during the early 1990s. *The pros. vs. Hadžić* IT-04-75. For the decision of the Tweede Kamer, see: Bojana Barlovac: "Dutch MPs refuse to ratify Serbia's SAA." *Balkaninsight* 8.6.2011.

260 "Serbia Aims to Beat EU Entry 'Speed Record'". Euractiv 4.1.2010.

261 "Address of Serge Brammertz, Prosecutor of the International Criminal Tribunal for the Former Yugoslavia to the Security Council on 18 June 2010". ICTY 18.6.2010.

262 "Address of Serge Brammertz, Prosecutor of the International Criminal Tribunal for the Former Yugoslavia 4 June 2009. ICTY, 4.6.2009.

263 Ibid.

264 Ibid.

265 "Commission welcomes Council decision to start the ratification process of the Stabilisation and Association agreement with Serbia". European Union Press Release, 14.6.2010.

266 Kurt Bassuener: "Here we go again". European Voice, 10.6.2009.

conclusions that they had acknowledged the Prosecutor's report, and then they broadly recommended that Serbia "follow the recommendations," [267] and surprisingly stated that "Serbia maintained its cooperation with the Tribunal with a view to delivering further positive results."[268] No mention was made of the specific criticisms by Brammertz, who later argued in an interview that it was "obvious that we are more critical in relation to the search for fugitives than in the previous report."[269] Instead of focusing on Serbia's deficits, the Council of the EU gave Belgrade a green light:

> Regarding Serbia, recalling its decision of 29 April 2008, and having regard to the efforts made by Serbia's authorities in their cooperation with ICTY with a view to delivering further positive results, the Council decided that the ratification procedures of the Stabilisation and Association Agreement should begin.[270]

In the report he made to the Security Council, he "reiterated to the Ministers that the support of the European Union in securing cooperation of States has not only been extremely effective in the past, but will remain essential in the future."[271] Brammertz' statement means, in plain language, that the European Union decided to move forward with its plans to bring Serbia into the bloc of nations, despite the criticism by the ICTY Prosecutor. The Netherlands, this time together only with Belgium, managed to introduce a small safeguard into the conclusions, according to which the SAA agreement would not be provisionally applied and member states were allowed to withhold actual ratification in parliament until a positive assessment of Serbia by the ICTY Prosecutor was made. A Dutch Ministry of Foreign Affairs source said, "we vetoed that alone for one and a half years, fully supported by our parliament."[272]

Those two documents, the ICTY report and the Council Conclusions, are written proof of the dynamics between the International Criminal Tribunal and the European Union, and reveal the extent to which the conditionality of full cooperation with the ICTY, understood here as referring to the capture of the main fugitives, was pushed into the background by the group of nations in favour of other interests. These included the situation in Kosovo, which acquired particular relevance, to the extent that one of the incentives to move EU negotiations forward was Belgrade's decision to soften its tone towards its former province.[273]

---

267 Council of the European Union. "3023rd Council Meeting". 14.6.2010.
268 Ibid.
269 Toby Vogel: "EU eases war-crimes conditions for Serbia". European Voice 8.7.2010.
270 Council of the European Union. "3023rd Council Meeting", op. cit.
271 Ibid. (Italic emphasis added)
272 Interview with official of the Dutch Ministry of Foreign Affairs, The Hague, May 2012.
273 Simon Taylor: "Serbia 'rewarded' for Kosovo resolution". European Voice, 13.9.2010.

It is telling that the EU stalled negotiations with Belgrade in May 2006 mostly because of Serbia's failure to capture Mladić and then, two years later, signed the SAA and initiated its most decisive process to date to bring Serbia into the EU despite Mladić still being at large. This is a major and easily noticeable transitional justice policy shift by the EU towards Serbia.

As far as the ICTY is concerned, this situation shows that the Tribunal had less leverage in Serbia's revitalized path to the EU. In 2006, an assessment by the Office of the Prosecutor was highly influential in stalling negotiations; subsequent reports were not so effective. The positive June and December 2009 reports by Brammertz were followed by positive change in the EU towards Serbia (the interim agreement was unblocked on December 7, visa liberalisation for Serbian citizens entered into force 12 days later, and Serbia applied for EU membership three days after that), but his negative assessment in June 2010 was not considered accordingly by the EU. Serbia still moved forward in spite of being negatively assessed.

The Transfer of Mladić and Hadžić

The town of Lazarevo, in Serbia's Vojvodina province, very suddenly became the centre of attention in May 2011. Its name appeared in all major newspapers around the world, and journalists were sent as special envoys to report the breaking news. What had just happened there was ground-breaking: after a 16-year manhunt, Ratko Mladić had been arrested by Serbian Special Forces when he was setting out to take a stroll before dawn. "I can only praise you," Mladić told the officers without putting up resistance. "You've found the one you wanted."[274]

During the following days, most influential actors on the global stage expressed their satisfaction at this important piece of news, and Serge Brammertz was no exception. At a press conference on June 1, two days before Mladić's first appearance in the ICTY, Brammertz acknowledged the Serbian authorities' success in arresting Mladić and then "particularly" thanked the European Union "for giving Serbia positive incentives to cooperate with the Tribunal."[275]

This last sentence by the ICTY Chief Prosecutor perfectly summarizes the process that led to the arrest and the reasons why Mladić was captured at that particular point in time. Although President Boris Tadić told BBC correspondent

274 "Ratko Mladić, what's next?" The Economist, 27.5.2011.

275 "Statement of the Prosecutor on the transfer of Ratko Mladić to the International Criminal Tribunal for the Former Yugoslavia". ICTY, Press release 1.6.2011.

Mark Bowden that Serbia had never calculated its search for the war criminal,[276] and then added in another interview that such thoughts were "rubbish",[277] Mladić's appearance in The Hague fits in particularly well with the chain of events that have recently brought Serbia even closer to the European Union.

First, the same day that Mladić's arrest was announced, Catherine Ashton, European Union High Representative for Foreign Affairs and Security Policy, was in Belgrade to promote EU-sponsored talks between Serbia and Kosovo. This "coincidence",[278] as Ashton called it, is particularly revealing, as good-neighbourly relations between Serbia and its former breakaway province are, together with the arrest of war criminals, one of the most relevant requirements that must be met in order to be eligible for European Union membership.

What does not seem a coincidence is the fact that Mladić's arrest was completed as Serge Brammertz was about to make his six-monthly report to the UNSC, on June 6, 2011.

Parts of that report had previously been leaked to the press and its contents had been qualified as negative, to the point that it was said that the ICTY's report would tarnish Serbia's intention to get candidate status in 2011, which is a landmark step on the road to accession. The leaked document, summaries of which are available online, highlights Serbia's failure to apprehend the two remaining indictees and reveals that it "undermines its credibility and the strength of its stated commitment to fully co-operate with the ICTY."[279] The arrest was seen as a move to soften that document.

A third element was also present, since at the time, the European Commission was planning to present a document in October 2011, based on the report by the ICTY Prosecutor, that would determine whether negotiations should be opened with Serbia. This was enough in itself to encourage the Serbian government to capture the war criminal, but it was strengthened by the fact that Croatia was about to complete its own negotiations with the EU (which happened in June). In short, as *The Economist* pointed out, "Mr Tadić was facing the prospect of a negative report by Mr Brammertz provoking a formal rejection of Serbia's membership bid just at the time when Croatia, its neighbor and former enemy, was about to be invited to become the EU's 28th member."[280] This was not only about competition between the former war enemies; it was

---

276 "Ratko Mladić arrested: Bosnia war crimes suspect held". BBC News 26.5.2011.

277 "Reaction to arrest of Ratko Mladić". Transcripts. CNN, aired 27.5.2011. http://transcripts.cnn.com/TRANSCRIPTS/1105/27/nwsm.01.html

278 "Nicked in the nick of time". The Economist, Charlemagne's Notebook. 28.5.2011.

279 Andrew Rettman: "War crimes report damages Serbia's EU bid". EU Observer, 26.5.2011.

280 Ibid.

about geopolitics, finance, and institutions at the same time. A country which joins the EU before a problematic neighbour can use its voting rights in the Council of the EU to block the accession of that neighbour. A new member country which, like Croatia, is likely to be a beneficiary of EU funds, can use its influence to prevent the latecomer from obtaining certain funds and to shape funding schemes in a way which makes them more profitable for the early bird than for the latecomer. In other words, newcomers can use the influence that membership grants to them in order to decrease membership benefits for latecomers. The strained relationship between some antagonistic new and old member states like Greece and Macedonia are a compelling example of this mechanism. Because Greece first entered the union, it could impose additional conditions on Macedonia. The EU uses this mechanism during accession negotiations when they concern more than one country. By negotiating separately with each candidate, the EU is able to play them off against each other. When one candidate increases its demands more than the others, negotiations with it are slowed down, which results in the respective government facing the threat of joining the Union later than the remaining candidates, which increases domestic pressure. In this way, the EU is able to use domestic pressure in candidate countries for its own purposes. This negotiation strategy is called "regatta" in European integration research.

It was therefore not only Brammertz' pressure on Serbia, but also the "regatta" context which explains why Mladić was found at exactly that time in his house in Lazarevo despite rumours, spread by leading politicians in Serbia, that Mladić was beyond their reach and hiding somewhere in Bosnia. But Serbia did not only receive words of praise for its cooperation. Once again, the Netherlands poured cold water on the Serbian government. "It is important," Dutch Prime Minister Mark Rutte meekly admitted. Mladić's arrest had been "an important precondition", but it did not mean "automatic membership."[281] The phrase meant that there still was one fugitive at large. Goran Hadžić might not have been as visible and relevant as Mladić or as Karadžić were during the wars in the Balkans, but his importance should not be underestimated. During Croatia's war of independence, Hadžić was the political leader of Serb breakaway regions and allegedly took part in a JCE between 1991 and 1993. He is considered responsible for one of the most atrocious crimes in the region, namely the murder of some 300 hospital patients and the subsequent

281 Quoted according to EurActiv: "Serbia's Eu prospects brighten after Mladić arrest." http://www.euractiv.com/enlargement/serbias-eu-prospects-brighten-mladi-arrest-news-505183

displacement of about 20,000 inhabitants of the city of Vukovar during a three-month siege in 1991.[282]

His current importance stems not only from his historical responsibility, but also because, after Mladić's arrest, Hadžić became the last remaining fugitive sought by the ICTY. If Serbia managed to capture him as well as Mladić, it would put an end to 18 years of diplomatic and political struggles with the ICTY and its prosecutors over the need to arrest the main figures in the tragic events of the 1990s. By doing so, it would also convincingly pave the way for more positive reports by the ICTY, and put pressure on the European Union to grant the country candidate status. Hadžić was indeed taken into custody soon after Mladić, on July 20, 2011. According to Serbian war crimes prosecutor Vladimir Vukčević (whose version was later denied by Hadžić's lawyer), an unusual element led to his capture: a stolen painting by the Italian modernist Amedeo Modigliani. The work could have come into Hadžić's possession during the war in Croatia, and recently, under pressure and penniless, he decided to sell it. But he failed, and unexpectedly alerted Serbian authorities, who captured him near the northern Serbian village of Krusedol. "Today," Brammertz explained later, referring to Hadžić's transfer – "every individual wanted by the Tribunal has been, or will be, brought to account. For the Tribunal – and for international justice – the arrest of Goran Hadžić is a milestone to remember."[283]

It was also a key moment for Serbia, as Brammertz praised Belgrade's "new phase" of cooperation and its "genuine commitment." He concluded: "Serbian authorities have fulfilled a key international commitment."[284]

In less than two months, Serbia had found the two fugitives it had not been able to capture in the three years since it sent Radovan Karadžić to The Hague. In less than two months, Serbia decisively proved what it is after. One player was responsible for triggering this evident change of attitude: the European Union and its enlargement process. "I will look my European counterparts in the eye and see if they make good on what they have promised,"[285] were Tadić's categorical words after Serbia fulfilled one of its international justice obligations.

---

282 *The pros. vs. Hadžić*, IT-04-75.

283 "Statement of Prosecutor Serge Brammertz on the transfer of Goran Hadžić". ICTY, Press release. 22.7.2011.

284 Ibid.

285 "Goran Hadžić's arrest: a turning point for Serbia?" BBC News. 22.7.2011.

Conclusions

In his December 6, 2010, report to the United Nations Security Council, ICTY Chief Prosecutor Serge Brammertz commented on the Tribunal's most relevant goal: "We have our eyes firmly fixed on the completion of our activities."[286] After 18 years of investigations, after 161 indicted persons, the Tribunal is fast approaching the end of its mandate.

Since it was brought to life by the UNSC in 1993, the ICTY has set out to bring justice to the Balkans and to end the havoc there, infamously but aptly called Europe's tinderbox. Moreover, its profile increased after it was officially linked at the turn of the century to the accession of Serbia and Croatia to the European Union. To what extent the Tribunal has played a defining role in that process is the central question that has been discussed in this part of the book. In short, has the ICTY been a principal of Europeanisation or has it been an agent thereof?

This question has been assessed by delving respectively into at least three policy shifts by the European Union towards Croatia and Serbia. Croatia's policy shifts mostly covered the period 2001-2005, whereas Serbia's shifts referred to decisions between 2006 and mid-2011. These time specifications are not strict, as policy shifts refer to processes which cause the EU to adapt or cancel previously established conditions or create new ones.

In Croatia's case, the first point which warranted analysis was the signing of the SAA in 2001 and the decisive influence that Croatian national politics had on that decision; this was followed by the analysis of the postponement of the opening of the accession negotiations in 2005; and it concluded by examining the about-turn nearly seven months later, when negotiations were surprisingly opened.

On the other hand, the first EU policy shift in Serbia alluded to the stalling of accession negotiations in May 2006; the second evaluated the EU reversal and the reasons for reopening them one year later; and the third policy shift concerned the signing of the SAA shortly before the capture of Radovan Karadžić, and the process which led to the capture of the other two remaining fugitives, Ratko Mladić and Goran Hadžić.

All these policy shifts illustrate underlying patterns in the role the ICTY played in the accession negotiations between the EU and Serbia and Croatia. The dynamics before and after each policy shift lead to the general conclusion that the ICTY influenced an EU decision the most when it spelled out as much

286 "Pressure to conclude trials, 'staff attrition' among obstacles cited as officials of international criminal tribunal's brief Security Council", UNSC, 6.12.2010.

as possible what type of cooperation it wanted from the respective states, and accompanied that definition with pressure on the states to comply with it. In other words, when the ICTY filled the concept of 'full cooperation' with clear content, it made conditionality much more accountable, and decisively influenced the EU in its application. This influence was frequently visible in specific EU documents which mention the conditions established by the ICTY. Thus, in many cases, the Tribunal acted as a principal.

Various examples exist which prove the Tribunal's influence. ICTY Prosecutor Carla Del Ponte's decision to indict Croatian General Ante Gotovina in 2001 and publicly press for his transfer to The Hague (for example with her reports to the UNSC) decisively influenced a shift in EU conditionality towards Croatia. Whereas key EU documents in 2002 and 2003, such as the Annual Reports, mention cooperation with the ICTY in broad terms and do not explicitly refer to Gotovina, relevant documents in 2004 and 2005 do refer to the general. This is the case, for instance, with the 2004 Opinion by the European Commission on Croatia's Application for Membership of the European Union, which mentions Gotovina twice, or the 2005 Croatia Progress Report, also authored by the European Commission, where the name of the general appears five times. Moreover, after a negative assessment of cooperation by the ICTY in March 2005, the Council of the European Union decided to cancel, for the first time in history, the opening of accession negotiations.

The influence of the ICTY can also be seen in Serbia. After the death of Slobodan Milošević, Carla Del Ponte raised the issue of Ratko Mladić to the top of her agenda. That interest was in line with the goals of the EU on this matter. A telling image was the fact that Carla Del Ponte and Commissioner for Enlargement Olli Rehn appeared together at a joint press conference in January 2006 to express the need to capture Mladić.[287] In May that year, after a meeting between Rehn and Del Ponte, a negative assessment by the ICTY confirmed that Serbia had failed to meet an EU ultimatum to capture the fugitive, and this was quickly followed by the stalling of negotiations and the resignation of the head of Serbia's SAA negotiating team. In short, the ICTY assessment of whether Serbia was cooperating with a view to handing Mladić over proved to be essential when negotiations were halted in 2006.

These examples of the leverage exerted by the ICTY go hand in hand with others where the Tribunal had little say in EU enlargement decisions and basically served as an agent. Those situations arose when the internal politics of Serbia and Croatia transgressed national borders and influenced the EU to

287 Teresa Küchler: "Serbia to choose Mladić or EU, Rehn and Del Ponte say". EU Observer, 20.1.2006.

generate a policy shift, and when internal EU dynamics (in particular, contradictory interests of member states) pushed ICTY conditionality into the background in order to favour other interests. Frederick Swinnen of the ICTY acknowledged this:

> When there are other interests, sometimes the ICTY plays a very little role and justice is shoved aside. That is a constant threat, we can raise our voice and publicly express concern, but in the end, we don't have coercive or political powers. We count on the effective support of states.[288]

One clear situation where the ICTY was pushed aside to the advantage of other issues was when Serbia and Croatia held elections and there was a danger of a nationalist backlash in one of these countries.

In Zagreb's case, the first presidential elections after Tudjman's death created new power dynamics between that country, the ICTY, and the EU. Croatia used its relationship with the ICTY politically – by delaying or unblocking assistance strategically – in order to get benefits from the European Union. The European Commission, for instance, in its Opinion on Croatia's Application for Membership of the European Union, praised Zagreb's progress and admitted that its commitment "was reflected in a rapid development of relations with the European Union."[289] This development was SAA, which was signed in 2001, only months after the ICTY's indictment of Ante Gotovina.

In Serbia, internal developments have often been catalysts of change in European Union policy. Apart from Kosovo's declaration of independence and the referendum in Montenegro, the periods surrounding elections are also clear examples of this phenomenon. The 2007 parliamentary elections were carefully analysed by the European Union, which feared the revival of the Radical Party led by Tomislav Nikolić. The decision to restart negotiation talks with Serbia was only made after the elections, as the 2007 Progress Report on Serbia confirmed. Something similar happened one year later: important decisions by the European Union (the signing of the SAA or the Roadmap for Visa Liberalisation) occurred in the periods surrounding the presidential or parliamentary elections.

But the fact that the EU was sometimes influenced by key political events in Serbia and Croatia is not sufficient for understanding the reasons behind the EU policy shifts studied here. It is important to stress that internal dynamics within the EU and, in particular, conflicting member states' interests have proven to be essential in luring the Balkans. A clear example can be seen with the

288 Interview with Frederick Swinnen, The Hague, April 2011.

289 Commission Of The European Communities. "Communication From the Commission. Opinion on Croatia's Aplication for Membership of the European Union", op. cit.

Netherlands, progressively left alone with its demands to keep the condition of full cooperation with the ICTY at the top of the EU enlargement agenda with respect to Belgrade. Only after it relaxed its stance, the EU was able to sign the SAA with Serbia, a decision that gave that country's accession prospects a new impetus.

Apart from EU member states' interests, an additional element is key in order to assess the enlargement process for the Western Balkan states and the dynamics between the EU, the ICTY, and the two Balkan countries, namely political conditionality (referring to the need to fully cooperate with the ICTY) and its effects on the main actors involved.

Conditionality was used by the EU in two ways: first, as a hard condition. In this case, fulfilment is a necessary, unavoidable step towards receiving a reward. An example is the suspension of negotiations with Croatia as a result of the lack of cooperation in capturing Gotovina (2005) and, with Serbia, after the failure to apprehend Mladić (2006). The second way was by giving the reward first as an incentive in order to encourage the country to meet the requirements. The clearest case was the capture of Radovan Karadžić (2008) after the SAA had been signed.

In both processes, the situation should be viewed critically. Although conditionality led to or influenced concrete results (war criminals in The Hague and two countries on the road to EU membership), it was hardly ever consistent and not always effective. It brought the best results, at least from the EU's viewpoint, when it was tied to concrete and immediate results.[290] The signing of the SAA with Croatia, in 2001, is a good example: with that important benchmark in sight, Zagreb's new government pledged to cooperate with the Tribunal.

On the other hand, there are also situations where conditionality proved to be ineffective. The first reason, as Florence Hartmann notes, is that conditionality was political in nature and, as such, it was sometimes subject to decisions by the EU that differed from the goals set by the ICTY.[291] A second reason refers to the lack of a definition of what it actually meant, and when it had to be used. This not only led to heated debates among member states that had different opinions on how conditionality should be achieved, it also made the whole process less clear and generated ambivalences.

Those ambivalences relate to the lack of consistency both with respect to Croatia and Serbia separately, and also when the two countries are compared. In

290 Dobbels, Mathias: "Serbia and the ICTY: How Effective is EU Conditionality". *EU Diplomacy Papers*, (6/2009). http://www.coleurope.eu.

291 Hartmann, Florence: "The ICTY and EU conditionality", in Batt, Obradović, War Crimes, Conditionality, 67.

the first case, one prominent example comes to mind: the negotiation talks with Serbia stalled in 2006 because of the failure to capture Ratko Mladić, but they were restarted one year later and progressed swiftly thereafter despite Mladić being at large.

When comparing conditionality in Serbia and Croatia, the effectiveness of this tool has also been criticised. As Geraldine Mattioli-Zeltner mentions, "what was demanded from Serbia compared to what was demanded from Croatia was completely different."[292] One case often mentioned refers to the fact that Serbia feels there is an anti-Serb bias both in the Tribunal and in the EU. In particular, some Serbs believe it is "unfair"[293] that Croatia was considered to be cooperating fully with the Tribunal in 2005 when its main fugitive, Ante Gotovina, was still at large, yet Serbia did not receive the same treatment with Karadžić and with Mladić. According to Mathias Dobbels, this "undermined the EU's credibility in holding on to a tough stance vis-à-vis Serbia as it gives the impression that conditionality is negotiable and variable from case to case."[294] Actually, as this part of our book shows, conditionality was negotiable – especially, when there were strong internal obstacles present in Croatia or Serbia or when EU member states were divided and did not specify exactly what "cooperation with the ICTY" meant. "Croatia and Serbia were not treated equally by the EU," Param-Preet Singh, Senior Counsel at Human Rights Watch,[295] admitted. This is an opinion that was shared by one of our Dutch diplomatic sources. It was due not only to a possible bias or policy preference at the ICTY or among member states, but also to the balance of power within the EU, where Croatia had adamant supporters but Serbia did not. A high-ranking Dutch diplomat said, "we had member states intervening for Croatia and we knew that not all member states agreed fully with our stance toward Serbia and the ICTY, but there was never a member state that exposed itself so much for Serbia as we did for the ICTY or others did for Croatia." In other words, there was never a real danger for The Netherlands of its veto being overruled by a concurrent one from another member state, as had been the case in the Austria – Britain standoff over Turkey and Croatia.

In the case of Serbia and Croatia, particular conclusions can be drawn from the analysis of the impact of the specific conditionality regarding full cooperation with the ICTY. From the perspective of international justice

---

292 Telephone interview with Geraldine Mattioli-Zeltner. April 19, 2011.

293 Dobbels, Serbia and the ICTY, op. cit.

294 Ibid.

295 Interview with Param-Preet Singh, Senior Counsel at the International Justice Program of Human Rights Watch in April 2012 in New York.

advocates, tying accession to the European Union to the obligation to hand over the main architects of the wars has been an assurance that most perpetrators will sooner or later face justice, and that with them in jail, some sort of truth can be obtained and victims can be redressed. In other words, it is a reminder that the only way forward for Serbia and Croatia is coming to terms with the past. The fact that EU conditionality was a driving force behind the capture of high-ranking officials, such as Ante Gotovina or Radovan Karadžić, proves this point right.

On the other hand, critics of applying conditionality address not only the point of strategic utilisation of the concept for goals not related to international justice obligations but also the effects of conditionality on countries' internal politics. John Hagan explains in this regard that "this exercise of structural conditionality polarized, mediated and contextualized Serbian politics."[296]

Hagan presents one powerful and illustrative example: Prime Minister Zoran Djindjić, who was in charge of transferring Milošević to The Hague and who worked closely with ICTY Prosecutor Carla Del Ponte, was assassinated in 2003 on the very same day that he was about to issue warrants for high-level arrests.[297] This shows the extent to which conditionality divided Serbian politics and stirred up nationalistic sentiments.

Finally, for the ICTY, conditionality has brought clear results. Carla Del Ponte, Florence Hartmann and also Frederick Swinnen view conditionality in a positive light. Swinnen, for example, recognizes that "without conditionality we would not be where we are today. It is thanks to the European Union that we are where we are today in terms of arresting fugitives."[298] Hartmann concurs,[299] while Del Ponte expressed the importance numerically: "90 per cent of all indictees brought to justice [before the ICTY] are direct results of conditionality applied by the EU."[300]

The fact the ICTY's interests were contractually bound to the interests of the European Union often provoked criticism. Del Ponte's statement shows the final outcome, but does not highlight the process. And that process was not always

296 Hagan, John: "The Political Economy of Genocide Intervention: Structural Conditionality, Collective Command Responsibility, and The Former Yugoslavia". *3rd Annual Conference on Empirical Legal Studies Papers* May 2008. http://ssrn.com/abstract=1132583.

297 Interview with a former security advisor of Zoran Djindjić in Belgrade in October 2009. The advisor saw Djindijić's decision to sign the warrants as the main reason for the assassination.

298 Interview with Frederick Swinnen, The Hague, April 2011.

299 Hartmann, The ICTY and EU conditionality, op. cit.

300 Ibid (quoting Carla Del Ponte).

transparent towards the ICTY. Both Serbia and Croatia sometimes resorted to particular strategies in order to delay, block or enhance cooperation, not necessarily because they were interested in meeting their international justice obligations, but because it represented a shortcut to receiving European Union rewards. From a moral perspective of how countries should deal with their violent past, this may be viewed negatively. Applying the principal-agent approach, EU rewards are the carrot and the withholding of benefits (like the stalling of negotiations) is the stick which makes conditionality effective. Conditionality was efficient when it was based on personalisation – when the EU clearly mentioned who should be apprehended and pinned a price tag on non-compliance. The decisive question is therefore: under what conditions could the ICTY get EU ministers to personalize their demands for compliance toward Serbia and Croatia? This was the case when no important internal constraints were present in both countries. When personalizing and rewarding an ICTY request was likely to stir up nationalist parties and endanger internal stability in one of these countries, the EU shirked and inverted structural conditionality. Instead of demanding concessions (the surrender of a fugitive) in exchange for a reward, the EU decided to give the reward in the hope of getting a payback after the nationalist threat had disappeared. This means that the ICTY could only act as a principal toward the EU if no internal constraints threatened the pro-EU conduct of the Croatian or Serbian government at that moment. In other words, the ICTY could only use EU conditionality as an efficient tool to coerce Serbia or Croatia into compliance if its influence was not counterbalanced by nationalist forces in both countries.

All in all, the effectiveness of conditionality in Serbia, Croatia, the ICTY and the EU takes on particular importance when this issue is viewed as an on-going phenomenon. The ICTY is drawing closer to the end of its mandate, which was originally planned for 2010 but has now been extended to 2014. In retrospect, it becomes clear that the Tribunal, despite a performance that sometimes resembled a roller-coaster ride, has been a central element in Serbia's and Croatia's aspirations to become EU members. It has certainly raised the cost of EU membership for both countries, because in addition to the political, legal and economic criteria for EU membership, they have also had to meet conditions that previous accession candidates did not face – to apply a retributive transitional justice policy, which sometimes endangered their internal stability. The cooperation between Carla Del Ponte and Prime Minister Djindjić, which ended with the latter's assassination, is a striking illustration of this fact. For the ICTY's role as a principal, this is a rather sombre view. It means that the ICTY was acting largely as the agent of the EU and its member states, and as a hostage of the internal situation in Croatia and Serbia. Only when EU member states were united in their interest toward the Balkans and no threat of a nationalist backlash in Zagreb and Belgrade was visible, could the ICTY hope to push the EU to adopt a personalized, precise and price-tagged demand, which would then be met by the target state. This may not seem like a lot, but it should be remembered that it was much more than the ICTR could hope for. The ICTY's counterpart in Arusha had no strong regional organisation that could issue credible ultimatums connected to the handing over of a specific suspect. Neither the UN nor the African Union had comparable sticks or carrots that they could use to enforce conditionality. As a result, the ICTR had to struggle with non-cooperative states even in cases when there was no internal obstacle to handing over a suspect.

Part II
External Influences on Judging at International Criminal Tribunals

Introduction

From a theoretical standpoint, a trial can be regarded from two perspectives: As the process of negotiating guilt, during which the prosecutor acts as a representative of the state (or, respectively, as a representative of the community, whose system of norms was violated), the defence counsellor acts as a representative of the defendant and the judge moderates the confrontation between the two parties, weighs the evidence and finally issues a verdict, possibly guiding a jury. These features broadly describe the adversarial system, which exists in the United States. In the inquisitorial system, which dominates on the European continent, it is the task of the judge (or the trial chamber) to establish the truth (rather than guilt alone) in a joint effort with the prosecution and the defence. Whether we reject this dichotomy or not, both systems' basic assumptions remain undisputed. One of them is the belief that the application of specific procedures facilitates the establishment of the truth about a certain controversial event (what happened and who did what).[301] Another one consists in the conviction according to which this procedure can only work smoothly and efficiently if all participants fulfill the role assigned to them by the law. A more specific and extremely essential requirement is the impartiality of the judge or the trial chamber. Another one is the expectation that verdicts should be based on deliberation rather than bargaining, which includes that the discussions of the judges (and, if applicable, the jury) should only be guided by the aspiration to discover the truth and not by the material interest of the participants. In order to guarantee the deliberative character of judges' and jurors' debates, both have to undergo lengthy and detailed investigations about their impartiality, and judges and jurors who give reason for suspicion about any conflict of interest with one of the trial parties must be excluded from the proceedings. Applying Jürgen Habermas' concept of deliberation, one could conclude that courts' verdicts are to be based uniquely on truth-seeking and consensus-building and should therefore exclude any possibility of compromise, defined as the outcome of a bargaining process concerning material, private or individual interests.[302]

---

301 We refer to this issue later in the theoretical introduction to chapter 3, where Peter Lambertz explains the role of "truth telling" and the production of truth in transitional justice.

302 Habermas distinguishes between bargaining, which is based on private, material interests (partikulare Interessen) and leads to a compromise on the one hand, and deliberation, which is deprived of material interests and is based only on the aspiration to find the truth or the best solution for all involved and includes only "general interests" (verallgemeinerungsfähige Interessen). Jürgen Habermas: Strukturwandel der Öffentlichkeit. Frankfurt / Main 1961, 38-47.

As has often been pointed out by Habermas' critics, this model is idealistic rather than realistic. Even in predominantly deliberative settings (like the jurors' discussion in a criminal trial), private or material interests can affect the outcome. The distinction between deliberation and bargaining is therefore relative, not absolute. We may discuss proceedings and how some are more deliberative than others, but we will never be faced with a procedure that is purely and totally deliberative. Even when no jury member is linked in any way to a defendant, private and material considerations of jury members (like their wish to go home before the last subway leaves) may affect their judgment (and prevent them from discussing all the evidence related to the case).

Another basic assumption of both legal systems refers to the need of judges (more than jurors) to base their conclusions about truth and guilt on evidence and legal considerations. According to the predominant public image of judges (and most judges' own concept of how justice works), verdicts should only be based on the consideration of evidence in the light of a narrow interpretation of the law. Judges are expected to apply the law, and in the classical legalist school of juridical reasoning it is the law and nothing but the law, which guides judges considerations when issuing verdicts. As Richard Posner has pointed out, embracing legalism in extenso would lead to a situation in which judges become unnecessary and can be replaced by computers, which, on the basis of allegedly objective criteria pertaining to the evidence, apply the law without any reference to personal interests, ideological bias, individual convictions or beliefs of any kind. From this perspective, the mere existence of judges is inconsistent with legalist claims. Of course, it is impossible to explain judges' decision-making by referring to only one theory of judicial behavior. Judges actually do apply the law, but at the same time, they do more than just that, and while applying the law, they react consciously and unconsciously to incentives from outside: to considerations about their image, their position within the legal hierarchy, the costs a decision involves for them, and the potential broader consequences of their verdicts. Judges are not computers, they are driven by emotions, convictions, and ideologies, while seeking the truth (or establishing the level of guilt), they are also labor market participants pursuing a career, and they often act like public figures, prominent judges even may act and behave like politicians.[303] Judges are human beings, and as such, they succumb to stereotypes, bias and thinking in terms of *pars pro toto*.

All these factors play varying roles in various theories of judicial behavior, and neither of them can explain or predict the way in which judges come to a decision and which verdicts they issue. Each of them, however, explains a part

303 Posner, Richard A.: How Judges think. First Havard University Press 2008, 19-124.

of the variance, which occurs when judges make decisions: some judges are more ideology–driven than others, younger judges may attach more importance to their career within the system than judges who are close to retirement, and judges from an authoritarian background may react more strongly to norm violation (and therefore issue relatively harsher verdicts) than judges who were socialized in a libertarian environment. Many of these theories – but far from all – can be applied to judges in international criminal tribunals.

Municipal courts, regardless of whether they deal with criminal or civil matters, can be considered actors in a principal-agent structure, in which the government defers certain tasks to courts (the solution of conflicts, for example), equipping its agent with a mandate (the law) and providing specific incentives, which should incline the agent to execute his task properly, i.e. according to the will of the principal.[304] The inherent contradiction in this model immediately becomes visible, since courts are not expected to execute the will of their respective governments. Rather, the opposite is true: judges are expected to apply the law no matter whether this suits the government or not. They are, however, expected to act according to the will of the legislator (e.g., the parliament) and they are rewarded for doing so by another principal: the government, which pays judges' salaries. Municipal judges face divided principals and differing incentives. The government may put gentle pressure on judges in order to incline them to go into one direction, whereas the legislator may try to push them in another direction by drafting laws accordingly. Additional incentives may come from the wider public, which may (depending on the level of public controversy, which a case may arouse) pressurize a judge to go in a third direction. No matter whose influence, if any, prevails, the fact remains that judges' behavior in municipal courts is likely to be shaped by the sides of this triangle.

For judges of international criminal tribunals, there is no such triangle. They are elected according to the procedures of the United Nations[305] and later, during their term, report to the Security Council.[306] Ad litem judges are elected for a specific term, permanent judges are elected for the time the tribunal is supposed to

304 More about the principal-agent dichothomy can be found in Thomas Sparrow-Botero's chapter on the ICTY as an agent or principle of europeanisation. Here we only mention the concept in order to clarify in how far this concept can be applied to judicial behavior.

305 About the selection of international judges see: Mackenzie, Ruth; Malleson, Kate; Martin, Penny and Sands, Philippe (eds): Selecting International Judges. Principles, Process, and Politics. Oxford University Press 2010.

306 Annual reports to the UNSC are delivered by the chief prosecutor and the president of the ICTY and ICTR.

exist. Salaries are fixed (according to the UN principles). If there is a principal for whom ICTY and ICTR judges could be agents, then it is the Security Council. We may regard the tribunal statute and the Security Council Resolutions as their mandate. But instead of a national public, which could use incentives to push the judges into one or another direction, we have a very dispersed and fuzzy international public sphere, where epistemic communities, international judges and lawyers from other international or internationalized institutions and the media from the countries of the tribunal's territorial jurisdiction as well as influent international media play the important roles. All these elements together suggest that judges of international criminal tribunals enjoy a much larger leeway than judges in municipal courts. Their mandate is relatively broad, since the tribunal statutes are elaborated for specific cases and do not emerge from century-old evolutions of primary and secondary law. The rules of procedures and evidence are established and can by altered by the judges who have to apply them, which provides them with more flexibility than any municipal judge could ever dream of. In national, historically grown legal systems, rules of procedure and evidence, which come mostly in the form of criminal codes, are complicated collections of laws, embedded in legal traditions, interpretations and decisions of higher instances, based on century–long experience and are therefore quite stable. The ICTY's rules of procedure and evidence have often been altered ad hoc, in order to adapt them to the changing circumstances of current trials. Between 1994 and 2010, the ICTY's rules of procedure and evidence were amended about 40 times, on average once every five months.

Compared to municipal judges, international judges are also confronted with different conditions regarding their career opportunities and their chances for promotion. International judges compete on a very narrow labour market. Opportunities for promotion within an international tribunal are very limited, since a trial judge can only be assigned to an appeals chamber and theoretically be elected as tribunal president. Judges seeking advancement can switch to another international tribunal (but then will most likely end up on the same level) or return to their country (but then cease to be international judges). We may therefore assume that labour market and promotion opportunities have a much weaker impact on international judges' decisions than we might expect in the case of municipal judges.[307] This is also due to the fact that for most

307 An additional argument may be that for the overwhelming majority of ICTY and ICTR judges, their post at these tribunals constituted the peak of their careers, after which they went into retirement. Career considerations seem to play a bigger role for prosecutors, who are often younger and return to their national justice administration after completing their term at an international tribunal. This was confirmed in several interviews at the ICTY.

permanent judges, their term at the ICTY is often their last position before retirement. One judge admitted: "Being appointed an international judge is the copestone of a judge's career." This, however, is only true for permanent judges. For judges *ad litem*, who after their term may return to their former posts in their country, career and labour market considerations may play a much bigger role.[308]

When it comes to their judgments, we may therefore expect international judges to rather be influenced by personal beliefs, convictions, stereotypes and ideologies, than by considerations concerning career, tenure, salary issues and constraints emanating from the judicial environment.

Since their autonomy is much bigger than the maneuverability of municipal judges, we can expect their judgment to reflect this difference. Even more: we should be able to observe the influence of additional factors on international judges' decisions, factors, which have little or no impact on municipal judges. Such factors are the opinions and moral judgments of a large, and disperse media community – which mostly ignores trials in municipal courts –, of powerful foreign governments (especially members of the UN Security Council), and of international non-governmental organisations. The latter may play a much bigger role than in trials before municipal judges, since they mostly concentrate on big, controversial issues, which provide opportunities for politicisation, polarisation, and the mobilisation of public opinion.[309] International NGOs are important for yet another reason. Some of them actively supported the tribunals, collected and submitted witness statements and evidence, and even helped to finance the tribunals during their initial period. The Open Society Institute supported the ICTY financially during the court's early days; Human Rights Watch sent researchers to Albania to collect witness statements and contact information, which were later submitted to the tribunal. Leading HRW-campaigners served as witnesses for the prosecution.[310] Richard Dicker, head of the Human Rights Watch international justice program, recalled: "The OTP saw us as assisting them and contributing to their mission, but we decided we would talk to both sides – but, at the same time, protect our sources." However, contacts with

308 Interview with Judge Christoph Flügge in May 2012 at the ICTY.

309 It is worth mentioning that many, if not all, factors, which are likely to influence adjudication in international tribunals, may also play a role in huge, controversial trials in municipal courts, which attract international media interest. Examples are the Dutroux trial in Belgium in 2003-2004 or the trial against Saddam Hussein. Since political trials before national courts are not the issue of this book, implications of such trials for sentencing and judicial behavior are neglected here.

310 Fred Abrahams: "Lifes. Face to face with Milošević." The New York Times Magazine, 21.7.2002.

the OTP were more intense than with defence counsellors.[311] Interaction between human rights organisations and the ICTY was close, but it was much closer in the case of the ICTR. According to Filip Reyntjens, this was due to the lack of knowledge of international judges and prosecutors at the ICTR during the initial stage of the tribunal. "Back in 1996, OTP members came to my house in Antwerp asking about the basics of Rwandan contemporary history. With Alison des Forges, I conducted a seminar in my living room, where Bernard Muna was present and during which we would call for pizzas, because it lasted so long. I guess I have spent the equivalent of six months full-time working for the tribunal. In May 2003, we were even invited to Arusha for a seminar with the funny title 'Encounters with Alison des Forges and Filip Reyntjens'. At the beginning, they wanted non-lawyers with a fact-based approach rather than legal experts to bring in their narratives." Reyntjens agreed that this was likely to shape the preconceptions of both prosecutors and judges. The impact of Alison des Forges, an expert and campaigner for Human Rights Watch as well as the author of the first concise history of the Rwandan genocide (which became the authoritative handbook for prosecutors and judges at the ICTY), was particularly strong.[312] Reyntjens would later become a prosecution witness in the *pros. vs. Bagosora et al.* and in *the pros. vs. Rutaganda.*[313] After he agreed to testify on behalf of the defence in *the pros. vs. Nyiramasuhuko et al.*, his relations with the OTP became tense. In 2005, he wrote a letter to chief prosecutor Hassan Jallow declaring that he would not agree to testify at the ICTY as long as the OTP did not investigate and prosecute crimes committed by the RPF.[314]

Whereas judges' and prosecutors' knowledge about the conflict had been much more widespread during the start-up phase of the ICTY, it was scarce in Arusha. ICTR prosecutors and judges seemed to be more open for outsider knowledge than their colleagues at the ICTY, where such pre-trial knowledge was rather suspected to cause bias and prejudice. One ICTY trial judge told us during an interview: "It is better to focus on what happens in the courtroom and

---

311 Interview with Richard Dicker in April 2012 in New York. According to Dicker, the establishment of the International Justice Program was a reaction to the Milošević trial.

312 Interview with Filip Reyntjens in Antwerp in April 2012.

313 ICTR-96-03-R.

314 According to Reyntjens, relations started to get complicated after the then prosecutor Carla Del Ponte had learned about his decision to testify for the defence in the Butare case. She made it clear, that she regarded Reyntjens as "hers", as the prosecution's witness and that she considered his testimony for the defence a kind of treason. After that, he was no longer invited to testify for the OTP, neither was he subpoenaed by the prosecution. Interview with Filip Reyntjens in Antwerp in April 2012.

on the evidence presented by the parties than to read books about the issue beforehand." Judge Gabrielle Kirk McDonald recalled, however, that there were also training sessions in the start-up phase of the ICTY: "I remember we received a lot of papers about the history of Bosnia, about Yugoslavia and the law there. I specifically remember one entitled 'no peace without justice' and a paper on sexual violence. At one point I thought, 'oh God, am I back in school?'"[315]

At the ICTY, influence on judges' preconceptions of the events relevant for a case were more likely to come through the prosecution, while at the ICTR it could be channeled directly from NGOs and media to the trial chamber in the form of reports, informal contacts and expert testimonies.[316] At the ICTR, the informal influence of experts was initially very strong. Before the ICTR became fully operative, prosecutors from Arusha asked some well-known academics for advice, even travelling to their private residences in Europe. As Filip Reyntjens, one of the academics, recalled, all these experts were Europeans and Americans. Alison Des Forges, who worked for Human Rights Watch, had carried out extensive on-site investigations in Rwanda already during the second half of 1994 and had written an academic handbook on the genocide, which subsequently became a bestseller and was admitted as a prosecution exhibit by ICTR trial chambers, was also there. Together with Reyntjens and French sociologist André Guichaoua, she conducted a number of introductory courses for prosecutors about Rwandan history and the time between 1990 and 1994. Guichaoua had been in Rwanda during the genocide, he had helped to save some prominent Tutsi politicians from being slaughtered and had excellent connections with the new government, which took power after the RPF had conquered the country. According to him, these history lessons were not limited to prosecutors, but also included judges. In the case of the ICTY, this kind of influence was formalized and took place mainly through witness testimonies of experts (among them also NGO activists). According to our interviews, the

315 Interview with Judge Gabrielle Kirk McDonald in June 2012. She had already undergone training on international criminal law by the Justice Department after her appointment as ICTY judge and prior to her departure to The Hague. Later on, during *the pros. vs. Blaškić, amici curiae* were called in order to assist the chamber in finding out whether and how the ICTY could subpoena states and state officials.

316 As Filip Reyntjens told us, during the early years in Arusha, the lobby of the local Novotel became the informal meeting place for prosecutors, judges, defence counsellors and expert witnesses, who would often drink beer together. He insisted that discussions with judges never touched upon issues connected to trials pending. Interview with Filip Reyntjens in Antwerp in April 2012.

ICTY seemed to be more insulated from the OTP, outsiders, defence counsellors and experts than was the case in Arusha.[317]

More leeway, the need for maximal flexibility, and a detached and flat hierarchy increase the likelihood of several phenomena, which occur quite seldom in municipal courts. International judges may be more prone to act as legislators and innovators, and they may be more eager to apply pragmatic adjudication. At the same time, the lack or relative weakness of external constraints on judges' decisions may increase the impact of internal factors, such as a stronger inclination to avoid conflict and controversy, to subordinate one's decisions to the guidance of superiors, informal authorities, and peers. The impact of these factors is the more important, the less international judges are constrained by issues connected to judicial method, the need to narrowly interpret and apply the law, and – a very important topic – the less they are constrained by evidence.

317 Interviews with Filip Reyntjens in Antwerp in April 2012, and with André Guichaoua in Paris in May 2012. See also Reyntjens, Ruling Under a Volcano, chapter "the ICTY", where he describes the consequences of the prosecutors and judges living together "in the promiscuity (sic!) of the 'village' that is Arusha."

Fact-Finding, Evidence and Testimony

In municipal courts, judges, prosecutors, defendants and witnesses come from the same cultural background, they usually speak the same language and their arguments are based on similar values. Communication problems, misunderstandings about basic issues, cultural differences between judges and witnesses occur during trials in municipal courts for example when involving immigrants from distant countries, or, in socially deeply divided societies, when judges and witnesses belong to extremely different classes or social groups. While racial, social, regional, ethnic and political bias may play a role in the relations between judges and defendants, they usually are less important in judge-witness relations. This is totally different in international criminal tribunals, where judges, who often belong to the social elite of their country, have to deal with evidence given by illiterate witnesses from deprived social or ethnic groups, who often do not even understand what they are expected to do in court. The probability of misunderstandings is the higher, the larger the socio-economic and educational distance is between a judge and a witness.

As Nancy Armoury Combs has shown, trial chambers in international criminal courts often ground their factual findings on witness statements, which are incomplete, incoherent, internally contradictory and, because of their vagueness, deprive defendants of important opportunities to attack the prosecution case, for example by preventing them from presenting an alibi.[318] The scope of these shortcomings inclined Combs even to suggest that judges in international tribunals should be allowed to attribute less importance to witness statements and to substantiate their judgments by applying a standard of proof, which is based on associational features rather than the traditional standard of fact-finding beyond a reasonable doubt.[319] There are indeed indications for the

318 Combs, Nancy Armoury: Fact-Finding Without Facts. The Uncertain Evidentiary Foundations of International Criminal Convictions, Cambridge University Press 2010.

319 Combs clearly points out one important issue, which relates to the difference between international and municipal courts. In municipal courts, usually the cost (or harm) of a conviction of an innocent is deemed higher than the cost of acquitting a guilty person. This can be seriously put into question with respect to many highly politicized international trials, where the cost (for society, for the court and important political stakeholders) of acquitting an innocent (but publicly blamed) accused may be much higher than the cost of sentencing an innocent (if the latter is widely regarded as guilty). As Combs convincingly points out, acquittals have detrimental psychological consequences for victims, no matter, whether the acquittals are grounded or not, whereas sentencing an innocent who is publicly taken for guilty (e.g., because of his influential position during the commission of crimes by his subordinates) will probably be limited to himself, his family and a part of his supporters. In cases where a relatively

(conscious or unconscious) use of associational features by judges. Combs suggests, that, given the same amount and quality of evidence, international judges tend to interpret institutional affiliations in exactly the opposite way than judges in municipal courts use to do. The higher the formal rank of an accused, the higher the likelihood of being found guilty; the lower his rank, the higher the probability, that judges will acquit him, provided that all other factors, which may influence sentencing, remain the same. [320] What Combs terms "the use of organisational liability as an evidentiary proxy"[321], is rooted in a specific "culture of conviction" at international criminal tribunals. Despite the high risk of perjury, communication breakdown in the courtroom, testimonial vagueness and translation errors, defendants in international criminal tribunals face a relatively high risk of conviction, which is illustrated by a 100 per cent conviction rate at the Special Court for Sierra Leone and a 97 per cent rate at the Special Panels in the Dili District Court in East Timor – the courts where the likelihood of erroneous fact finding due to cultural differences, communication problems, perjury and misunderstandings are highest. The ICTR runs a 74 per cent conviction rate, whereas the ICTY has so far issued 13 acquittals as opposed to 64 convictions.[322] This culture of convictions can be traced back to the different incentive structure to which international judges are subordinated when compared to their colleagues in national courts, and it actually reflects their different assessment of the cost of acquittal as opposed to the cost of conviction. This different assessment is even visible in UNSC Resolution 827, which declares, "to establish an international tribunal for the *sole* purpose of *prosecuting* persons (emphasis by the authors) responsible for serious violations of international humanitarian law." [323] In the language of principal-agent approaches, one could say that the only formal and clearly identifiable principal, to whom international tribunals are subordinated, the UNSC, issues a clear signal to the judges that in case of any doubt, they are expected to opt for

low numbers of perpetrators caused a relatively high number of victims, the relative cost of acquittal of a guilty person will be even higher than the relative cost of convicting an innocent. See Combs, Fact-Finding, 229-232, 257-260, 245-350., 356-357.

320 Combs, Fact-Finding, 235-270.

321 Combs, Fact-Finding, 235.

322 Data for the Special Court and the Special Panels come from Combs, Fact-Finding, 221, rates for the ICTR and ICTY were established by us and reflect the situation in July 2011 according to both tribunals' websites. The ratio for the ICTY is blurred by a high number of suspects whose indictments were either withdrawn or became obsolete due to the death of suspects (36), and whose indictments were referred to national jurisdictions according to the ICTY's completion strategy (13).

323 UNSC Resolution 827.

conviction rather than acquittal. This signal is strongly reinforced by a general punitive tendency of (international and local) media, international NGOs and the international human rights community. The relatively (when compared to municipal courts) strong presence of former human rights activists in the trial chambers of international tribunals shows that these punitive influences should not be regarded merely as externalities. They may also have an influence during *in camera* discussions between judges, when the stabilizing force of consensus prevents dissenters from uttering their reservations.[324]

If we compare international judges to municipal ones, it becomes immediately evident that most external constraints which are likely to influence judicial behavior are much weaker: due to the vagueness of statutes and the relative autonomy of international tribunals, legalist ramifications are rather weak and judges' leeway is relatively broad. Labour market, salary and career considerations are unlikely to constrain judges' autonomy and the lack of clearly identifiable principals, of accountability mechanisms and narrow mandates make international criminal tribunals agents on a very long and flexible leash. Compared to agents in other principal-agent relations, their autonomy is very broad.[325] But there are also incentives which shape judicial behavior of international judges, but only weakly, if at all, affect decision-making in municipal courts. Judges may be guided by their own prejudices, bias, religious or non-religious beliefs, their hierarchy of values, by ideology, personal characteristics and psychological limitations, by socialisation, education and personal experience. These features are likely to affect the decisions of any judge, whether international or municipal, but due to the weakness of externalities in international tribunals, we may expect them to play a bigger role there. In municipal courts, it is more probable that judges' personal, internal

324 Posner, How Judges Think, 374. What Posner calls "stabilizing force of consensus" is to a large extent the result of an intergroup process, which in public opinion research is known as the "spiral of silence", developed by German pollster Elisabeth Noelle-Neumann. The theory describes how potential dissenters refrain from taking part in a discussion when they realize they are in a minority position. In such cases, opinion polls tend to underestimate the actual level of dissent. The same mechanism may prevent a judge of a trial or appeals chamber from opposing a dominant opinion (or erroneously taken as such), or from writing a dissenting opinion, thus signaling to the public a higher level of consensus than actually is the case. See: Elisabeth Noelle – Neumann: Die Schweigespirale. Öffentliche Meinung – unsere soziale Haut. Langen Müller, München 1980.

325 Posner, How Judges Think, 39, mentions other principle-agent relations, where independency of the agent is intended by the principle and an indispensable prerequisite of the relation, like with physicians and commissioned salesmen. One could also add journalists as agents of editors.

features are to a certain extent counterbalanced by externalities pertaining to principals, narrower mandates, and legalist and career considerations. There is also at least one factor, which throws its mostly invisible shadow over international tribunals and which is almost totally absent in municipal courts – institutional interest. Institutional interest should not be confused with cooperative interest (the economic interest of judges as professionals of a certain kind). Considerations about cooperative interest have to be seen as part of career, salary and labour market considerations, which may affect judgment, but have already been dealt with above. Institutional interest describes the tendency of judges, to include considerations about the standing, prestige and future of "their" tribunal. As history has shown, international criminal tribunals often suffer from a high degree of institutional instability due to shortages in funding, policy shifts of important contributors and external pressure. The ICTY faced financial shortages during its early days, and later, during the terms of George W. Bush as US president, was forced to elaborate a completing strategy and exposed to public criticism for being expensive and wasting money. The most striking example of how institutional interest can affect decision-making in international criminal tribunals comes from the ICTR.

In one of the most controversial verdicts, the appeals chamber in the Barayagwiza case[326] reversed the judgment of the trial chamber, ordering the immediate release of a high ranking suspect without prejudice, because his rights had been violated irremediably by detaining him extensively before his trial. The judgment caused outrage in Rwanda, where the government refused to issue a visa to the (newly appointed) chief prosecutor Carla Del Ponte, although she had not been involved in the case. Rwanda suspended all cooperation with the ICTR. In a hearing about a review of the appeals chamber's decision, Carla Del Ponte made it clear that the decision to release Barayagwiza constituted a threat to the very existence of the tribunal: "whether we like it or not, we must come to terms with the reality that our ability to continue our investigation depends on Rwanda", and without it, "we might as well open the doors to the prison. It is my hope that Barayagwiza will not be the one to decide the fate of this tribunal."[327] Later on, the appeals chamber reversed its ruling,[328]

326 *The pros. vs. Barayagwiza et al.* IT-99-52-A.

327 Quotes according to Moghalu, Kingsley: Rwanda's Genocide. The Politics of Global Justice. New York: Palgrave MacMillan 2005, 117.

328 It was not exactly the same appeals chamber, since Gabrielle Kirk McDonald, the presiding judge of the chamber, had left the tribunal before the second appeals chamber ruling, and a year later became arbiter at the Iran-United States Claims Tribunal in The Hague. See: Moghalu, Rwanda's Genocide, 106-109 and the webpage of the Iran-US Claims Tribunal: http://www.iusct.org/english/page18/mcdonald.html. In our interview

substantiating it with new facts which the prosecution had managed to introduce, and changed the initial decision to not allow the prosecutor to bring any charges against the accused. Barayagwiza was not released but put on trial for genocide together with two other suspects, and finally sentenced to life imprisonment for genocide, crimes against humanity, and violations of the Geneva Conventions.[329]

The Barayagwiza case constituted a striking example of the link between the specific incentive structure, the agency of international judges and what Combs called "the culture of conviction". Compared to the situation of municipal judges, contingent pressure from their principals and the wider public inclines international judges much more to convict suspects than to acquit them. Unlike municipal courts, they are much less expected to solve conflicts, or to establish a truth than they are supposed to punish perpetrators. Their institutional interest runs a greater risk when they decide to release a suspect (rightly or wrongly) regarded as guilty by principals and the public than in cases when they decide to convict a suspect whose guilt is disputed in public. The opposite case – that a suspect is convicted, despite being taken for innocent by the public – almost never arises in international criminal tribunals, because the public almost always tends to regard people who have been indicted or arrested (or both) as guilty. Studies show that high-ranking suspects in international tribunals usually cease to enjoy the benefit of the presumption of innocence as soon as they become suspects.[330] Some lawyers support a pragmatic approach to solve the tension between the tendency of the media and the public to refer to strict and sharp normative distinctions and to state who is a victim and a perpetrator on the one hand, and the need to uphold the presumption of innocence as a vital tool for the administration of justice that is more than just legally enshrined scapegoating on the other hand. They argue that the presumption of innocence should be confined to the courtroom only, a point which, once applied, would leave it to

with Judge Kirk McDonald in June 2012, she was critical of the reversal given her firm belief in the importance of safeguarding the rights even of those defendants that are accused of committing heinous crimes.

329 The trial chamber decreased this sentence as a reaction to the decision of the Appeals Chamber, to compensate the infringement of his rights before the trial either financially (in case he would be acquitted) or by lowering his prison term (in case he would be found guilty). After taking into account the time already served in jail by Barayagwiza, the ultimate sentence amounted to 27 years of imprisonment. At the time when sentence was passed, Barayagwiza was 53 years old. *The pros. vs. Nahimana, Barayagwiza and Ngeze* ICTR-99-52-T.

330 More on the presumption of innocence (especially with regard to the genocide charge in *the pros. vs. Milošević*, see: Nielsen, Christian Axboe: "Can We Salvage a History of the Yugoslav Conflicts from the Milošević Trial?" In: Waters, Timothy (ed): The Milošević Trial. An Autopsy. Oxford University Press 2013, chapter 23.

the incriminated person alone to deal with the damage of his public image after being acquitted.[331] The presumption of innocence as such is never absolute, and courts have frequently set out its ramifications. The presumption of innocence may be subordinated to other considerations (for example concerning the security of witnesses, jurors and trial judges), as long as this does not impede a fair trial. It neither prevents a prison administration from applying restrictions to a prisoner, nor does it inhibit a judge from keeping details about jurors confidential, when revealing them might enable defendants to intimidate members of the jury.[332] Whereas a limitation of the presumption of innocence at a pre-trial stage may not endanger the right of an accused to a fair trial, the massive undermining of the presumption by the media and the public is likely to exercise undue impact on judges and jurors. The potential impact on the latter has frequently been recognized by courts and has led to numerous cases in which courts were unable to find jurors not influenced by excessive (and biased) media coverage or had to refrain from judging a suspect, because a fair trial had no longer be possible. The link between one-sided media coverage before a trial and its influence on jurors is quite uncontested in the literature, but at the same time, hardly anyone would be ready to extend this suspicion of bias to professional judges. It is doubtful, though, that judges are totally immune to any external influences coming from public opinion and the media. Since international judges are exposed to much more one-sided (punitive, convictive) incentives than municipal judges, we also may expect them to be more influenced by them (though maybe less than jurors would be).

When external factors are weaker, we can expect personal factors and external factors to increase, and judges to develop more judicial initiative than they would in a municipal setting. As Posner already pointed out, the probability of judges abandoning a strict and legalistic way of applying the law and acting as occasional legislators by bringing in legal innovations is the higher, the higher the position of their court in the hierarchy of the legal system. International judges are to a large extent detached from any national hierarchy

---

331 As an example: Jones, Ashby: The Presumption of Innocence Belongs Only in the Courtroom. Discuss. The World Street Journal 27.2.2009. http://blogs.wsj.com/law/2009/02/27/the-presumption-of-innocence-belongs-only-in-the-courtroom-discuss/

332 Abramovsky, Abraham: "Juror Safety: The Presumption of Innocence and Meaningful Voir Dire in Federal Criminal Prosecutions – Are They Endangered Species?" *Fordham Law Review* vol 50 issue 1 (1981), 33-39. http://ir.lawnet.fordham.edu/cgi/viewcontent.cgi?article=2501&context=flr&sei-redir=1#search=%22media%20presumption%20innocence%22 Abramovsky mentions a number of cases in which courts agreed to somehow suspend the presumption of innocence before and during trial when other important interests were at stake.

and they have actually delivered a number of legal innovations, which have been intensely discussed in legal literature. Among them is the application of the concept of "Joint Criminal Enterprise" in international criminal law, the introduction of rape as a count of crimes against humanity in the Foča case[333] and as a count of genocide in *the pros. vs. Akayesu.*[334] These innovations are controversial, but for the purpose of our argument here, it is crucial to state that despite their relatively short existence, the ICTY and ICTR strongly contributed to the development of novel concepts in international criminal law. Judges actually acted as legislators, creating new notions and concepts, which were later applied in municipal law (e.g., under universal jurisdiction) and by other institutions. One of the most far-reaching novelties of international criminal tribunals is the enlarged definition of the four protected groups, enumerated in the Genocide Convention and the ICTR statute.[335] In *the pros. vs. Akayesu* and *the pros. vs. Ruzindanda and Kayishema*, the ICTR found that adherence to the four protected groups cannot exclusively be based on objective criteria, but also on perception, or, as it sometimes is called, on ethnicity as a social construction. From the perspective of this subjective approach, it is no longer essential whether Tutsi and Hutu were actually different ethnic groups in 1994, but whether they regarded each other as such. This approach enabled the ICTY to establish that in 1994, genocide had in fact taken place in Rwanda, a finding that later served as an "adjudicated fact" in other trials.[336] While there is no problem establishing that ICTY and ICTR judges actually acted as occasional legislators and did not feel particularly constrained by legalistic rules, it is much more difficult to show their inclination for pragmatic decision-making. We tried to

---

333 *The pros. vs. Kunarac, Kovač and Vuković* IT-96-23 and 23/1.

334 *The pros. vs. Akayesu*, IT-96-3-T. On the ICTY's legal innovations see also: Feinberg, Gary: The International Criminal Tribunal for the Former Yugoslavia: The Establishment and Evaluation of a Unique Concept in International Justice Administration. War Crimes, Genocide & Crimes against Humanity. Volume 2 (2006): 87-113; and Engle, Karen: "Feminism and Its (Dis)contents: Criminalizing Wartime Rape in Bosnia and Herzegovina", *The American Journal of International Law*, Vol. 99, No. 4. (Oct., 2005), 778-816.

335 These are racial, ethnic, religious and national groups. The attempt to destroy them "in whole or in part" is punishable under the Genocide Convention. Since Hutu and Tutsi in Rwanda were of the same nationality (Rwandan) and differed in neither religion nor race and could not be regarded as different ethnic groups, attempts to eliminate all or some Tutsi because of their Tutsi identity could not be regarded as genocide.

336 For a discussion of the ICTR's genocide definition and the significance of this subjective approach, see: Verdirame, Guclielmo: "The Genocide Definition in the Jurisprudence of the *ad hoc* tribunals." *International and Comparative Law Quarterly*, vol. 49, July 2000, 578-598.

address this issue through the lens of both tribunals' claim to further reconciliation. As we will show, some concepts of reconciliation require judges to adopt a pragmatic stance by, for example, taking into consideration non-legalist approaches to sentencing, which might run contrary to the requirement of prosecuting and punishing. As the final part of this book will show, judges only exceptionally applied pragmatic adjudication in situations in which there was a dilemma between punishment and reconciliation.

One of the potential consequences of international judges' specific incentive structure is their relatively strong exposure to the external influences of international media, governments and international non-governmental organisations. We are now testing whether such an influence can be empirically observed in the judgments and sentencing of both tribunals with regard to publically salient and controversial cases, during which such external influence was present. In order to do this, we have selected four cases – two from each tribunal – which had several features in common: they all attracted enough media attention to incline international media to produce a number of frames about the underlying events; they all aroused the awareness of governments and provoked them to issue statements, from which frames could be derived; they all were important enough to incline international human rights organisations to issue reports and statements about the trials and the underlying events, which we could use for our analysis.

Minor cases before the tribunals were often only reported by specialized agencies and went unnoticed by NGOs and foreign governments, and it would therefore be difficult to expect these organisations to impact judges' decision-making. Even if there were such an influence, it would probably be impossible to measure. The cases we selected for analysis are the events in Račak 1999, the fate of the Dutch peacekeepers (Dutchbat) in Srebrenica in July 1995, the murder of Belgian paratroopers at the onset of hostilities in Rwanda in April 1994 and the events in Taba, west of Kigali, which were dealt with in *the pros. vs. Akayesu*.

This chapter proceeds as follows: First, we briefly present the four cases and explain the selection criteria by pointing to the interest and awareness of external actors in these cases. We also explain how and where these events were reflected in the tribunals' proceedings. Next, we present the method for comparing these stakeholders' interpretations of the events with the ones used by the judges (trial chamber and appeals chamber). Our method is based on a specific form of content analysis drawn from media and public opinion research, and well known in the literature as "frame analysis." We then compare the frames used by external actors, prosecutors and judges in order to assess whether the judges adopted interpretations (frames) used by external actors, in part or in whole. This method does not enable us to assess any direct influence of these actors on particular judges; rather, it helps to exclude such influence in cases where our analysis does not reveal any similarities. In cases where external actors' interpretations of the underlying events were channeled into judgments or judges' public statements, we do not claim that judges were influenced by these external actors. All we can say is that such an influence cannot be excluded and that the interpretations of the judges were close or even identical to those of the external actors. This method also makes it possible to assess the differences in influence exerted by external actors. We will be able to infer, for example, whether the interpretations in judges' statements concerning the Taba rapes were closer to the interpretations of a particular government, or closer to the interpretations of Human Rights Watch.

Four Case Studies of External Influence and Judges' Frames of the Conflicts

Our first case study deals with the killing of the Belgian paratroopers on the day following the assassination of the presidents of Rwanda and Burundi, who were on-board of an airplane, which was shot down whilst approaching Kigali airport. At the time, Rwanda was hosting the United Nations Assistance Mission for Rwanda (UNAMIR) peacekeeping force, which was supposed to oversee the formation of a broad based transitional government previously agreed upon by the Rwandan government and the RPF. This UNAMIR force was made up of military contingents from various countries (Bangladesh, Canada, Ghana, Tunisia), with the 450 strong Belgian paracommando contingent forming the backbone of the force.[337] On 7 April 1994, ten Belgian peacekeepers were dispatched alongside five Ghanaian soldiers to the premises of the Rwandan Prime Minister Agathe Uwilingiyimana as additional security. Members of the Rwandan Presidential Guard and other military contingents repeatedly attacked the premises, and the Belgian and Ghanaian peacekeepers were disarmed and taken to the Rwandan military headquarters at Camp Kigali.[338] Here the Belgians were assaulted and beaten by Rwandan soldiers and finally killed. Since the Belgians were Western foreigners and Belgium an important troop-deployer in Rwanda, the incident was likely to evoke a lot of media awareness and comments from foreign governments, from the Rwandan conflict parties and from international media and international non-governmental organisations. We chose this case, because it seemed likely to deliver a lot of different frames, which could be traced again in indictments and judgments.

The ICTR trial chambers dealt with these events in two cases, in *the pros. vs. Ntuyahaga* and in *the pros. vs. Bagosora et al.* Bernard Ntuyahaga was an officer of the Rwandan Army who had been initially indicted by the chief prosecutor (then Louise Arbour) of the ICTR in 1998 and had subsequently surrendered to the tribunal in Tanzania. Louise Arbour decided to withdraw the indictment against him, convinced that it would be possible to hand him over to the Belgian authorities, which were eager to prosecute him for the participation in the murder of the 10 Belgian peacekeepers.[339] Instead of extraditing him to

337 Dallaire, R. A.: Shake Hands With The Devil: The Failure of Humanity in Rwanda, London, Arrow Books, 2004, 113, 144.

338 International Criminal Tribunal for Rwanda, *The Prosecutor vs. Bagosora*: Amended Indictment, Case No. ICTR-96-7-I, 12 August 1999, 37, paragraph 6.22.

339 Moghalu, Rwanda's Genocide, 102-103. The count of the indictment referring to the killing of the Belgians had been the only one of 10 counts, which had previously been confirmed by a judge of the tribunal. Arbour had therefore decided to withdraw the

Belgium, the trial chamber ordered Bernard Ntuyahaga's release, against the will of the accused, who feared for his life and was searching for a safe host country. He was finally sent to Tanzania in a small ICTY-owned aircraft and set free there. A few days later, Tanzanian authorities arrested him again, and – in order to avoid a conflict with Belgium and Rwanda, whose authorities sought his extradition – decided to prosecute him in Tanzania. After lengthy negotiations with Belgium and Rwanda, Tanzania finally denied Rwanda's request and allowed Ntuyahaga to go to Belgium, where he turned himself in to the authorities. In 2007, he was sentenced to 20 years of imprisonment for the murder of the paratroopers, but acquitted on several other counts of the indictment. He unsuccessfully appealed against the verdict.[340]

The Belgian government followed the case closely, since the whole course of events, beginning with the shooting of president Habyarimana's plane, the murder of the paratroopers and of Prime Minister Uwilingiyimana, and the subsequent withdrawal of the majority of UNAMIR (which had been triggered by the Belgian government) had become a very controversial topic in Belgian internal politics and subject to investigations by a special committee of the Belgian parliament.[341]

The Belgian authorities and the public also closely followed the so-called Military Trial at the ICTY, which also encompassed the deaths of the 10 UNAMIR Belgian peacekeepers. This group trial concerned Colonel Théoneste Bagosora, directeur de cabinet of the Ministry of Defence, General Gratien Kabiligi, head of the operations bureau of the army general staff, Major Aloys Ntabakuze, commander of the elite Para Commando Battalion, and Colonel Anatole Nsengiyumva, commander of the Gisenyi operational sector. The Prosecution charged each of these men with conspiracy to commit genocide, genocide, crimes against humanity, and war crimes, based on direct or superior

---

whole indictment and leave it to the Belgian authorities to prosecute him. See: *The pros. vs. Atuyahaga IT-98-40.*

340 Several specialized agencies reported on the case, amongst them Swiss Hirondelle: http://www.hirondellenews.com/content/view/9427/26/
Also Trial Watch (also Swiss based): http://www.trial-ch.org/en/resources/trial-watch/trial-watch/profile.html?tx_jbtrial_pi2[tab]=legal-procedures&tx_jbtrial_pi2[profile]=bernard_ntuyahaga_477&cHash=7a48b8f232 and Universal Jurisdiction: http://www.universaljurisdiction.org/cases/rwanda/1076-bernard-ntuyahaga
See also: Angelique Chrisafis: "Rwanda major jailed for murder of Belgian peacekeepers." The Guardian 6.7.2007.

341 For the Belgian debate about the paratroopers' deaths, see: Lefèvre, Patrick and Jean-Noël: Les militaires belges et le Rwanda 1916-2006. Tielt: Lannoo Uitgeverij 2006, 199-206.

responsibility for crimes committed in Rwanda in 1994.[342] The Military I trial commenced on 2 April 2002, and the verdict was delivered on 18 December 2008. In the ICTR indictment delivered on 12 August 1999, Colonel Bagosora was charged with one count of conspiracy to commit genocide, one count of genocide, one count of complicity in genocide, six counts of crime against humanity, and three counts of serious violations of Article 3 Common to the Geneva Convention and Additional Protocol II. [343] Bagosora was held responsible for the murder of the ten Belgian peacekeepers on count 5 (crime against humanity), and count 11 (serious violation of Article 3 Common to the Geneva Convention and Additional Protocol II). None of the other accused military officials were indicted in relation to the deaths of the Belgian peacekeepers.[344]

Our second case study deals with the events in Taba in April 1994. After the crash of the presidential airplane on April 6, violence immediately spread to the whole Rwandan capital. Militias connected to the ruling party erected roadblocks on road crossings in and around Kigali, swarmed the city's quarters in search for enemies they would then beat down, rob and eventually decapitate or otherwise mutilate. This wave of politically motivated violence would extend to the whole country, but it started in different regions at different times and was triggered by numerous factors. One of them was the policy of the self-declared interim government, which had constituted itself after the president's death in order to prevent a constitutional succession of power. It was the policy of the government to set up self-defence forces all over the country to assist the army and the police in detecting alleged spies and partisans supporting the Rwandan Patriotic Forces (RPF), which had crossed the Ugandan border and were now advancing quickly, wreaking havoc in the ranks of the government army. At the same time, the government incited its radical supporters to denounce RPF supporters associated publicly with the Tutsi minority of the population. As a consequence of this policy, militias like the Interahamwe were set up in various places, and armed government supporters were sent from Kigali and bigger provincial towns to smaller places in order to bring these places under the control of the interim government.

---

342 *The pros. vs. Bagosora et al.*: Oral summary of the Judgment and Sentence, Case No. ICTR-98-41-T, 18 December 2008, paragraph 5.

343 *The pros vs. Bagosora et al.*: Amended Indictment, Case No. ICTR-96-7-I, 12 August 1999, pp. 54-63.

344 This interpretation of events is taken from *the pros. vs. Bagosora et al.*: Oral summary of the Judgment and Sentence, Case No. ICTR-98-41-T, 18 December 2008, paragraphs 22-30.

These developments put the local authorities under considerable pressure and confronted them with the dilemma to carry out their duties toward the local community, or, where the orders coming from Kigali demanded otherwise, to abandon their duties, tolerate atrocities or even participate in looting, killings and the persecution of alleged government opponents.

According to evidence disclosed during the ICTR's proceedings, testimonies of witnesses and earlier accounts of the events east of Kigali in April 1994, more or less the same happened in Taba, a small town of the Gitarama district. Here, everything remained peaceful until April 19. The local prefect charged the major of Taba, Jean-Paul Akayesu, with ensuring the security of the local population, which Akayesu did, according to all testimonies, including his own. The situation changed, however, with more and more internally displaced persons arriving to Taba from other places. These internal displacements were caused by the advance of the front between government forces and the RPF, by atrocities committed in Kigali against the civilian population, and by the looting and robberies of armed gangs, which had managed to seize weapons in the turmoil and now extorted contributions from the population. Also in Taba, armed militias were set up and their local leader, Silas Kubwimana, quickly started to compete with Akayesu for power and control over the town. On April 18, Akayesu was summoned to a meeting in Gitarama, where he allegedly received instructions to set up an armed guard in order to fight alleged RPF insurgents and people suspected of supporting them. The next day, Akayesu read out a list of names at a rally in Taba, which had been prepared by pro-governmental radicals in order to stir up the local population against alleged RPF-supporters. This seems to have been the turning point in the recent history of Taba. From now on, armed gangs, linked to the government parties, took control of the town, started to beat up people they regarded as potential enemies or identified (rightly or wrongly) as Tutsi, looted, killed and raped. Violence was not only directed against potential local opponents of the government, but also against intellectuals and internally displaced persons, who had found refuge in the town, in churches and hideouts in and around Taba. Numerous survivors of the atrocities later testified that Akayesu had stayed indifferent toward crimes committed in his presence, had tolerated abuses or even taken part in atrocities. His successor as major, who came to power after the liberation of Taba by the RPF, blamed him for the death of several of his relatives. Women came forward and testified; he had supported, abetted and participated in cruelties against them, including sexual abuses. During early April and the end of June 1994, about 2000 people were killed in and around Taba, most of them Tutsi. When the RPF approached Taba, Akayesu fled to neighboring Zaire and from there to Zambia, where he was apprehended and transferred to Arusha on the request of the ICTR. In February 1996, Jean Paul Akayesu was charged with genocide; complicity in genocide; direct and public incitement to commit genocide; and extermination, murder, torture, rape, inhumane acts (crimes against humanity); and murder, cruel treatment and outrages upon personal dignity including rape (violations of the laws and customs of war). He was also the first defendant that stood trial at the ICTR. The Akayesu judgment marks the first time that an international tribunal enforced the 1948 Genocide Convention. It is also the first time that rape was considered constitutive of genocide, if committed with the intent to destroy in whole or in part a specific group.[345] The trial, during which Akayesu pleaded not guilty, saw a strong mobilisation of media and human rights organisations and – as the first ICTR trial against a suspect from Rwanda – evoked a lot of media interest. It also led to the creation of a number of frames of different stakeholders, which can be compared with the ones contained in the indictments and judgments.

The third case we chose deals with the role of Dutch peacekeepers in and around Srebrenica in July 1995. Srebrenica (a small town in Eastern Bosnia) came under siege by Bosnian Serb forces already at the onset of the conflict in Bosnia and subsequently was declared a safe area by the UN. The small Dutch battalion of UN peacekeepers (Dutchbat), which was stationed in the town in summer 1995, was regarded by the population as a protective force, but its mandate was much narrower, specifying that Dutchbat was entitled to shoot only in self-defence. Its main task was to supervise the fragile ceasefire between the besiegers and the weak and ill-equipped defenders of the town. The ceasefire was violated by both sides, by the forces under the command of the Bosnian Serb entity, which frequently shelled the town, and by armed groups from within the town, which would raid surrounding Serb villages in order to get food and other scarce commodities that could be sold on Srebrenica's black market.[346] The conflict reached a devastating climax between 12-14 July, when the Bosnian Serbs upped the ante by pushing aside (and firing upon) the small force of 429 Dutch blue helmets. They took control of the town and immediately began to separate men and boys from the women and girls. As was later revealed, the buses containing the men and boys – organized and provided beforehand – never reached the territory controlled by the Bosnian government in Sarajevo, because they were directed to abandoned farms outside the town, where the prisoners were executed by death squads. The corpses were buried in mass graves. The buses with women and girls reached government-held territory. About 7000 inhabitants of Srebrenica were killed, mostly in

345 The Hague Justice Portal http://www.haguejusticeportal.net/eCache/DEF/8/778.html

346 Hagan, Justice in the Balkans, 14.

executions, or in shootings and manhunts when they tried to escape the enclave through the mountains and forests surrounding the town – many contaminated with landmines – by night. On July 16, it was negotiated that the Dutch peacekeepers could leave the area, although they had to leave behind all of their weapons and supplies. Some of the members of Dutchbat had witnessed atrocities against civilians while still there, however, they were unaware of the killing sites outside the town. The first news about mass killings were revealed only weeks later, after Dutchbat officers and soldiers had been debriefed in the Netherlands and complaints from Bosnia about missing relatives of evacuated women reached the UN.

The fall of Srebrenica quickly became a hot topic in Dutch, US and French politics. As a reaction to the conquest of the town by Serb forces, French president Jacques Chirac called for a reconquest of Srebrenica by a freshly formed French-British Rapid Reaction Force.[347] In France and the Netherlands, the events after the fall of Srebrenica led to several parliamentary inquiries and government investigations, which in the latter case, caused the resignation of a whole cabinet in 2002, when the Dutch Institute for War Documentation (Nederlandse Instituut voor Oorlogsdocumentatie, NIOD) published a vast report which exposed severe dysfunctions and errors of the Dutch reaction in 1994.[348] The United Nations launched an inquiry, too, whose findings were later published, exposing the shortcomings and delays in decision-making in summer 1995.[349]

At the ICTY, the massacres after the fall of Srebrenica constituted the largest single issue to be investigated and prosecuted by the tribunal. 17 of 126 cases judged by the ICTY were connected to the events in Srebrenica. Due to the political repercussions in Western Europe and the US the events in Srebrenica had evoked, we found a multitude of different frames created by a plethora or political stakeholders. The ICTY dealt with the role of Dutch peacekeepers for the first time in *the pros. vs. Krstić*.[350] Krstić, against whom a secret indictment had been issued, became "the first (indictee) with major

347 Silber, Little, The Death of Yugoslavia, 351-352.

348 For the Netherlands see the NIOD report on Srebrenica, which can be retrieved from the special NIOD website www.srebrenica.nl. For France, see: Srebrenica, rapport sur un massacre. Tom 1, rapport et annexes, Tom 2: Auditions. Les documents d'information de l'Assemblée Nationale N3413 2001.

349 Report of the Secretary General Persuant to General Assembly Resolution53/35. The Fall of Srebrenica. A54/549 15.11.1999. www.un.org/peace/srebrenica.pdf

350 See: International Criminal Tribunal for the Former Yugoslavia: *The pros. vs. Krstić*: Initial Indictment, 30 October 1998.

command responsibility"[351] being tried by the ICTY and the first defendant in a case involving genocide. The trial against Krstić was in closest proximity to the events in Srebrenica and the first during which the events in Srebrenica, including the actions of Dutchbat, were debated.

Finally, we analyse a very specific case which, despite its rather limited character, provoked a huge media echo and led to the creation of an immense number of diverging frames issued by governments, human rights defenders, the media, and the conflict parties. Our final case study focusses on the town of Račak in Kosovo in early 1999. This refers to armed clashes between the Serbian police and members of the Kosovo Liberation Army (KLM). In a police action that took place on January 15, 1999 in the village of Račak, 45 Kosovo Albanians were killed. Conflicting views on whether the conflict was a legitimate anti-terrorist action by the Serbian police or a massacre of Albanian civilians are the outcome of different political interests, contradictory information published in the mediam and different conclusions of the autopsy conducted by both sides. Being highly active in the region, KLA was assumed to have headquarters in Račak. After the series of clashes in the neighouring municipalities of Suva Reka and Uroševac, a security cordon in the immediate area had been established by Yugoslav security forces. Reports by the Kosovo Verification Mission (KVM) about the killings of civilians in Račak on January 15, 1999 evoked the attention of the international community[352]. While the official version of the Serbian Government held that the Račak victims were members of the Kosovo Liberation Army, KLA, killed in combat in a police action, the other interpretation coming from KLA and the head of the Kosovo Verification Mission, ambassador William Walker, described the conflict as a "massacre of innocent civilians."[353] The events in Račak heightened tensions between the international community and Yugoslavia at the time, and attracted huge media attention. Numerous reports of human rights organisations, the Organisation for Security and Cooperation in Europe (which had deployed the Kosovo Verification Mission) elaborated reports about the alleged Račak massacre. The public attention that was given to the case set off a chain of events which ultimately led to a NATO intervention. It is believed to be a turning point that served as a rhetorical argument directed against FRY and as a legal and moral justification for the NATO bombings.[354] It also strongly

351 Hagan, Justice in the Balkans, 154.

352 Joksimović, Vojin: Kosovo Crisis: A Study in Foreign Policy Mismanagement, Graphics Management Press, 1999, 171.

353 op. cit. 171-172.

354 Wolfgram, Mark A.: „Democracy and Propaganda: NATO's War in Kosovo." *European Journal of Communication*, June 2008 vol. 23 no. 2, 153-171.

contributed to the delegimisation of the Yugoslav government's policy in Kosovo and the Serbian claims on Kosovo as an integral part of the Republic of Serbia. It caused a shift in media coverage, which no longer saw Albanian nationalism in Kosovo and the KLA as clandestine and overtly criminal phenomena linked to organized crime in Western Europe, instead beginning to see the "Kosovo issue" in terms of a legitimized struggle of a poor David against a repressive and cruel Goliath.

Framing the Past in International Criminal Tribunals

Consumers of media outlets tend to confront narratives and opinions in newspapers and electronic media with what they perceive as true and consistent with established facts and common knowledge. Analysts of the media take a very different approach, which avoids establishing a truth with which the media coverage is confronted. Instead of assuming that reporting is by definition derived from some prior, objective and univariate reality, they ask why certain media describe things in one way, while other media do so in a different way. The basic assumption of this approach is that every media outlet and every reporter can choose from a multitude of options when they decide to present a specific issue. Through the very act of writing about an identified issue, media draw upon and refer to cognitive schemes, called "frames," which provide categories, order, and chronology that allow the reader (and author) to organize fragmented information and attribute meaning to it. By emphasizing certain aspects of an event and embedding its description in headlines, pictures, the structure of a page, a film or a radio program, media instruct us both what to think, and how to think about it.[355] Such frames act as patterns of interpretation, which affect problem definition, moral evaluation, and causal interpretation, and may even imply particular solutions for the identified problem. Viewed through this lens, journalism appears to be a far more discretionary and constructed exercise than the traditional professional image of reporting facts.

Applied to our cases, for instance, the events in Srebrenica can be described as the heroic story of Bosnian Serb warriors, who, after years of siege, finally managed to eliminate a security risk for the local Serb population, or as a narrative about the suffering of the innocent civilian population, harassed and terrorized by a vicious foreign army. It can be described as the failed attempt of

355 Cohen refers to these two respectively as "priming" and "framing." Cohen, B. C.: The Press and Foreign Policy, quoted according to Roessler, Patrick: "Agenda-Setting, Framing and Priming" in: Donsbach, Wolfgang; Traugott, Michael W. (ed): The Sage Handbook of Public Opinion Research 2008, 210-212.

the international community to live up to its commitments to protect the Bosnian population, as an example of how "the West" abandoned Muslims (by not providing air support to Dutchbat), and as an example of how the West for years actually protected Muslims (during the years before the fall of the town). Much depends on the definitions chosen: whether one speaks of "Muslims" or "Bosniacs", of "civilian population" or "the defenders of Srebrenica", of "Bosnian Serbs" (which would involve the responsibility of all Serbs in Bosnia) or the "Bosnian Serb Army" (which would involve only militaries), "the Serbs" (which suggests responsibility, or even guilt, of all Serbs). As we shall see later, authors of some texts even refrained from any references to the ethnic and religious backgrounds of Srebrenica's population, simply using the terms "people" or "civilians".

The same approach can be used for each of the four case studies presented here. In every instance, we will be able to identify the choice made by an author, when describing events and embedding them into a larger narrative. The conflict in Rwanda can be described as a "genocide" of Hutu against Tutsi (which is the dominant version at the moment), as a "civil war" in which all sides committed atrocities against each other and the civilian population, as a "foreign intervention" (from Tutsi emigrés with Ugandan citizenship), or "Ugandan aggression" assisted by internal "Rwandan traitors", as the breakdown of an internationally brokered ceasefire agreement, or as the outbreak of archaic ethnic violence, which led to a fight of "everybody against everybody." Depending on which narrative is chosen, events in Taba may therefore been interpreted as the violent reaction to huge migrations, a (failed) attempt to secure order and stability, a transition of local power, or the extension of a murderous policy to a provincial town.

These frames potentially contradict each other, though each may also overlap with one or several others. All of these frames have some features in common. In each case, there is an attempt to tell a story, to attribute meaning to the events and to embed them in larger narratives – how Serbia is allegedly subjugated and victimized by the West, how the ICTY manages to enforce its policy in Serbia, or about the progress of international criminal justice, how Rwanda suffers from its colonial legacy, how poorly minority rights are rooted in the country, or how the international community failed to stop violence and prevent genocide (another very popular media frame). Frames used in the media and by lawyers tend to include very strong normative assumptions, shifting blame and attributing guilt; they are often dichotomous or even Manichean, and make strong claims about causality and impute specific intentions to actors. For this exercise in framing to function, certain conditions must be fulfilled. An overarching narrative must exist, in which the respective frame can be embedded; the event to be framed must possess certain features that allow the author to ascribe meaning to it and to interpret it normatively. Events that lack these conditions tend to be neglected by journalists and are often incomprehensible to the audience. The same is true for events that do not lend themselves to consistent moral judgment.

Frame analysis as a method of desegregating and comparing content that has been widely used by media analysts and public opinion researchers in qualitative and quantitative research. By now, it has become so widespread in other disciplines, such as psychology, communication research and even in negotiation studies,[356] that it is already difficult to say what the concept of frame and framing actually does and does not encompass. Frames are treated by some authors as dependent variables, which may lead to specific consequences (framing effects)[357] and – like in this part of the book – as dependent variables, which result from decisions and choices and influences on those who make these choices. In all of these cases, different definitions of what a frame is (or is meant to be by an author in a specific research design) are used, ranging from the most general and vague ones to very specific and narrowly conceptualized ones.[358] In media and communication studies, framing is usually understood as "selecting and highlighting some facets of events or issues and making connections among them so as to promote a particular interpretation, evaluation and/or solution."[359] In order to impact actors, such a frame must be culturally salient, emotionally loaded, prominent and repetitive. Media researchers tend to assume the existence of a pluralistic and transparent environment for the creation of frames. They also presuppose frames to emerge and exercise their influence within a large audience (a society, a media system on a national or transnational level). From such a perspective the requirement of cultural salience and prominence makes sense, since it is not very likely that politicians are influenced by frames

356 For example Donohue, William R.; Rogan, Randall G.; Kaufman, Sandra (ed): Framing Matters. Perspectives on Negotiation Research and Practice in Communication. New York, Washington, Baltimore, Bern, Frankfurt, Berlin Brussels, Vienna Oxford 2011.

357 Rothman, Alexander J., Updegraff, John A.: "pecifying When and How Gain- and Loss-Framed Messages Motivate Healthy Behavior: An Integrated Approach." In: Keren, Gideon (ed): Perspectives on Framing. New York and Hove 2011, 257-278; Bruine de Bruin, Wändi: "Framing Effects in Surveys: How Respondents Make Sense of of the Questions We Ask." In: Keren, Gideon (ed): Perspectives on Framing. New York and Hove 2011, 303-324.

358 Donohue, William R., Rogan, Randall G., Kaufman, Sanda: "Introduction. Framing in Negotiation. State of the Art." In: Donohue et al. (eds): Framing matters, 1-6.

359 Entman, R. M.: "Cascading Activation. Contesting the White House's Frame after 9/11." *Political Communication*, 20, 2003, 415-432.

issued only once by marginal media in a culturally incomprehensible way which does not appeal to emotions. When applying the concept to the interaction and communication in international courts, one must be aware of the limitations the specific international judicial context imposes on the concept, especially if one studies the impact of external frames on judges' decision-making. In such a case, the judges are the audience – a very specific, atypical and extremely small one. There is hardly any public sphere surrounding the decision-making process, since international criminal courts are very much detached from any audience and their actual decision-making procedures are mostly kept secret, although the rules which they claim to apply are completely transparent. Communication between external actors, prosecutors and judges is extremely limited, and the professional ethics of judges require it to be deprived of emotions as far as possible. The requirement of cultural salience and repetition is problematic, too, due to the different cultural, ethnic, linguistic, national or even religious origin of the actors. What sounds convincing in the framework of a country's public sphere may be much less compelling in the framework of an international court. It would therefore be premature to hypothesize about the conditions and characteristics, which make frames powerful in an international court, since these conditions and factors may very much differ from the ones which may function within the public sphere of a specific country, where all (or most) members of the audience share the same cultural background.

Despite all these reservations, it is possible to treat not only media content as frames, but also government declarations, press releases and NGO reports as textual products which contain frames. If so, they may also be compared to the narratives, which emerge from juridical proceedings, such as indictments and judgments. They fulfil the same requirements: Indictments and judgment have to fit into pre-existing narratives, they are strongly normative and attribute meaning and interpretation to disperse and often unrelated facts, which emerge from the investigations (in the case of indictments) and from the trial proceedings (in the case of judgments). Finally, they "tell a story", which is based on fact selection. It is therefore possible to compare which facts from the indictment are selected in order to substantiate the arguments of a judgment, and it is also possible to compare the narrative contained in a judgment to the one offered by an NGO report, a government press release, the speech of a minister or a press report.[360]

---

360 One of the main differences between such frames and the ones used in media analysis is the lack of recipees for the future, which most media frames contain. Judges and prosecutors (opposite to NGOs) usually do not present remedies to problems even if they identify problems. The usual "remedy" they offer, are punishment and, to some

The underlying hypotheses of this chapter claims that the specific incentive structure, to which judges in international criminal tribunals are exposed, renders them receptive to influences from external actors, such as NGOs, the media and governments and this influence may be (but not necessarily needs to be) channelled through the prosecution. The objective of this chapter is to establish whether such influence can be excluded. If the frames used by judges in their oral statements and judgments differ significantly from the ones used by external actors and the prosecution, we will regard the hypothesis as falsified. If we encounter considerable similarities between the frames used by one or several external actors and frames from judges' oral statements and judgments, we will claim that receptivity cannot be excluded. Even in this case the results of our research will not entitle us to claim any direct influence. They will only allow us to not exclude it.

The main criteria according to which our frames are examined concern the way crimes and perpetrators of crimes are described, whether the description follows the presumption of innocence or not, how and to whom guilt is attributed, and how a specific group is divided into perpetrators, victims, witnesses, bystanders and collaborators, who is alleged to have started the conflict, and how and when the conflict is said to have ended. Special attention is given to the causes and reasons frames use for rationalizing a conflict, for example, whether a frame merely provides a description of atrocities ("after the assault on the village, men were rounded up and shot") or constructs causes, reasons and explanations for it ("in order to eliminate potential enemy fighters, all men were rounded up and shot"). Additional criteria refer to the use of command responsibility, aggravating and mitigating circumstances and the character of the conflict (internal, international, civil war etc.). We do not search for legal notions in media coverage. These notions should be understood in a broader meaning: "command responsibility" may be contained in a legal document (e.g., in an indictment or judgment), but it may also show up in a newspaper comment claiming, for instance, "that Slobodan Milošević cannot deny his responsibility, since he occupied the highest constitutional position in Serbia when these crimes happened." Another important criterion is the way perpetrators and victims are framed. For instance, armed men trying to prevent

---

extent, compensation and acknowledgement for victims. But where elitist media tend to propose political measures for solving the problems which they have identified, judges and prosecutors usually do not comprise such recommendations into their indictments, judgments and decisions. For this component of frames, see Entman, Cascading activation, 415-432. One of the few prescriptions, which sometimes can be found in judges' verdicts, pertains to reconciliation. We deal with this issue, which is specific for the ICTY and the ICTR, in the last part of this book.

the fall of Srebrenica in July 1995 can be framed as "Muslims", "Bosniacs", "government soldiers", "defenders of Srebrenica", "armed militias", and in many other ways, of which each one involves different meanings, normative judgments and fits into different narratives. Whenever we find a certain frame in a judgment, which was previously used by an external actor or by the prosecution, we claim that in such a case it cannot be excluded that the judges were influenced by the actors who used this specific frame. We acknowledge that this method is a more adequate tool for comparing the strength of different external actors on judges than analysing whether judges were actually influenced or not. It is very important to understand the limitations of our approach. It neither proves the bias or prejudice of judges, nor does it prove that judges were indeed influenced by a clearly identifiable external actor. It only shows whether the frames used by judges are closer to the frames used by one actor or another. This comparison can – but doesn't need to be – inconclusive, for example, when all frames compared do not reveal any differences, because a specific frame is so widespread and generally accepted that it is used by all actors involved (e.g., the frame describing atrocities in Rwanda as a genocide).

How do frames emerge, how are they disseminated and channelled into the communication of specific institutions? There is a large amount of literature dealing with the creation of frames by media and journalists, but there is much less about the journey frames take after they leave the office desks and printers and are disseminated among the audience of the medium – and beyond that. Especially the latter aspect is crucial for this research, because we assume frames to impact not only the direct audience of a medium, but also people who may not even be among its occasional readers. What is merely undisputed is that frames (together with agenda-setting and priming effects) shape public perceptions about events and signal, about what should be seen as positive and negative. They transport certain normative implications, but also meaning, interpretation and causal connections. These implications continue to exist, spreading further (by means of gossip, rumours, fragmentary communication) among smaller audiences, such as families, circles of friends and colleagues, or even among random groups that exchange views on a subject, as it sometimes happens when bus passengers comment on a piece of news on their way to work. This way, people may be influenced by frames that they never directly consumed, be it in the form of an article, a TV programme, or something else. It is also quite undisputed that in the media world, different actors take different forms of influence on audiences. There are strong and influential agenda-setters, whose topics are taken over by other media, and there are weak ones who endorse frames from these agenda-setters. It is therefore difficult, or even impossible, to identify the original source of a frame and to follow this frame (and its possible alterations) to the audience. A reporter of the New York

Times in Central Africa may endorse a frame which he found in a local newspaper, which then, due to the strong agenda-setting power of the New York Times, may be channelled into a CNN report and spread all over the world, ultimately shaping the frames of media in Bulgaria, Georgia or even in the municipality in which the New York Times correspondent originally picked the frame. It would be impossible to follow the whole chain of frame transmission, and even if it was possible, no one could ultimately claim with certainty whether the resulting frame actually stemmed from a village in Central Africa, or was developed by the New York Times or CNN, since even the original frame from the village could – in the age of internet and satellite TV – have emerged as the result of frames, which a local journalist might have accidentally picked up from a film, an e-mail message or an oral story told to him by villagers. We therefore do not claim that our analysis will reveal the origins of frames and show their path from the source to the final destination. We assume that influential frames are more likely to be produced by well known, renowned and wealthy media than by weak, local and isolated ones, and we concentrate our research on frames from media more likely than others to influence the cosmopolitan, well-educated and highly mobile personnel of international criminal tribunals. We selected international human rights organisations like *médecins sans frontières*, Human Rights Watch, Amnesty International and the Coalition for Women's Rights in Conflict Situations in the case of *the pros. vs. Akayesu*, as far as they undertook considerable activities to influence outcomes at the ICTY and the ICTR, either through direct lobbying, or through advocacy and the dissemination of their frames to the media and the general public. What's more, we chose media outlets which we expected to be consumed by tribunal personnel and which had a relatively high coverage of tribunal matters. Here, the New York Times clearly outperformed the Washington Post and, of course, all weeklies in English. Due to the fact that English and French are the official languages at both tribunals (and the ability to communicate in these language is a precondition for their personnel), we also included Le Monde as the most international daily among the French press. We did not take into account frames from Neue Zürcher Zeitung, Frankfurter Rundschau, Süddeutsche Zeitung, El Pais and other media, which are consumed only by a small minority of tribunal staff.[361] We explicitly do not claim any direct relation between media frames and

361 According to information obtained from the ICTY library, until May 2012 the ICTY had subscribed to the following newspapers and weeklies: The (British) Times, Le Monde, The International Herald Tribune, Frankfurter Allgemeine Zeitung, BBC Monitoring, Balkan Inside, Media Monitoring in Yugoslavia, Time Magazine, Newsweek. The New York Times was not among these outlets. We included it nonetheless, because given the strong presence of Anglo-American staff at the ICTY, it is likely to be read anyway by staff members who participate in drafting indictments and judgments.

judges or prosecutors, since, according to the information obtained during our interviews, indictments, judgments and sentences are to a large extent the result of teamwork, during which a large part of the drafting is done by collaborators of prosecutors and judges, who oversee and direct the work. Since they concentrate on legal issues, one should not overestimate their influence on the shape of legally non-relevant frames. Such a frame may make its way into a judgment, because one or several staff members were influenced by a media report, although the judge himself was not. In the case of legally relevant frames (which, for example, describe guilt), such a windfall effect is rather unlikely.[362] In the same way indictments should not be seen as the individual work of one prosecutor. They are collaborative projects, in which a number of staff members take part, and which are sometimes used in several trials.[363] However, when it comes to direct dissemination of frames from the prosecution to the trial chamber, the most important channel available at the ICTY seems to be the courtroom. According to the judges and members of the OTP, informal contacts between both branches of the ICTY's judiciary are reduced to the minimum, and an informal code of conduct prevents judges and prosecutors even from sitting at the same canteen table. As Judge Flügge explained: "Judges are not supposed to enter the prosecution aisle of the building and prosecutors should not enter the judges' aisle. However, they interact with the prosecution, but not directly, face-to-face, but through the prosecution staff and the legal officers of the trial chambers, mostly by e-mail." Frederick Swinnen confirmed that: "We never speak with judges about a pending case outside of the courtroom."[364] According to our sources in Arusha, this division between the branches of the tribunal is less strict at the ICTR.

---

362 The information about the drafting of judgments stems from an interview with Judge Christoph Flügge, conducted in May 2012 in The Hague. According to him, each trial chamber at the ICTY can rely on about 5 to 7 staff members to whom the judges can delegate the drafting of judgments, but also the written assessments of evidence and witness testimonies after each day of trial. According to information from Gabrielle Kirk McDonald, during the early years of the ICTY, trial chambers only had between one and two collaborators and the staff of the ICTR always was much smaller than at the ICTY: "The ICTR was, compared to the ICTY, a kind of second-class citizen."

363 The chapter concerning the events in Račak describes how exactly the same wording of a part of one indictment was copied into other indictments in the course of the proceedings against several accused. The information about the drafting of indictments come from an interview with Frederik Swinnen, political advisor to ICTY chief prosecutor Serge Brammertz, and an interview with Serge Brammertz himself, both carried out in May 2012 at the ICTY.

364 Interview with Frederik Swinnen, political advisor to ICTY chief prosecutor Serge Brammertz, conducted in May 2012 in The Hague.

Another methodological disclaimer is needed here. All explanations about frames and frame analysis so far only refer to what frames are and what frame analysis can achieve. We deem it necessary to emphasize what frame analysis is not and what it cannot do. Using frame analysis, it is not possible to detect any kind of truth about the events and actors which are framed. By analyzing frames created by actors on the ground about the events in Srebrenica in July 1995, one is unable to establish what really happened there. Historians may come close to such a kind of truth when comparing frames to the context, to empirical evidence and material sources such as documents, artefacts or even forensic evidence. Frame analysis does not pretend to lead to any objective, univariate truth independent of time, space and context. Frame analysis only shows why, how, and when certain actors decided to put forward specific interpretations (and what these interpretations contained) about these events, no matter whether and how these events actually came about. On the basis of frame analysis, we can only reach conclusions about who said or wrote what, why, how and when and how this relates to other actors' discourse, but we can never hope to find out what really happened. This disclaimer runs in both directions: Because frame analysis does not even aim at the truth about the events which were framed by actors, it is no valid challenge to frame analysis to put forward the argument that judges or prosecutors developed specific frames just because they were true or reflected reality. "Truth" and "reality" are beyond the scope of what frame analysis can do and references to both do not invalidate the results of frame analysis but its very basis. By claiming that a judge created a frame because it was true, one eliminates any possible basis to establish other reasons why he might have done so. And one assumes – just like any legalist would do – that a different judge in the same situation would interpret the same events in exactly the same way.[365]

The Frames Concerning the Conflict in Rwanda in April 1994 and the Death of Belgian Soldiers in Rwanda in 1994

According to most sources and historians, dealing with the events in Rwanda in 1994, the genocide started after President Habyarimana's plane was shot down above Kigali airport on 6 April 1994, and lasted roughly 100 days.[366] After the death of the president, Prime Minister Agathe Uwilingiyiama, a Hutu, like the

365 We would like to thank James Gow for his reservations about the frame-concept in a judicial context. They inclined us to add these explanations, which may help non-media-researchers to understand it better.

366 Moghalu, K. C.: Rwanda's Genocide: The Politics of Global Justice, New York, Palgrave Macmillan, 2005, 16-17.

deceased heads of state, would have been the legal successor, but she never took office. Instead, a military interim government consisting of Hutu radicals and militaries took power. On 7 April 1994 ten Belgian peacekeepers were dispatched alongside five Ghanaian soldiers to the premises of the Rwandan Prime Minister Agathe Uwilingiyimana as additional security. The premises were repeatedly attacked by elements of the Rwandan Presidential Guard and other military contingents and the Belgian and Ghanaian peacekeepers were eventually disarmed and taken to the Rwandan military headquarters at Camp Kigali.[367] Here the Belgians were assaulted and beaten by Rwandan soldiers and eventually killed. Some of them managed to withdraw to a building within the Camp Kigali military barracks, to disarm a soldier and fight back for some hours before they were killed.

During the following days, Rwandan Government forces and Hutu militias, such as the Interahamwe, attacked and killed mainly Tutsi and a larger number of Hutu, who were later labelled moderate. On the other hand, the rebel forces of the Rwandan Patriotic Front (RPF), consisting mostly of Tutsi, began their campaign of conquering the country from its positions in Northern Rwanda. At the same time, Rwanda was host to the United Nations Assistance Mission for Rwanda (UNAMIR) peacekeeping force, which was supposed to oversee the formation of a broad based transitional government previously agreed to by the Rwandan government and the RPF. This UNAMIR force was made up of military contingents from various countries (Bangladesh, Ghana, Tunisia), with the 450 strong Belgian paracommando contingent forming the backbone the force.[368]

The death of the Belgian soldiers never was a cornerstone of the ICTR. However, the killing of the Belgians quickly became an important issue in Belgium and for the Belgian government, since it triggered the immediate withdrawal of all Belgian blue helmets and inclined the Belgian government to urge other UN members to withdraw their contingents, too. As more and more UN personnel was being evacuated, the number of observers of the on-going massacres declined and more and more UN sites, where civilians had found refuge, were deprived of their armed protectors. This sequence of events later made Belgian Prime Minister Guy Verhofstadt apologize for the policy of his predecessor during a visit to Rwanda.[369] From 1994 on, Belgium had a special

367 International Criminal Tribunal for Rwanda, *the pros. vs. Bagosora et al.*: Amended Indictment, Case No. ICTR-96-7-I, 12 August 1999, 37, paragraph 6.22.

368 Dallaire, R. A.: Shake Hands With The Devil: The Failure of Humanity in Rwanda, London, Arrow Books, 2004, 113, 144.

369 "Belgian apology to Rwanda." BBC News 7.4.2000.

interest in prosecuting those responsible for the killing of the Belgian soldiers. When in 1998 Bernard Ntuyahaga, an officer of the Rwandan Army, surrendered to the ICTR after being indicted for the murder of the 10 Belgian parachutists, the prosecutor of the court withdrew the indictment against him to enable Belgium to demand his extradition. After a lengthy and complicated legal battle between the judges, the prosecutor and the justice departments of the governments of Rwanda, Tanzania and Belgium, Ntuyahaga finally stood trial in Belgium and, in 2007, was sentenced to 20 years of imprisonment by a Belgian court.[370] The court acquitted him with respect to the assassination of the Rwandan Prime Minister, but sentenced him for the participation in the killing of the Belgian paratroopers.[371]

The Ntuyahaga trial, called "the Rwanda trial" by the Belgian media, aroused immense attention in Belgium, across the cleavages dividing the French and Flemish public spheres. Flemish and French newspapers together with the official news agency Belga followed every stage of the trial.[372] In 1997, the Belgian Senate created a special commission of investigation (commission d'enquète), dealing with the events which led to the death of the Belgian paratroopers and the withdrawal of the blue helmets.[373] Of course, the Belgian public also followed all other attempts to elucidate the criminal responsibility for the killings of the soldiers. When in 1996 the Cameroon authorities arrested several suspects, among them Théoneste Bagosora, the Belgian government demanded Bagosora's extradition from Cameroon – competing with Rwanda, whose Ministry of Justice had also sent such a request. While Belgium withdrew its request after the ICTR had asked Cameroon to hand over Bagosora, Rwanda put pressure on the ICTR chief prosecutor, Richard Goldstone, to step back and agree to have the colonel tried in Kigali. Bagosora was regarded as the military mastermind of the genocide and a kind of "Milošević of Rwanda", as Goldstone later recalled.[374] Goldstone did not acquiesce and Bagosora was finally delivered to Arusha, where his trial started years later. The Belgian government later

370 Guichaoua, André: Rwanda 1994. Les politiques du génocide à Butare. Paris: Karthala 2005, 294.

371 "Bernard Ntuyahaga jugé coupable." Le Soir 4.7.2007.

372 Jean Pierre Borloo: Le troisième procès Rwanda à Bruxelles. Le Soir 19.4.2007. and the special internet-dossier of the Flemish daily *De Morgen* about the so-called Rwanda – Process: www.demorgen.be

373 Belgian Senate. Session of 1997-1998, December 6 1997. Parliamentary commission of inquiry regarding the events in Rwanda. Report in the name of commission of inquiry by Mr. Mahoux and Mr. Verhofstadt. http://www.senate.be/english/rwanda.html

374 Quoted according to Peskin, International Justice, 173.

asked the trial chamber to admit its representatives as "friends of the court" and to hear witnesses and see evidence proposed by Belgium.[375]

One can therefore clearly recognize the Belgian government as an important and potentially influential producer of frames, which were likely to shape the frames adopted by the judges in their verdict.

Due to the immense attention all trials directly or indirectly concerning the deaths of the Belgian paratroopers attracted in the Belgian public, every cabinet must have been interested in ICTR attempts to hold suspects accountable for the events in April 1994 in Kigali. It is therefore likely that frames used by Belgian ministers, the Prime Minister and other members of the government may have permeated into the frames used by the trial chamber. Unfortunately, it is impossible to conduct such an analysis with respect to the appeals chamber judgment. Bagosora's defence went to appeal after the trial chamber had sentenced the accused to life long imprisonment in 2008, but at the time when this book was being prepared for printing, the appeals chamber still had not issued a verdict in the case.

The Belgian government is not the only one whose frames may have impacted frames of the trial chamber in *the pros. vs. Bagosora et al.* We also can't exclude that early frames, as used by international media, international non-governmental organisations dealing with the events in Rwanda 1994, the UN and the US (whose government was pressed to intervene in 1994) pre-established interpretations of the events in 1994, which might have been adopted by judges even prior to their assignment at the ICTR. We therefore also looked into the frames of the US government as issued during the conflict and into documents of the UN. The Rwandan government also must have had an interest in acting as an agenda-setter in the framing of the trial, since it had shown such a great interest in the apprehension of Bagosora and his extradition to Kigali rather than Arusha.

The time frame for these analyses spans between the conflict in 1994 and the trial verdict in 2008. The trial in which responsibility for the deaths of the 10 UNAMIR Belgian peacekeepers was assigned is often referred to as the Military I trial. This group trial concerned Colonel Théoneste Bagosora, directeur de cabinet of the Ministry of Defence, General Gratien Kabiligi, head of the operations bureau of the army general staff, Major Aloys Ntabakuze, commander of the elite Para Commando Battalion, and Colonel Anatole Nsengiyumva, commander of the Gisenyi operational sector. The Prosecution charged each of these men with conspiracy to commit genocide, genocide,

---

375 Decision on the *amicus curiae* application by the Government of the Kingdom of Belgium. 6.6.1998, *the pros. vs. Bagosora et al.*, IT-96-7-T.

crimes against humanity and war crimes, based on direct or superior responsibility for crimes committed in Rwanda in 1994.[376]

The Belgian Government's Frames

When the Special Commission of the Belgian Senate investigating the death of the 10 Belgian paratroopers in Kigali issued its final version in 2007, the media had already revealed before to what extent the Commission's report was infected by partisan politics and inter-party bargaining. Nevertheless, the huge report also brought some interesting insights for frame analysis, because it developed several hypotheses about the reasons why the Belgian blue helmets had been killed. The version favoured by the commission members can be labelled as "mutiny frame". According to the report drafted by Philippe Mahoux and Guy Verhofstadt (the later liberal Prime Minister), there had been no direct preparation for the killings. Immediately after the assassination of the Rwandan president, rumour had spread in Kigali, but also among the Rwandan Hutu community in Belgium and the Rwandan embassy, according to which a Belgian special unit, which had been stationed near the airfield, had launched a rocket that hit the president's plane. This rumour was based on earlier reports about an alleged Belgian plan to assassinate the Rwandan president.

The commission report rejected other hypotheses, such as the version according to which the Belgians were killed because they had been witnesses of the Prime Minister's murder (who is predominantly addressed as "Mrs Agathe" in the report). According the commission's findings, she had fled her residence during the raid by the presidential guard and attempted to hide in building in the immediate neighbourhood. She was later brought back to her residency, where she was killed at a point when the Belgian paratroopers had already left. According to the commission report, they had never witnessed the murder. The commission then described the events leading to the death of the blue helmets. After being brought to Camp Kigali, they faced a mutiny among the ranks of the government soldiers of the garrison, which had been caused by the rumour (spread, among others, by Ntuyahaga) claiming the president had been killed by Belgians. According to the testimonies collected by the commission, the soldiers, who began to beat and hit the Belgians, acted without orders from superiors and even attacked other Rwandan soldiers, who attempted to hold them back: "De nombreux militaires rwandais qui s'interposent sont blessés."[377]

376 International Criminal Tribunal for Rwanda, *the pros. vs. Bagosora et al.* Oral summary of the Judgment and Sentence, Case No. ICTR-98-41-T, 18 December 2008, paragraph 5.

377 Parliamentary commission of inquiry; op. cit.

In the report, the relevant section is entitled "Le meurtre des dix paracommandos" and the actions against the Belgian soldiers are described as a "massacre". The rumour about Belgian involvement in the president's assassination "aurait rapidement engendré une mutinerie et un soulèvement général pour le lynchage des militaires belges." In the meantime, handicapped war veterans and other soldiers had attacked the blue helmets with stones and bayonets, causing the death of four soldiers. The remaining paratroopers managed to withdraw into a building, where they stayed together with five Ghanaian soldiers. Due to the intensive shelling from outside, the Belgians and the soldiers from Ghana were forced to hide under the beds. After some time, the Ghanaians were allowed to leave. They joined UNAMIR in a nearby building, escorted – but not harmed – by Rwandan soldiers. They finally managed to inform the UNAMIR commanders about the fate of their Belgian colleagues and then were brought to the UNAMIR headquarters.

When the Belgian government filed its *amicus curiae* brief to the ICTR trial chamber dealing with *the pros. vs. Bagasoro et al.*[378], the word the government officials most frequently used for the description of the events was then "assassination". In 2000, Prime Minister Guy Verhofstadt went to Kigali and decided to pay tribute to the victims of what by then was almost unanimously labelled genocide; his speech did not reveal the intimate knowledge of the events which he had acquired as rapporteur of the parliamentary commission. Verhofstadt refrained from blaming any specific person or group for the massacres: "Man, not history, bears the guilt."[379] He started by reminding his audience about the assassination of the paratroopers: "The families of the soldiers and the Belgian civilians, who were assassinated in Rwanda during these terrible days of 1994, accompany me today."[380] Next, he called the massacres of 1994 a genocide: "Nobody in the world ignores the horrors of the Rwandan genocide."[381]

378 Décision relative a la demande du Royaume du Belgique de comparaitre en qualité d'amicus curiae, *the pros. vs. Bagosora et al*, Tribunal penal international pour le Rwanda, 2, 08/07/1998.

379 "Ce n'est pas l'Histoire qui est coupable. C'est l'Homme qui est coupable." Discours du Premier Ministre belge, M. Guy Verhofstadt, Kigali, 7 avril 2000, Ambasade de Belgqiue, http://www.diplomatie.be/kigalifr/default.asp?id=25&mnu=25&ACT=5&content=36

380 "Les familles des soldats et des civils belges qui ont été assassinés au Rwanda pendant ces terribles jours de 1994 m'accompagnent aujourd'hui." Discours du Premier Ministre belge...op. cit.

381 "Nul au monde n'ignore les horreurs du génocide rwandais." Discours du Premier Ministra belge, op. cit.

> "I confirm: the international community as a whole carries an enormous responsibility. A dramatic amount of neglect, carelessness, incompetence, reluctance, and errors created the preconditions for an unspeakable tragedy. I accept here in front of you the responsibility of my country, of the political and military authorities of Belgium. Belgium was at the heart of the UN's operation. The genocide started in front of their eyes. Belgium and the international community must acknowledge the errors they have committed. I don't know, and I will never know, whether it was possible to prevent those terrible events of 1994, but I am convinced that we should have done more and we should have done better. In order to enable Rwanda to turn toward the future, towards reconciliation, we first have to accept our responsibility and acknowledge our failures. In the name of my country, I ask you for forgiveness."[382]

These were the words, which then spread across the world's news media as the Belgian apology for the policy of the Belgian government of 1994, which had been confronted with the massacres and decided to withdraw all its soldiers. Verhofstadt – who had not been involved in the decision-making, but later admitted that he too would have withdrawn the soldiers (but without pushing other countries to do the same)[383] – finally addressed the issue of guilt. "Those guilty of the Rwandan genocide, who thought they would find a save haven in Belgium and so avoid justice, will not escape from it. Our country will continue to cooperate with all its force with the International Criminal Tribunal for Rwanda."[384] He refrained from any accusations concerning the death of the Belgian soldiers.[385]

---

382 "Je l'affirme: la communauté internationale tout entière porte une immense responsabilité. Un dramatique cortège de négligences, d'insouciance, d'incompétences, d'hésitations et d'erreurs a créé les conditions d'une tragédie sans nom. J'assume ici devant vous la responsabilité de mon pays, des autorités politiques et militaires belges. La Belgique était au cœur de l'opération onusienne. C'est sous ses yeux que le génocide commença. La Belgique et la communauté internationale doivent reconnaître les erreurs commises. Je ne sais pas, ou je ne saurai jamais, si ces événements terribles de 1994 pouvaient être évités, mais je suis convaincu que nous aurions dû faire plus, que nous aurions dû faire mieux. Pour que le Rwanda puisse tourner son regard vers l'avenir, vers la réconciliation, nous devons d'abord assumer nos responsabilités et reconnaître nos fautes. Au nom de mon pays, je m'incline devant les victimes du génocide. Au nom de mon pays, au nom de mon peuple, je vous demande pardon." Discours du Premier Ministre belge, op. cit.

383 Verhofstadt appeared as a witness in the "Rwanda-Trial" against Ntuyahaga in Belgium. Stephane Detaille: „Verhofstadt accable Dehaene." Le Soir 26.5.2007.

384 Les coupables du génocide rwandais, qui ont cru trouver refuge en Belgique et ainsi se soustraire à la justice, n'y échapperont pas. Notre pays continuera à collaborer de toutes ses forces à l'action du Tribunal pénal international."Discours du Premier Ministre belge, op. cit.

385 Discours du Premier Ministre belge, op. cit. About the reactions in Kigali to the speech: Colette Braeckman: Au nom de mon pays, je vous demande pardon. Le Soir 8.4.2000

Verhofstadt's speech provided a kind of non-frame, similar to the way in which the Dutch government would behave between the commissioning and the publication of the NIOD report on Srebrenica. His speech did not provide any rationalisation or explanation, neither for the genocide nor for the assassination of the paratroopers. It is most interesting to depict what Verhofstadt avoided to frame in his speech. He did not identify a specific group (for example: the Hutu, "extremists" or "radicals") as culprits.

The Frames of the Rwandan Government

The radical factions of the Hutu-dominated political establishment were conducting the war against the RPF from a position of ethnic exclusionism, drawing a clear and impermeable division between the Hutu as the in-group and Tutsi as the out-group. Much of the propaganda radical Hutu ethnocentrist media like Kangura and Radio des Milles Colinnes spread in the country aimed at making this line between in-group and out-group as prominent and insurmountable as possible. Compromises between the groups were denounced as treason and any attempt to cross the line was treated in the same way.

The RPF was unable to pay back with the same coins. Ethnic exclusionism of the same sort would have confined the Tutsi population into a minority position, which it would never be able to leave. Whereas Hutu exclusionism could be linked (and was linked) to formal democracy (primitively understood as the rule of the majority), Tutsi exclusionism would have forced the RPF to adopt autocracy and dictatorship openly – and would probably have irrevocably damaged its image in the world. The RPF leadership solved this problem by promoting an anti-exclusionist agenda, which appealed to all Rwandans to overcome ethnic divisions and cooperate on a national rather than an ethnic basis. From the beginning, the RPF tried to avoid any elements of ethnic hatred (at least in its propaganda). In the territories which came under its control in late April 1994, RPF officers used various methods – from persuasion to coercion – in order to recruit members of the Hutu population into its units. Hutu politicians, who had renounced the Habyrimana regime, gone into exile or kept distance to the government, were invited into the political leadership. In some cases, RPF officers and commissioners even requested the local population, "to forget, who is a Hutu and who is a Tutsi" and to build a common Rwanda.[386] Such

386 Des Forges, Alison: Kein Zeuge darf überleben. Der Genozid in Ruanda. Hamburg 2002, 815.

attempts to overcome long-lasting and deeply entrenched dividing lines usually need some kind of historical legitimacy to be successful. The RPF leadership tried to create such a kind of legitimacy by rewriting Rwanda's history from one dominated by ethnic division within the country (which had been put forward by subsequent Hutu governments after the countries independence) into a history dominated by national unity, which had been disturbed by external enemies. According to the dominant version of Rwandan history favoured by Hutu–exclusionists, the Tutsi had been these external culprits, oppressing the allegedly indigenous Hutu population for centuries and collaborating with the colonialists. The RPF could not strike back in the same way, so it presented the colonialists as the only culprits to its audience – they had invented ethnic divisions, which were basically foreign to Rwandans. This interpretation of history was based on the assumption of a predominantly harmonious history of Rwanda prior to colonialism, on which RPF rule would draw. Such a harmonious vision of the future could also count on more support in a country rampaged and impoverished by war than the antagonistic vision of Hutu hardliners who had led to that war. On the other hand, such a vision of a future non-exclusionist, harmonious Rwanda, devoid of any ethnic conflict, revealed chiliastic traits well known from European totalitarian movements and ideologies. It entrapped the RPF into a potentially totalitarian understanding of history and an extremely broad definition of genocide. The latter was due to the on-going power struggle, in which the country had become embroiled even after the massacres had ended.

The RPF, which came to power after pushing the government forces, militias and the Presidential Guard to the south of the country, forcing them into emigration, immediately claimed to have liberated the country from the perpetrators of genocide. Fighting the *génocidaires* within and outside the country (in the numerous refugee camps in Zaire) became a major issue of post-war Rwanda and one of the most powerful sources of the new regime's legitimacy. It was a relatively easy justification for foreign intervention in neighbouring countries, where alleged and actual perpetrators had found refuge in camps and started to mobilize political and military support against the new government in Kigali. Denouncing enemies as *génocidaires* became a convenient tool for stripping enemies, both political and military, of legitimacy. This was easier, the broader the definition of genocide was. The international community, international media, non-governmental organisations and genocide and conflict researchers tend to fix the start of the genocide at the earliest at April 7 and assume it to have ended after a three-month period. For the RPF, the genocide dates back to the colonial period, where its seeds were sown, coming up in the Habyiarimana period and culminating in the mass killings of 1994. If the roots of genocide were so deeply entrenched, their eradication would be a huge task for the state, one that might in fact take generations. In a document, which was officially issued by the Rwandan Senate in 2006, the authors claim: "In 1994, Rwanda experienced a genocide, which cost more than a million human lives. It was the product of a genocidal ideology, which was manifest throughout the massacres. Despite the efforts of the Rwandan state to consolidate national unity, the ideology of genocide unfortunately persists in the middle of society."[387]

These implications had a strong impact on the frames the Rwandan government started to produce once it had taken power in the whole country. The RPF was one of the first actors who decided to label the events after April 6 genocide; despite its preference to present the conflict as political rather than ethnic.[388] The inherent contradiction is obvious. Explaining the conflict in terms of genocide made it necessary to use the same ethnicized vocabulary, which the RPF had previously defined as a cause of the conflict, and it required an explanation of the numerous Hutu casualties of the massacres in 1994. The RPF solved that problem by introducing the notion of "moderate Hutu", who were also regarded as victims of the genocide alongside the Tutsi. Thus, the genocide became a series of centrally organized massacres of Hutu against Tutsi and some other Hutu, called "moderates". The difference to other genocide-frames, invoked for example by international media or Gourevitch, is obvious: from their perspective, the genocide was carried out by Hutu and directed against Tutsi between April and August 1994. From the perspective of the RPF's construction of the past, Hutu *génocidaires* had organized genocide against Tutsi and "moderate Hutu", whose roots dated back to colonialism and had culminated in the killings of 1994. Paraphrasing the relevant article of the Genocide Convention, one could say that for the RPF, genocide had become the attempt to "destroy in whole or in part one ethnic group and the moderate part of another ethnic group." On May 30, Théogène Rudasingwa, the RPF's secretary general, claimed in an interview that the RPF was the only force, which could stop the genocide, "and also know all the Hutu, who are victims

387 Senat: Rwanda – ideologie du génocide et stratégies de son eradication. Kigali 2006, 3.

388 The authors of a special inquiry into the conduct of the UN in Rwanda 1994 mention a RPF statement of as early as April 13th, which described the ongoing conflict as genocide. Report of the independent inquiry into the actions of the United Nations during the 1994 genocide in Rwanda. S1999/1257 from 15.12.1999, 38. www.un.org/news/dh/latest/rwanda.htm

in the same way as the Tutsi."[389] Asked, who was guilty, Rudasingwa answered: "Not the Hutu, but a dictatorial clique, which, together with its army, militias and death squads wants to stay in power." He blamed the colonialists and the post-independence governments, for continuing colonial divisions, claiming that Hutu and Tutsi had lived together peacefully for centuries, until colonialists had started to divide them.[390] It is worth mentioning, that the way, the Rwandan government constructed the genocide in recent years, differs considerably from the version, it used to promote in the public during the nineties. The official version of the past in nowadays Rwanda is a twofold and and contradictory one. Etnicity is no longer an issue, and even symbollically or rethorically dividing the population into Hutu and Tutsi can entail criminal consequences for (oppositional) politicians, intellectuals and academics, because it is now regarded as divisionism and an element of genocide ideology. But simultaneously, the genocide has ceased to be one carried out by Rwandans against other Rwandans and has become "the genocide of the Tutsi", with the Hutu population fulfilling the role of a collective culprit. Hutu victims are totally erased from public memory; not only those, who fell victim to RPF retaliation in 1994 or later in Eastern Kongo, but also those, who were killed by Interahamwe and soldiers during the genocidal campaign.[391]

389 Interview in the German weekly *Der Spiegel*, titled "Wir werden das Morden beenden. Interview mit Rebellenführer Théogène Rudasingwa über den Bürgerkrieg." Der Spiegel 30.4.1994. http://www.spiegel.de/spiegel/print/d-13685251.html

390 The original quote: "Nicht die Hutu, sondern eine diktatorische Clique, die sich mit ihrer Armee, ihren Milizen und ihren Todesschwadronen an der Macht halten will." (...) "Tutsi und Hutu sind über viele Jahrhunderte miteinander ausgekommen. Sie verbindet eine Sprache, eine Religion. Die Spannungen begannen in der Kolonialzeit, als die Belgier sich der Tutsi-Elite als Kollaborateure bedienten." Der Spiegel 30.4.1994.

391 When asked about the percentage of Hutu among the members of the genocide survivor organisations for which Ibuka is an umbrella, Ibuka president Dusingizemungu explained, that except for some Hutu widows of Tutsi, who were killed during the genocide, the survivor organisations did not include any Hutu: "It was the genocide of the Tutsi, so why would we have Hutu members". Klaus Bachmann's Interview with Jean-Pierre Dusingizemungu, president of *Ibuka*, Kigali, July 2012. More about the current public discourse and the official historical policy of Rwanda can be found in Phil Clarks and Zachary D. Kaufmans edited volume: After Genocide. Transitional Justice, Post Conflict Reconstruaction and Reconciloiation in Rwanda and Beyond. London: Hurst & Co. 2008; especially the chapters written by Lemarchand, Hintjens, Buckley-Zistel, prosecutor general Martin Ngoga and the preface written by president Paul Kagame.

The Rwandan government never created any specific frame interpreting the death of the Belgian soldiers in April 1994 before they became subject of an ICTR verdict. In this respect, one cannot expect to reveal any influence on prosecutors' or judges' frames of these events. Given the enormous role cooperation with Rwanda used to play for the ICTY, we may expect to observe an impact of the RPF's genocide frame on prosecutors' and judges' interpretation of the preconditions, development and the duration of the genocide and its implications as well as about the genocidal ideology the RPF used to allege.

The New York Times Frames

The New York Times' coverage of the conflict in Rwanda is a fine and instructive example of the emergence of the genocide frame in international media. The day after the plane crash in Kigali, an article written by Richard Perez-Pena – a portrait of Burundi's head of state, Cyprien Ntarymira, who now, as a victim of the assassination, was presented as a mediator and peacemaker, and a democrat who had tried all he could to end ethnic strive in the country – appeared in the newspaper. At that stage, being Hutu was not yet associated with being a genocidal perpetrator, and the reader was left with the impression that the deceased president had been a democrat and statesman who looked beyond ethnic cleavages; a Hutu who had been "unable to gain control of the Tutsi-led military, (...) and could not put an end to the violence." Neighbouring Rwanda was described as "plagued by war between Hutu and Tutsi".[392] The second victim of the air crash, the Rwandan president, was also portrayed in a way which suggested, that the authors were strongly inspired by the rule *de moribus nihil nisi bono*. "The initial years of Mr. Habyarimana's leadership were marked by considerable development and economic progress. But he also faced repeated attempts to overthrow his Government, mostly by rebel invaders from adjoining Uganda", the author wrote. Habyarimana was alleged of having "excelled at strengthening ties to the West and attracting foreign aid and investment at a time when a number of other African leaders were being accused of running corrupt and inefficient governments. (...). In 1990, he sought to make a major break with the past by authorizing the formation of a multiparty political system in what was largely a feudal society. But his efforts to reach a peaceful settlement were not successful." The conflict in Rwanda was presented as a "civil war" between

392 Richard Perez-Pena: "Cyprien Ntaryamira, 39, Tried to End Burundi's Strife." The New York Times 7.4.1994.

a Hutu majority and a Tutsi minority.[393] Two days later, on April 9, the events in Kigali were framed still as a kind of civil war, with the capital tormented by "terror", "vicious battles" and "heavy fighting". The report relied mostly on international sources like the UN and Western embassies and state sources: "Rival tribal factions waged vicious street battles Friday for control of the city, reports from Rwanda said. The death toll of civilians, Government ministers and soldiers – including at least 10 United Nations peacekeeping troops – was estimated to be in the thousands." This "civil war"-frame remained in force for weeks. A report from April 21 spoke about "the fighting, provoked by a suspicious plane crash on April 6 that killed the Presidents of Rwanda and neighbouring Burundi, both Hutu, has been fed by tribal hatred between the majority Hutu and the minority Tutsi. But the killing, at least in its initial stages, was mostly politically motivated, set off by hard-line Hutu who disapproved of a new Government that integrated Hutu and Tutsi." The picture painted by the newspaper resembled a tribal war, during which Tutsi and Hutu attacked each other, rather than a genocide, which consists of one side killing the other one.[394]

The New York Times electronic archives reveal that the "g-word" was used for the first time in connection to Rwanda in an opinion piece written by Jerry Gray as early as on April 9. Subsequently, the reference to genocide reappeared frequently in comments, but not in the news coverage of the newspaper and not before the end of April.[395] On April 23, genocide was once again mentioned in an article without a by-line entitled "Cold Choices in Rwanda", where it is stated that "what looks very much like genocide has been taking place in Rwanda."[396] However, the newspaper avoided framing the conflict as genocide for a very long time, and even when the "g-word" was used in an opinion piece, it was never connected to any broader narrative which would stipulate who killed whom, why, for what purpose and in what kind of context.

With respect to the Belgian peacekeepers, The New York Times was not as ignorant of their fate as many other media outlets were, disregarding the killing of the ten paratroopers as a minor detail in the on-going tribal conflict, civil war or general chaos. The day after their deaths, William E. Schmidt, apparently writing from his desk in New York, claimed in a large article entitled "Troops Rampage in Rwanda; Dead Said to Include Premier" that there had been "a

393 Ronald Sullivan: "Juvénal Habyarimana, 57, Ruled Rwanda for 21 Years." The The New York Times 7.4.1944

394 Donatella Lorch: "The Massacres in Rwanda: Hope Is Also a Victim." The New York Times 21.4.1994.

395 Jerry Gray: "2 nations joined by common history of genocide." The New York Times 9.4.1994.

396 (No author): "Cold Choices in Rwanda." The New York Times 23.4.1994.

sudden convulsion of violence" (...) "leaving it unclear who was in charge and even who was battling whom." (...) "In telephone and radio reports reaching the outside, residents and relief workers inside Kigali described a city that appears to have been given over to anarchy, with gangs of young men wielding clubs and machetes rampaging through streets, looking to settle old scores." He framed the conflict as one between "two sides of a guerrilla war", which had been going on between Tutsi and Hutu for centuries. "According to the United Nations, the peacekeepers tried today to get armoured vehicles to the home of a United Nations staff member where Ms. Uwilingiyimana had sought refuge, but they were held up by roadblocks. Under rules of engagement that allowed them to fire only in self-defence, the peacekeeping troops did not use force to get through. United Nations diplomats said the Prime Minister's guards were overpowered by the Presidential Guards, who took her away and killed her." (...) "The United Nations diplomats said 'unruly elements' of the army were responsible for killing other Belgian peacekeepers."[397]

The Frames of Le Monde

Le Monde's first frames, which contain specific interpretations of the events that unfolded in Rwanda after the airplane crash of April 6, appeared in a short report two days later and were based on information collected by Jean Hélène, who was presented as the newspapers "regional correspondent". Much of the content of the report was in sharp contradiction to the facts which later became evident. Similar to other media outlets, Le Monde assumed the conflict in Rwanda to be a civil war. The massacres in the capital were presented as the "blind revenge" of Habyarimana's presidential guard, whose officers had been recruited mainly from the North of the country, for his death. There was no mention of genocide in Le Monde at that stage. The report claimed that the entire opposition was being targeted, including the Democratic-Republic Movement, which represented the Hutu from the South. Concerning the death of the Belgian peacekeepers, the report contained two contradictory interpretations. According to the first one, the Belgian paratroopers had been apprehended while covering the escape of Prime Minister Agathe Uwilingiyimana, who, in line with the report's subtitle, had been killed. According to the second explanation, the Belgians had been killed by members of the presidential guard, who had

397 William E. Schmidt: "Troops Rampage in Rwanda, Death said to include Premier." The New York Times 8.4.1994

apprehended and disarmed them when the Belgians were heading for the airport in order to investigate the airplane crash.[398]

Three days later, genocide still was not mentioned, and the whole situation was described as an on-going civil war with numerous atrocities committed by the military and the presidential guard. The reporting, a highly emotional piece with detailed descriptions of various atrocities, made no mention of the Belgians.[399] Two months later, Rwanda had become “a country full of horror” and the civil war frame was replaced by one depicting the conflict as a clash resulting from ethnic strive, exacerbated by colonisation and power struggles within the ruling elites and their tribal structures.[400] The article first elaborated the question of guilt for the airplane crash, and then attempted to explain the current violence in the country through the heritage of colonialism. Guilt was attributed to both sides, the RPF and the Habyariamana government for “pogroms” and “reprisals” carried out against the civilian population of the other side, and the international community was blamed for reducing its personnel when hostilities started after the crash of the presidential airplane. However, the article did not explain why this reduction had occurred and made no reference to the fate of the Belgian paratroopers.

Le Monde’s coverage of the conflict was very specific. For a relatively long time, the newspaper refrained from taking sides and blaming one side of the atrocities; it also stopped short of calling them genocide. The reasons for Le Monde’s specific framing may be found in its country of origin and its ideological embedding (previous French governments had supported Habyarimana’s government and had armed his military)[401], but also to the environment, in which Le Monde’s correspondents were working. French journalists had no problems entering government-controlled parts of the country; they could relatively easily work in Kigali, because their presence was tolerated

398 Le premier ministre a été assassiné lors des massacres qui ont suivi la mort du chef de l’Etat. Le Monde 9.4.1994. Actually, one group of Belgians went to the airport and ended up in a stand-off with the Presidential Guard, which held the Belgians for hours; another group went to the Prime Minister’s residence. It was the second group that was killed. See: Dallaire, Romeo: Shake Hands with the Devil. The Failure of Humanity in Rwanda. Brent Beardsley Books 2008 (kindle edition), chapter 10.

399 Jean Hélène: Le Rwanda à feu et sang. Le Monde 12.4.1994.

400 Frédéric Fritscher: Rwanda. Un pays habité par l’horreur. Le Monde 22.6.1994.

401 In early 1994, France was governed by the so-called second cohabitation, with socialist François Mitterand as president and the rightist Eduard Balladur as Prime Minister. Le Monde was definitely more sympathetic toward Mitterand than towards Balladur, and foreign policy was traditionally the domain of the president rather than the Prime Minister (also due to the strong involvement of the presidential office in African affairs and Mitterand’s personal interest in Africa).

by the army and the police, whereas Belgians were regarded as supporters of the FRP insurgents in the capital, chased away and persecuted.[402] Where other media outlets would already shift the blame for atrocities to the interim government and to "Hutu radicals", Le Monde's reporters described the situation from the perspective of Kigali's civil population, which was, according to these reports, exposed to indiscriminate RPF mortar attacks and the fury of the Interahamwe.[403] Le Monde mostly framed its coverage on Rwanda in terms of a civil war and massacres, or as in an article in late April, as a face-off (affrontement) between two rival forces.[404] The "g-word", which later became so popular in describing the massacres in Rwanda, sometimes shows up in Le Monde's articles, but it is impossible to detect any specific frame related to it.[405] Le Monde used massacre frames and civil war frames, but hesitated for a long time to adopt a genocide frame to the situation in Rwanda. On May 17, the daily even published an interview of its Rwandan correspondent, Jean Hélène, with one of the leaders of the Interahamwe, Robert Kajuga, who rejected accusations of genocide, explaining the massacres which had occurred by "popular outrage of our people about the assassination of our president."[406] The way the newspaper presented the interview to its readers revealed the reservation of the journalists about the allegations of Kajuga and suggested the possibility of genocide in the country, contrary to Kajugas claims. The first larger article containing a genocide frame appeared in early June and even mentioned the "g-word" in the title. Jean Hélène had started travelling with the advancing RPF units in their conquest of the country, and in almost every place which the RPF soldiers cleared of government forces, they met survivors, people who had managed to escape the killings, had been hidden by friends or relatives, or had been injured and left behind by the militias, who had taken them for dead. They

402 Jean Hélène: Le Rwanda à feu et sang. Le Monde 12.4.1994.

403 Frédéric Fritscher: La situation au Rwanda. Le Monde 02.07.1994.

404 Jean Hélène: Après la rupture des deux cessez-le-feu au Rwanda . Des affrontements à l'arme lourde continuent d'opposer Hutu et Tutsi . Le Monde 29.4.1994.

405 For example in the comment which appeared in Le Monde on 15.4.1994, in which the anonymous author uses the word genocide, but in a context which makes it impossible to assess whether he actually claims that a genocide is taking place in Rwanda and whom he regards as the perpetrator. The relevant phrase reads: "Le combat des pays démocratiques du Nord ne doit pas s'arrêter au rapatriement de ses ressortissants. Stopper l'action à ce stade serait laisser se poursuivre un véritable génocide de tous ceux qui ont voulu contribuer à la paix en refusant les extrémismes ou encore, de manière plus insupportable, de tous ceux qui n'ont pas eu la chance de naître dans la bonne ethnie, qui n'est pas la même pour tous les extrémismes."

406 Jean Hélène: En dépit de nombreux témoignages Le chef des milices rwandaises réfute les accusations de génocide : Le Monde 17.45.1994.

were eager to tell their stories, and the picture which emerged from their perspective was a strong contrast to the balanced approach the newspaper had taken during the weeks and months before, when the government version of the events had been more easily available to journalists working in Kigali. The new frame no longer contained distanced notions about a confrontation between two rival (and therefore basically equal) parties, a civil war and massacres committed by both sides. Now, the general interpretation was that the advancing RPF had liberated and saved genocide survivors, had detected trenches, mass graves and killing sites, and chased away a nightmare. "In each village conquered by the RPF, such testimonies can be found time and again, when the survivors leave there hidings. Some have watched their whole families being massacred. In each settlement, small heaps of soil reveal the existence of a mass grave, where the militiamen have hurried to obscure their atrocities with a bulldozer."[407] There were no equal conflict sides any more. When Le Monde's special correspondent arrived in Nyamata, a small town in the southern district of Bugesera, and managed to talk to several survivors and people who were searching for their relatives, he wrote: "Nyamata, the martyr town, now symbolizes the genocide of the Rwandan Tutsi."[408] The journalist realized that the surroundings of the town were almost empty. The article suggested strongly that the RPF soldiers were the good guys in the story, and accused the government army to leave behind a string of plundered villages. As Rwanda's south was overwhelmingly and disproportionally populated by Hutu, it was far from obvious, why the army and the militias of a radical Hutu nationalist government would pillage and plunder the villages and farms of their own people and why these people – after their possessions had been ravaged by the militias – would nevertheless escape with them. The journalist explained this obvious contradiction by alleging that the withdrawing militias and soldiers of the government army had forced the Hutu villagers and farmers to come with them. According to the newly emerged genocide frame, everything the withdrawing Hutu militias and the government army did was deprived of

407 Jean Hélène: Rwanda: sur la route du génocide a mesure qu'ils avancent, les combattants du Front patriotique rwandais découvrent l'étendue des massacres qui ont frappé la communauté tutsie. Le Monde 8.6.1994. "Dans chaque village conquis par le Front patriotique rwandais (FPR, le mouvement armé de la minorité tutsie), les témoignages comme celui-ci se multiplient au fur et à mesure que les rescapés sortent de leurs cachettes. Certains ont vu toute leur famille massacrée. Dans chaque localité, un monticule de terre trahit la présence d'une fosse commune, où les miliciens ont hâtivement dissimulé leurs atrocités au bulldozer, tel un monument aux morts dédié aux civils."

408 Ibid.

rationality and aimed at wreaking havoc and destruction, whereas all the RPF did was dictated by security concerns and by the objective to shelter the civilian population. When the newly appointed political commissioner for Bugesera ordered the local Hutu population to be concentrated in camps, the journalist affirmatively quoted his explanation that "this way, it will be easier to help them." Helping them also meant forcing them to abandon "ethnic propaganda".[409]

Finally, a few days before the 4th anniversary of the air crash, Le Monde published a huge series of reports on the events, which by now had become an unquestionable genocide. As the first article of the series stipulated, "more than a million Tutsi were exterminated in Rwanda in spring 1994. This genocide, first contested by the Western powers, has been acknowledged as such by the UN, which have created an international criminal tribunal, whose first verdict will be issued before summer." By then, the story about atrocities committed by both sides of what had once been a civil war or an ethnic strive had become an attempt to exterminate Tutsi by Hutu, during which – as one isolated sentence claimed – "also Hutu opponents had been eliminated." The events of spring 1994 were now embedded in a context which comprised Cambodia's "killing fields", "crimes against humanity" in the former Yugoslavia, and even the Nuremberg Tribunal. The author directly compared the German involvement in the Holocaust and the attitude of Rwandans in the genocide: "The genocide in Rwanda was a popular one. If the Germans participated in the genocide of the Jews like so many elements of a deadly chain, the contribution of the Rwandans, spontaneous or not, was of an unprecedented cruelty."[410]

More than ever, the genocide now became one in which "the Hutu" were the perpetrators and "the Tutsi" the victims. "Hordes of rural Hutu went to massacre their neighbours, clutching machete."[411]

It is not clear whether the author was aware of the origins of the stereotypes on display in his text when he rowed the Tutsi who had been killed with "the sheep that went to the slaughterhouse."[412] Le Monde provided many different

409 Ibid.

410 "Le génocide au Rwanda fut un génocide populaire. Si les Allemands ont participé, comme autant de maillons d'une chaîne de la mort, au génocide des juifs, la contribution des Rwandais, spontanée ou non, fut d'une cruauté sans précédent." Ibid.

411 "Des hordes de paysans Hutu sont allées, machettes à la main, massacrer leurs voisins Tutsi." Ibid.

412 The rationalisation of the apolitical Hutu majority's behaviour during the genocide was in line with the secular policy which the newspaper had always followed: "Des décennies d'apprentissage de la soumission et de la ferveur religieuse ont contribué aux comportements extrêmes de 1994. Des paysans Hutu qui n'avaient pas l'âme de

rationalisations for the behaviour of specific groups during the genocide, but the article lacked any explanation about a possible rationale of the events, similarly to most accounts of the events in Srebrenica a year later. No explanation was given for the motives and reasons of the perpetrators. Violence and destruction were explained by referring to psychological notions, by pointing to a general prevalence of obedience in Rwanda and an allegedly deep-rooted culture of impunity and crime.[413] Despite various comparisons with the Holocaust in Europe, the author refrained from identifying general psychological and human patterns of perpetrators', bystanders' and victims' behaviour, and instead strove to identify local factors which allegedly explained the events. This attempt inclined him to adopt an ethnological lens, which, at the same time, painted a picture of a society which seemed to be very distant from the individualist Western European human rights culture in which the author had been socialized. When the author put the blame on certain societal tendencies, which he had previously identified as typical for Rwandan society (such as authoritarianism, mutism, submission and deeply entrenched ethnic hatred), the genocide became exotic – it had taken place in an exotic country, where exotic habits had facilitated it; it had been carried out in an exotic way (in a chaotic, emotional and bottom-up way, which differed so much from the well-organized, top-down enterprise the Holocaust had been) and it had caused exotic outcomes, like a silent, withdrawn society, where, for pragmatic reasons, murderers had to live side by side with victims, unable to reconcile and deterred by force from resorting to violence again.

Le Monde never created any frame explaining the fate of the Belgian paratroopers. The death of the Belgians was a complete non-topic in the newspaper's coverage of the Rwandan conflict.[414] The newspaper created some

---

meurtriers n'ont pas refusé de participer au crime. Et les Tutsi, au lieu d'organiser une résistance dans les collines, se sont réfugiés devant les bureaux communaux et les églises, symboles de l'autorité, alors que les bourgmestres organisaient le génocide à l'échelon local et que les prêtres Hutu s'y sont rarement opposés. Des agneaux sont allés à l'abattoir..." Rémy Ourdon: Au pays des âmes mortes. Le Monde 31.3.1998.

413 The topic of "deeply entrenched violence", which quickly became a popular explanation for Rwanda's alleged inclination to genocide, was put into the mouth of one of Le Monde's interlocutors, who was quoted as follows: "Il y a eu génocide parce qu'auparavant il y a eu impunité, commente Alice Karekezi, une militante des droits de l'homme. Certains racontent sans malice combien de personnes ils ont tuées. Ici on a tué ses voisins, les gens avec lesquels on partageait la boisson... Ce n'était pas le système nazi. Le crime était presque intégré au quotidien depuis des décennies. Certains savaient qu'ils allaient mourir et d'autres qu'ils allaient tuer. C'est le bilan de l'impunité." Ibid.

414 Running the terms "Rwanda+Dallaire+parachutistes" through the search engine of the electronic archive yields only 7 articles, which all deal with Dallaire's testimony at the

frames about Bagosora and the so-called military trial. Bagorosa was frequently labelled "the mastermind of the genocide" (le cerveau du génocide)[415] and, quoting Roméo Dallaire's testimony, even called "the devil".[416]

The Frames of the US Government

The responses of the US government to the events in Rwanda in spring 1994 belong to the most intensely researched topics connected to the genocide topic, especially with respect to the reluctance of the State Department and the White House to denounce these events as genocide. Several works deal predominantly with this topic.[417] They mostly focus on the reluctance or even unwillingness of the US State Department and the White House to use the "g-word" in public,

---

Akayesu Trial of the ICTR and the French involvement in Rwanda, but are without any reference to the Belgian paratroopers.

415 Jean Philippe Remy: Le cerveau du génocide Rwandais devant la justice; Le Monde 9.11.2003 and (by the same author): A Arusha, Roméo Dallaire dompte ses peurs et accuse le colonel Bagosora. Le Monde 27.1.2004. The latter article contains the sentence: "Devant le Tribunal pénal pour le Rwanda, l'ancien chef des casques bleus est confronté au 'cerveau' du génocide."

416 The quote about Bagosora as a "devil" comes from Dallaire's testimony from December 1998. See: Stephen Smith: En jugeant le 'diable', le tribunal d'Arusha joue sa crédibilité. Le Monde 4.4.2002 It was repeated in several articles: "Je sais que Dieu existe parce que j'ai rencontré le diable: c'est par ces mots que Roméo Dallaire, qui commandait les forces des Nations unies à Kigali en avril 1994, a évoqué le colonel Théoneste Bagosora lors de sa déposition devant le Tribunal pénal international. Considéré comme l'un des «cerveaux» du génocide, le colonel Bagosora était directeur de cabinet du ministre de la défense au moment du drame. Parti en exil en juillet 1994, d'abord dans l'est du Zaïre, avec les responsables Hutu, le colonel Bagosora a circulé dans toute l'Afrique avant de se fixer au Cameroun. Il a été arrêté à Yaoundé en mars 1996 et transféré à Arusha début 1997." Jean Philippe Remy: Le colonel Théoneste Bagosora est jugé devant le Tribunal pénal pour le Rwanda. Le Monde 4.4.2002

417 Fitzsimmons, Daniel: "Following The Leader: The Impact of the Mass Media on American Foreign Policy in Somalia, Rwanda, and Kosovo." *Conference Papers – International Studies Association*, 2007 Annual Meeting. Peterson, Shannon: Stories and past lessons: Understanding United States decisions of armed humanitarian intervention and nonintervention in the post-cold war era (Somalia, Rwanda, Bosnia and Herzegovina.) [Dissertation]. Ohio State University 2003. http://etd.ohiolink.edu/send-pdf.cgi?osu1047933325; Crocker, Chester A.: The Lessons of Somalia: "Not Everything Went Wrong." *Foreign Affairs* vol. 74 nr 3/2004, 2-8. A chapter of Samantha Power's Pulitzer Prize-winning book "A Problem from Hell. America and the Age of Genocide", London, New York, Toronto, Sidney 2003, is also dedicated to the responses of the US government to the crisis in Rwanda 1994, see 329-390.

since (as this reluctance is usually explained) it would oblige the US to intervene in Rwanda in accordance with the requirement of the Convention against Genocide. The dilemma of whether genocide had occurred in Rwanda or not didn't only become relevant after April 7. The day after the plane crash, when violence spilled over in Kigali, the US State Department organized a press conference in order to reveal its plans to evacuate US citizens from the country. The way the news was phrased by The New York Times sometimes makes it impossible to find out whether a specific frame was actually used by Deputy Assistant Secretary of State for African Affairs Prudence Bushnell, who conducted the conference, or was ascribed to her: "She added that there is no indication that any of the 255 Americans living in Rwanda are being targeted by the country's warring tribes." However, at that stage, it was obvious that the US treated the conflict in Rwanda as a civil war rather than a genocide of one side. "There is fighting and there is chaos," Ms. Bushnell said, and asked about the details of the intended evacuation, she continued: "There is no date, there is no time. We're looking to see how best we can do this." [418]

According to Samantha Power, genocide in its legal meaning was first used in a report sent to the UN by Roméo Dallaire at the end of April, and then made its way through Reuters and CBS.[419] Throughout May, the US government avoided mentioning genocide, because it had become apparent that this could negatively affect the image of the government and coerce it into intervening, which it did not want to do. Using the word genocide would immediately create a legal obligation and raise public expectations, urging the government to do something about it. In the days and weeks that followed, US State Department officials even directly quoted from the Convention in order to prove that the circumstances did not cover all elements necessary to define the events in Rwanda as genocide. Behind closed doors, when experts and officials discussed action in the UN Security Council, they were much blunter than during press conferences: "The events in Rwanda clearly seem to meet the definition of genocide."[420] It was only on May 21 that US Secretary of State, Christopher Clarke unblocked the "g-word" and US diplomats could start using it.[421]

By that time, the US government had long lost agenda-setting power about the framing of the Rwandan events in public opinion and the international media. When it started to publicly talk about "acts of genocide" (which were

418 William E. Schmidt: "Terror convulses Rwandan Capital as Tribes battle." The New York Times 9.4.1994.

419 Power, A Problem from Hell, 358-359 and 567.

420 Quote from Power, A Problem from Hell, 361, where she refers to a cable from the US representation at the UN to the State Department from April 27.

421 Power, A Problem from Hell, 361.

still regarded as something different from genocide), other frame producers had long before labelled the events in Rwanda as genocide. Already on April 9, The New York Times had published an opinion piece by Jerry Gray, in which he looked at Rwanda and Burundi through an ethnological lens (which was often used by journalists not familiar with the area), explaining the bloodshed during and after April 7 by referring to long lasting tribal tensions. In the article entitled "2 Nations Joined by Common History of Genocide", he claimed that "the bloodletting in Rwanda and Burundi runs through the history of both countries as fluidly as the meandering Akanyaru River that marks their common border. Tribal problems exist in virtually every African country. But modern weapons, the centuries-old feud between the Hutu and the Tutsi and a competition for land unlike anywhere else in Africa have led to genocidal orgies in Rwanda and Burundi." On May 1, Human Rights Watch published a fifteen-page report entitled "Genocide in Rwanda".

In 1994, the US government did not create any specific frames concerning the death of the Belgian blue helmets who had intended to protect the Rwandan Prime Minister.

Other Frames: Gourevitch and Dallaire

During the time preceding the trial chamber's verdict in *the pros. vs. Bagosora et al.*, three important books came out – their content can be presumed to have influenced the frames used by the prosecution and the trial chamber: Philip Gourevitch's report on post-genocide Rwanda, the memoirs of Luitenant General Roméo Dallaire, which later became the basis of a Canadian paradocumentary film, and Human Rights Watch's Alison des Forges' *Leave none to tell the story*, which saw numerous editions. Dallaire and Des Forges are most important here, since they also appeared in court several times as crime-based (Dallaire) and expert witnesses (Des Forges), which increases the likelihood of influence on trial chamber's frames. All these publications approach the events of spring 1994 from different angles.

Dallaire almost meticulously avoids any ethnic frame and refers to the conflict parties he had to deal with as political and ideological entities. He almost never uses ethnic labels to categorize actors, but instead uses labels such as "radical", "moderate" or attaches political affiliations. Caught in the logic of peacekeeping, which requires decision-makers to remain neutral, keep an equal distance and avoid culpabilisation, Dallaire analyses threats to the peace process, mounting tension and the escalation of violence, but refrains from putting blame on one ethnic group. The massacres, which emerge from the escalation after the air crash, are, in his eyes, the result of the conscious and deliberate politics of an inner circle of government officials and the military leadership, but they are not actions carried out by and on behalf of one ethnic group against another one. Even the victims are not described as Tutsi, but as victims of the radical forces' violence. According to Dallaire, they were killed by Interahamwe, not, for example, by a "Hutu militia". In a scene dealing with the situation in the city centre after the beginning of the atrocities which followed the air crash, Dallaire writes: "The RPF was still following the rules and we were only facing rogue RGF [Rwandan Government Forces] units." No mention is made of ethnic alignments; all of the actors, even those on whom he puts blame, are linked to their official institutional or political affiliation.[422] When Dallaire received Kagame's ultimatum in the afternoon of April 7, he calculated: "Last light in Rwanda fell at about six o'clock, which meant I had less than four hours to bring the situation under control, or the nation would sink back into civil war."[423] For Dallaire, Rwanda still was "a nation" and the conflict the start of a civil war, not genocide.[424]

When it comes to the death of the Belgian paratroopers, Dallaire quotes a military driver, an RGF major, who, while driving the Canadian through the deserted inner city of Kigali to Bagosora, attempted to prevent him from entering the RGF barracks at Camp Kigali, because "the troops inside the camp were out of control." Dallaire seems to believe him, or at least to suggest that such a belief would have been a reasonable reaction to the facts, as far as they were known to him at that time. He leaves it open, whether he also regards this interpretation as justified from an ex-post perspective in the light of the evidence, which at the time was not available to him. He regards the havoc in Kigali after April 7 as the result of the presidential guard's vengeance. The guard had, according to him, been deprived of its highest commander and symbolic father.[425] Daillaire provides a very different explanation for the death of the Belgian paratroopers. Months earlier, Dallaire had been informed by an insider from the core group of radicals of the preparations for a final onslaught against the RPF and the places where secret weapon depots were kept as well as

422 Dallaire, Shake Hands with the Devil, (Kindle Edition) chapter 10.

423 Dallaire, op. cit.

424 In the context of his mandate (which allowed him to only use force when fired upon) he frequently refers to the atrocities as possible crimes against humanity – never as genocide. Dallaire, op. cit. The events after April 7 are labelled genocide; on the day of the plane crash, Dallaire only sees massacres of the Presidential Guard, the party militias and mutineering members of the RGF, with loyal soldiers and the gendarmerie trying to get them under control.

425 In fact, Habyarimana was often referred to as "the father" or the "the father of the nation."

plans to scare off the blue helmets by targeting the Belgian paratroopers. The death of the Belgians was therefore the result of an "extremist plot" whose objective was to diminish the possible number of observers and witnesses before the massacres were launched at full scale. "The aim was to secure first a Belgian, then an UN withdrawal. The extremists had taken their cue from the grim farces of Bosnia and Somalia."[426]

But Dallair's book is never clear on this issue – he quotes Bagosora and his aides claiming the abuse of the Belgians was brought on by mutineers, whom the Army could not get under control. He also quotes them claiming to have lost control over the presidential guard and the radical militias (or not yet regained control over them), but clearly expresses doubts whether they actually intended to get things under control: "Bagosora was either the coldest fish in Africa or he was the ghost of Machiavelli executing a subversive plan."[427] The book also leaves open the question of whether Bagosora and his aides knew about the death of the Belgians before they were found dead in the hospital underground and whether they had ordered or tolerated the killings. Dallaire interprets them as the result of a hardliner conspiracy to get rid of the most capable part of UNAMIR, but when quoting his military interlocutors, he never casts a doubt on their claims that the killing of the ten Belgians was committed by disobedient soldiers and furious war veterans. Interestingly, the Belgians who died in Camp Kigali were heroes, not victims, for Dallaire, which stands in sharp contrast to most other frames used for the interpretation of their fate: "They were and remain heroes of Rwanda." [428]

Gourevitch is much more outspoken on ethnicity and genocide than Dallaire, and his book, which first appeared in 1998, is a great source of frames, many of which are much more moralizing, normative and concentrated on guilt than the few put forth by Dallaire. On the first pages of *We Wish to Inform You That Tomorrow We Will be Killed with our Families*, Gourevitch claims that in Rwanda, "the government had adopted a new policy, according to which everyone in the country's Hutu majority group was called upon to murder everyone in the Tutsi minority. The government, and an astounding number of its subjects, imagined that by exterminating the Tutsi people they could make the world a better place, and the mass killing had followed."[429] Throughout the book, Gourevitch leaves no doubt about whom he blames for the events, who,

---

426 Dallaire, op. cit.
427 Ibid.
428 Ibid.
429 Gourevitch, Philip: We Wish to Inform You That Tomorrow We Will Be Killed With Our Families. Stories from Rwanda. London, Basingstoke and Oxford 2000, 6.

according to him, was a perpetrator and who was a victim. Paul Kagame, the RPF commander who, after the three-month period of massacres in Rwanda, became president of the country, is his hero. Gourevitch despised the Hutu refugees from Rwanda, most of whom he subsumed under the roof of "Hutu Power", but also those who helped them (including the UN who delivered food and medicine to the camps in Zaire, neglecting the politicisation and militarisation of the camps) and a large part of his book is dedicated to the correction of alleged misinterpretations and misrepresentations of Rwanda's situation by the media and politicians who refuse to understand that Kagame's measures are crucial for preventing a repetition of the genocide. This may be due to his references to the Holocaust in German-occupied Europe, which he regards not only as the predecessor of the Rwandan genocide, but even as the inspiration for its Hutu perpetrators:

> "It has become a commonplace in the past fifty years to say that the industrialized killing of the Holocaust calls into question the notion of human progress, since art and science can lead straight through the famous gate – stamped with the words 'Work Makes You Free' – to Auschwitz. Without all that technology, the argument goes: the Germans could not have killed all those Jews. Yet it was the Germans, not the machinery, who did the killing. Rwanda's Hutu Power leaders understood this perfectly. If you could swing the people who would swing the machetes, technological underdevelopment was no obstacle to genocide. The people were the weapon, and that meant everybody: the entire Hutu population had to kill the entire Tutsi population. In addition to ensuring obvious numerical advantages, this arrangement eliminated any questions of accountability which might arise. If everybody is implicated, the implication becomes meaningless. Implication in what? A Hutu who thought there was anything to be implicated in would have to be an accomplice of the enemy."[430]

As much as he imputes "Hutu Power" intentions of genocide from the very beginning, as much he also ascribes solely noble intentions to the RPF: "The RPF had never really expected to win its war on the battlefield; its objective had been to force a political settlement, and at Arusha it appeared to have done that. When Gourevitch quotes interlocutors from "Hutu Power", he does it with distance, or even disapproval and disdain. When he quotes RPF representatives, no sign of detachment or reservation can be found.[431]

The death of the Belgian paratroopers was not Gourevitch's main topic, so he dealt with it in a rather short and superficial manner. Contrary to his claim about a plan of "Hutu Power" to make all Hutu kill all Tutsi, he asserts that on

430 Gourevitch, We Wish, 96.
431 Op. cit., 99.

April 7, the first aim of "Hutu Power" was to kill moderate Hutu opponents with political influence, among them Prime Minister Agathe Uwilingiyimana. "A contingent of ten Belgian UNAMIR soldiers arrived on the scene, but the Prime Minister fled over her garden wall and was killed nearby. Before the Belgians could leave, a Rwandan officer drove up and ordered them to surrender their arms and to come with him. The Belgians, outnumbered, were taken to Camp Kigali, the military base in the centre of town, where they were held for several hours, then tortured, murdered and mutilated. After that, the wholesale extermination of Tutsi got underway, and the UN troops offered little resistance to the killers."[432] As can easily be seen, this frame differs considerably from the others, which claim the killing of the Belgians was an attempt to scare off the UN and its troop-deploying member states and trigger the withdrawal of UNAMIR. In Gourevitch's book, hardly any explanation or rationalisation is given about the death of the Belgians, almost no motivation is imputed to the perpetrators and the only possible motive, one can deduce from these phrases is the assumption, that the Rwandan soldiers killed the Belgians in order to break possible resistance of UNAMIR to the genocide, which, according to Dallaire's memoirs, would have totally overstretched UNAMIR's military capabilities at the time.

The Frames of the UN

In the case of Rwanda, the United Nations was among the most active creators of frames of the events. Secretary General Boutros Ghali was among the first voices to label the events genocide. In a speech held in Oslo on May 3, he asked African countries to commit to a peacekeeping troop for Rwanda, arguing that only that way would it be possible to "defuse the conflict, to stop the genocide."[433] After the killings in Rwanda had ended, several members of the Security Council, among them the Czech representative, urged the UN to establish an ad-hoc criminal tribunal for the prosecution and punishment of the main perpetrators. Several Security Council resolutions reveal how the majority of the Council framed the conflict. In the first resolution concerning the ICTR, the Council expressed its "grave concern at the reports indicating that genocide and other systematic, widespread and flagrant violations of international humanitarian law have been committed in Rwanda." The first version of the ICTR's statute, drafted by the Council, explicitly stated that a genocide had

432 Op. cit., 114.

433 Quoted according to Paul Lewis: "U.N. Chief Asks Rights Aide To Take On a Role in Rwanda." The New York Times 3.5.1994.

taken place in Rwanda and eventually also beyond the borders of Rwanda during the period between 1.1.1994 and the end of that year – thus limiting the temporal framework (and the *ad temporae* jurisdiction) of the ICTR to one year.[434] In the following resolution about Rwanda, the Security Council also used the word genocide with respect to the events during 1994.[435]

Not surprisingly, neither the Secretary General nor the Security Council delivered any specific frames about the deaths of the Belgian soldiers. However, we find such frames in a report which Boutros Boutros-Ghali's successor Kofi Annan commissioned in early 1999 on the events in Rwanda. This inquiry about the conduct of the UN during the conflict was carried out by several high-ranking and publicly well known politicians and experts, who delivered their findings in December 1999. The report was sent to the Security Council and then disclosed to the general public.[436]

The report adopts the view that the genocide started immediately after the airplane crash of April 6 and ended with the one-sided ceasefire declaration of the RPF and the swearing in of a new government in Kigali a hundred days later.[437] According to the report's authors, this genocide was premeditated and intentional.[438]

The death of the Belgian soldiers at Camp Kigali on April 7 is described on various occasions as "tragic,"[439] but the authors do not provide any explanation or rationalisation for the "tragic killings". According to the report, the Belgians had surrendered as demanded by officers by the presidential guard who had surrounded the Prime Minister's residence. They had subsequently been transported to Camp Kigali, abused and killed. The report lacks any reference to the Belgians having defended themselves at Camp Kigali and denounces the killings as "brutal murder".[440]

---

434 UN Security Council Resolution 955 (1994), from 8.11.1994. S/RES/955 (1994), http://www.unictr.org/Portals/0/English%5CLegal%5CResolutions%5CEnglish%5C955e.pdf

435 See: S/RES/978 (1995). 27 February 1995. It may be worth mentioning that the Security Council did not preclude the occurrence of genocide when it established the ICTY.

436 The authors were Ingvar Carlsson, former Prime Minister of Sweden, Han Sung-Joo, former Foreign Minister of South Korea and General Rufus Kupolati of Nigeria: "Report of the independent inquiry into the actions of the United Nations during the 1994 genocide in Rwanda." S1999/1257 from 15.12.1999. www.un.org/news/dh/latest/rwanda.htm

437 Op. cit., 29.

438 Op. cit. 33.

439 Op. cit. 17, 36.

440 Op. cit. 16, 36.

The Organisation of African Unity's Frames

The UN was not the only international organisation which commissioned an inquiry into the events in Rwanda and provided interpretations of what had happened there. This inquiry is probably the only one which overtly admits its total failure to understand, explain and rationalize the massacres in Rwanda in 1994: "But when it came to trying to understand the actual act of killing, we confess our total failure. We acknowledge from the outset this failure. We have grasped the insidious process by which people were stirred up. We understand how they were manipulated and how they came to accept the demonisation and dehumanisation of others. We studied the literature, some of it highly controversial, that attempts to account for collective human breakdowns in which ordinary citizens turn into monsters. We have arrived at a certain comprehension of the complex series of factors at work. But we do not pretend for a moment that we have reached any understanding of the act of one neighbour or one Christian or one teacher actually hacking another to death. Perhaps, some day, answers will emerge. But for now, we are able to offer little illumination on the first questions that so many people reasonably ask." The report mostly dealt with the possibilities of preventing genocide in Rwanda, the role of external factors and the UN, and the knowledge the outside world had or could have had before April 1994. It mentioned the death of the Belgians, calling it "murder", but refrained from any broader framing of the incidents leading to their deaths. The Organisation of African Unity (OAU) also supported the view that the genocide had been planned beforehand with the intent of preventing the Arusha accords from entering into force by annihilating the Tutsi community of Rwanda.

The Frames of Human Rights Watch

Human Rights Watch belongs to the first organisations to create a clear-cut genocide frame about the conflict in Rwanda. Strong language and clear messages, which cover up any potential doubt the authors of HRW's report might have had while drafting it, are the organisation's hallmark and contribute greatly to its agenda-setting power in a professional and international media environment. Even if HRW's frames are not always endorsed by other influential actors (such as governments and international media) and sometimes appear to contradict facts established by the organisation itself, they immediately raise attention and attract awareness, thus inclining media to quote from HRW's reports and ask HRW experts for statements and interviews.

HRW's first report on Rwanda comprised all of these attributes. Entitled: "Genocide in Rwanda April – May 1994", it contained a table of contents that left no doubt about HRW's message: "Systematic slaughter" is one chapter title, other formulations include: "the worst, but not the first massacre", "slaughter immediately after the crash", "extending the massacres".[441] The report included an executive summary, which outlined the authors' main points: "The death of president Juvénal Habiarymana of Rwanda in a suspicious plane crash on April 6 1994 was the pretext for Hutu extremists from the late president's entourage to launch a campaign of genocide against the Tutsi, a minority of about 15 per cent of the population of Rwanda. The extremists also killed Hutu who had shown that they were willing to cooperate with the Tutsi in forming a more democratic government. Six weeks later, the killing continues. At least 200 000 and as many as 500 000 unarmed and unresisting civilians have been slain. The international community has failed to take any effective action to stop the slaughter."[442] The summary provides all of the classical elements of an international conflict frame: it is strongly normative, puts blame on one side, divides between the good and the bad guys, labels the atrocities in strong, unequivocal terms (which are not necessarily legal ones), uses emotional language and accuses an unspecified "international community" of negligence and inaction. Nevertheless, there are some elements which deviate from similar frames: HRW regarded a more inclusive government (comprising Tutsi) as "more democratic", explained the persecution of Hutu by other Hutu by the former's political engagement and partisanship (they were alleged to be ready to cooperate with the Tutsi and to support democracy). Persecution, according to this frame, was political rather than ethnic or racial – a claim in contrast to the general frame, which suggested the conflict to be one between two rival ethnic groups. Throughout the report, the period preceding the plane crash was described as a civil war in which the conflict parties were political (the RPF against the government). When Tutsi were mentioned, they were described as victims. Resistance came from members of the local elites (mostly governors and mayors) who tried to protect the Tutsi population. There was no Tutsi resistance in the government-held territories – a frame which is strikingly similar to the famous (and often criticized) "lambs to the slaughterhouse" – frame in connection to the Holocaust in Europe. The RPF was blamed for "less systematic abuses" against members of the Hutu population in the territories under its control. Only a small part of the report was dedicated to the killing of the Belgian paratroopers: "When Prime

441 Human Rights Watch: "Genocide in Rwanda April – May 1994." May 1994. HRW Africa, vol. 1994, vol. 6 no. 4.

442 Ibid.

Minister Agathe Uwilingiyimana fled for her life to a UN compound, UNAMIR dispatched ten soldiers, part of the Belgian contingent, to rescue her. They encountered a hostile and armed crowd and three were disabled. The others requested instructions from headquarters and, according to a press account, were told to put down their arms and attempt to negotiate with the crowd. They were slaughtered. The Belgian government then withdrew its troops, who were the best equipped of those available to the UNAMIR force. Subsequently Bangladeshi troops also left, some of them in panic before orders were given for their withdrawal." The failure of UNAMIR was explained by its weak mandate and insufficient equipment.

In July 1994, Human Rights Watch used the White House Conference on Africa to issue a voluminous report attacking the Clinton administration's Africa policy and its alleged negligence of human rights. The report not only reproduced the same frames about Rwanda, but also copied the same wording from the May report into the new document. This time, though, the aim of the report was not to denounce the situation in Rwanda and the Habariyama government's actions, but to incline Clinton to improve the human rights record of his policy and correct his allegedly inappropriate policy toward Rwanda (and other African states): "President Clinton's failure to make the prevention and punishment of genocide in Rwanda a priority reflects the low level of American interest in Africa. The fact that US objections and foot-dragging caused critical delays in the deployment of African peacekeeping forces which might have saved tens of thousands of Rwandan lives, that no senior administration official has visited Rwanda during the ten-week-old crisis, that virtually no public action has been taken to stigmatize and isolate the rump government, and that no serious efforts have been made to provide American military technology to jam the Rwandan radio stations that have promoted ethnic slaughter, suggest that human rights abuses in Africa do not become priorities, even when they amount to genocide."[443]

These were minor contributions to the international media and policy debate on Rwanda 1994. The biggest and probably the most influential contribution came in the form of a huge volume written by HRW expert Alison Des Forges, who had been a frequent visitor to Rwanda, had followed and commented on the Arusha peace process and had been called during the atrocities by friends in Rwanda who had urged her to take action, speak out on what was happening

---

443 Human Rights Watch Africa vol. 6, no. 6, July 1994.
Alison Des Forges died on February 12, 2009 in an airplane crash and leading international newspapers immediately published large orbituaries, among others The New York Times and The Economist.

and, if possible, help them find shelter. Some of them had been targeted by killer commandos because of their political or human rights engagements. After the RPF had conquered most of the country and the killings had stopped, Des Forges led HRW efforts to hold the perpetrators accountable and to establish a precise and detailed record of what had happened. Fluent in French and Kiniyarwanda, she was not only able to conduct inquiries in Rwanda and speak to leading members of the political establishment, but also to interview rural people and members of the towns' populations, the clergy, and the local elites in different parts of the country. Her whole research, carried out together with a huge number of HRW staff all over the world, was published in 1999 in a huge volume entitled *Leave None to Tell the Story. Genocide in Rwanda*[444] and was subsequently translated into many other languages. Her role during the 1994 events, her research, contacts, and the book, which quickly became a bestseller, made her an international authority on the Rwandan genocide. Much of the evidence she and her collaborators from HRW and local and European human rights activists had collected was given to the OTP of the ICTR and facilitated the drafting of indictments and enabled prosecutors to get access to important witnesses. According to information from HRW itself, she was called as an expert witness 11 times in various ICTR trials.[445] Her influence on the prosecution was huge. As Wilson claims, the ICTR's Office of the Prosecutor did not have a high profile analyst group comparable to the leadership research group at the ICTY, strongly relied on Des Forges' expertise in Rwandan history and on her and HRW's research into the genocide conducted for the book. The OTP and the subsequent ICTR trial chambers fuelled Des Forges' version of intergroup relations in Rwanda into their indictments and judgments, and *Leave None to Tell the Story*, became "the official version of Rwandan history at the Tribunal," Wilson claims.[446] However, in *the pros. vs. Akayesu*, the judges might have been under the impression of Des Forges testimony (which they frequently quoted in the judgment), but they could not yet have read her book, which appeared only a year after the trial chamber verdict.

Much of her book was dedicated to proving that the events following April 6, 1994 were not the outburst of century-long ethnic rivalries or just another

444 Des Forges, Alison: Leave None to Tell the Story. Genocide in Rwanda. Human Rights Watch 1999.

445 Georgette Gagnon: "Response to The New York Times article on genocide." Human Rights Watch 18.5.2009.

446 Wilson, Richard Ashby: Writing History in International Criminal Trials. Cambridge University Press 2011, 172-180. The eminent role of Alison Des Forges was confirmed in our interviews with Filip Reyntjens and André Guichaoua in Antwerp and in Paris in May 2012.

African tribal conflict, but a well-prepared genocide, by which a relatively limited group within the ruling establishment of the Habyarimana government had attempted to prevent a power-sharing accord between the forces supporting the government and the political opposition, including the RPF. The Arusha accords, Des Forges argued, would have forced the government to share power within the country not only with the RPF, but also with the emerging oppositional Hutu parties whose strongholds were mostly in the south of the country, whereas the inner circle of the Habyarimana government predominantly came from the north and north-east and represented the interest of the local population there. At the same time, the president himself (and his highly elitist, well-trained, privileged and powerful presidential guard) would have lost much of his power as the ultimate authority in internal strife within the ruling establishment after such a power-sharing deal had come into force. Therefore, Des Forges claimed, the plane crash in early April had only been the pretext, but not the reason for the explosion of atrocities. These had been previously planned in detail. In accordance with Dallaire's account, she identified Théoneste Bagosora as the main instigator and the brain behind the events which followed the plane crash. The genocide was not only a means to get rid of political competitors in the fight for power, but also a means to strengthen the (ethnic) solidarity within the Hutu camp, which threatened to fall apart into different political currents due to the pluralisation of the country's political landscape. By imposing a strong and insurmountable division between Hutu and Tutsi and by making this division the borderline between those who could live and those who were doomed to die, the main perpetrators managed to eradicate the cleavage which had emerged among the Hutu population and which had been strengthened by the RPF's political appeal to Hutu opposition parties.

With respect to the killing of the Belgian peacekeepers, Des Forges meticulously reconstructed the events around Prime Minister Uwilingiyimana's residence and Camp Kigali. At 5.30 in the morning of April 7 when a UNAMIR patrol first tried to reach her, Rwandan government soldiers shot at the patrol and immobilized two of the four vehicles. At 8.30, the Prime Minister tried to reach a neighbouring building, which belonged to a US diplomat. After being prevented from going there, she reached another building belonging to a UN officer. Before 9.00, Rwandan troops surrounded the UNAMIR soldiers who had tried to protect her, and drove them to Camp Kigali. There, soldiers attacked the Belgian paratroopers, believing Belgians had been responsible for the shoot-down of Habyarimana's airplane. Here, Des Forges based her account mostly on Dallair's testimony (who had not been an eyewitness of the killings), claiming, "most of the Belgians had been beaten to death". A small group had withdrawn into a small building, where they managed to kill and disarm a Rwandan soldier and to defend themselves for several hours. Des Forges did not decide whether they had been victims or heroes, but – contrary to many other accounts - she provided enough evidence to show that they had not remained passive. Killing them was, according to Des Forges, part of a plan to get rid of a forceful UNAMIR, by targeting its most professional, well-trained and equipped core. Though she did not explicitly say so, it is obvious from her account that she did not regard the rumours about Belgian complicity in the airplane crash the reason for mutiny, but rather as an element of a plan which aimed at infuriating the soldiers against the Belgians, so that they would be ready to kill them.

The Prosecutor's Frames

In the original indictment against Ntuyahaga, the then prosecutor of the ICTR, Louise Arbour framed the actions he was alleged of having committed in the following way: According to the indictment signed by deputy chief prosecutor Bernard Muna, the attack on the Belgian paratroopers was the culminating point of earlier attempts to target them, dating back to January 1994, long before the assassination of Rwanda's president. The indictment alleges that UNAMIR "was perceived as an obstacle by certain members of the extremist political circles. Certain eminent figures in this circle thus adopted a strategy intended to provoke the Belgian military contingent, UNAMIR's most effective and best-equipped contingent. Their ultimate goal was to force them to withdraw."[447] For this purpose, the indictment claimed, a propaganda campaign was staged against UNAMIR in nationalist media such as *Kangura* and the *Radio et Télévision des Mille Collines*. Confusingly, the indictment draws a direct line between alleged preparations of high militaries from January 1994 and the assissination of the paratroopers, which actually took place months later. It is even more confusing that the indictment does not mention any participation of the accused in these preparatory meetings.[448]

When it comes to April 6, the Ntuyahaga indictment further claims the Belgians were dispatched for the protection of the Prime Minister at her residence. There, the Belgians were forced to surrender their arms and were subsequently transported to Camp Kigali, where, upon arrival, Bernard Ntuyahaga held a speech during which he accused the Belgians of having assassinated president Habyarimana. Then, it is further alleged, the Rwandan

447 *The pros. vs. Ntuyahaga* ICTR-98-40.

448 The indictment also mentions a meeting in January during which plans were developped to use the Interahamwe militia against the paratroopers, whereas on April 7, it was in fact an Army unit that killed them.

soldiers started to physically abusing the Belgians. Four Belgian soldiers died immediately, the others "withstood several attacks for a number of hours before being killed." As the indictment points out, Colonel Théoneste Bagosora was present in Camp Kigali, participated in a meeting a hundred metres away from the place where the Belgians were killed, and was informed by the Camp Commander Lieutenant Nubaha "that the Belgian UNAMIR soldiers were under risk of death."

In the indictment of *the pros. vs. Bagosora et al.*, the events were described in more detail. The Office of the Prosecutor now regarded Hutu, Tutsi and Twa as "ethnic or racial groups", but without any further explanation of how these categories were related to the definition of protected groups in the ICTR statute. Then the OTP presented the postcolonial history of Rwanda as a sequence of ethnic clashes and civil wars between the two major groups up to 1990. In the light of the dispute described earlier in this book about the character of the conflict, it may be surprising that the OTP's analysis provided some substantiation for critics of the genocide frame, which, at the time when the indictment was drafted, was already firmly established in Rwanda, in the epistemic community dealing with Rwanda in 1994, and in international media. According to the indictment, the Hutu-Tutsi cleavage was far from being the only one which cut across Rwandan society in the early 1990s, and the ethnic dividing line was by no means clear. The authors of the indictment framed the conflict as political rather than racial, pointing to a relatively small group of Hutu from Rwanda's north-west who had enjoyed a privileged position under president Habyarimana and were linked to the so-called "power factions" of the Hutu political parties and the inner circle of Habyarimana's entourage, the so-called *Akazu*.[449] For this group, the Arusha accords had been – according to the indictment – a threat to their position and privileges, and that was the reason why they had opposed the peace settlement and why they had prepared a final crackdown on their antagonists. But they had not only listed Tutsi as enemies, but also Hutu from parts of the country other than the northwest. "Determined to avoid the power-sharing prescribed by the Arusha accords, several prominent civilian and military figures pursued their strategy of ethnic division and incitement to violence. They targeted and labelled as RPF accomplices the entire Tutsi population, and also Hutu opposed to their domination, particularly those from regions other than northwestern Rwanda." Taken seriously, this claim meant that the same conflict which the prosecution had framed as genocide had actually occurred between a small ruling elite of Hutu close to president Habyarimana as the perpetrators, and the overwhelming majority of the Tutsi

449 *The pros. vs. Bagosora et al.* indictment, ICTR-98-41-T.

and the Hutu population (most of whom did not live in northwestern Rwanda and did not support this small circle), who had become victims of this genocide. The indictment specifies that killings had been carried out on the basis of regularly updated proscription lists, but failed to explain the contradiction between such targeted killings on the one hand, and the extremely broad and indiscriminate approach to killing in the framework of genocide on the other hand.

When it comes to the death of the Belgian peacekeepers, the Bagosora indictment is also much more detailed than the Ntuyahaga indictment. It contains the same phrases about the perpetrators' rationale: "This United Nations military force was perceived as an obstacle by certain members of the extremist political circles. Certain eminent figures in this circle thus adopted a strategy intended to provoke the Belgian military contingent, UNAMIR's most effective and best-equipped contingent. Their ultimate goal was to force them to withdraw." It then continues by attributing the perpetrators with the intention of causing everything which happened in consequence of their deeds: since the murder had led to the withdrawal of the Belgians and other peacekeepers, the perpetrators had attacked the Belgians, in order to get rid of the peacekeepers. The indictment repeats and elaborates more widely on the conspiracy to provoke the Belgian peacekeepers by killing some of them during a demonstration in January 1994. According to the prosecution, the attempt failed because the peacekeepers did not show up. The indictment remains silent about why the period between January and April went by without any further provocation or attacks of government-related forces against the Belgian units. Then, in the night of April 6/7, some of the paratroopers were ordered to protect the Prime Minister who wanted to go to the National Radio Station and address the people. "When they arrived at the Prime Minister's residence at around 5.00 a.m., they were attacked by FAR[450] personnel, including elements from the Presidential Guard, the Paracommando Battalion and the Reconnaissance Battalion. Later, the ten Belgian paracommandos, along with the five Ghanaian soldiers who were guarding the Prime Minister, were disarmed and arrested." They were then taken to Camp Kigali, where they were immediately attacked and beaten by Rwandan soldiers in front of Rwandan Army officers." Once again, the indictment of *the pros. vs. Bagosora et al.* repeats the same phrases as the Ntuyahaga indictment, adding that Bagosora and other senior officers did nothing to prevent the Belgians from being killed. The indictment also contains a frame about the death of Prime Minister Agathe Uwilingiyimana. She had

450 FAR is the abbreviation for "Forces Armées du Rwanda", the forces loyal to the interim government.

been, according to the indictment, "tracked down, arrested, sexually assaulted and killed by Rwandan Army personnel, more specifically, members of the Presidential Guard, the Paracommando Battalion and the Reconnaissance Battalion."

The Frames of the Trial Chamber in *the Pros. vs. Bagosora et al.*

The trial in which responsibility for the deaths of the 10 UNAMIR Belgian peacekeepers was established is often referred to as the Military I trial. This group trial concerned Colonel Théoneste Bagosora, directeur de cabinet of the Ministry of Defence, General Gratien Kabiligi, head of the operations bureau of the army general staff, Major Aloys Ntabakuze, commander of the elite Para Commando Battalion, and Colonel Anatole Nsengiyumva, commander of the Gisenyi operational sector. The Prosecution charged each of those men with conspiracy to commit genocide, genocide, crimes against humanity and war crimes, based on direct or superior responsibility for crimes committed in Rwanda in 1994.[451] What is of key importance for our research is the role Theoneste Bagosora played in the deaths of the 10 Belgian peacekeepers.

The Military I trial commenced on 2 April 2002, and the verdict was delivered on 18 December 2008. In the ICTR indictment delivered on 12 August 1999, Colonel Bagosora was charged with one count of conspiracy to commit genocide, one count of genocide, one count of complicity in genocide, six counts of crime against humanity, and three counts of serious violations of Article 3 Common to the Geneva Convention and Additional Protocol II.[452] Bagosora was held responsible for the murder of the ten Belgian peacekeepers on count 5 (crime against humanity), and count 11 (serious violation of Article 3 Common to the Geneva Convention and Additional Protocol II). None of the other accused military officials were indicted in relation to the deaths of the Belgian peacekeepers.

Contrary to the trial chamber in the *pros. vs. Akayesu*, which extensively discussed the question whether genocide had occurred and whether Tutsi and Hutu were different ethnic groups, the trial chamber in the Military I Trial refrained from a larger discussion of this issue, pointing instead to other

451 International Criminal Tribunal for Rwanda, *The pros. vs. Bagosora et al.*: Oral summary of the Judgment and Sentence, Case No. ICTR-98-41-T, 18 December 2008, paragraph 5.

452 International Criminal Tribunal for Rwanda, *The prosecutor vs. Bagosora et al.*: Amended Indictment, Case No. ICTR-96-7-I, 12 August 1999, 54-63.

verdicts: "Leaving aside the particular facts in this case, it is clear that a genocide occurred. The Tribunal has convicted a high number of individuals in completed cases for genocide committed in various parts of the country. The Appeals Chamber has even concluded that the genocide in Rwanda in 1994 is a fact of common knowledge which there is no reasonable basis to dispute."[453]

However, in its findings about when exactly this genocide occurred, the trial chamber deviated from many pre-existing frames whose authors regarded the early nineties as the time when the inner circle of the government and the military had started to plan the extermination of all Tutsi in the country. Among the frames the judges rejected were also Des Forges' interpretations, according to which the genocide had already been planned in 1990. It is worthwhile to quote the judges' arguments in extenso, because they constitute an impressive attempt to establish an interpretation in opposition to the opinion of the defence, the prosecution, and at least some of the Western expert witnesses who had been called during the trial. Whereas the prosecution had tried to prove the main perpetrators' intention of committing genocide before to 1994, the defence regarded the escalation of violence after April 6 as a direct consequence of the RPF's advance into the government-held territories. The defence seemed more inclined to blame the RPF than to disprove the evidence pointing towards the accused. This was a political rather than a legal strategy, similar to the one Slobodan Milošević was following at the same time in The Hague, where he was eager to shift blame for the massive displacement of Kosovo civilians on NATO bombings and KLA terror, and away from himself and his government. Both frames, the "conspiracy to genocide" frame and the frame blaming the RPF, overlooked a more apparent one which one could derive from the cleavage between "intentionalists" and "functionalism" in literature on the Holocaust.[454]

453 In *the pros. vs. Karemera et al.*, Decision on Prosecutor's Interlocutory Appeal of Decision on Judicial Notice (AC), 16.6.2006, para. 35, the Appeals Chamber had characterized the events of 1994 as "a campaign of mass killing intended to destroy, in whole or at least in very large part, Rwanda's Tutsi population".

454 In a few words,"intentionalists" assume the existence of a genocidal intention of Hitler and the core of the political establishment of Third Reich, whereas "functionalists" regard the Holocaust as the incremental escalation of systemic tensions, which emerged from the regime's racial policy. For intentionalists, the Holocaust took place because the regime had planned it before and then carried it out. For functionalists, the Holocaust happened because it was the intrinsic result of the needs and constraints the regime had created before and which had escalated; the regime endorsed it without a clearly identifiable prior intent or plan. It was an escalation of the mechanisms the regime had set in motion and which then became self-executing. On Intentionalism and functionalism, see: Hayes, Peter; Diefendorf, Jeffry M.: Lessons and Legacies: New currents in Holocaust research. Northwestern University Press 2004, 235-250.

The trial chamber endorsed the latter frame. "When viewed against the backdrop of the targeted killings and massive slaughter perpetrated by civilian and military assailants between April and July 1994 as well as earlier cycles of violence, it is understandable why for many this evidence takes on new meaning and shows a prior conspiracy to commit genocide. Indeed, these preparations are completely consistent with a plan to commit genocide. However, they are also consistent with preparations for a political or military power struggle. The Chamber recalls that, when confronted with circumstantial evidence, it may only convict where it is the only reasonable inference. It cannot be excluded that the extended campaign of violence directed against Tutsi, as such, became an added or an altered component of these preparations." In other words, the judges did not want to rule out that the massacres, which the appeals chamber in *the pros. vs. Karemera et al.* had defined as genocide, had occurred as the result of an initially unintended, but then accepted escalation of a power struggle, but which at the roots had not been genocidal.

The trial chamber also developed a detailed interpretation of the Belgian peacekeepers' deaths, it described the death of Prime Minister Agathe Uwilingiyimana, and the events at Camp Kigali. Contrary to prosecution claims and earlier interpretations about a conspiracy to oust the Belgians, the judges were sceptical about these intentionalist frames and left it open whether the killing of the ten soldiers had been part of an earlier established plan or the result of a spontaneous escalation among insubordinate government soldiers and war veterans. For the legal reasoning and for Bagosora's responsibilities as a commander, who had been informed about the events, but had failed to prevent them (and had failed to punish the perpetrators), this was a minor question. From the perspective of frame analysis, it is nevertheless worth mentioning. In this case, the judges seemed to follow Dallaire's and the Belgian parliamentary commission's mutiny frame more than the other frames (including the prosecution's) which had alleged the death of the ten paratroopers to be the result of a conspiracy dating back to 1990. The judges wrote: "The Chamber accepts that the initial assault on the peacekeepers after they were brought to the camp may have resulted from insubordination. The evidence that a number of officers unsuccessfully tried to intervene equally supports this proposition and suggests that these killings were not part of a highly coordinated plan. Nevertheless, the Chamber has found that Bagosora had authority over the Rwandan army at the time of the attack. It also concluded that he was aware of the threat posed to the Belgian peacekeepers around 10.45 a.m. when Colonel Nubaha informed him of the unrest at Camp Kigali. In any event, he was fully apprised of the dire situation facing them when he personally visited the camp between 12.15 and 2.00 p.m. after the conclusion of the meeting and saw the bodies of the dead peacekeepers. At the time, many of the peacekeepers were still alive in the UNAMIR office at the camp." The judges blamed Bagosora for not using violence to end the mutiny and save the Belgians, despite the presence of a loyal elite unit in the camp which could have been used for that purpose. They also rejected the *ex post* rationalisation, which inferred intentions from mere chronology. The fact that the Belgians' death had triggered the departure of most of the UNAMIR troops was not enough for the judges to conclude that making them leave had been the intention of those who had killed the Belgians. The Chamber was not satisfied beyond reasonable doubt that "the attack formed part of a concerted strategy to further the massacres by forcing the withdrawal of the Belgian peacekeeping contingent. As mentioned above, the evidence suggests that these killings were not necessarily part of a highly coordinated plan. It remains possible that the animosity towards the Belgian contingent followed from anti-colonial sentiments and their perceived support of the RPF." At the end of the day, Bagosora was sentenced for genocide, but acquitted of conspiracy to genocide.[455] The killing of the Belgians was not regarded as an element of genocide, opposite to the prosecution's claims that the killings were intended to trigger the departure of all peacekeepers in order to facilitate the killings and carry them out without witnesses. The trial chamber dismissed the claim "that this is the only reasonable inference to be drawn from the killing of the Belgian peacekeepers. Accordingly, the Chamber does not find that these killings constituted genocide. It also has not been proven that they were committed with the requisite genocidal intent in order to substantially assist other acts of genocide." Instead, the judges found that the murder of the Belgians "formed part of widespread and systematic attacks against the civilian population on ethnic and political grounds." This amounted to a crime against humanity, not a war crime, since the judges had earlier argued that the peacekeepers had been disarmed before they were killed and could not be regarded as combatants.[456]

---

455 This was also due to the narrow intepretation of the ICTY's jurisdiction, which had been limited by the Security Council to the year 1994. Earlier evidence could be heard in court and used as circumstancial evidence, which provided information about conduct, intentions of actors and help to understand subsequent events, but it did not empower the court to judge the acts of an accused prior to 1994.

456 Withdrawing to the barrack, killing a Rwandan soldier and defending themselves with his weapon also did not make them combatants, the judges argued, since this had been undertaken as an act of self-defence in reaction to the killing of the four paratroopers who had been disarmed and killed beforehand. The distinction between civilians and persons *hors de combat*, which was used in the judgment, was derived from the appeals chamber judgment in *the pros. vs. Martić* IT-95-11.

Resisting Powerful External Frames

The trial chamber in *the pros. vs. Bagosora et al.* is an extreme case of judges' resistance against external frames used by outside actors who strive to shape public opinion and – indirectly and probably unintentionally – to shape the trial chamber's interpretations. This resistance emerged in two forms – as a resistance of the judges against the intentionalist interpretations of Human Rights Watch, Alison Des Forges, the authors of the UN and OAU reports, which all constructed a far-reaching genocide plan, which allegedly led to the events following the airplane crash. At the same time, the judges also rejected the less strong and less widely used premeditation frame about the death of the Belgian peacekeepers. Here, the trial chamber endorsed the mutiny frame rather than the interpretation entailing a plan which had been developed years before in order to get rid of the Belgians, either because the perpetrators wanted to scare off the UN troops, or because they regarded the Belgians as the strongest potential obstacle to their genocidal plans. In opposition to almost all pre-existing frames (but with some congruence with the frames used in Le Monde and The New York Times), they interpreted the genocide as the consequence of a power struggle, which emerged due to the logic of escalation in, on one hand a civil war, and on the other hand an escalating power struggle within the ruling political establishment. Except for the general endorsement of the dominant genocide frame, which they accepted only in a very narrow definition, the judges demonstrated almost complete immunity to outside influences.

It was no surprise that the Rwandan government reacted furiously to the verdict. The first official reactions were rather mixed and concentrated on the life-long sentence for Bagosora[457], but intellectuals and politicians close to the government quickly discovered that the ruling was a blow to the official version of a premeditated and well-planned genocide. But for the government in Kigali, things went even more awry. Bagosora and his co-accused Anatole Nsengiyumva appealed. Only co-defendant Gratien Kabiligi, who had been acquitted, did not appeal. On December 14, 2011, the appeals chamber rendered its verdict. It found Bagosora not guilty of some of the counts in the indictment and sentenced him to 35 years of imprisonment. And it did not challenge the interpretations of the trial chambers about the ramifications of the genocide and the deaths of the Belgians. As usual, the appeals chamber limited its investigations to two questions: whether the trial chamber had erred in fact or in law while assessing the evidence. The five judges had no reason to put the trial chamber frames into question, since none of the appellants had challenged them.

457 George Kagame: "Mixed feelings as ICTR delivers landmark ruling." The New Times 20.12.2008

The prosecutor and the Rwandan government had not appealed, but they were the only putative actors that could have had an interest in challenging the trial chamber's factual findings about when and why the genocide took place and whether it had been planned in advance. The relative lowering of the sentence for Bagosora stimulated the outrage in Kigali even more. Now, the reactions were no longer ambiguous, they were openly hostile. President Kagame criticized the verdict, as did Jean de Diu Mucyo, the executive secretary of the National Commission for the fight against genocide, saying: "I was shocked by the decision; it's nothing but an insult to Genocide survivors; however, I need to read the ruling thoroughly to know the exact basis of the judgment."[458] Jean-Paul Kimonyo, an advisor to Kagame, wrote: "The clearing of Bagosora's guilt on the account of conspiring to commit genocide has less to do with what happened before and during the genocide than with what was happening in 2008. This judgment was pronounced in the midst of a revisionist campaign launched two years earlier by the French judge Bruguière asserting that it was the RPF that shot Habyarimana's plane and provoked the genocide. A thesis defended by Bagosora and his co-accused presenting the genocide as a collateral damage of a legitimate, genuine, political and military course of action against 'state enemies'. A thesis the Chamber has shamefully endorsed." He called the ruling "ridiculous". His article in The New Times was entitled: "On Bagosora, the ICTR ended up with adopting his ideology."[459] A month later, Evariste Kalisa, deputy speaker of the parliament, called for a revision of the verdict: "That is completely wrong because the Genocide was prepared, even before the plane was downed. Every Rwandan knows that".[460]

---

458 The New Times 16.12.2011 and http://www.rwandagateway.org/spip.php?article1319

459 Jean-Paul Kimonyo: "In Bagosora, the ICTY ended up with adopting his ideology." The New Times 23.12.2011.

460 James Karuhanga: "MP calls for review of Bagosora's trial". The New Times 12.1.2012

The Frames in *the Prosecutor vs. Akayesu*

The case against Akayesu led to a huge amount of diverging frames, but those were not as comprehensive as the ones in use in the case of Srebrenica and the events of April 1994 in Kigali. Nevertheless, the events in Taba and their juridical follow-up in *the pros. vs. Akayesu* led to the creation of some unique frames and to unique circumstances, under which these frames permeated into indictments and judgments. This happened despite the initial lack of public interest in the case. Before the trial started, *the pros. vs. Akayesu* was interesting only for one reason – it was the ICTY's first full scale trial.

The Frames of International Media

When the conflict in Rwanda broke out violently after April 6, 1994, rape was no important issue in the news coverage of international media, such as The New York Times, Le Monde, Time Magazine, or Newsweek.[461] Of all media analysed here, The New York Times dedicated the most articles to Rwanda at the time, but only 6 of these articles contained the keywords "Rwanda" and "rape". From the very beginning, The New York Times was also quite emphatic of the Rwandan Patriotic Front and negative about the actual (Hutu) government of country. In a piece dealing with the causes of the relatively rapid advance of the Rwandan Patriotic Front into the central and southern parts of Rwanda in 1994 and the defeat of the government commanded militias and the Rwandan Army, the RPF was associated with a multitude of positive adjectives, describing it as "better led and trained", "highly motivated and disciplined", whereas the other side of the conflict was presented as "soldiers and militiamen", who "were undisciplined, and that drinking and rape were condoned by their officers."[462] The whole conflict was described in the article as one between the Army and governmental militia, who "slaughtered" Tutsi civilians on the one hand, and, on the other hand, "rebel forces" that targeted the militia: "Although combat casualties were small compared with the slaughter of

---

461 We chose these outlets because of two basic criteria, which are important for the research questions we want to answer. First, because they are international (as opposed to national) because they are addressed and consumed by a relatively international audience, i.e. by readers in countries other than the countries of their origin, and second, because they were likely to be read (either directly or indirectly through news ageny reports, press summaries and broadcasting) by prosecutors, judges and the staff of the ICTR, so they were more likely than others going to influence frames used by them.

462 Donatella Lorch: "Rwanda Rebels' Victory Attributed to Discipline." The New York Times 19.7.1994.

200,000 to 500,000 Tutsi civilians by Hutu military and militia units, the war between the Rwandan Patriotic Front and the Government was vicious, and often involved modern weapons." Frank Smyth, a book author and military expert, was later quoted in the article saying, "I think the RPF's primary goal was to target the militias more than the army," (...)"Those were the ones doing the killing." The picture painted by a Time Magazine article in May 1994 was quite different. There, Rwanda appeared to tumble into a spiral of violence, a chaos caused by a civil war, with no good and bad side and actually no one to blame. In the article, "slaughter" just "occurs" and "killing takes place", but there is no indication of who is the victim and who the perpetrator, and no hint is given, which would enable readers to attribute blame to one side or to specific actors. "The horrifying slaughter is another explosion in a mainly ethnically based civil war that outsiders understand imperfectly if at all – and therefore do not know how to solve. No one is even certain what sort of diplomatic efforts might persuade the Rwandan factions to halt the bloodletting."[463] In all articles, atrocities, killings and "slaughtering" were mentioned, but not mass rape campaigns or massive human rights violations of women. When orphans were mentioned, they were presented as children whose parents had been perished during the killings, not as survivors or offspring of raped mothers.[464] Later in 1994, the perpetrator/victim divide in news coverage somehow became obfuscated, when Time Magazine wrote about an internal UN report, accusing "the putative good guys" in Rwanda, the RPF, of having committed atrocities against civilians during the military invasion of the country. "The report, by the U.N. High Commission on Refugees (UNHCR), claims 'an unmistakable pattern of killings and persecution' by Tutsi victors of Rwanda's civil war", Time revealed, presenting the RPF as the "victor of a civil war", rather than as liberators of the country or saviours from genocide. [465]

The Frames of International Non-Governmental Organisations

The first conflict frames to contain explicit allegations of gender-specific violence during the events in Rwanda during and after April 1994 stem from a report of *médecins sans frontières*", the international organisation of physicians,

463 Time (no author indicated): "Kind words but not much more." Time Magazine, 16.5.1994.

464 Claire Brisset: Le silence des enfants rwandais. Le Monde 15.12.1994.

465 Time (no author): "Rwanda... Are the "good guys" bad guys, too?" Time Magazine 27.9.1994. http://www.time.com/time/nation/article/0,8599,1866,00.html#ixzz1TDdoFgPs

published in May 1995.[466] A news report published in Le Monde in February of the same year highlighted for the first time the issue of orphans of genocide in Rwanda – the fate of thousands of young children who had lost their parents during the atrocities and were now raised in orphanages all over the country. Both frames – the one about rape as a specific and organized form of crime against women and the one about orphans – would later merge into one and constitute a new frame, which would prove extremely influential.

Meanwhile, Jean-Paul Akayesu was apprehended in Zambia on behalf of the new, RPF-led Rwandan government. Invoking its primacy over national jurisdiction, the ICTY submitted a request to the Zambian government to keep Akayesu in custody. At that time, no indictment had been drafted against him. Richard Goldstone, the South African chief prosecutor of the ICTR, managed to file an indictment against Akayesu on February 13 of the following year, which was confirmed by a judge three days later and then transferred to the Zambian government by the tribunal registrar. Akayesu arrived in the detention unit in Arusha in late May 1996, more than two years after the genocide had started and more than 7 months after his arrest. What followed can only be described as a striking and extremely successful case of lobbying a court – a massive campaign, orchestrated by international media (mostly The New York Times) and international human rights organisations, which strove to make the Akayesu trial a trial against rape and gendered violence. The campaign started with a report by Human Rights Watch entitled "Shattered Lives – Sexual Violence during the Rwandan Genocide and its Aftermath", which contained allegations about the use of rape as a weapon in the conflict. The first sentences of the report read: "During the 1994 genocide, Rwandan women were subjected to sexual violence on a massive scale, perpetrated by members of the infamous Hutu militia groups known as the Interahamwe, by other civilians, and by soldiers of the Rwandan Armed Forces, including the Presidential Guard. Administrative, military and political leaders at the national and local levels, as well as heads of militia, directed or encouraged both the killings and sexual violence to further their political goal: the destruction of the Tutsi as a group. They therefore bear responsibility for these abuses."[467] The report uses a multitude of different frames, including one which presents the conflict as an ethnic struggle between Hutu and Tutsi, during which the Hutu are the perpetrators and the Tutsi the victims. According to this frame,

466 Donatella Lorch: "Wave of Rape Adds New Horror To Rwanda's Trail of Brutality." The New York Times 15.5.1995. Lorch quotes the report. The original could not be retrieved from *médecins sans frontières*.

467 Human Rights Watch: "Shattered lives – sexual violence during the Rwandan genocide and its aftermath." September 1996, http://www.hrw.org/legacy/reports/1996/Rwanda.htm

Hutu used rape as a weapon for achieving various objectives in the struggle. The report is extremely rich in such explanations, which elaborate on the reasons and aims of the rapists:

> "Throughout the world, sexual violence is routinely directed against females during situations of armed conflict. This violence may take gender-specific forms, like sexual mutilation, forced pregnancy, rape or sexual slavery. Being female is a risk factor; women and girls are often targeted for sexual abuse on the basis of their gender, irrespective of their age, ethnicity or political affiliation. Rape in conflict is also used as a weapon to terrorize and degrade a particular community and to achieve a specific political end. In these situations, gender intersects with other aspects of a woman's identity such as ethnicity, religion, social class or political affiliation. The humiliation, pain and terror inflicted by the rapist is meant to degrade not just the individual woman but also to strip the humanity from the larger group of which she is a part. The rape of one person is translated into an assault upon the community through the emphasis placed in every culture on women's sexual virtue: the shame of the rape humiliates the family and all those associated with the survivor. Combatants who rape in war often explicitly link their acts of sexual violence to this broader social degradation. In the aftermath of such abuse, the harm done to the individual woman is often obscured or even compounded by the perceived harm to the community. During the Rwandan genocide, rape and other forms of violence were directed primarily against Tutsi women because of both their gender and their ethnicity."[468]

Thus, the authors of the report added a second cleavage to the already prevailing one in dominant media frames about the conflict in Rwanda. A gender-divide was added to the Hutu-Tutsi-divide, which, in accordance with the prevailing tendency in international media, was declared "ethnic". At that stage, it was already obvious that things had not been that simple in Rwanda. The authors admitted that a few sentences later, pointing to the fact that Hutu women had also been raped during the conflict, a fact which was in slight contradiction with the frame describing "Hutu aggressors raping Tutsi women because of their gender and ethnicity." Rapes of Hutu women by Hutu militiamen and government soldiers could hardly be explained by referring to ethnicity and to the Hutu/Tutsi cleavage. The authors solved this problem by mentioning yet marginalizing cases of rape that did not fit into the dominant frame: "Some Hutu women were also targeted with rape because they were affiliated with the political opposition, because they were married to Tutsi men, or because they protected Tutsi. A number of women, Tutsi and Hutu, were targeted regardless of ethnicity or political affiliation. Young girls or those considered beautiful were particularly at the mercy of the militia groups, who were a law unto themselves and often raped indiscriminately." It is worth mentioning, that the

468 Ibid.

first trace of rape as a weapon in the conflict appeared in an Amnesty International report from 1994, which accused the RPF of atrocities against the civilian Hutu population during the RPF's invasion from Uganda. AI remained rather reluctant to join the campaign for making rape the dominant issue of the Akayesu trial. Counter to the AI approach, RPF soldiers (or, as they were often called, "rebels") raping Hutu women were no issue for HRW. What AI and HRW frames (and all other remaining NGO frames dealing with rape) had in common was the construction of women as victims rather than heroes, survivors, or victors of the conflict. HRW's *Shattered Lives* report (the title itself emphasizes victimhood) mentioned the huge imbalance in post-conflict Rwanda, which made women 70 per cent of the population and heads of 50 per cent of all households. But these statistics were a mere illustration of the burden women would have to carry in the years to come; they did not incline the authors to discuss the putative consequences for upward social mobility and womens' emancipation. This was even more astonishing with respect to the inherent logic of the report, which, by suggesting that a relatively big part of the population (Hutu men) had raped a relatively small part of (Tutsi) women, automatically imposed the conclusion that many more women would have the chance to take the social, professional and political posts of men than could have been raped. In other words: since nearly all rape victims were Tutsi women and the overwhelming majority of Hutu women had not been raped (according to HRW's frame), women as such were more likely to be beneficiaries of the new situation than men.[469] Nevertheless, in NGO reports dealing with mass rape in Rwanda, women were present only as stigmatized victims, carrying traumas, isolated by their families and struggling with health problems. "In Rwanda, as elsewhere in the world, rape and other gender-based violations carry a severe social stigma. The physical and psychological injuries suffered by Rwandan rape survivors are aggravated by a sense of isolation and ostracisation. Rwandan women who have been raped or who suffered sexual abuse generally do not dare reveal their experiences publicly, fearing that they will be rejected by their family and wider community and that they will never be able to reintegrate or to marry. Others fear retribution from their attacker if they speak out. Often, rape survivors suffer extreme guilt for having survived and been held for rape, rather than having been executed."[470]

469 In fact, Rwanda is today one of the most advanced countries with respect to the legal and political empowerment of women, competing only with countries such as Norway, Sweden, and Finland.

470 HRW, Shattered Lives, op. cit.

Yet another element surfaced in the report – the fate of children born as a result of rapes. HRW dedicated only a few sentences to the issue, which would later become much more salient, and these sentences reveal that the report's authors once again had problems placing the issue in their prefabricated frame of "ethnic and gender violence". The passage reads: "A large number of women became pregnant as a result of rape during the genocide. Pregnancies and childbirth among extremely young girls who were raped have also posed health problems for these mothers. The 'pregnancies of the war,' 'children of hate,' 'enfants non-desirés' (unwanted children) or 'enfants mauvais souvenir' (children of bad memories) as they are known, are estimated by the National Population Office to be between 2,000 and 5,000. Health personnel report that some women have abandoned their children or even committed infanticide, while others have decided to keep their children. In some cases, the mother's decision to keep the child has caused deep divisions in the family, pitting those who reject the child against those who prefer to raise the child." However, there were other cases, and the report leaves it open how to weigh the two versions and which one better characterized the situation of mothers and children in post-war Rwanda: "In others, the child is being raised without problems within the community." In other parts of the text, general problems emanating from the conflict for men and women, girls and boys, parents and children are also pressed into the gender frame, suggesting that these general problems were either the specific problems of rape victims, or predominantly burdens women would have to carry.[471]

The final part of the report, which deals with recommendations for the UN field mission in Rwanda, the ICTR and the Rwandan government, is most striking. Recommendations concerning the improvement of the situation of female rape victims only occupy a small part and are dealt with in a cursory way. The overwhelming majority of recommendations is dedicated to the advocacy of punitive measures against rapists and the facilitation of testimonies by rape victims in court. The recommendation addressed to the ICTR specify that "[t]he International Tribunal must fully and fairly investigate and prosecute sexual violence. Rape, sexual slavery and sexual mutilation should be recognized and prosecuted, where appropriate, as crimes against humanity, genocide crimes, or war crimes." Then the authors point out that "the International Tribunal must step up its efforts to integrate a gender perspective into its investigations. Previous investigative methodology and procedures,

471 For example, the fragments dealing with heritage problems arising from the fact that most genocide victims had not been able to designate heirs to their property or had just disappeared and could therefore not be declared dead.

which have failed to elicit rape testimonies, must be amended.[472] In particular, the Tribunal must ensure that the issue of violence against women is treated with the same gravity as other crimes against humanity within its jurisdiction." Finally, Human Rights Watch issued a clear message to the public and the ICTY as to how precisely it expected the ICTR to ease the fate of rape victims, who, according to the report, remained deprived of the retribution they demanded for their torturers. "Existing indictments should be amended, where appropriate, to ensure that rape, sexual slavery and sexual mutilation charges are brought. If need be, further investigation should be conducted by the Tribunal investigators to collect information on sexual violence previously overlooked." This also would prove a very influent frame at a later stage – the allegation that firstly, there had been large-scale gender violence of a specific character, which, secondly, had been "overlooked" by the tribunal (despite the fact, that the tribunal had, as HRW admitted in the report, a special "Sexual Assault Committee") and that, thirdly, indictments did not comprise gender-related charges. Such crimes would therefore require more intense investigation and their legal categorisation would have to be altered in order to include rape and related violations in the jurisdiction of the ICTR. It is worth mentioning that at the time, such crimes could already be prosecuted by the ICTR, since rape surely entails "causing severe bodily harm" (which can be an element of genocide)[473], whereas enslavement, torture and rape were already included in the definition of crimes against humanity[474] and, if committed against protected persons during a war, "outrages upon personal dignity, in particular humiliating and degrading treatment, rape, enforced prostitution and any form of indecent assault" also were part of the war crimes definition in article 4 of the ICTR statute.[475]

In late September of that year, The New York Times climbed upon the bandwagon, printing a large report about mothers who had given birth to children after being raped and were now "struggling to care for children fathered by their tormentors, often the same men who killed the women's entire families." The highly emotional and strongly personalized report also quoted the Human Rights *Shattered Lives* report, but it went much further. Where HRW had only claimed

---

472 It remains unclear what HRW intended to indicate here, since there hardly was any "previous investigative methodology" at the ICTR. The Akayesu Trial was the first trial the ICTR conducted.

473 Art. 2 of the ICTR statute. See: UNSC Resolution 955 (1994), adopted by the Security Council at its 3453rd meeting, on 8 November 1994.

474 Art. 3 of the ICTR statute, op cit.

475 Article 4 of the ICTR statute, dealing with violations of Article 3 common to the Geneva Conventions and of Additional Protocol II. op. cit.

that some women had been killed after being raped,[476] The New York Times now found that "almost all of the women were raped after witnessing the deaths of their loved ones."[477] The main frames of the report were identical to the ones used in the HRW report. Women appeared as the poor victims of ethnicized and gendered violence, and the whole conflict was presented according to the "Hutu-Tutsi" cleavage, but elements that did not fit into this frame and had been mentioned by Human Rights Watch were now omitted. The article gained more sharpness and provided a clear and unambiguous message to the reader, confronting him with a Manichean picture where Hutu rapists were on the bad side and raped Tutsi women and their innocent children were on the good side. The reportage strongly emphasized a frame that had only played a marginal role in the HRW report. It was the trauma of the mothers, the rejection of their babies (partly by themselves and by their families and friends), and their social stigmatisation.

Until then, no media report had explicitly demanded the ICTR to undertake particular legal steps relating to sexual violence in Rwanda. The Human Rights Watch report had been the first to advocate gender-related investigations and a change of prosecutorial strategy. At the time when it was published, Richard Goldstone headed the Office of the Prosecutor in The Hague and in Arusha. He had drafted the first indictment against Jean-Paul Akayesu and pressed for his extradition to the ICTR. But in October 1996, Canadian lawyer Louise Arbour replaced him. Back in 1996, Arbour was known in Canada, but she had no international standing. As a member of the Ontario appeals court, she had signed a verdict which forbade using the sexual past of a rape victim as an argument for a rapist's defence and had given prisoners the right to vote. These decisions had built her image in Canada, but, according to press coverage from Canada at the time, it had been US support that had ultimately assured her nomination by the Security Council.[478] Nine days after she had taken over duties from Goldstone, the Akayesu trial started, prepared on the basis of Goldstone's indictment and by an OTP, which was far from being a professional office and an efficient institution. Ten days after the trial had started, The New York Times ran another heart-rending story about Rwandan rape victims, who struggled with the ignorance of their government and were scared by the internationally

476 "These crimes were frequently part of a pattern in which Tutsi women were raped after they had witnessed the torture and killings of their relatives and the destruction and looting of their homes. According to witnesses, many women were killed immediately after being raped." Human Rights Watch: Shattered Lives, op. cit.

477 James C. McKinley Jr.: "Legacy of Rwanda Violence: The Thousands Born of Rape." The New York Times 23.9.1996.

478 Cruvellier, le tribunal des vaincus, 35-37.

brokered return of (Hutu) refugees from their camps in Zaire to Rwanda.[479] The article repeats most of the earlier frames on rape in Rwanda, but it also adds some new elements to the pre-existing ones, elucidating the role of men in Rwandan society and shedding new light on the issue of refugee returns. What is more relevant for the purpose of this chapter is the way statistics are dealt with. Generally, statistical accounts about rape, "children of bad memories" (as children born out of rape are frequently labelled) were then based on the results of a survey, which was carried out in 1994 and 1995 in Kigali and seven other prefectures among 304 women. The percentages retrieved from the survey were then extrapolated; according to the results, 15,700 women had been raped during the conflict, of whom 10,000 had become pregnant, 1,100 had given birth to children, and 5,200 had undergone abortions. These numbers were published by *médecins sans frontières* in 1995 and taken over by The New York Times in the article from May 15, 1995. In 1995, Human Rights Watch estimated the number of children born from rape in its *Shattered Lives* report to 2000 to 5000, basing these estimates on information from the Rwandan National Population Office and a UN report. It then assumed that statistically, 100 rapes lead to one pregnancy, the number of raped women in Rwanda in 1994 amounting to between 250,000 and 500,000, indicating that these numbers seemed exaggerated. They were in stark contradiction to the estimate of 15,700 by a *Reporters Without Borders* report of 1995. The New York Times story from October 1996 no longer reflected Human Rights Watch's own hesitation concerning the 250,000 to 500,000 estimate, instead it claimed that "more than 250,000 women" had been raped during the genocide. The author Elisabeth Royte, a writer who later became famous for books popularizing scientific and natural issues, did not realize how much her own assumptions about the events in Rwanda contradicted the statistics which she used for illustrating them. At one point, she claimed that "the country had become 70 per cent female, 60 per cent of whom were widows." Given an 85 to 15 relation between Hutu and Tutsi, even the elimination of all Tutsi women from Rwandan society could not have caused a situation in which 60 per cent of all women were widows. So either the Manichean divide between Tutsi and Hutu had not been that sharp (and more Hutu than Tutsi had been killed during the conflict) or the percentage of widows had to be lower than indicated by Royte.[480] As

479 Elisabeth Royte: "The outcasts." The New York Times Magazine, 19.10.1996.

480 Even in case of the elimination of the total Tutsi population, the percentage of widows within the overall female population of postwar Rwanda could (given, that women constituted 70% of the population) only amount to a maximum of 40%.

emotional as her account was, it neither formulated any recommendations for the ICTY, nor did it suggest steps to be undertaken by the ICTR. The New York Times coverage on the rape issue was addressed to a wide audience; it was, to put it into the language of lobby analysis, rather "noise" than "voice".[481] But it coincided with a first targeted intervention by a coalition of human rights organisations, which was much more "voice" than "noise". In August 1996, the "Coalition for Women's Human Rights in Conflict Situations" (hereinafter as the *Coalition*), filed a first *amicus curiae* brief to Richard Goldstone.[482] It did not cause any detectable reaction.

This changed dramatically in spring 1997, after Goldstone had left the post of chief prosecutor. In March, the *Coalition* filed another brief, this time to the new chief prosecutor, Louise Arbour. Hillary Clinton subsequently travelled to Arusha with her daughter Chelsea, who attended a workshop on sexual violence organized by Louise Arbour.[483] The *Coalition's* letter contained a number of references to legal sources and UN documents, illustrating the need to address gender-specific violence. Then, it directed a clear request to the tribunal:

> "Accordingly, *amici* call upon the Trial Chamber to exercise its supervisory authority, under the Tribunal Statute and the Rules, to call upon the Prosecutor to amend the indictment against Jean-Paul Akayesu to charge rape or other serious acts of sexual violence as crimes within the competence of the Tribunal; evaluate whether to supplement the record on such charges either through calling its own

---

481 "Noise" describes lobby action addressed to a wide and disperse audience, which aims at changing public attitudes toward an issue, whereas "voice" describes approaches targeted to specific, precisely defined groups and decision-makers, which avoid the public and try to bring about changes in a critical juncture of the decision-making process. See: Mendell, Margarite: "Empowerment. From Noise to Voice." *Universitas Forum*, Vol. 2, No. 1, September 2010. http://www.universitasforum.org/index.php/ojs/article/view/50/194
Beyers, Jan: "Voice and Access. Political Practices of European Interest Associations." *European Union Politics*, June 2004 vol. 5 no. 2, 211-240.

482 The *amici* briefs are not published on the ICTR website. The main one, filed later, can be retrieved from the Coalition website: http://www.womensrightscoalition.org/site/advocacyDossiers/rwanda/Akayesu/amicusbrief_en.php
The Coalition website now seems to be inoperative. Our attempts to obtain more information from the Coalition were unsuccessful. We managed to contact Binaifer Nawrojee, but did not get any further information from her. The information about the 1996 letter to Goldstone can be found in: Van Schaack, Beth: "Engendering Genocide: The *Akayesu* Case Before the International Criminal Tribunal for Rwanda." *Santa Clara University School of Law Legal Studies Research Papers Series. Working Paper* No. 08-55, July 2008 (Revised 9.11.2008), 9-11. http://papers.ssrn.com/sol3/papers.cfm?abstract_id=1154259

483 Moghalu, Rwanda's Genocide, 60-61, 65.

> witnesses pursuant to Tribunal Rule 98, or through calling upon the Prosecutor to consider supplementing the investigation and/or evidence in this case; examine why none of the indictments issued thus far have included charges of rape or other forms of sexual assault, despite reliable reports documenting widespread rape and other forms of sexual violence committed by the Hutu as part of the widespread and genocidal violence, and, thereby, indicating the availability of probative evidence."[484]

This intervention amounted to nothing less than either to incline the prosecution to include charges of rape as counts of genocide in the indictment against Akayesu, or, if the prosecution would refuse, to get the trial chamber to impose such a change upon the prosecution. It is worth mentioning that the trial was already in progress, and, as the *Coalition* had rightly pointed out, until then no gender-related charges had been included. Neither the existing indictment, nor the *Coalition*'s *amicus* brief alleged that Akayesu himself had raped someone or aided or abetted others to rape. Actually, NGO reports and testimonies before the court had confirmed that women in Taba had been raped during the conflict and that some of the victims had been raped even in the *bureau communal* of the mayor. As Cruvellier emphasizes, the Akayesu Trial was based on witness testimonies. No documents linked Akayesu to crimes. The indictment was built on two pillars: Witness testimonies, many of which were inconclusive, contradictory and vague[485], and Akayesu's official position as mayor. During the trial, his defence counsellors were eager to diminish his actual power and responsibility as a mayor, shifting the blame to Interahamwe gangs from outside the municipality and radical local politicians who allegedly sidelined Akayesu, whereas the prosecution (and the *Coalition* in its brief) tried to present Akayesu as the one who actually wielded power in Taba and controlled the situation. Only in the latter case could he be held accountable for the atrocities, which took place in his presence. Only then would he be punished for allowing the genocide to happen in Taba, and for failing to protect the victims. What the *Coalition*'s brief intended was therefore not to hold Akayesu accountable for rape as such, but to prosecute him for not only tolerating murder and torture in a genocidal situation, possibly aiding and abetting it and for failing to punish the perpetrators, but to hold him accountable for tolerating, aiding and abetting a specific element of genocide – rape and sexual mutilation. Here, the *Coalition* went even further than Human Rights Watch, which, in its *Shattered Lives* report, had demanded to prosecute rape as a crime against humanity. The

---

484 Coalition for Women's Human Rights in Conflict Situations: Amicus Brief Respecting Amendment of the Indictment and Supplementation of the Evidence to Ensure the Prosecution of Rape and Other Sexual Violence within the Competence of the Tribunal.

485 Combs, Fact-Finding Without Facts, 257-260.

Coalition additionally wanted it to be treated as an element of genocide: "In addition, the Prosecutor should consider charging Akayesu with rape as an act of genocide pursuant to Article 2(2)(b), (c) and (d) of the Statute."[486]

The brief states explicitly that "Akayesu is criminally responsible for this violence under Article 6(1) and 6(3) of the Statute", a sentence in opposition with the presumption of innocence. The authors of the brief realized that in the final part of their conclusions in which they stated: "In sum, *amici* cannot purport to judge whether the evidence in the record is sufficient to establish the guilt of Jean-Paul Akayesu for rape and other sexual violence in the Taba Commune" (...) "There is unquestionably sufficient evidence before the Prosecutor and the Trial Chamber to prosecute Jean-Paul Akayesu on charges of rape."

The Frames of the Prosecution

While The New York Times articles and the Human Rights Watch campaign had probably increased public awareness of the rape issue in Rwanda in 1994, the *Coalition*'s intervention considerably raised the awareness of a few key decision-makers at the ICTR. Shortly afterwards, Arbour responded to the *Coalition* letter from The Hague. She informed the *Coalition* that the trial prosecutors had been instructed to amend the indictment in light of the newly discovered evidence.[487] This exchange of letters took place during the first phase of the trial, when the prosecution presented its evidence. Arbour and her collaborators waited until the end of the prosecution case to apply for leave to amend the indictment in order to include the rape charges.

In the new indictment, several additional charges were included, all of which concerned sexual violence, which was now treated as a crime against humanity. Especially the events at the bureau communal were now widely exposed and described in detail. Since Akayesu was the mayor in charge and wielded a position of power and authority in his municipality at the time of these events, and since he had been present when women were being raped and abused, he must have known about these acts and had not prevented them, the prosecution argued now. "By virtue of his presence during the commission of the sexual violence, beatings and murders and by failing to prevent the sexual violence, beatings and murders, Jean-Paul Akayesu encouraged these

486 Coalition Brief, ibid.

487 Letter from the OTP to the Coalition, 30.7.1997. Retrieved from: http://www.womensrightscoalition.org/site/advocacyDossiers/rwanda/Akayesu/Akayesu_970630.pdf

activities."[488] The OTP did not amend the genocide charges against Akayesu with rape as genocide, as the *Coalition*'s brief had requested; it included the rape charges in crimes against humanity.[489]

The judges accepted her motion and postponed the trial until the end of October, in order to allow the parties to adapt to the new situation and to enable Akayesu to plead to these new charges. The decision amounted to a prolongation of the prosecution case. A week before the trial resumed, the *Coalition* sent another brief to the ICTR. In the meantime, members of the *Coalition* had met with Arbour, who had declared to revise all current indictments in order to find out whether sexual charges could be included.[490] Now, the *Coalition* asked the OTP to reform its witness protection and Sexual Assault Bureau in order to ensure more security for rape victims.

When the trial resumed and the prosecution called additional witnesses to substantiate the charges added to the amended indictment, The New York Times published another article at issue, whose author, James McKinley, had already previously dealt with genocide orphans. This time, however, the testimony of a rape victim only served as the graphic introduction to a harsh critique of the ICTR, which was described as a tribunal tormented by intrigue, administrative inability, corruption and nepotism, unable to advance reconciliation in Rwanda because of its cumbersome proceedings and the slow pace of its first trial.[491] Readers now learned that Akayesu had been charged with "ordering rape and sexual mutilation of Tutsi women" and a courageous witness had testified in the trial about "how militiamen acting on Mr. Akayesu's orders raped and killed the three Tutsi women." [492] The frame presenting prosecution witnesses as courageous and brave – opposite a defiant and arrogant accused –, which emerged from the article was a popular frame often used by journalists once trials had progressed and were delving into the details of evidence. The frame was typical for a trial stage, which was difficult to transform into thrilling coverage. The same frame emerged in the Milošević Trial before the ICTY,

488 *The pros. vs. Akayesu*, ICTR-96-4-I.

489 Van Schaack argues that a formal inclusion of rape in genocide was not necessary, since "causing bodily harm" was already part of the genocide definition of the ICTR statute. Van Schaack, Engendering, 12.

490 NGO Coalition On Women's Human Rights In Conflict Situations: Witness Protection, Gender and the ICTR. Letter to Justice Louise Arbour, Chief Prosecutor of the ICTY and ICTR. 17.10.1997

491 James C. McKinley Jr.: "On 1994 Blood Bath in Rwanda, Tribunal Hews to a Glacial Pace." The New York Times 21.11.1997.

492 Ibid.

when the initial media coverage about the duel between a self-confident and energetic female prosecutor and "the butcher of the Balkans" had expired.[493]

The Frames of the Trial Chamber

On September 2, 1998, the trial chamber issued its verdict. A day before, the *Coalition* issued a short press release, claiming that testimony had emerged from the trial about "Akayesu's prominent role in the rapes" and expressing hope that "the Akayesu decision will hopefully lead to further prosecution for crimes of sexual violence by the ICTR."[494] A verdict including charges of sexual violence would be a milestone for international criminal justice, the *Coalition* argued. The next day, the milestone was achieved. Jean-Paul Akayesu was found guilty on almost all charges, except for the ones concerning war crimes, and including the ones linking rape to genocide and crimes against humanity. His main crime had been, that "he did not attempt to prevent killings of Tutsi. Whether he had the power to do so is not at issue, as he never even tried and as there is evidence establishing beyond a reasonable doubt that he consciously chose the course of collaboration with violence against Tutsi rather than shielding them from it."[495] The judges went on: "The Accused, having had reason to know that sexual violence was occurring, aided and abetted (...) acts of sexual violence, by allowing them to take place on or near the premises of the *bureau communal* and by facilitating the commission of such sexual violence through his words of encouragement in other acts of sexual violence which, by virtue of his authority, sent a clear signal of official tolerance for sexual violence, without which these acts would not have taken place."

With regard to rape and sexual violence, the Chamber underscored that in its opinion, they constituted genocide "in the same way as any other act as long as they were committed with the specific intent to destroy, in whole or in part, a particular group, targeted as such." With respect to the legal construction of rape as a count of genocide rather than merely crimes against humanity, the chamber fully followed the line of the *Coalition*'s *amicus* brief. The trial chamber sentenced him to life imprisonment, a verdict which was sustained on appeal in 2001. Akayesu was transferred to Mali, where he is currently serving his sentence. Despite his relatively low position and the fact that the next accused

---

493 Bachmann, Framing the Trial of the Century, op. cit.

494 Coalition for Women's Human Rights in Conflict Situations. Rwanda, verdict in the case of Jean-Paul Akayesu. September 1, 1998. http://www.womensrightscoalition.org/site/newsReleases/1998-9-rwanda_en.php

495 *The pros. vs. Akayesu,* ICTR-96-4-I, Judgment.

appearing before the judges would be Rwanda's former Prime Minister, Jean Kambanda, Akayesu became a synonym of a *génocidaire* for the public. As Cruvellier recalls, people in the streets of Arusha tended to point at the UN vehicles transporting suspects to trial and say that "another Akayesu" was on his way to the court.[496]

The *Coalition* and other members of the international Human Rights community celebrated the verdict as a victory for women's rights. The *Coalition*'s press release after the verdict stated: "The victory that the Akayesu judgment and sentencing represent was hard won. When Akayesu was first charged in 1996, the 12 counts in his indictment did not include sexual violence, despite documentation of the widespread rape during the genocide in general and in his commune in particular. The charges of rape were only added to the Akayesu indictment mid-trial, following concerted pressure by non-governmental organisations and an amicus curiae brief filed by this *Coalition* in May 1997." Human Rights Watch "applauded" the Rwanda rape verdict and claimed that "history was made today". The press release was almost identical to the one the *Coalition* had issued. And HRW claimed the verdict a victory for NGO-pressure on the ICTY, too. "Under pressure from Rwandan and international rights groups, the Office of the Prosecutor finally amended the charges against Akayesu to include sexual violence in June 1997."[497] In 2001, the ICTR's appeals chamber dismissed Akayesu's motion for appeal in a final ruling, which dealt mostly with legal and procedural matters and did not create any new frames about the events described above in this chapter.[498]

What Powerful Frames Can Achieve

It would be too easy and one-dimensional to assume that international NGOs such as the *Coalition* and Human Rights Watch had actually been the only external players to successfully influence the prosecution and the trial chamber and that the inclusion of rape into the genocide verdict were due only to their actions. There also was a strong component of institutional interest involved in

496 Cruvellier, le tribunal des vaincus, 55.

497 Human Rights Watch: "Human Rights Watch Applauds Rwanda Rape Verdict. Sets International Precedent for Punishing Sexual Violence as a War Crime" [sic]. 02.09.1998.

498 *The pros. vs. Akayesu IT-96-4-A*,, appeals judgment on 1.6.2001. Only the index can be derived from the ICTR website: http://www.unictr.org/Portals/0/Case%5CEnglish%5 CAkayesu%5Cdecisions%5Cindex.pdf
The whole text is available on the UNHCR's website: http://www.unhcr.org/refworld/ publisher,ICTR,,,4084f42f4,0.html

the chambers decisions: The ICTY dearly needed a verdict, and, given the tension between the ICTY and Rwanda and the pressure from the public, such a verdict could only be a guilty verdict. Nevertheless, the Akayesu case constitutes a striking example of efficient judicial lobbying, since all other factors, which probably could have contributed to the final outcome were comparatively weak. Given the low rank of the suspect, no important state interests were involved. And finally, even if there was an underlying interest of the Rwandan government (and from Rwandan public opinion) to have Akayesu convicted, it is unlikely that this would have triggered the prosecution to charge him and the judges to convict him precisely of rape as genocide, as requested by the *Coalition* and HRW. It is difficult to imagine that Akayesu be acquitted and set free, it is even more difficult to imagine, that his case be dismissed for not falling under the jurisdiction of the ICTR (in case the judges concluded that the conflict in Rwanda had not been a genocide), and it is also difficult to presume that Akayesu was convicted of rape as elements of genocide and crimes against humanity because of pressure from Rwanda or another government. There is no evidence to support such a claim.

However, a detailed comparison of the frames used by media and NGOs on one hand and by the prosecution and the judges on the other hand, reveals that the victory of human rights groups was not limited to the verdict only. The OTP and the trial chamber used a number of frames, which from today's perspective may appear as natural and inevitable, but were much less common and less generally accepted in the years following 1994.[499] Today, speaking of the events in Rwanda in 1994 in other terms than genocide can expose a person to accusations of negationism. But back in 1997 or 1998, before the respective rulings of the ICTY, the conflict was often described as a civil war, as indiscriminate killings, and a blood bath, where everyone fought against everyone, or even as an invasion or a war. As already mentioned earlier, The New York Times' frames presenting the conflict as ethnic violence between Hutu oppressors and Tutsi liberators were not universally accepted, as can be seen in Time Magazine's coverage of the conflict or the reports of Amnesty International, which both avoided putting blame and guilt on only one side of the conflict. When violence ended in Rwanda, women's conditions also could be framed in many different ways, as some of them had helped their husbands to commit genocide, had instigated crimes, whereas others had become victims of these crimes, observed them, had fled or taken advantage of the situation and

---

499 For example, it is difficult today to find a recent publication estimating the number of genocide victims lower than 800,000. At the time of the Akayesu trial, most sources spoke of about 500,000 victims.

improved their own social and material status. Women depicted as the poor and stigmatized victims of a genocide was one of an endless number of other possible frames, each of which was as true or untrue as any other, and the frame of the "rape victim" was neither more nor less representative of women's situation in post-war Rwanda, than the frame of the "refugee woman" or the "woman hero" (who had hidden potential victims or her own husband).

Nevertheless, the frames used by HRW, the *Coalition* and The New York Times were the ones to prevail over the ones used by Time Magazine and Amnesty International, and a comparison with the frames used in court clearly shows that they proved extremely influential. The prosecution and the trial chamber's frames collided with respect to the characterisation of the conflict as an "internal one", during which "Hutu soldiers and militia" had committed genocide against "Tutsi civilians" and raped Tutsi women. Both the prosecution and the chamber endorsed the HRW version, according to which a second cleavage had overlapped the conflict between both ethnic groups[500], one which divided Hutu men and Tutsi women and led to sexual violence, which was shaped either by ethnicity or gender. In a part of the trial chamber's judgment, the court declared to be satisfied that all women who had been raped in Taba had been Tutsi. This permitted the court to regard the rapes as part of an attempt to harm members of an ethnic group. By doing so, the court actually excluded the possibility of incidental, non-ethnic or simply private and non-political sexual violence in Taba. Both the prosecution and the chamber also rejected frames other than the one describing the conflict as an internal one, despite the considerable influence of external factors, like Uganda, the UN, or France.

It is not the intention of this chapter to prove that the trial chamber erred in its decision to convict Akayesu, since this is beyond the scope of our research. *The pros. vs. Akayesu* has been criticized for a lack of fairness and consequence by some authors, but this criticism is based on shortcomings in legal procedure and directed against (alleged) errors in law and facts, which have nothing to do with the rape-as-genocide issue.[501] However, it is our intention to show that from a multitude of possible frames, the prosecution and the trial chamber (and ultimately also the appeals chamber) picked exactly the same frames as were

500 The fact that the Twa, a third and very small group ethnic group, also inhabited Rwanda was never mentioned.

501 Cruvellier, 50-58, argues, that the court overestimated Akayesu's power during the criticial days in Taba, whereas Reyntjens criticizes the negligence of the prosecutor and the appeals chamber to take into account the alleged perjury committed by a crucial prosecution witness (protected witness BBB) and the possibility of a perjury conspiracy mounted by victims organisation *Ibuka*. See: Reyntjens, Ruling under a volcano, the chapter about the ICTR.

previously used by The New York Times, Human Rights Watch, and the *Coalition*. This is not really astonishing, given the support of human rights groups for the creation of the ICTR and their eagerness to fight impunity after violent conflicts and to internationalize criminal responsibility. This support did not end when the ICTR came into being. The prosecution case in *the pros. vs. Akayesu* rested on two pillars – on expert witnesses, who were expected to brief the judges on the general background, the history and the character of the conflict, and on crime-based witnesses, who were supposed to link the accused to specific crimes. The five expert witnesses the prosecution called all came from Western countries. Two were journalists, one was the Canadian commander of the blue helmets, Roméo Dallaire, whose task it had been to oversee the ceasefire agreement in 1993. One was Alison Des Forges, a Human Rights Acitivist and expert on Rwanda, who was under contract at Human Rights Watch. The second was Dr. Ronie Zachariah from *médecins sans frontières*, the organisation, which had published the first report about rape during the genocide. In their verdict, the chamber largely relied on their interpretations and frequently quoted their explanations when deciding whether Hutu and Tutsi were ethnic groups and the conflict could therefore constitute genocide. It is remarkable that the prosecution and the judges (who had to approve the prosecution witness list) apparently regarded Western testimonies concerning the situation in Rwanda as more reliable than evidence provided by local experts. The prosecution also called Western witnesses concerning the situation in and around Taba, although some of them could only describe the climate in the region and had had no contact with the accused. The strong reliance on Western expert witnesses confirms Combs' observations about international judges' inclination to regard Western witnesses as more trustworthy than local ones.[502]

The frames from the indictment and the verdict were previously used by HRW and The New York Times, but this does not mean that there was no difference in framing between the human rights organisation and the prosecution and judges. Prosecutors did not endorse the request of the *Coalition* to charge Akayesu with rape as genocide, and they refrained – in the same way the judges had – from any attempt to explain rape. Opposite to the HRW's *Shattered lives* report, no indications are given for the motives of rapists. Prosecutors and judges in *the pros. vs. Akayesu* were not guided or manipulated by external actors. They used their discretion to deviate from the frames, to which they had been exposed. This chapter should therefore not be read as a description of how external actors manipulated judges, interfered with the administration of justice

502 Combs, Fact-Finding Without Facts, 259.

or provoked a miscarriage of justice. Prosecutors don't act in a political and social vacuum, they are members of a society and they are open to a multitude of external influences. Judges seldom admit being influenced, since being independent and immune to interference is part of their professional ethics. Nevertheless, judges, trial chambers and courts are not totally detached from society and the mere evolution of jurisprudence demonstrates that they are open to value changes in society. External influence on judges is therefore inevitable, and isolating courts completely from any external influence would lead to outcomes contrary to social expectations about what justice is. If the norms applied by judges, are the result of societal value orientations, then judges must be exposed to these value changes, otherwise their verdicts and decisions would quickly cease to be understood, accepted and respected by the society, whose hierarchy of values they are supposed to reflect. Within this diffuse and often fuzzy path of socially accepted values, judges exercise their discretion when applying the law. Sometimes they may transgress this path, causing outrage, political dispute and professional criticism. But these exceptions are then discussed in public exactly because they are deviations from the rule, which stipulates that in general, jurisprudence flows in accordance with the current of social value change, not against it.

Since jurisprudence decides in many cases about the redistribution of scarce resources, power and recognition, it is only natural that social actors attempt to influence the application of the law by courts. From this perspective, judges' decisions to a certain extent also reflect the balance of power between important social and political groups, influential actors and political cleavages. In such a rationalist and political view, a judge acts as a mediator in conflicts, as a political referee, and it is in his best interest to solve these conflicts in a way that strengthens his authority. While social expectations pull him into a position close to the mainstream of social values, his own self-interest pushes him in the same direction. For these reasons, even judges who boast their independence and pretend to be immune against any external interference will be receptive to external signals, which inform them what society may expect from them. By doing so, they become open to the subtle external pressure of agents, who try to influence their decision by pretending that their interests, beliefs and convictions belong to the mainstream of social values, which prevails in society. This is the moment when courts become targets of lobby interests. Courts may be lobbied by diffuse and untargeted "noise"-campaigns in the media (which is the case when, after a dramatic and strongly mediatized crime, the public cries out for punishment) or by purposive and well-directed initiatives like "voice"-approaches (when protestors start to shout "guilty" in the court room, or demonstrate in front of the judges' apartments). An important access point for such "voice"-approaches is the possibility introducing *amicus curiae* démarches and to call witnesses in cooperation with the prosecution or the defence.

This is what Human Rights Watch and the *Coalition* did during the Akayesu trial. They used the trial of an individual suspect to advance their goal of turning international criminal tribunals into vehicles for the punishment (and possibly deterrence) of sexual violence against women in conflict situations. They applied a strategy, which prior to them had been used by the US civil rights movement and the South African anti-apartheid movement in order to delegitimize racial segregation. Some observers rejected that as judicial activism, which, as Moghalu has labelled it, "has brought the goals of the feminist movement under the umbrella of international legal protection."[503] But Moghalu is right in stipulating that in such a case, "it would be no different from the inclusion of the rights of other groups under the tent of international law." It is no novelty that lobby groups try to influence a court in order to further their goals and it was no novelty when this was achieved in *the pros. vs. Akayesu.* What actually is a novelty is the fact that they managed to do so not in a municipal court, but during an international trial. Until then, the jurisdiction of international tribunals was usually the result of interstate bargaining and reflected the lowest common denominator of state interests, which could sometimes be altered when bold judges exploited their discretionary power to the maximum. In the Akayesu trial, this lowest common denominator was surpassed by transnational legal activism, which achieved an outcome that would have been much more difficult and costly to obtain by using national access points and by lobbying national governments in order to increase their lowest common denominator. By instead lobbying the ICTR, they obtained a new legal concept, which was subsequently adopted by other trial chambers, inclining the OTP to alter other indictments (and include sexual violence charges) and which strongly influenced jurisprudence of other international criminal tribunals as well as municipal courts acting under universal jurisdiction. Students of European Integration may realize here that HRW and the *Coalition* applied a top-down approach for bringing about legal change, which is similar to the way transnational actors in the EU take advantage of the EU's system of multilevel governance. It is beyond the scope of our study to assess whether international criminal courts and their legal and institutional environment can be regarded as a multi-layered system of governance, but it certainly provides intriguing incentives for considering them as such.

---

503 Moghalu, Rwanda's Genocide, 83.

The Frames Concerning the Behaviour of Dutchbat in Srebrenica in July 1994

The attention and controversy caused by the fall of Srebrenica was practically unequalled during the violent breakdown of Yugoslavia. Similar to the events following the crash of the presidential airplane at Kigali airport in 1994, Srebrenica became a synonym for genocide, although the killings, which were later incriminated as genocide, took place after the city had already been conquered by units of the Bosnian Serb Army and were carried out outside the city. The controversies surrounding the events in July 1994 in and around the enclave mainly concern the questions of whether the fall of Srebrenica could have been prevented, whether the Dutch peacekeepers would have been able to prevent the events, whether they had behaved appropriately during and after the fall of the town, and whether they were in possession of information about an on-going massacre in and outside the town and had delivered the information to their superiors in The Hague, and, finally, how the government in The Hague had dealt with the information about the killings once it had reached The Hague. There were also other stakeholders with an interest in the framing of these events. The French government was one of them, since one of the controversial issues pertained to the role of French General Bernard Janvier, who had denied so-called "close air support" for Dutchbat, thus facilitating the advance of the Bosnian Serb unities which were closing in on the city. Due to the weak capabilities, Dutchbat had been equipped with, close air support by NATO was crucial for Dutchbat's ability to confront the attacking units efficiently. After the information about the killings following the fall of Srebrenica had caused outrage and public debates in several NATO countries, the French parliament instituted a special commission charged with investigating the involvement of Janvier and the French government in the events.

The second stakeholder interested in promoting specific interpretations about the events, was the UN, which was swiftly accused by the media, victims and survivor organisations of having "abandoned" the population of Srebrenica and having facilitated the killings. The UN commissioned an investigation and published a report on the events in 1999.[504] The third, and – from the perspective of this research – the most important stakeholder with an interest in shaping the public understanding of the events was the Dutch government. Its members and spokespersons commented on the events almost immediately after they had

504 Report of the Secretary General pursuant to General Assembly Resolution 53/35 "The Fall of Srebrenica". http://daccess-dds-ny.un.org/doc/UNDOC/GEN/N99/348/76/IMG/N9934876.pdf?OpenElement

taken place, and during the months and years that followed the fall of Srebrenica, several investigations were carried out either by individual politicians acting under official mandates, or by parliamentarian committees.

The Dutch Government's Frames Concerning Srebrenica

In July 1995, the Dutch government did not yet know about the fate of several thousand inhabitants of Srebrenica who had disappeared in buses, which had been delivered by the Bosnian Serb forces. This was due to the fact that the military command of the Dutch army withheld evidence from the government, which had emerged in the soldiers' debriefing. The Dutch government concentrated on the behaviour of its soldiers and whether there was evidence for misbehaviour or even criminal acts committed by Dutchbat. It avoided the attribution of guilt in legal terms and only "condemned" the Bosnian Serb attacks on the enclave, without formulating this condemnation in legal terms.

During the following months, more and more details surfaced, and the government came under public pressure to disclose more information and to take a stronger stance. In December 1995, the Dutch "Second Chamber" held a debate on the events, during which the government delivered more information. However, it only became apparent in 2002, when the Netherlands Institute for War Documentation (NIOD) published its final and very huge report, that the Army had had evidence of genocide already in summer of 1995. As a result, several ministers who had been members of the 1995 cabinet stepped down, triggering the collapse of the whole government. By then, the events following the fall of Srebrenica were widely regarded as genocide. During recent years, the Dutch government has frequently been accused of cowardice in Srebrenica and of covering up immoral actions of Dutchbat there. Survivors and relatives of survivors have sued the Netherlands in a Dutch court and claimed compensation. On July 5, 2011, a Dutch court, acting pursuant to a private lawsuit of Srebrenica survivors, sentenced the Dutch government for failing to protect the relatives of three Bosniac UN employees, who had been working for Dutchbat in July 1995. They had sued the Netherlands because Dutchbat officers had ordered their relatives to leave the Dutchbat compound in Potočari after the town had been conquered by units of the Bosnian Serb Army and occasional killings had been reported in the town. Until then, the Dutch government had rejected compensation claims by victims, shifting the blame to the UN, which had allegedly failed to provide Dutchbat with the support needed to carry out its mandate in Srebrenica.[505]

505 BBC News: Dutch state 'responsible for three Srebrenica deaths', 5.7.2011.

The official version of the events in the Netherlands, promoted on several occasions by the government, is contradictory and largely inconsistent, thus reflecting the deep division of the Dutch public in the interpretation of the events. The events are mostly described as Bosnian Serb genocide against the Muslim or Bosniac population of the enclave, and the actions of Dutchbat in July 1994 are regarded as weak, reluctant and even half-hearted. But at the same time, Dutchbat officers were given awards in public. The media described them as cowards who surrendered to the Serbs instead of protecting the population and fighting back, and many media outlets overtly sympathized with victims' organisations, criticizing the Dutch government and blaming the Dutch state for the fate of their relatives. But the Dutch media also published extensive stories about individual soldiers and officers, presenting them as victims suffering from post-traumatic stress disorder, self-reproach, feelings of guilt and inferiority as well as depression.

Yet for another reason, the Dutch government can be regarded as an important stakeholder in the juridical investigation about Srebrenica. The Hague is one of the most important hosts to international juridical institutions, and every Dutch government in the last decades did its best to uphold and raise the prestige of The Hague as a world capital of international law. All the recent Dutch governments have supported the establishment of international courts in The Hague and are very supportive of them. The Netherlands provided the court building and the detention facility for the ICTY where suspects are imprisoned awaiting trial and verdict. Many famous Dutch lawyers work at the tribunal (mostly as defence counsellors) and the media dedicate a lot of awareness to these tribunals' proceedings.

It is vital to establish the appropriate time frame for the analysis of the Dutch government's frames, which could have been channelled into prosecution and trial chamber frames. Since the frames from *the pros. vs. Krstić* are used here as the dependent variable, only Dutch government frames prior to the sentencing hearing can be used. General Radislav Krstić was arrested on December 2, 1998 and was held in custody until March 13, 2000, when his trial started. The trial chamber's judgment was issued on August 2, 2001, the appeals chamber rendered its judgment on April 19, 2004. If we intend to detect frames used by the Dutch government or other state institutions concerning Srebrenica in the Krstić indictments and judgments, we should examine the frames falling into the period prior to 2001 and 2004, which includes the frames used in the immediate aftermath of the fall of Srebrenica.

At that time, the Dutch government was not at all occupied with the fate of Srebrenica's inhabitants, mainly concentrating on the behaviour of its own troops. The first legal notions that were mentioned (in public and behind closed doors) concerned allegations about “withholding help from civilians”, “xenophobic behaviour of some of the Dutch soldiers” and “lack of medical help” for civilians. No one even spoke about war crimes or genocide due to the fact that the first reports about atrocities from soldiers were not handed over to the government by the military command.[506] In July 1995, the Dutch minister of defence spoke in Parliament about the “war crimes” committed and the alleged “forced removal of civilians from their homes” in Srebrenica. The minister spoke about “summary executions” (“standrechtelijke executies”), “war crimes”, and “human rights violations”.[507]

From today’s perspective, it may be striking that during the first days after the July events, government officials avoided casting blame on anyone. In their first reactions, government officials found that “there are no good and no bad guys there”, and that Srebrenica was “a humanitarian catastrophe” the Dutch troops could not deal with, since they were “let down by the UN.”[508] Only once was guilt attributed to “the Bosnian Serbs”, who “attacked safe areas” and other enclaves, a behaviour which “has to be condemned in the strongest possible way.”[509] The victims were mostly labelled as civilians, in some cases as “men”

506 This is a finding from the NIOD report. See: NIOD report, Srebrenica, vol. 6, 3003-8.

507 “Dutchbat heeft vele mensenlevens gered, maar niet kunnen voorkomen dat in Srebrenica de mensenrechten ernstig zijn geschonden. Het grootste deel van de bevolking van Srebrenica, volgens de jongste schatting van UNHCR 38 000 mensen, is met geweld van huis en haard verdreven. Hetstaat vast dat er oorlogsmisdaden zijn gepleegd, ook al valt door de beperkte waarnemingsmogelijkheden van Dutchbat-militairen weinig met zekerheid te zeggen over de schaal waarop. Zij hebben well de standrechtelijke executie van ten minste tien mannen kunnen vaststellen. Er moet rekening mee worden gehouden dat met het beschikbaar komen van nieuwe informatie, onder meer van blauwhelmen, ook andere oorlogsmisdadenaan het licht komen.“ (...) “De opluchting over de terugkeer van Dutchbat laat onverlet dat Bosnisch-Servische aanvallen op «veilige gebieden» in Bosnie¨ en de gedwongen evacuatie van de plaatselijke bevolking van Srebrenica, en nu ook Žepa, scherp moeten worden veroordeeld. De rechten van de mens zijn ernstig geschonden.“ Tweede Kamer der Staten-Generaal, Vergaderjaar 1994-1995, 22181, “De situatie in Joegoslavie¨ Brief van de minister van defensie aan de Voorzitter van de Tweede Kamer der Staten-Generaal.“ ’s-Gravenhage, 27 juli 1995.
http://www.sp.nl/service/dossiers/srebrenica/briefkabinet27795.pdf

508 Brief van de minister van defensie, op. cit. 27 juli 1995.
http://www.sp.nl/service/dossiers/srebrenica/briefkabinet27795.pdf

509 “De aanwezigheid van Unprofor was er van meet af aan vooral op gericht de Bosnische Servie¨ rs ervan teweerhouden de enclaves in te nemen“ (...) “De Bosnische Servie¨rs hadden in het voorjaar van 1993 gedreigd Srebrenica onder de voet te lopen“ (...) “Van meet af aan was duidelijk dat de enclave niet tegen een aanval van de Bosnische Servie¨ rs zou kunnen worden verdedigd.“ Brief van de minister van defensie... 27.7.1995

and "defenders of Srebrenica". Other categories were "local personnel" (lokale personeel), "the population of Srebrenica" (de bevolking van Srebrenica), which according to the source, suffered "in a way impossible to describe." Dutchbat soldiers were to a large extent described as "helpless bystanders" and witnesses.[510] The frame concerning the characteristics of Dutchbat would later undergo big changes, being replaced by the "cowardice frame", which, instead of emphasizing helplessness and victimhood, would then highlight reluctance, hesitance, xenophobia (toward the population of Srebrenica), and opportunism (toward the invaders). A first wave of criticism had come from the French government, whose members accused Dutchbat of having surrendered to the invaders without any important resistance. The statement caused outrage and inclined the Dutch government to take a firm stance backing its soldiers in the second half of July 1994.[511]

With respect to the context and the sources of the conflict which had led to the fall of Srebrenica and the subsequent events in July 1994, the Dutch government emphasized attempts of the "Bosnian Serbs" to conquer the enclave already in 1993. The underlying conflict was framed as an internal struggle between "Bosnian Serbs" and defenders of Srebrenica, under the involvement of external factors, such as NATO, UNPROFOR, and the UN. The possible involvement from the Republic of Serbia or other countries was not an issue at that time.

The events in Srebrenica became subject of a number of parliamentary enquiries by special commissions and a commission of the Ministry of Defence, which did not reveal any major shortcomings or errors. In 1996, the government charged the Netherlands Institute for War Documentation (Nederalandse Instituut voor Oorlogsdocumentatie, NIOD) with writing a report about Srebrenica. The report appeared in summer 2002 and revealed serious failures in the chain of command (information about crimes was not passed on), problems with the coordination of the with , the experience and preparation of the soldiers, and a lack of a feasible exit-strategy. Days after the 7000-page report had been published, two ministers, who had already been members of the cabinet back in 1994, resigned. This triggered a chain reaction and finally forced Prime Minister Wim Kock to go to the Queen and to propose her the resignation of the whole cabinet. NIOD and most of the foreign media were quite surprised by these events.

Between 1994 and 2002, the government had refrained from formulating any coherent interpretation of the events in Srebrenica in 1994, and had always

---

510 Brief van de minister van defensie, op. cit. 27.7.1995.

511 NIOD Report, 2374-2376.

postponed such statements until the completion of the NIOD report. Once NIOD had published its report, the government endorsed it unconditionally. For the new cabinet, accepting the report was much easier, since it did not involve any direct political responsibility, which the cabinet under Kok had taken over when stepping down. There was yet another reason why the acceptance of the NIOD report no longer bore any political risk. Its volume of 7000 pages made it a perfect object for cherry-picking. Whatever someone wanted to prove, invoke or illustrate, it could be found in the NIOD report. Subsequently, the report was used in ICTY trials in several cases by the prosecution and the defence.[512]

Although several ministers had deemed the report embarrassing enough to step down in 2002, all subsequent prime ministers were eager to underline that the Netherlands were not guilty of the events in Srebrenica and therefore did not need to apologize for them. They too could point to the NIOD report. Such statements were usually accompanied by confessions about the failure of the international community, which had let down the population of Srebrenica and the UN "safe haven". Dutch responsibility was placed in such a context – the Netherlands had failed not individually, but together with the UN and other countries, and were therefore as responsible as the others.[513] The Dutch

512 Karen Meirik: "Controversial Srebrenica Report Back on Table. Dutch report on events surrounding the massacre is so broad that both prosecution and defence witnesses are using it." IWPR report 9.11.2005.

513 "Toenmalig minister-president Kok heeft op 16 april 2002 gesteld dat de ernst van de bevindingen van het Niod, bevindingen die betrekking hebben op een periode waarin opeenvolgende kabinetten van uiteenlopende samenstelling verantwoordelijkheid hebben gedragen, niet zonder politieke consequenties mogen blijven. Daarom heeft het kabinet zijn ontslag aangeboden aan HM de Koningin. Daarbij heeft de minister-president de volgende verklaring publiekelijk afgelegd. «Het NIOD-rapport is volstrekt duidelijk over de vraag wie verantwoordelijk moet worden gesteld voor de val van Srebrenica en de daarop volgende massamoord: de schuld daarvoor ligt bij de Bosnische Serviërs, in het bijzonder bij generaal Mladić. Mladić is een oorlogsmisdadiger. Hij en andere verantwoordelijken mogen niet ontkomen aan berechting voor het Joegoslavië-tribunaal hier in Den Haag. De internationale gemeenschap is tekortgeschoten in het bieden van voldoende bescherming aan de mensen in de zogenaamde safe areas. Daarmee is ook de Nederlandse regering als lid van die internationale gemeenschap tekortgeschoten. De consequenties die thans worden getrokken zijn níet verbonden aan één specifieke gebeurtenis of één specifiek moment, maar vloeien voort uit de opeenstapeling van tekortkomingen gedurende verschillende kabinetsperiodes. Met dit besluit wordt integraal verantwoordelijkheid genomen voor het gevoerde beleid gedurende een reeks van jaren. Nederland neemt nadrukkelijk níet de schuld op zich voor de gruwelijke moord op duizenden Bosnische moslims in 1995. Wél wordt op deze wijze de politieke medeverantwoordelijkheid van Nederland voor de situatie waarin dit kon gebeuren zichtbaar gemaakt. «De

government extended financial support to victims and supported the commemoration of the events in the town. It also pledged to grant asylum to survivors of Srebrenica who had arrived in the Netherlands after 1995. This pledge has often been a subject of controversy in parliament, when members of the opposition accused subsequent cabinets of deporting people who had survived the massacre.[514]

After the NIOD report, a new frame emerged whose constitutive elements can be derived from statements of government officials and cabinet members in public and in meetings of parliamentary committees, which tried to sort out what had gone wrong in 1994.

According to this new frame, the killings during and after the fall of Srebrenica could neither have been predicted, nor anticipated by anyone. The killings were now labelled as "infamies committed by Mladić", a reaction to the indictment of Mladić by the ICTY and the on-going hunt for the former head of the Bosnian Serb military.[515] The events of 1995 were labelled as "mass murder" and "war crimes" and "cruel murder". In many other documents and speeches, they are also called "drama" and "aggression".[516] Dutchbat would not have been able to prevent them. The government claimed that "Dutchbat had fulfilled its task honourably and painstakingly."[517]

Cabinet members speaking before a parliamentary committee only used to mention "Mladić" and "Karadžić" as perpetrators linked to the events in Srebrenica. In a speech before his abdication, Prime Minister Kok called them "mass murderers". He said explicitly, "it is of greatest interest to declare them guilty in the legal sense of the word, too." He called both "guilty" and urged to judge them by the ICTY together with others responsible for "the mass

---

internationale gemeenschap» is anoniem en kan niet op een zichtbare manier verantwoordelijkheid nemen tegenover de slachtoffers en nabestaanden van Srebrenica. Ik kan – en doe – dat wél.» Het kabinet ziet geen aanleiding kanttekeningen bij deze overwegingen te plaatsen." Tweede Kamer, kamerstuk 28506, 137, 138.

514 The pledge to facilitate the immigration of Srebrenica survivors did not incline the Dutch authorities to remove some of the obstacles for Bosnian journalists to attend the ICTY trials connected to the events in Srebrenica. See: Thomas Verfuss: "Trying Poor Countries' Crimes in a Rich City. The Problems of the Press from the Former Yugoslavia." *Journal of International Criminal Justice* 2004, 509-515.

515 The first indictment against Mladić dates back from July 25, 1994 and had been drafted and confirmed less than two weeks after the fall of Srebrenica. See: *the pros. vs. Mladić* IT-09-92.

516 Tweede Kamer, kamerstuk 28 506, Enquête Srebrenica, nr. 8 Lijst van vragen en antwoorden, 27 februari 2003, 131-133. www.tweede-kamer.nl

517 "De regering is met de commissie van mening dat de leden van Dutchbat III hun taak naar eer en geweten hebben uitgevoerd." Tweede kamer, kamerstuk 28506, 133.

murder".[518] His successor, Prime Minister Jan Peter Balkenende, individualized guilt in the same way. In a speech during the plenary debate of the Tweede Kamer in 2003, which was entirely dedicated to the Srebrenica enquiry, he mentioned Mladić and Karadžić as the culprits, but also added that "the Serbs, the Bosnian Serbs" had "a role" in the events, stopping short of attributing guilt to them.[519] Defence Minister Henk Kamp was much more emotional when he addressed the chamber during the same session.

"The Prime Minister and the Minister of Foreign Affairs commemorated the sad fate of the victims of the Bosnian Serbs' aggression during the days when the Srebrenica enclave fell. More than 7,500 are missing, most likely they are dead, of which 6,000 were murdered in unimaginable mass executions. A mass murder in 1995 in Europe. These events, which are so repugnant for victims and their relatives and others involved, and the inability of our country to stop the aggressor, shall always remain a part of our history."[520] The minister extensively elaborated on the situation and dilemmas of Dutchbat in Srebrenica in July 1995, arguing that conditions on the ground went far beyond simple divides between good and bad. His speech mentioned the seldom-acknowledged fact that "Muslim fighters" had attacked villages around the city in order to confiscate food, and that Serb villagers had been killed during these raids. Their aim had been, according to Kemp, to "keep the Bosnian Serb Army busy, so that she could not be used in other parts of Bosnia." Kemp was probably the only person who attempted to provide a rationalisation of the killings by suggesting that they might have been a retaliation of Bosnian Serb units against the raids of these "Muslim fighters". "Thousands of Muslim fighters of the 28th division, who remained in the enclave against the agreement, also did not care about

518 Kok's speech can be derived from the electronic archive of the Dutch Broadcasting Foundation NOS (Nederlandse Omroep Stichtung) on: http://nos.nl/archief/2004/nieuws/index.html#@http://nos.nl/archief/2004/nieuws/dossiers/val_kabinet/2002/april/1604_toespraak.html. It was held in the *Tweede Kamer* on 16.4.2002.

519 Prime Minister Balkenende's speech during the *Tweede Kamer* debate about the results of the NIOD report: Tweede Kamer, vergaderingen, behandeling van het Rapport van de Enquêtecommissie Srebrenica (kamerstuk 28506) (debat met de regering). Vergadering van 17 juni 2003.

520 "De minister-president en de minister van Buitenlandse Zaken hebben stilgestaan bij het treurige lot van de slachtoffers van de Bosnisch-Servische agressie in de dagen na de val van de enclave Srebrenica. Meer dan 7500 vermisten, hoogstwaarschijnlijk doden, van wie er 6000 bij onvoorstelbare massa-executies zijn vermoord. Een massamoord in 1995 in Europa. De afschuwelijke gebeurtenissen voor slachtoffers en nabestaanden en andere betrokkenen en het onvermogen van ons land om de agressor een halt toe te roepen, zullen altijd onderdeel van onze geschiedenis blijven." Minister Kamp during the plenary session of 17.6.2003, Tweede Kamer, vergaderingen (kamerstuk 28506).

Dutchbat. At given times, they carried out their actions outside the enclave in order to restock and to hit Serb targets. The mountainous, wooded landscape between the fairly isolated Dutchbat observation points provided good opportunities for doing that. NIOD has convincingly shown that it was a considerable strategic aim of the Muslims to tie the Bosnian Serbs to the Eastern enclaves, so that their troops could not be used for the siege of Sarajevo. According to NIOD, this was an important reason for Mladić and his people to launch the attack on Srebrenica in July 1995. At that time, countless accounts were already being settled. While in the Netherlands the stereotypical picture of good and bad, of Muslims against Serbs, dominated the political and public opinion, the reality with which Dutchbat was confronted was much more contradictory."[521]

It is striking that in most statements of government officials, armed men who fought on behalf of the government of Sarajevo were described in religious terms ("the Muslims", the "Muslim fighters", the "Muslim men"), whereas victims remained without any religious, political or ethnic affiliation ("the victims of Srebrenica", "the population"). Alleged perpetrators were mostly described in ethnic and regional terms as "the Bosnian Serbs". Except for Kamp's contribution to the debate, there never was any attempt to explain or rationalize what was consequently called a "massacre". Even Kamp limited his explanation to the attack and the invasion of Srebrenica, but stopped short of giving any reasons why the invaders had carried out massacres of prisoners of war and civilians. The military explanation (to distract soldiers from Sarajevo)

521 "De duizenden moslimstrijders van de 28ste divisie die zich tegen de afspraken in ophielden in de enclave, trokken zich evenmin ook maar iets van Dutchbat aan. Op gezette tijden voerden zij acties uit buiten de enclave om voorraden aan te vullen of om Servische doelen te treffen. Het bergachtige, beboste terrein tussen de betrekkelijk geïsoleerde observatieposten van Dutchbat bood daarvoor alle mogelijkheden. Het NIOD heeft overtuigend aangetoond dat het een belangrijk strategisch doel van de moslims was om de Bosnisch-Servische troepen bij die oostelijke enclaves te binden, zodat deze troepen door de Bosnische Serviërs niet konden worden ingezet voor de belegering van Sarajevo. Voor Mladić en de zijnen was dat, aldus het NIOD, uiteindelijk een belangrijke reden om begin juli 1995 de aanval op Srebrenica in te zetten. Bovendien waren er tegen die tijd onderling talloze rekeningen te vereffenen.Terwijl in Nederland het stereotiepe beeld van goed en kwaad, de moslims tegenover de Bosnische Serviërs, de publieke en politieke opinie bleef domineren, ondervonden de Dutchbatters dat de werkelijkheid veel weerbarstiger was." Minister Kamp during the plenary session of 17.6.2003, Tweede Kamer, vergaderingen (kamerstuk 28506). The notion "28th division" should be understood as the 28th division of the Bosniac Army (loyal to the government in Sarajevo), "the agreement" refers to the ceasefire agreement in force during the attack on Srebrenica.

would not have been sufficient to explain that. The only element of his speech, which could give a hint about the attackers' motives, was the conjecture concerning "settling accounts" for previous raids into Serb villages.

What emerged from the debate about the NIOD report was basically a frame comprising the following elements: Dutchbat had found itself in a fight between two parties, "Muslim fighters" in the enclave, and attacking "Bosnian Serbs", for which the Dutch soldiers had not been prepared. Let down by the international community, they were overrun by the Serb attackers and had become helpless bystanders. Mladić and Karadžić were the ones to blame, whereas Dutchbat was innocent. The Netherlands, which had failed together with the international community, were responsible for not preventing the massacre, which had been in retaliation of earlier "Muslim" raids. This new frame filled the vacuum left by former governments' reluctance to explain the events in a coherent way. It was almost deprived of strong normative elements, except for the condemnation of Mladić and Karadžić.[522] Where other frames created strong divides between "good Muslims" (or Bosniacs), and "bad Serbs" (or Bosnian Serbs), between evil attackers and innocent victims, the official Dutch version refrained from attributing collective guilt to one side only – including the Dutch side. The frame was complex enough to blur responsibilities and dilemmas. For instance, it did not address the tricky question concerning the selection of people who were allowed to enter the Potočari compound, after the latter had become a shelter for civilians when Mladić's troops had taken over control of the town.[523] Both the government frames as well as the ones used by NIOD stopped short of labelling the events in and around Srebrenica as genocide. As Karen Smith points out, the omission was intentional and both the French parliament's commission investigating Srebrenica and its Dutch counterpart had decided to not use terms, which they regarded as reserved for the judiciary.[524]

---

522 This consensus between different actors in the Netherlands about Mladić and Karadžić as the main culprits of the situation in Srebrenica contributed strongly to the hardening of the Dutch position toward the integration of Serbia into the EU and allowed subsequent governments to justify their reluctance toward an EU membership of Serbia in public. See Thomas Sparrow-Botero's chapter on Serbia's EU accession and conditionality linked to ICTY compliance. This link also was confirmed in an interview with a high official of the Dutch Ministry of Foreign Affairs, responsible for EU affairs, which was carried out in The Hague in May 2012.

523 This dilemma had to be solved by the judges in the trial in July 2011, who concluded that Dutchbat had no right to send relatives of civil Bosnian Dutchbat employees out of the compound.

524 Smith, Karen E.: Genocide and the Europeans. Cambridge University Press 2010, 128-129.

Human Rights Watch's Frames

As usual, HRW's frames were much more blunt and unambiguous. In October 1995, HRW published a report entitled "The Fall of Srebrenica and the Failure of UN Peacekeeping", which put the main bulk of the blame onto the "Bosnian Serbs" and drew the origins of the conflict back to 1993, when the Bosnian Serb side had attempted to conquer the enclave for the first time. Where the Dutch government linked the "Muslim fighters' raids" to the atrocities committed after the fall of Srebrenica, HRW saw the fall of Srebrenica as an element of a Serb sponsored "ethnic cleansing campaign", which had been "typical of Bosnian Serb military conduct to date."

The report continued:

> "Abuses attending the occupation of the 'safe area' included the terrorisation of women, children and the elderly and the premeditated mass executions of men and boys. The trek through Bosnian Serb-controlled territory that men fleeing the enclave hoped would lead them to safety instead led to ambushes and executions of hundreds and possibly thousands of men in numerous locations. We have based our accounts of these atrocities on the testimony of survivors who have identified locations and sites of mass executions both within the Srebrenica region and in various areas stretching between Bosnian Serb-controlled and Bosnian government-controlled territory. We report on the mishandling of the crisis by the U.N.'s Bosnia peacekeeping force UNPROFOR — from the craven decisions of its field commanders prior to the fall of Srebrenica, to its apparent suppression and destruction of evidence of massive human rights abuses immediately after the fall of the 'safe area.' We also report on the Dutch Defence Ministry's 'mislaying' of a crucial list of missing Bosnian men and boys and its destruction of a video tape showing Bosnian Serb soldiers engaged in extrajudicial executions as Dutch U.N. troops looked on."[525]

For Human Rights Watch, the conflict about the enclave was a further step in Serb efforts to ethnically cleanse Bosnia, which had begun with the hostilities in Bosnia: "In April and May 1992, the Bosnian Serb army - with the active assistance of the Yugoslav Army and paramilitary groups from Serbia proper - began a drive to 'ethnically cleanse' all non-Serbian inhabitants from much of Bosnia. As part of its 'ethnic cleansing' campaign, Bosnian Serb forces used tactics such as siege warfare, systematic persecution involving widespread torture, murder, rape, beatings, harassment, *de jure* discrimination, intimidation, forced displacement of people, confiscation and destruction of property, and the destruction of cultural objects such as mosques and Catholic

525 Human Rights Watch: The Fall of Srebrenica and the failure of UN peace keeping." 15.10.1995.

churches. With the fall of Srebrenica and Žepa, Bosnian Serb forces have virtually completed the 'ethnic cleansing' of eastern Bosnia. The abuses perpetrated during the 'ethnic cleansing' of eastern Bosnia constitute war crimes and crimes against humanity as that term was defined at the Nuremberg trials and within the meaning of customary international law. Moreover, the fact that the abuses associated with 'ethnic cleansing' were 'committed with intent to destroy, in whole or in part, a national, ethnical, racial or religious group,' and that such acts were perpetrated systematically, that no one was held accountable for such crimes, and that they appear to have been premeditated in some cases, would indicate that the 'cleansing' of eastern Bosnia and of the Srebrenica 'safe area' in particular was part of a larger attempt by Bosnian Serb forces to commit genocide against the Bosnian Muslims and other non-Serbs."[526] Human Rights Watch identified two main culprits in the reports, the Bosnian Serbs, who were condemned for waging war, attacking the UN safe areas and committing genocide and crimes against humanity, and the UN for failing to stop them and to protect the enclaves efficiently. The Dutch government was blamed for neglecting and destroying evidence of the Bosnian Serbs' crimes. The report uses extremely emotional language and its authors side with witnesses and victims from within the enclave, whose statements are mostly left without further comment, whereas quotes from other actors are either used as proof of their bad intentions or their attempts to obfuscate the obvious. Statements about "Bosnian Serbs" are frequently embedded in a negative context and surrounded by emotional and derogatory adjectives. Dutchbat soldiers appear as helpless bystanders and victims of the Serb assault. Similarly to the Dutch governments frame, victims are described in religious categories (the "Muslims"), while alleged perpetrators are presented in ethnic terms ("Bosnian Serbs", "Bosnian Serb forces"). Raids against Serb-held villages from within the enclave are reported but trivialized, either by quoting witnesses claiming these raids were private initiatives and had been rejected by the population, or by claiming they had been necessary for bringing food into the town. The HRW report also rejects the Dutch interpretation of atrocities being committed in retaliation for the raids and sees the killings as cold-blooded and planned: "The July 1995 attack on the U.N.-declared 'safe area' of Srebrenica by Bosnian Serb forces was planned well in advance and abuses perpetrated after the fall of the enclave were systematic and well-organized." The formula anticipates elements of JCE as later used by the OTP. But the only alleged perpetrator whom the report mentioned by name was Ratko Mladić.

---

526 Human Rights Watch: The Fall of Srebrenica, op. cit.

HRW later returned to the Srebrenica topic. Two years after July 1995, Human Rights Watch launched a short-term campaign against impunity, which included press conferences in several Western capitals and the release of letters written by human rights activists to political leaders. HRW's executive director Kenneth Roth argued that the West's reluctance to bear the cost of apprehending suspects at large would undermine national reconciliation, because politicians like Mladić and Karadžić would continue to prevent refugees from returning to their homes and "undermine the peace process". The press release did not contain specific frames linked to the events in Srebrenica 1995, except for saying that "Srebrenica has become a symbol of the atrocities committed during the war in the former Yugoslavia and of the inaction of the international community. It is time for the international community, after having failed for far too long to stop the killing in Bosnia and Herzegovina, to ensure at least that the killers are brought to justice."[527] A few days later, SFOR troops tried to arrest several suspects who had been under confidential indictments, among them a senior police official of Republika Srpska, who had allegedly overseen several detention camps in the Prijedor region, and Simo Drljača, who was shot after he had fired on the troops who wanted to arrest him. Another suspect, the former director of the Prijedor hospital, Milan Kovačević, surrendered without resistance.[528] On July 11, The International Herald Tribune published a comment written by Kenneth Roth, which comprised several elements of the former press release, including the following descriptions of key actors: "General Ratko Mladić, who personally presided over the slaughter in Srebrenica, and Radovan Karadžić, the political mastermind of the Bosnian genocide."[529] Thenceforth, HRW continued to lobby for more efforts to apprehend accused at large, and became a strong and consequent supporter of EU conditionality, lobbying, among others, the Council of the EU in order to link any rapprochement between the EU and Serbia to the latter's compliance with ICTY requirements, especially the demands to arrest and transfer Mladić

527 Human Rights Watch: "Human Rights Watch Calls on NATO to Apprehend the War Criminals in the Former Yugoslavia." 7.7.1997.

528 Human Rights Watch: "Human Rights Watch applauds NATO efforts to apprehend war criminals." 10. July 1997. Kovacevic's trial commenced in July 1998. He plead not guilty two times to counts in the (once amended) indictment charging him with genocide, crimes against humanity and war crimes and died in August 1998 in the detention unit in Scheveningen. Marlise Simmons: Heart attack kills Serb on Trial for genocide. The New York Times 2.8.1998.

529 Kenneth Roth: "Two years after Srebrenica, the killers remain free." International Herald Tribune 11.7.1997.

and Karadžić to The Hague.[530] HRW seldom referred to the events in detail. One exception was a press release from July 10, 2005, entitled "The Legacy of Srebrenica", which contained a quite precise and coherent frame about the event in Srebrenica ten years earlier, including elements which attempt to rationalize the killings and provide moral judgments about the role of Dutchbat in Potočari. According to this frame, Srebrenica was not conquered for military reasons and victims were not killed in retaliation, but these events had to be seen as the culminating point of a campaign of hatred and omnipotence by the Bosnian Serb leadership. "The 1995 massacre in Srebrenica occurred because Bosnian Serb leaders, intoxicated by hatred and an illusory sense of omnipotence, lashed out savagely against the country's Muslim population."[531] The elements of the frame concerning Dutchbat had also changed and lost clarity and cohesion. Whereas Dutchbat had been framed in earlier HRW releases and reports as helpless bystanders and victims of Bosnian Serb aggression, they were now presented as a force which had been capable of stopping the aggression, but had failed to do so: "The Dutch United Nations Protection Force (UNPROFOR) battalion based in Srebrenica failed to take the military action necessary to save the town."[532] A few paragraphs later in the same release, the old frame was recycled: "The four hundred lightly armed Dutch soldiers in and around Srebrenica had neither the authorisation nor the capacity to repulse the Serb offensive. The Netherlands later launched an investigation into the shattering failures of that time: but the responsibility was much broader than that. The world simply looked away." [533]The last sentence belongs to a frame, which is very popular and widely used by media and non-governmental organisations whenever they try to explain and denounce states' reluctance to intervene during humanitarian crises. One could call it a "world's indifference frame". The reluctance to intervene is explained as the result of moral indifference, not as a plot of diverging interests, a lack of resources or domestic support, as risk avoidance or by capability shortages of

530 Human Rights Watch: "Bosnia's most wanted remain free." 28.6.2005.
Human Rights Watch: "Safe Areas" for Srebrenica's Most Wanted. A Decade of Failure to Apprehend Karadžić and Mladić." A Human Rights Watch Briefing Paper. 29.6.2005
Lotte Leicht and Richard Dicker: "Letter to EU Foreign Ministers on Establishing Closer Ties with Serbia." HRW 11.6.2010.
http://www.hrw.org/news/2010/06/10/letter-eu-foreign-ministers-establishing-closer-ties-serbia

531 HRW: Bosnia's most wanted, op. cit. The same sentence also appears in another text from 11.7.2005, titled: The Legacy of Srebrenica.
http://www.hrw.org/news/2005/07/10/legacy-srebrenica

532 Ibid.

533 Ibid.

crucial actors. In the HRW report, this "indifference frame" was additionally reinforced by the subsequent sentences: "But the international community also bears responsibility for the worst crime in Europe since World War Two. After promising protection to the inhabitants of Srebrenica, the United Nations and NATO allowed the 'safe area' to fall. That responsibility is compounded by the continuing failure to bring to justice Radovan Karadžić and Ratko Mladić, the two men indicted as the principal architects of the Srebrenica genocide." This also is a classical tool for raising public awareness and mobilizing support, which consists of using blame in order to arouse feelings of guilt, which are meant to incline the reader to 'take action' and increase his moral self-esteem.

The United Nations' Frames

Already in 1992, the UN's Commission of Human Rights appointed the former Polish Prime Minister Tadeusz Mazowiecki special rapporteur. He was charged with the collection of information not only about human rights violations, but also about violations of International Humanitarian Law. He himself regarded his duty as "helping the people."[534] This tension drove him to resign after the fall of the enclaves of Srebrenica and Žepa in summer 1995. Until then, he had submitted 18 reports. Only the last one covered the events in July 1995 in Srebrenica. It is important to mention that Mazowiecki drafted his last report at a point when there were still considerable doubts about the character of the events. The report therefore mentions the separation of men and women after the fall of the enclave, incidental executions and abuses within the town, the separation of men and women in buses and mass executions on sites outside the town. Mazowiecki also mentioned that 10,000 people were missing, but indicated that this number should not be regarded as the overall number of casualties. It is also worth mentioning that his report is the only document which attempts to precisely define the term of "Bosnian Serb". In the document, the special rapporteur makes a difference between Serbs fighting for the then-government in Pale and Serbs loyal to the government in Sarajevo. Mazowiecki framed the column which left town after the fall, trying to get through the Bosnian Serb Army's lines, as a predominantly unarmed one. He also indicated that making a distinction between civilians and combatants in this column would later encounter considerable legal problems, since groups of unarmed civilians used

534 Letter from Tadeusz Mazowiecki to the Commission of Human Rights and the Secretary General dated 17.7.1995. Retrieved from: http://www.unhchr.ch/Huridocda/Huridoca.nsf/0/4382f1156088a2ea8025669d00503b39?Opendocument (the letter could not be found on the website of the UN)

to be accompanied by smaller groups of armed men. "In order to establish a violation of international humanitarian law, such attacks must be against civilians. Attacks against combatants are permitted in the course of normal warfare. This poses a problem in the situation in question as the initial column and subsequent splinter groups were comprised of a mixture of civilians and combatants. Thus it would be necessary to determine on a case-by-case basis whether each individual attack on a particular group constitutes a violation of international humanitarian law. An important factor to be taken into account in making this determination is the proportion of civilians to combatants. Combatants who have surrendered are to be considered as prisoners of war and are to be protected under the Geneva Convention relative to the protection of prisoners of war of 1949."[535] For Mazowiecki, the events in and around Srebrenica started with the fall of the enclave, and no mention was made in the 18th report about raids of armed men from within the enclave into Serb villages surrounding Srebrenica. He mentions cases in which Bosnian Serb soldiers were overwhelmed by small units of armed men who tried to escape from the enclave. "Reports certainly indicate that some of these attacks by Bosnian Serb soldiers were against groups comprised only of Bosnian Government soldiers. Armed combat took place, and witnesses reported that on occasion Bosnian Serb soldiers were killed or captured."[536]

Mazowiecki does not offer any rationale for the atrocities committed after the fall of Srebrenica, which he frames in neither legal nor moral terms. The relevant paragraph reads: "There is significant direct and circumstantial evidence indicating that summary executions took place, both of individuals and small groups of people. On the question of mass executions of large numbers of people at one time, the evidence so far obtained leads to the chilling conclusion that these may have occurred. Further conclusions particularly in terms of the total number executed and the fate of those unaccounted for cannot be drawn without access to the territory under the control of the Bosnian Serb *de facto* authorities, the examination of the sites in question, the exhumation and examination of corpses which may be found, and until further information is available on those still reported missing." For Mazowiecki, the main issue was not what happened after the fall of the town and whether this was a crime, he was mainly concerned with the negligence

535 Situation of human rights in the territory of the former Yugoslavia. Final periodic report on the situation of human rights in the territory of the former Yugoslavia submitted by Mr. Tadeusz Mazowiecki, Special Rapporteur of the Commission on Human Rights, pursuant to paragraph 42 of Commission resolution 1995/89.

536 Ibid.

of the UN and the international community, which had allowed a safe area to be conquered and the inhabitants to be abused and driven away. It was this motive, not protest against the mass executions, which inclined him to resign in protest: "The character of my mandate only allows me to further describe crimes and violations of human rights. But the present critical moment forces us to realize the true character of those crimes and the responsibility of Europe and the international community for their own helplessness in addressing them. We have been fighting in Poland against a totalitarian system with a vision for the Europe of tomorrow. How can we believe in a Europe of tomorrow created by children of people who are abandoned today?"[537] Surprisingly, Mazowiecki did not at all discuss the behaviour and role of Dutchbat in the enclave.

More than three years later, on November 30, 1998, the UN General Assembly decided to charge the Secretary General with conducting an enquiry into the events leading to the establishment of safe areas in Bosnia and their later fate. The investigation lasted for a year and ended with the presentation of a report of the Secretary General, submitted to the General Assembly on November 15, 1999.[538] The report is the UN's most precise, detailed, and coherent attempt to assess the events around the Dutchbat compound in July 1995 in Srebrenica to-date. From the perspective of frame analysis, it is a somehow equivocal document, since it not only presents frames whose channelling into prosecutorial documents and judgment at the ICTY can be examined, but a part of its descriptions and conclusions was also shaped and influenced by earlier ICTY decisions, specifically the indictments of *the pros. vs. Karadžić*, *the pros. vs. Mladić* and the testimony of Dražen Erdemović, who was tried between March 1996 and 1998.[539]

The UN report paints a surprisingly neutral picture of the developments which preceded the fall of Srebrenica and provides an unengaged, balanced account of the atmosphere in and around the enclave before July 1995. According to the report, the town was circled by the Serb Bosnian Army (throughout the report, only "Serbs" and "Bosnian Serbs" are used synonymously), which had cut the population off from food, fuel and other vital commodities, and which in return triggered numerous attempts of armed men to

537 Letter from Tadeusz Mazowiecki, op. cit. to the Commission of Human Rights and the Secretary General dated 17.7.1995.

538 Report of the Secretary General persuant to General Assembly Resolution 53/35 "The Fall of Srebrenica".

539 *The pros. vs. Erdemović* IT-96-22. His guilty plea from the trial is extensively quoted on page 101 of the UN report.

raid the (Serb-populated) area surrounding the town.[540] The situation had set in motion a spiral of violence with mutual accusations, whose accuracy UNPROFOR had been unable to assess. The Bosnian Serb forces are described as well equipped, though outnumbered by the forces in Srebrenica (which are called "Bosniacs" throughout the report). These "Bosniac forces" are described as demoralized, poorly trained, undisciplined and badly equipped. According to the report of the UN General Secretary, neither side was fully compliant with the demilitarisation agreements which had been brokered by the UN in 1993. It also claims that the Army of the Republic of Bosnia and Herzegovina (ARBiH) in Srebrenica did not pose a major threat to the Bosnian Serb Army and largely dismisses the argument according to which the Bosniac defenders of the town raided the vicinity in order to distract Bosnian Serb troops from Sarajevo. This assumption is rejected as a Serb exaggeration. "The extent to which this pretext was accepted at face value by international actors and observers reflected the prism of 'moral equivalency' through which the conflict in Bosnia was viewed by too many for too long."[541]

Between these two conflict parties, Dutchbat soldiers were stuck in a desperate position. "In contrast to the lightly armed Netherlands peacekeepers, the Serbs were prepared for war."[542] Dutchbat was exposed to differing and opposing expectations: The Bosnian Serb Army wanted Dutchbat to disarm the Bosniac fighters in the town, in order to prevent them from raids outside the area. The Bosniac fighters refused to disarm, supposing that Dutchbat would not be able or willing to defend the town on its own. The local civil population expected Dutchbat to guarantee their security and to defend the town against the beleaguerers. The report confirms the reluctance of Dutchbat to confront the invaders, once they had begun to dismantle the observation points around the town and to close in on the valley from the south. "It is true that the UNPROFOR troops in Srebrenica never fired at the attacking Serbs. They fired warning shots over the Serbs' heads and their mortars fired flares, but they never fired directly on any Serb units." These sentences were frequently invoked as a confirmation for the cowardice and hesitance of Dutchbat, to stop the Bosnian Serb advance.[543] However, this is not what the Secretary General intended to say

540 The UN report mentions these raids, but, based on interviews with members of the civil administration of Srebrenica, also confirms that these raids were subject to controversy, because a number of citizens regarded the raids as provocations of the Serb forces, leading to more violence.

541 UN report, 103-104.

542 Ibid.

543 Compare: Dion van den Berg's article: "Rekindling the National Debate: How Public and Private Recognition Can Shift the Dutch Discourse on Srebrenica." Opening

in his report, as the subsequent fragment demonstrates: "Had they engaged the attacking Serbs directly it is possible that events would have unfolded differently. At the same time, it must be recognized, that the 150 fighting men of Dutchbat were lightly armed and in indefensible positions, and were faced with 2000 Serbs advancing with the support of armour and artillery." [544]In the hours and days after the fall of the enclave, the Dutch soldiers were confronted with a "selection dilemma", which is typical for blue helmets in rapidly deteriorating peacekeeping settings. Like in several places in Rwanda 1994 and many other locations where peacekeepers were literally overrun by huge waves of refugees, they were forced to decide under conditions of very imperfect information whom to save and whom to hand over to potential killers. Kofi Annan is probably the only one who ever discussed the possible alternatives for the reaction of Dutchbat: "It is easy to say with the benefit of hindsight and the knowledge of what followed that the Netherlands battalion did not do enough to protect those who sought refuge in its compound." He suggested the soldiers could have admitted everyone into the compound and then formed a "human shield" around it, which, however, also could have inclined the invaders to shell the whole compound.[545] "Ultimately it is not possible to say with any certainty that stronger actions by Dutchbat would have saved lives, and it is even possible that such efforts could have done more harm than good. Faced with this prospect and unaware that the Serbs would proceed to execute thousands of men and boys, Dutchbat avoided armed confrontation and appealed in the process for support at the highest level."[546] The report is critical of Dutchbat, but this criticism is not related to the battalion's reluctance to stand up and fight, but to the delay to report about "sinister indications" of the war crimes some of soldiers had encountered.

The UN report is also a rare attempt to disentangle the motives of the Bosnian Serb Army for overrunning the enclave from the motives behind the

---

address at the "Transforming Images of the Enemy" seminar in Utrecht, the Netherlands on Oct. 8.9.2009, 2. It can be retrieved from http://www.scribd.com/doc/57273277/ Rekindling-the-National-Debate

The author is an activist of the Interchurch Peace Council (Interkerkelijke Vredesberaad), probably the strongest critic of Dutchbat's involvement in Srebrenica. See: Nettlefield, Courting Democracy, 176-117. The organisation supported compensation claims for Srebrenica victims. The same kind of criticism, concerning alleged corwardice and "failure to confront the Serbs" was issued by the French Parliament in its report about Srebrenica in 2001 and by several French politicians in 1995.

544 UN report, 102-104.

545 Ratko Mladić had threatened to do so in case NATO airplanes fired on his soldiers.

546 UN report, 102.

subsequent killings. It identifies a number of reasons for invading the enclave, all of which are based on a contemporary UNPROFOR report and all of which involve strategic considerations. According to them, the Bosnian Serbs had overrun Srebrenica in order to gain control of the roads between the enclaves in Eastern Bosnia and Zvornik, in order to change the military balance of power around Sarajevo, to get the whole area under its control, including the vibrant black market in Srebrenica, and to get access to the natural resources in and around Srebrenica.[547] These possible motives did not explain why Mladić's troops proceeded to mass executions after they had won the battle and achieved all their military objectives linked to the town.

Annan leaves open how many of the ultimate victims were killed as a result of deliberate and planned massacres of prisoners of war (like the ones described by Erdemović), how many fell victim to the hardship and duress caused by the attempts of many to "fight their way through" to government-held territory near Kladanj and how many were killed in Srebrenica before the evacuation of started. He embeds the killings into a larger context, revealing some affinity with the concept of JCE. The Bosnian Serbs had "a central war aim". They intended "to create a geographically contiguous and ethnically pure territory along the Drina, while freeing their troops to fight in other parts of the country." The key issue behind the security of the "safe areas", the report claims in its conclusions, had been "the essential nature of ethnic cleansing." "As part of the larger ambition for a 'Greater Serbia', the Bosnian Serbs set out to occupy the territory of the enclaves; they wanted the territory for themselves. The civilian inhabitants of the enclaves were not the incidental victims of the attackers; their death or removal was the very purpose of the attacks upon them. The tactic of employing savage terror, primarily mass killings, rapes and brutalisation of civilians, to expel populations was used to the greatest extent in Bosnia and Herzegovina, where it acquired the now infamous euphemism of 'ethnic cleansing'. The Bosnian Muslim civilian population thus became the principle victim of brutally aggressive military and paramilitary Serb operations to depopulate coveted territories in order to allow them to be repopulated by Serbs." While the elements concerning Dutchbat were quite similar to the ones used by the Dutch government and Human Rights Watch, the elements of the UN-frame about the killings were quite different from any other frame. There was neither mention of retaliation nor of revenge for earlier raids against Serb villages. The killings were part of a larger plan, which included strategic military and demographic objectives and whose main idea was to get hold of the town, but without its population. The account left one important point open

547 The report mentions bauxite mines. UN report, 67.

(which had also not been addressed by any other frame): Bosnian Serbs, as all other sides in the war, had tried to forcibly remove large parts of the other war parties' population. These attempts had often involved persecution, terror, torture, hate propaganda and orgies of violence. But in Srebrenica, these attempts culminated in meticulously organized genocidal mass executions, for which no strategic or even rational reason was apparent.

Other Frames

The case of Srebrenica is a rather unusual subject for frame analysis. According to the underlying theory and the research design of this chapter, we could expect external actors' frames to influence the frames used at the ICTY. Traces of such influence were shown in the preceding subchapters. The basic logic of this approach requires a situation where external frames emerge prior to the tribunal frames. But in the case of Srebrenica, it is rather the other way around. As demonstrated above, the Dutch government largely refrained from frame-creation in the early days after the fall of Srebrenica, partly because it was deprived of the information needed to create sustainable and coherent frames, partly because it decided to shift the burden of interpretation to NIOD. Human Rights Watch reacted only in autumn 1995, issuing the first report. The media were caught on the wrong foot, too. During the days and weeks that followed the fall of Srebrenica, events on the ground developed so quickly and dynamically that monitoring the fall of the other enclaves, observing the diplomatic turf wars between Washington, London, Paris, Bonn, Moscow, and the Balkans required an immense amount of resources, which at some time even seemed to exhaust a media corporation like The New York Times. What is more important here: it left neither the space nor the time for contemplating a larger, coherent narrative which could have survived beyond the following days. After the fall of the other enclaves in Eastern Bosnia, the decision of NATO to launch air strikes against positions of the Bosnian Serbs, the advance of the Bosnian government army, the launch of operation "Flash" and "Storm" by Croatia and units of the Bosnian Croats in north-western Bosnia, which led to the biggest refugee crisis in Serbia since the begin of the war and totally emptied the traditional Serb territories in Croatia within a few days, no one managed to focus on the fate of several thousand refugees who had gone missing after the fall of Srebrenica. Initially, UN officials estimated the number of missing people at 20,000, but it was obvious that many of them might have reached territory held by the government in Sarajevo. There were allegations about rape and about executions of refugees, but due to the absence of Western media in Srebrenica, these allegations could not be verified. Instead of reporting about killing fields and massacres in

Srebrenica, reporters barely mentioned "allegations" and "accusations" of mostly unnamed camp inmates, who suffered from severe stress and told inconsistent and contradictory stories. Even when the first attempts of more systematic investigations were made[548], it remained uncertain whether and how the killings differed from atrocities which were taking place in other parts of Bosnia at the time. The first accounts of atrocities in Srebrenica focused more on cases of rapes than on mass executions; killings were described as "episodes" and individual cases rather than as centrally organized and well-planned actions. On July 23, a correspondent of The New York Times who had spoken to Dutchbat members in Zagreb sent a story to his head office, in which Dutch soldiers confirmed incidental killings, but denied having witnessed cases of rapes.[549] Two days later, Tadeusz Mazowiecki confirmed that Bosnian Serb forces had committed "wide-scale acts of barbarism when they seized the 'safe area' of Srebrenica."[550] But Mazowiecki, too, spoke only of "very serious violations of human rights on an enormous scale that can only be described as barbarous." He did not invoke genocide or crimes against humanity. Against this background, the only impression that could potentially emerge from these diverging accounts was one of ubiquitous turmoil and violence, similar to the Times' frame about Rwanda during the days following the airplane crash in Kigali.[551]

This gave the ICTY the unique opportunity to act as an agenda-setter and to establish and promote its own frames. Less than two weeks after July 15, the OTP announced the release of 5 new indictments against a total of 24 accused, including Mladić, Karadžić and Milan Martić, a leader of the Croatian Serbs in Krajina. The hurriedly-drafted press release enumerated a number of crimes, ranging from firing several rockets into Zagreb by Martić, to hostage taking,

548 Stephen Kinzer: "Bosnian Refugees' Accounts Appear to Verify Atrocities." The New York Times 17.7.1995.

549 Alan Cowell: "Peacekeepers at Fallen Enclave Confirm Some Atrocities but Say They Saw No Rapes."
The New York Times 24.7.1995.

550 Raymond Bonner: "U.N. Official Accuses Serbs of 'Barbarous' Acts." The New York Times 25.7.1995.

551 Many of the later accounts about Srebrenica and the ICTY seem to exaggerate the knowledge judges and prosecutors could have had in the early days after the fall of Srebrenica. Hazan claims that a judge at the ICTY had told him about the "horror" felt at the tribunal about the Security Council's reluctance to act. The phrase suggests the judges already had a complete picture about what had happened in and around Srebrenica, which they could not have had at that time. Hazan, Pierre: Justice in a time of war. The True Story Behind the International Criminal Tribunal for the Former Yugoslavia. Texas University Press 2004, 65.

torture and ethnic cleansing. It ended with counts of genocide for the Bosnian Serb military and political leadership and for suspects, who were accused of having run concentration camps in Prijedor and Keraterm.[552] Srebrenica was mentioned once – in the context of the 1993 shelling. It was not yet linked to genocide, and OTP investigators had just been deployed to the area. But in November 1995, the OTP was ready. It drafted an indictment for genocide, committed by Karadžić and Mladić, and pertaining to the events following the fall of Srebrenica.[553] According to the press release, judge Fouad Riad had commented on the evidence in the following way:

> "After Srebrenica fell to besieging Serbian forces in July, 1995, a truly terrible massacre of the Muslim population appears to have taken place. The evidence tendered by the Prosecutor describes scenes of unimaginable savagery: thousands of men executed and buried in mass graves, hundreds of men buried alive, men and women mutilated and slaughtered, children killed before their mothers' eyes, a grandfather forced to eat the liver of his own grandson. These are truly scenes from hell, written on the darkest pages of human history."[554]

In this case, emotional language reflects the feeling that the ICTY was in imminent danger to be sidelined by political events and by the states, which had created it. When judge Riad spoke, the Dayton negotiations were going on and there was a strong fear among many ICTY officials that justice and the punishment of perpetrators would be sacrificed for peace, and amnesty would be granted to political and military leaders, against whom ICTY prosecutors had collected evidence. It is beyond the scope of our book to discuss the mutual moral, political and legal implications between war, peace and justice, and we cannot delve into the interplay between the OTP's indictment policy and the role negotiators at Dayton ascribed to the ICTY. These matters have been extensively dealt with by Hagan, Hazan, Peskin and others[555]. For the purpose of this chapter, it is important to state that the ICTY used several strategies to reinforce its position in the peace process and to counter the threat of being sidelined. One of these strategies consisted in conducting so-called rule 61 hearings.[556] These public hearings were organized

552 ICTY Press release on 15.7.1995, The release was so hastily drafted that it contained many errors. Even Srebrenica was written "Srebenica".

553 *The pros. vs. Karadžić and Mladić*, IT-95-5-I

554 ICTY press release 16.11.1995

555 Hagan, Justice in the Balkans; Hazan, Justice in a Time of War; Peskin, International Justice in Rwanda and the Balkans (all op. cit.)

556 Other elements of the strategy employed by Goldstone at the time were public statements against impunity and the preparation of new indictments against Karadžić and Mladić, which would contain charges of genocide for Srebrenica. See: Peskin, International Justice, 42-44. Goldstone also threatened to resign if Dayton included amnesty.

when a state had failed to serve an arrest warrant issued by the ICTY. During these *ex parte* hearings, the prosecution had to present evidence, which would allow for the reconfirmation of the indictment and the issuing of international arrest warrants by the judges. Even among prosecutors, the procedure was controversial, since it seemed to provide a tool for practically conducting trials *in absentia*, which was contrary to the intention of the ICTY's founders, the UN legal culture, and the concept of the Security Council.[557] The rule 61 hearings have been discussed by many authors from different legal perspectives, however, one non-legal yet crucial aspect has almost completely been neglected. These hearings were a powerful tool for bringing the ICTY into the public realm by making it an important agenda-setter in the debate about the peace process and by enabling the OTP to set the agenda of public discourse. In other words: Judge Riad could create whatever frame he wanted with the of strong, emotional language, but he had no chance of influencing the public discourse, as long as his frames did not attract media attention. The reluctance of other key players to create and promote their own frames about Srebrenica fostered the agenda-setting power of the ICTY during the Dayton talks. The states and conflict parties were not eager to speak about Srebrenica, since it only could endanger the negotiations and damage their case[558]. Their reluctance fostered the agenda-setting role of the ICTY, because it deprived the ICTY frame of competition. This could be observed in an article of The New York Times, which appeared shortly after the start of the rule 61 hearings and reproduced exactly the same frame (and even the precise wording) used by judge Riad. On November 20, the newspaper published a piece which was largely based on an interview with Richard Goldstone, but ended with a reference to the rule 61 hearings which the the author had added: "Our conversation took place the day after the

557 One of the opponents of rule 61 hearings was Gabrielle Kirk McDonald, who argued against them from a human rights perspective. For her arguments see: Kirk McDonald, Gabrielle: "Problems, Obstacles and Achievements of the ICTY." *Journal of International Criminal Justice* 2 (2004), 558-571. Louise Arbour, who succeeded Goldstone, also was critical of rule 61 hearings, but mainly for reasons linked to trial economy and the alleged detrimental influence of rule 61 hearings on the discipline of prosecutors. She argued that the possibility to expose evidence to the public which cannot be challenged by the defence disclosed it to the suspects, enabling them to intimidate witnesses or manipulate evidence, and provided the trial prosecutors with a false impression about the strength of his evidence. Arbour, Louise: "The Chief Prosecutor's dual role." *Journal of International Criminal Justice* 2 (2004), 394-402.

558 The only exception was the Bosnian government in Sarajevo, which actually spoke about Srebrenica, using a specific "treason frame" blaming all other actors for crimes (the Bosnian Serbs) or for the betrayal of Srebrenica (the UN and the Western states which had provided troops there).

International War Crimes Tribunal for the former Yugoslavia indicted Dr. Karadžić and General Mladić for the second time, charging them with genocide and crimes against humanity. These charges stem from the massacre of thousands of Bosnian civilians after the Serbs seized the supposed safe area of Srebrenica in July." Then Anthony Lewis, the author of the article, directly quoted judge Riad's famous phrase about the "scenes from hell, written on the darkest pages of human history" and even adding the detail from the hearing about "a grandfather forced to eat the liver of his own grandson." He concluded the article with the sentence: "Before our conversation, I thought the issue of surrendering Dr. Karadžić and General Mladić to the tribunal should not stand in the way of an agreement in Dayton. I am convinced now that there can be no meaningful peace without that commitment to justice."[559] By using the instrument of rule 61 hearings, the ICTY had managed to bring its own counter-frame into the game, which was opposite to the pragmatic frame preferred by diplomats and politicians.

Strikingly, there is no Bosnian government frame on Srebrenica dating beyond July 1995. The government in Sarajevo refrained from issuing any moral judgment on the fall of the town, it did not even condemn it, indirectly supporting the allegations according to which it had tolerated or even contributed to the cleaning up of the maps and sacrificed Srebrenica.[560] Because of the government's silence, Prime Minister Haris Silajdžić even offered his resignation on August 3.[561] The Bosnian government framed its own version of the events much later. Even in the genocide lawsuit, which the Bosnian government filed against the Republic of Serbia at the International Court of Justice already in 1993,[562] but which did not attract media attention before the case started in February 2006, and is therefore unlikely to have influenced prosecutors' or judges frames prior to that date.[563] The original application did

559 Anthony Lewis: "Abroad at home, no peace without justice." The New York Times 20.11.1995.

560 There is some support for the thesis that at that time, the fall of Srebrenica created a militarily more sustainable situation for all conflict sides (except, of course, for the population of the town). It should be kept in mind that this assumption concerns the military situation, not the humanitarian one, and does not allege the Bosnian government of having accepted the ethnic cleansing and the massacre of the male population of Srebrenica by units of the Bosnian Serb Army. Support for the "sustainability-thesis" can be found in Rohde, endgame and Silber, Little, the death of Yugoslavia, 345-363.

561 (No author): "Bosnian Premier offers to resign." The New York Times 3.8.1995,

562 Subotić, Hijacked Justice, 135-140.

563 Application of the Convention on the Prevention and Punishment of the Crime of Genocide (Bosnia and Herzegovina v. Serbia and Montenegro). The final verdict was issued on 27.2.2007. http://www.icj-cij.org/docket/files/91/13685.pdf

not even contain charges relating to Srebrenica 1995, since it was tendered two years before the fall of the enclave. In 2007, the court found that Srebrenica had been the only case of genocide in Bosnia, but cleared the Republic of Serbia of the genocide charges, blaming Bosnian Serbs for the crime and the Republic of Serbia for not having prevented it.[564]

Another frame was much more likely to influence indictments and judgments at the ICTY. The BBC not only covered the events in Srebrenica extensively, it also produced a highly suggestive TV series, which was later sold commercially and accompanied by a bestseller whose subsequent editions can still be bought in libraries in Croatia, Serbia, and Bosnia. Fragments of *The Death of Yugoslavia* documentary were even shown in the courtroom in a number of trials, among them *the pros. vs. Milošević, the pros. vs. Prlić, the pros. vs. Stanišić, the pros. vs. Tadić, the pros. vs. Dokmanović*[565]. Several BBC reporters testified in court, such as Jacky Rowland (in *the pros. vs. Milošević*[566]), Martin Bell in the *pros. vs. Blaskić, the pros. vs. Naletilić, the pros vs. Prlić, the pros. vs. Karadžić* and *the pros. vs. Dragan Milošević* and *the pros. vs. Perisić.*[567] Jeremy Bowen was a witness in the *pros. vs. Naletilić*. Another BBC documentary, *The Cry from the Grave* (1999), dealing with the events following the fall of Srebrenica, was used in *the pros. vs. Tolimir.*[568]

---

564 The verdict saved the Republic of Serbia from the need to pay compensations to Bosnia. Since then, there has been an ongoing discussion in the public of Serbia and Bosnia and within the epistemic community dealing with transitional justice and international law on whether the verdict would have been different had the ICJ had access to the minutes of the so-called "Supreme Defense Council", which had been delivered to the ICTY and kept under seal. According to some authors, these documents directly linked Milošević (and thus the Republic of Serbia) to the genocide in Srebrenica. Others contest this interpretation. For the discussion see: Subotić, Hijacked Justice, 139; Prelec, Marko: "Body of Evidence: The Prosecution's Construction of Milošević." In: Waters, The Milošević Trial, chapter 25. It should be kept in mind that the ICJ had to decide about a conflict between two states based on international law, which required him to apply standards different from the ones applied by a criminal court, which bases his findings on international criminal law and individual responsibility. In the second case, failure to prevent genocide by an accused, in whose power it was to prevent it, may lead to a guilty verdict.

565 *The pros. vs. Prlić at al.* IT-04-74, *the pros. vs. Stanišić and Župljanin* IT-08-91, *the pros. vs. Tadić* IT-94-1, *the pros. vs. Dokmanović* IT-95-13a.

566 *The pros. vs. Milošević* IT-02-54.

567 *The pros. vs. Blaskić* IT-95-14, *the pros. vs. Naletilić and Martinović* IT-98-34, *the pros. vs. Prlić et al.* IT-04-74, *the pros. vs. Karadžić* IT-95-5/18-I, *the pros. vs. Dragomir Milošević* IT-98-29/1, *the pros. vs. Perisić* 04-81.

568 *The pros. vs. Tolimir* IT-05-88/2.

The Death of Yugoslavia was registered and written too early to contain precise frames about the killings after the fall of the town, but it contains some very specific and explicit interpretations about the siege, the role of Dutchbat, and the purely military events. Once again, Dutchbat soldiers appear as helpless bystanders and victims rather than traitors of the population. The conquest of the town is explained by two basic motives – "Serb" strategy for eliminating a source of insecurity (reference is made to Orić's raids) and retaliation for preceding raids into Serb villages. The book makes French general Janvier the main culprit for the lack of close air support. This element is part of a larger conspiracy frame, according to which the fall of the town is the result of a congruence of interests between Bosnian Serbs (who allegedly wanted to achieve their strategic goals), the Sarajevo government (who sought to drop the enclave, because it was regarded as too vulnerable and too exposed for efficient defence), Western powers, including the US government (which wanted to achieve a sustainable division of territory before Dayton). The frame lacks emotional elements, but collides with the main elements of the Bosnian government's frame. There is one important exception: Whereas the Sarajevo government used to blame all other stakeholders involved of having "sold out" Srebrenica, the BBC frame also includes the government in Sarajevo in its conspiracy frame.[569] While the killings described later by Erdemović do not play any major role in the book (they are called genocide anyway), *The Death of Yugoslavia* describes the fate of the column heading for government-controlled territory in the north of the enclave, suggesting that most of it consisted of armed men, who fought their way through minefields and ambushes. This element is largely consistent with the corresponding element in the UN report's frame.

It must be mentioned, that the construction of the book *The Death of Yugoslavia* differs considerably from the film, which is a TV series divided into six parts, each of about 45 minutes. While the book presents a bottom-up version of Yugoslavia's disintegration, which starts with political liberalisation in Slovenia and ends with Dayton, the TV series offers a top-down approach, starting with Milošević's Gazimestan speech and his power struggle against Ivan Stambolić, Milošević's main antagonist within the leadership of the League of Communists of Yugoslavia during the late eighties. Only then the focus shifts to Slovenia. It is worth mentioning, that the prosecution used the same approach

569 It should be mentioned that the word "conspiracy" does not appear in the book. The sequence of events leading to the fall of Srebrenica is rather explained by referring to congruence of interest between the main stakeholders, and no allegations are made about any formal agreement or plot between them.

when presenting its case in *the pros. vs. Milošević,* showing fragments of the BBC documentary in court and presenting Milošević's speech as the trigger of Yugoslav disintegration and the launch of his alleged Joint Criminal Enterprise. More than the book, the TV series emphasizes Serb guilt, for example, when Croat nationalist policy is presented as something evoked by Serb threats. The documentary usually only refers to "the Serbs" and often neglects to explain whether they mean Bosnian Serbs, Serbs in Serbia proper, Krajina Serbs or all Serbs in the former Yugoslavia. Serbs are framed as separatists (in Croatia and Bosnia), who want to consolidate all Serb-populated territories, but Croats "pray for peace". The conflict in Bosnia is not explained as a division of the republic along ethnic lines, which escalates due to radicalism and unwillingness to compromise, instead the authors claim "that Serb forces prepared for their next target – Bosnia." The documentary concentrates on two main issues in Bosnia – the siege of Sarajevo and of Srebrenica. There is no mention of concentration camps in central Bosnia, neither of pro-Serb Muslim forces in north-western Bosnia.

The July indictment against Mladić and Karadžić had already charged both with genocide, crimes against humanity and war crimes, but it had focused on counts pertaining to the siege and sniping of Sarajevo, to the creation and maintenance of "detention facilities" in Bosnia, and the destruction of property and unlawful confinement of civilians. It did not specify any charges connected to Srebrenica. Those came with the second indictment in November, which was overtly labelled the "Srebrenica indictment". In both indictments, the victims were described as "Muslims". The later indictment did not elaborate on the causes and reasons of the events in Srebrenica. It was limited to the very general statement that "after war erupted in the Republic of Bosnia and Herzegovina, Bosnian Serb military forces occupied Bosnian Muslim villages in the eastern part of the country, resulting in an exodus of Bosnian Muslims to enclaves in Goražde, Žepa, Tuzla, and Srebrenica."[570]

There was no specific frame concerning Dutchbat. Since Goldstone did not intend to incriminate the Dutch soldiers for any crimes, he concentrated on the actions of the two accused persons in the indictment. This focus reduced the role of Dutchbat practically to zero. The events in Potočari are framed in such a way that Dutchbat doesn't even take on the role of helpless bystanders; it is practically non-existent. The indictment only alleges that their observation posts were attacked and that later "several thousand women, children and some mostly elderly men fled to the UN compound in Potočari, located within the safe area of Srebrenica, where they sought the protection of the Dutch battalion responsible

570 *The pros. vs. Karadžić & Mladić*, IT-95-18-I.

for the compound." Thus, the indictment does not even decide whether it was Dutchbat's obligation to protect the refugees and whether those seeking protection actually found protection in the compound. Executions around the compound had caused panic among the refugees and had either inclined them to commit suicide or to leave the town on their own. The indictment then shifts its focus to the fate of this second group:

> "A second group of approximately 15,000 Bosnian Muslim men, with some women and children, gathered at Šušnjari during the evening hours of 11 July 1995 and fled, in a huge column, through the woods towards Tuzla. Approximately one-third of this group consisted of armed Bosnian military personnel and armed civilians. The rest were unarmed civilians." (...) "As soon as the column reached Bosnian Serb held territory in the vicinity of Buljim, Bosnian Serb military forces attacked it. As a result of this and other attacks by Bosnian Serb military forces, many Muslims were killed and wounded and the column divided into several smaller parts which continued towards Tuzla. Approximately one-third of the column, mostly composed of military personnel, crossed the Bratunac-Milici road near Nova Kasaba and reached safety in Tuzla. The remaining Muslims were trapped behind the Bosnian Serb lines."[571]

Then the indictment enumerates the killing sites described earlier by Erdemović, who had been a witness during the rule 61 hearings. "Many of the Bosnian Muslims who were captured by or surrendered to Bosnian Serb military personnel were summarily executed by Bosnian Serb military personnel at the locations of their surrender or capture, or at other locations shortly thereafter."

The indictment was amended several times, but it only became operational after Radovan Karadžić was arrested in Belgrade in summer 2008. Until then, the frames from the initial indictments had not changed. From the beginning, they comprised "ethnic cleansing" as an element of a JCE. Ethnic cleansing was allegedly a means to "permanently remove Bosnian Muslim and Bosnian Croat inhabitants from the territories of BiH claimed as Bosnian Serb territory." In the operational Karadžić indictment

571 Goldstone and his collaborators apparently did not decide whether attacking the column was a crime under the jurisdiction of the ICTY, they even refrained from assessing whether the column was to be regarded as a group of combatants rather than a civil group of refugees. Later in the indictment, the killing of persons who already had surrendered or were incapable of offering resistance is regarded as a war crime, but the formulations lack a characterisation of the column as military or civilian. This point later became very controversial, when in 2002 the NIOD report claimed that the column mainly consisted of armed fighters, which by then was strongly disputed by survivor organisations and the Bosnian government in Sarajevo. Nettlefield, Courting Democracy, 115-116.

from February 2009, it was alleged that Karadžić, together with others, had "participated in the below charged crimes in order to secure control of those areas of Bosnia and Herzegovina which had been proclaimed part of the Serbian republic". The notion of "permanent removal" was changed to another one, stipulating that Karadžić and others "were engaged in a variety of actions to significantly reduce the Bosnian Muslim, Bosnian Croat and other non-Serb populations of these municipalities." This was an attempt to explain various atrocities committed during the war against other ethnic groups, it was not an explanation of the specific escalation after the fall of Srebrenica. In the indictment against Mladić, which was the result of the severance of the Mladić indictment from the Karadžić indictment[572], it is alleged that the JCE, in which Mladić participated, consisted of implementing a plan of the Bosnian Serb leadership, to separate a distinct Serb entity within Bosnia, link it with Serbia proper and give it access to the sea.[573] "The objective of the joint criminal enterprise within BiH was the elimination or permanent removal, by force or other means, of Bosnian Muslim, Bosnian Croat, or other non-Serb inhabitants from large areas of BiH through the commission of crimes (...)". It remained unclear as to how these objectives were related to the systematic killings of all men and boys, who were captured after the fall of Srebrenica.

Long before Mladić and Karadžić were apprehended and transferred to The Hague, another indictment became operational. General Radislav Krstić was arrested in early December 1998 by British Special Forces, which acted on the basis of a secret indictment. In agreement with ICTY judges, Louise Arbour had refrained from publishing indictments in cases in which she suspected the relevant state not to cooperate. Krstić had been the chief of staff and deputy commander of the Drina Corps and a subordinate to Mladić during the conquest of Srebrenica.[574] In the first indictment against Krstić, confirmed on October 30, 1998, the OTP literally repeated the background introduction of

572 *The pros. vs. Mladić* IT-95-5/18-I.

573 The indictment refers to a project Radovan Karadžić presented on 12 May 1992, at the 16th session of the Bosnian Serb Assembly, and which included six strategic objectives of the Serbian People in Bosnia and Herzegovina, among them, to establishment of a state border separating the Serbian people from the other two ethnic communities, setting up a corridor between Semberija and Krajina, establishing a corridor in the Drina River valley in order to link the Serbian entity with the Republic of Serbia, establishing a border on the Una and Neretva rivers, divide the city of Sarajevo between Muslims and Serbs and ensure access to the sea for Republika Srpska.

574 More about the problem of secret (or "sealed") indictments see: Hagen, Justice in the Balkans, 110-102 and 129-130.

the Mladić and Karadžić indictments, framing the events before the fall of Srebrenica in exactly the same way. No new elements were added to the very parsimonious fragments which described Dutchbat. The notion of "Bosnian Serb forces" from previous indictments had now been replaced by "VRS forces".[575] These forces were under the "command and control of Ratko Mladić and Radislav Krstić" and alleged to have "participated in numerous incidents of opportunistic killings [sic] of Bosnian Muslim men shortly after they had been captured, as well as systematic summary executions of Bosnian Muslim men who were initially detained and then transported to various execution sites throughout the territory under the control of the VRS Drina Corps. The VRS forces, under the command and control of Ratko Mladić and Radoslav Krstić, executed thousands of Bosnian Muslim men." The killings were presented as the continuation of an "ethnic cleansing plan", which had been pursued since 1992. Due to the discovery of crime sites, which had been investigated since the early indictments against Mladić and Karadžić and due to new evidence from US satellites and from Erdemović, the indictment against Krstić was much more detailed and enumerated a number of killing sites around Srebrenica, and described the transport of victims from Srebrenica to different places. The elements of the frame pertaining to the column, which had left Srebrenica after Mladić's conquest of the town, had not changed. The column still was described as one third of its members being armed. In the amended indictment, already signed by Carla Del Ponte in October 1999, additional details about the internal organisation of the Bosnian Serb Army and the Drina Corps were added, but the frame describing the events had not changed. Still, the indictment mentioned "opportunistic killings" and lacked a rationalisation of the alleged genocide.

Tab. 1: Frames Used Before the Trial Chamber Judgment in the pros. vs. Krstić

Frame elements	Dutch government 1995	Human Rights Watch	UN report	BBC	Bosnian government	Prosecution frame from Karadžić, Mladić and Krstić indictments
Origin of the conflict around Srebrenica						

575 Meaning Vojska Republike Srpske, the Army of the Republika Srpska, the Serb entity in Bosnia.

"Bosnian Serbs" strive for conquest since 1993	X	X				
"Bosnian Serbs' hatred and omnipotence"		X				
Bosnian Serbs' propensity for "ethnic cleansing"						X
Attribution of guilt prior to Serb attack	Equidistance	Bosnian Serbs guilty	equidistance	Serbs guilty	Bosnian Serbs guilty	Bosnian Serb military forces guilty
Role of Dutchbat						
Helpless bystanders and victims	X	X	X	X		
Failed to protect and fight		X			X	
Failed only to deliver information about crimes		X	X			
Coward and craven		X				
Alleged reason for conquest						
Strategic and military	X		X	X		
Alleged reason for killings after fall						
Retaliation for defenders' raids	X			X		

Ethnic cleansing		X	X			X
Column leaving Srebrenica framed as[576]		civilian	military	military		Civilian
Perpetrators are	Bosnian Serbs	Bosnian Serbs	Serbs	Serbs		Serbs
Victims are	Population, defenders, men	Muslims	Bosniacs	Muslims		Muslims
Legal assessment	War crimes, forced removals, martial executions and Human Rights violations	War crimes, crimes against humanity, war crimes	attempted genocide	genocide	genocide	War crimes, crimes against humanity, genocide

The table shows that most actors agreed on three basic elements: the guilt of (Bosnian) Serbs prior to the fall of Srebrenica (afterwards this assessment was unanimous), that Dutchbat soldiers were helpless bystanders, and that the perpetrators of the killings were (Bosnian) Serbs. Whereas the victims were mostly framed in religious terms (Muslims rather than Bosniacs or "population" etc.), the perpetrators were defined in ethnic categories; in the case of the BBC and UN frames, they were even labelled solely "Serbs", as if the responsibility for the killings extended to all Serbs, no matter if from Bosnia or elsewhere. There is also a strong congruence with respect to the framing of the fighters inside the town, who are mostly regarded as "Muslims", and concerning the rationalisation of the town's conquest. Mostly strategic and military reasons are given for the military attack on the town (rather than psychological reasons like a propensity for retaliation or, as in the HRW frame, "hatred and omnipotence"), whereas "ethnic cleansing" is the prevailing rationalisation for the killings after military actions had ceased. The table also shows that the most substantial frame was the one from HRW, which addressed the majority of other frames' elements (to the extent of comprising contradictions), whereas the Dutch government's frame from 1995 scores very weakly, leaving most aspects of the events unexplained.

576 "Civilian" means the column is described as comprising more civilians than fighters, "military" means, it is considered to have comprised more members of the military.

The Frames of the Trial Chamber in *the Pros. vs. Krstić*

The trial chamber in *the pros. vs. Krstić* issued a verdict of 260 pages. It starts with a strong normative part, rather unusual for legal documents, which demonstrates the psychological impact of the trial on the judges:

> "The events surrounding the Bosnian Serb take-over of the United Nations ('UN') 'safe area' of Srebrenica in Bosnia and Herzegovina, in July 1995, have become well known to the world. Despite a UN Security Council resolution, declaring that the enclave was to be 'free from armed attack or any other hostile act', units of the Bosnian Serb Army ("VRS") launched an attack and captured the town. Within a few days, approximately 25,000 Bosnian Muslims, most of them women, children and elderly people who were living in the area, were uprooted and, in an atmosphere of terror, loaded onto overcrowded buses by the Bosnian Serb forces and transported across the confrontation lines into Bosnian Muslim-held territory. The military-aged Bosnian Muslim men of Srebrenica, however, were consigned to a separate fate. As thousands of them attempted to flee the area, they were taken prisoner, detained in brutal conditions and then executed. More than 7,000 people were never seen again. The events of the nine days from July 10-19 1995 in Srebrenica defy description in their horror and their implications for humankind's capacity to revert to acts of brutality under the stresses of conflict. In little over one week, thousands of lives were extinguished, irreparably rent or simply wiped from the pages of history. The Trial Chamber leaves it to historians and social psychologist to plumb the depths of this episode of the Balkan conflict and to probe for deep-seated causes. (...) The Trial Chamber cannot permit itself the indulgence of expressing how it feels about what happened in Srebrenica, or even how individuals as well as national and international groups not the subject of this case contributed to the tragedy."[577]

Despite the elements of this frame, which pointed to the collective guilt of the Bosnian Serbs for committing "hostile acts", the judgment went back to the early 1990s, summarizing in a rather neutral way the breakup of Yugoslavia and then drawing the line of events back to the events of 1993, avoiding shifting the blame to one side. Similarly to the UN report, it stated that both sides, the "Muslims" and the "Serbs", had violated the UN provisions for the safe area and attacked the other side. Raids from inside the enclave against Serb villages were mentioned. "In January 1993, Bosnian Muslim forces attacked the Bosnian Serb village of Kravica. Over the next few months, the Bosnian Serbs responded with a counter-offensive (...) severing the link

577 *The pros. vs. Krstić* IT-98-33-A. The strong normative part of the judgment is less astonishing given that one of the trial judges was judge Fouad Riad, the person to issue the most emotional statements during the rule 61 hearings in 1995.

between Srebrenica and Žepa and reducing the size of the Srebrenica enclave to 150 square kilometers".

Only when it comes to the events of 1995 was guilt attributed to a group, and this group was defined in ethnic terms. In three instances are the perpetrators referred to as the Bosnian Serb Army, whereas the abbreviation VRS appears in the document 241 times, "Bosnian Serbs" are denounced 57 times, the "Drina Corps" – even 662 times, and a special chapter was dedicated to its role in the crimes committed in and around Srebrenica (Section II-B of the judgment). Nevertheless, the judgment tries to attribute guilt to a specific member of that group, General Krstić. The victims are referred to as "Bosnian Muslims". The judges differentiate between Bosnian Muslim men (or Bosnian Muslim males, or the male population of Srebrenica), on the one hand, and Bosnian Muslim women, children and elderly, on the other.

In many ways, the judgment constitutes a new frame. With respect to the column which had decided to leave the enclave, the judges repeated the indictment, claiming that about one third of the men had been soldiers, "not all armed" and that their intention had been to fight their way through enemy lines. During the trial, the defence had challenged the genocide charge by proposing the interpretation that the fate of the column provided evidence that not all men and boys of military age had been targeted by the killings. Actually evidence showed that a subcommander of the Drina corps had agreed to let the spearhead of the column cross the line to government-held territory near Tuzla, and that some of the column members had been treated in a humane way and had survived. The judges dismissed this as apparent exceptions to the rule and (in the case of the subcommander) as an individual decision, taken without consultation from above and due to the military capacity of the column's front line, which had been too strong to be contained. Exceptions to the rule, the judges argued, could be due to attempts of "the Bosnian Serbs" to avoid attracting international suspicion. "For example, on 13 July, a report prepared by Colonel Janković of the Main Staff noted that over 50 wounded Bosnian Muslims had been placed in the Bratunac hospital and that an UNPROFOR officer had stayed at the hospital to ensure the men were accorded proper treatment." The defence had claimed only men, who posed a threat to the beleaguerers, had been killed. The judges refuted that: "Overwhelming evidence has shown that the Bosnian Serb forces went to great lengths to seize Bosnian Muslim men at virtually every opportunity, whether they posed a military threat or not." The trial chamber found that all men and boys had been targeted "regardless of whether they chose to flee to Potočari or to join the Bosnian Muslim column. The operation to capture and detain the Bosnian Muslim men was well-organised and comprehensive." Here for the first time a frame emerged, according to which the whole operation had neither been an attempt to retaliate, nor an overreaction, but an operation carried out in cold blood and meticulously anticipated, planned and carried out with a huge organisational effort. "The Trial Chamber finds that, following the take over of Srebrenica in July 1995, the Bosnian Serbs devised and implemented a plan to execute as many as possible of the military aged Bosnian Muslim men present in the enclave." The judges also proposed a specific explanation for the genocidal executions, which were difficult to explain in terms of military strategy. They quoted Bosniac General Sefer Halilović[578], who had suggested that the mass executions there had taken place because Srebrenica was situated in the Drina valley and because the Republika Srpska had the intention of abolishing the Drina as the border between Bosnia and the Republic of Serbia. "I think that today there are more than 60 settlements of Bosniac population mainly who wish to go back to their homes, but those who were executed no longer have any chance of going back home, and that area was removed from the face of the earth. It was cleansed ... and [it was] an area which was between two Serb states." Just like the prosecution had done in the indictment, he referred to the "the decisions issued by the Serbian Assembly in Banja Luka", suggesting that the male part of the Srebrenica population had been killed in order to prevent any attempts of the population to return to the town and reinstate an enclave, which could threaten the link between Serb territory in Bosnia and the Republic of Serbia.

Concerning the military plans to conquer Srebrenica, the judges discussed the defence thesis about a "deal" between Sarajevo and the Bosnian Serb leadership about an exchange of territory, but held that even if such a deal had existed, it did not justify the atrocities committed in the aftermath of the town's fall.

The Frames of the Appeals Chamber in *the Pros. vs. Krstić*

On April 19, 2004, the Appeals Chamber issued its verdict in *the pros. vs. Krstić*[579] in reaction to the defence's appeal, which had challenged the previous trial chamber's verdict of 45 years of imprisonment and had argued that the Trial Chamber had not found sufficient evidence to establish that Krstić had been a member of a joint criminal enterprise with the intent to commit genocide. Krstić's lawyers also defended the idea of a parallel chain of command in the

578 Halilović was years later indicted for war crimes committed against Croats in the Neretva valley, but acquitted. *The pros. vs. Halilović* IT-01-48.

579 *The pros. vs. Krstić* IT-98-33-A.

Bosnian Serb Army and claimed that Krstić's right to a fair trial had been violated. The Appeals Chamber reduced his sentence, finding that he had in fact lacked genocidal intent, instead finding him guilty of aiding and abetting genocide, and sentenced him to 35 years, lowering his sentence by 11 years. Krstić was transferred to the UK and detained in Wakefield Prison. He once again hit the headlines in 2011, when two Muslim inmates, one from Nigeria, the other from Albania, entered his prison cell and attacked him. Both were accused of attempted murder in a court in Leeds. The prosecutor alleged that the men had inflicted the injuries to punish him or take revenge, since his involvement in the Srebrenica massacres was known to them.[580]

Judge Riad was no longer involved in the case, since he had been member of the Trial Chamber in *the pros. vs. Krstić*. Still, he seemed to have made quite an impact on the style of the appeals judgment, which contained a strongly emotional introduction, reminiscent of the rule 61 hearings 9 years ago. It recalled, "Srebrenica has also lent its name to an event the horrors of which form the background to this case. The depravity, brutality and cruelty with which the Bosnian Serb Army treated the innocent inhabitants of the safe area are now well known and documented." Since the appeals chamber restricted its argumentation to issues raised by the defence, the verdict did not deal with many of the frame elements, which had emerged earlier in the public sphere. The overwhelming majority of the 126-page paper concerned legal issues, discussing the trial chambers findings which were attacked by the defence. There were some minor differences between the appeals chamber's and the trial chamber's frames. The five judges described the victims as "Bosnian Muslims of Srebrenica" and "of Eastern Bosnia", when characterizing the group that had been the target of genocide. They also delivered a rationalisation of the genocide, which, they emphasized, had taken place at Srebrenica. The rationale they attributed to the actions of the Drina Corps of the Bosnian Serb Army (which they regarded as the executor of the genocidal plan), was closely connected to the military aims of the Bosnian Serbs, as the judges saw them. "Without Srebrenica, the ethnically Serb state of Republica Srpska they sought to create would remain divided into two disconnected parts, and its access to

---

580 "Inmates plotted to kill war criminal Radislav Krstić." BBC News 7.2.2011. In September 2012, Polish media informed their readers, that due to security considerations, the ICTY had decided (and the Polish judiciary agreed) to transfer Krstić do Poland, where his life would be less endangered, because the country hosted much less Muslims in its prisons than many other countries, which had signed an agreement about prisoners with the ICTY. Gazeta Wyborcza: "Serbski zbrodniarz będzie siedział w Polsce", 20.9.2012. http://wiadomosci.gazeta.pl/wiadomosci/1,114871,12516790,Serbski_zbrodniarz_bedzie_siedzial_w_Polsce.html

Serbia proper would be disrupted. The capture and ethnic purification of Srebrenica would therefore severely undermine the military efforts of the Bosnian Muslim state to ensure its viability, a consequence the Muslim leadership fully realized and strove to prevent." Apparently, the judges understood the events as the result of a conflict over territory, during which the viability of a state of either Bosniac Muslims or Bosnian Serbs was at stake. This explained why one of the two conflict parties had conquered the town, but it did not explain why then this party – the Bosnian Serb military – had not stopped short of killing the male inhabitants instead of taking them prisoner or chasing away the entire population. The trial chamber established that it was the mere seize of the enclave that had attracted tens of thousands of civilians from other parts of Bosnia which explained why ethnic cleansing had led to genocide. This was sustained by the appeals chamber. "Because most of the Muslim inhabitants of the region had, by 1995, sought refuge within the Srebrenica enclave, the elimination of that enclave would have accomplished the goal of purifying the entire region of its Muslim population." In other words: the judges suggested that the Drina Corps had just taken advantage of seizing such a large number of Bosniacs, whose elimination they had intended anyway, at once. But the judges explained the reasoning: "The elimination of the Muslim population of Srebrenica, despite the assurances given by the international community, would serve as a potent example to all Bosnian Muslims of their vulnerability and defencelessness in the face of Serb military forces. The fate of the Bosnian Muslims of Srebrenica would be emblematic of that of all Bosnian Muslims." However, military necessity was not the only motive which drove the perpetrators to genocide: "The Trial Chamber also found that some of the victims were severely handicapped and, for that reason, unlikely to have been combatants. This evidence further supports the Trial Chamber's conclusion that the extermination of these men was not driven solely by a military rationale."

The appeals judges then constructed a chain of command, which ran from the Bosnian Serb leadership (with Radovan Karadžić on top) through Mladić, to the Drina Corps, which, in some cases, had been the instrument for carrying out the massacres, in other cases was circumvented by Mladić. The judges linked the mass executions to a directive issued by the Bosnian Serb government to the Army (so-called "directive 7") and which ordered the Army "to make the situation unbearable for the Bosnian Muslims in Srebrenica, both military and civilian." Based on that directive, Mladić allegedly wanted to secure the surrender of the Bosnian government forces by taking the civil population hostage and threatening to retaliate against it if the Army did not surrender. The genocidal executions after the fall of the town were therefore the consequence of the Bosniac Army's failure to surrender.

Not surprisingly, this new frame (largely based on the ones the trial chamber had created) did not address the main question raised by Richard Butler, one of the many military experts of the Office of the Prosecutor, who had testified in the Krstić trial: Why did the Bosnian Serb Army, which had become famous for taking hostages at every occassion, refrain from using the incredibly valuable bargaining chip it had obtained after the fall of the enclave? Why did Mladić and his officers throw away such an asset instead of using it in order to "get significant political leverage"?[581] Neither the trial chamber, nor the appeals chamber were able to provide a satisfying answer to this question, which also remained open in many other frames that attempted to explain the events in and around Srebrenica in July 1995.[582]

Judges as Agenda-Setters

According to the legal procedures of the ICTY, the chief prosecutor is the agenda-setter of the decision-making process, and pre-trial chambers (while confirming indictments), trial chambers and appeals chambers act as potential veto players, which can reject indictments in whole or in part before and during the trial, or acquit an accused. With regard to media and public opinion, it is also usually the chief prosecutor who sets the agenda by issuing indictments and making moral and legal judgments in public or accusing a person or a state (for example for non-compliance). Carla Del Ponte became famous for using her

581 Richard Butler, quoted according to Nettlefield, Courting Democracy, 81.

582 For a surprisingly compelling discussion of possible rationales behind the massacres of the male adult population of Srebrenica see: Wilcoxson, Andy: "No evidence for "Srebrenica Genocide" Verdict." The Balkan Monitor 12.4.2011. http://www.balkanstudies.org/articles/no-evidence-srebrenica-genocide-verdict. Wilcoxson doubts whether the claim of a genocide at Srebrenica could be substantiated by evidence if it was compared to the genocide tests applied by ICTY appeals chambers. He seems to favour a "military frame", according to which the men and boys were killed in order to eliminate future combatants. The "mens rea" of the perpetrator was, according to him, not the intention to eradicate the whole group of Bosnian Muslims, but only their potential future fighters. Wilcoxson errs when he finds that this kind of "mens rea" cannot be regarded as genocidal, since the the perpetrators would still intend to destroy a protected group "in part" (although not in "whole"). See *the pros. vs. Krstić* trial chamber judgment, paragraph 587, where the judges set out this argument, pointing to Whitaker, Benjamin: "Revised and Updated Report on the Question of the Prevention and Punishment of the Crime of Genocide, United Nations, Economic and Social Council, Commission on Human Rights, Sub-Commission on Prevention of Discrimination and Protection of Minorities", E/CN.4/Sub. 2/1985/6, 02.07.1985. The report can be retrieved from: http://www.preventgenocide.org/prevent/UNdocs/whitaker/

agenda-setting power to determine public discussion about the ICTY, making strong normative statements and putting blame on other actors. The tribunal president, the trial chambers and appeals chamber may contain or hamper the prosecutor in his activities, but due to the institutional and legal constraints and the self-imposed reluctance of judges to make public statements as well as their anxiety to avoid the impression of any bias, their agenda-setting power is much weaker.

The case of Srebrenica shows that judges can act as powerful agenda-setters, too. Due to the reluctance of other actors (except Human Rights Watch) to make clear and unequivocal statements and create simple frames, which could be taken over by the public, it was judge Riad who took the initiative and imposed his frame, which determined the way other actors and his fellow judges later presented the events. While in *the pros. vs. Akayesu* the court followed the line prescribed by international human rights organisations and international media, the ICTY's handling of the Srebrenica events shows a high level of autonomy. There is a certain congruence between the judges' frames about Srebrenica and the strong normative language of Human Rights Watch's October report, but the latter's frames were so broad that this congruence occurred with respect to almost all other frames present in the public at the time. By endorsing the Halilović-argument and putting forward strategic reasons for the massacres, the judges also distanced themselves from the psychological "omnipotence" frame HRW had ascribed to "the Bosnian Serbs".

The ICTY could become an agenda-setter mainly for two reasons: because it reacted quickly and issued strong, emotional frames which were easy to endorse by other actors, and because most other potential frame producers remained silent or created weak frames, which were deprived of emotions, contained complicated explanations and did not provide simple, moralizing explanations. The UN reports about Srebrenica with their differentiated analysis about Dutchbat's, Mladić's and the Srebrenica defenders' behaviour is a typical example. Such reports are almost perfect sources for historians and analysts, but they usually do not have a big impact on public opinion. The NIOD report had the same fate – it was so holistic, that it could be used for almost any purpose.

Nevertheless, the judges' frames in the Srebrenica case were not really original or new. They built on some presumptions which had already been dominant in the public realm before. The cornerstones of this overarching narrative, which the frames fit into, consisted of the conviction about (Bosnian) Serb guilt, the frame of Dutchbat as "helpless bystanders" (which was only briefly challenged in HRW's reports), and Muslims as victims. These elements were well established already before July 1995, but the events and their framing by the ICTY strongly reinforced them in public discourse. The same is true of the exposure of two men as the main culprits of the massacres. The Dutch frames were inconsistent and incomplete, but they were unanimous when it came to blaming of Karadžić and Mladić. Both quickly became the personification of genocide, and their names were inextricably linked to Srebrenica in public discourse.[583] It is striking that the ICTY, which was weak and in danger of being sidelined by diplomacy and the logic of the Dayton peace in 1995, carried out its agenda-setting power toward public opinion much more vigorously and successfully than it did after 2000, when more and more suspects arrived in The Hague, when Croatia and Serbia started to cooperate, and the trial chambers on the Churchillplein were working at full tilt. By then, media coverage had become much more critical and the ICTY seemed to be helpless against the rising criticism from the US, and as a result almost completely refrained from even trying to set the agenda of public debates. There are strong indications that this was due to the Milošević Trial.[584]

583 This is true only with respect to public discourse. As the practice of the ICTY shows, many more people were accused and sentenced for the events in Srebrenica (whose names remained much less – if at all – associated with the Srebrenica genocide frame, especially in Western media coverage).

584 More about the trial and its implications for the ICTY's public image and the agenda-setting power of the tribunal in later years in Waters, The Milošević trial, part III "Reporting the Demise".

The Frames of the Račak Events in Kosovo

On January 15, 1999, forces of the Serbian Ministry of the Interior advanced on Račak, a village in southern Kosovo. The village was known as a stronghold of the Kosovo Liberation Army (KLA), which had been founded during the mid-1990s by radical Albanian nationalists who disagreed with the pacifist autonomy movement headed by Ibrahim Rugova. The attack on Račak was a reaction to KLA attacks on police stations, during which three policemen had died during the days preceding the attack on Račak. According to eyewitness accounts collected later, Serb forces shelled the village and then conducted house-to-house searches. They were accompanied by a reporter of Associated Press.

Before and during these events, a special unarmed deployment of the Organisation of Security and Cooperation in Europe (OSCE), the so-called Kosovo Verification Mission, was present in Kosovo and had been invited by the Serbian forces to observe the attack. KVM observers could observe the events only from outside; they were not allowed to penetrate the village before the following day. On January 16, they were able to enter the village, inspect the scene and talk to villagers. By then, they had discovered 45 bodies with numerous mutilations and wounds, including the bodies of several women and that of a 12-year old boy. These bodies were later taken away by a Serb forensic team to Priština and examined by Finnish, Belorussian and Serb forensic expert teams.

Two Antagonistic Frames From Governments

When William Walker, an US career diplomat, former CIA agent and head of the KVM, arrived at the scene and had been briefed by his observers, he denounced the events as an "unspeakable atrocity" and "a crime very much against humanity", blaming the Serb government for the killings and demanding them to be investigated and the perpetrators punished. In the tense climate of escalation, which prevailed at that time in Kosovo, Walker's words contributed to a polarisation of positions between Western governments and the federal government of Yugoslavia under Slobodan Milošević. After the news about a massacre in Račak had reached Western media and government offices, a fierce battle concerning the interpretation of the events started, revealing two opposite and mutually exclusive sets of frames about what had happened.

The first set, whose agenda had been set by William Walker, claimed that unarmed civilians had been slaughtered by Serb forces in an exaggerated and disproportional attack on a civilian settlement in the village. The frame left open whether the alleged massacre was caused by overzealous local commanders or in accordance with orders the police and military forces had received from Belgrade. The various “massacre frames” differed with respect to this question. Walker’s version claimed Yugoslav (rather than Serb) security forces were responsible for what he called a “massacre”. He also alleged three women and a child to be among the victims, and in emotional language accused the Yugoslav authorities of badly returning a favour the KLA had done to them the days before, when the organisation had released 8 Yugoslav soldiers.[585]

The opposite frame claimed that Serb forces had conducted an anti-terrorist intervention, which was justified by previous KLA activities in the region and had been proportional to the threat it intended to eliminate. During this intervention, only KLA fighters had been killed and the alleged crime scene had been manipulated by the KLA, which had removed and replaced bodies in order to create the impression that unarmed civilians had been massacred. This “hoax frame” did not leave room for variation.

Supporters of both frames used extremely emotional language in their interpretations of the events. The Serb government described the events as an “anti-terrorist action” or a “police operation”, and the crimes the police had dealt with as “acts of terrorists”. It refrained from applying precise legal notions to the alleged crimes of the KLA, contrary to William Walker, who had immediately suggested that the crimes he imputed to the Serb forces fell under the ICTY’s jurisdiction as crimes against humanity.[586] Whereas Walker’s first statements were strongly emotional, the first press releases of the Serb Ministry of the Interior were formulated in almost neutral language, presenting the police action in Račak as the result of an attempt to arrest a “terrorist group”, which had attacked a police station in another village in the vicinity the day before and had killed a policeman.[587] The problem with this official version was that it changed rapidly over time. This, of course, could be due to new information the Ministry received from its structures in Kosovo; it also could be due to propaganda efforts aiming at presenting the events in more favourable light. On January 16, the Ministry claimed its forces had been fired upon and had responded to this fire, killing 10 “terrorists”, most of whom had been in KLA uniforms.[588] Leading politicians’

585 Op. cit, 289.

586 BBC: World: Europe. “Nato crisis talks on massacre.” 17.1.1999.

587 Ministarstvo unutrašnjich poslova Respublike Srbije, Priština, saopštenje za javnost, 15.1.1999, according to Simić, Ilija: Istina o Račku, Beograd 2006, 294.

588 Ministarstvo unutrašnjich poslova Respublike Srbije, Priština, saopštenje, 16.1.1999, according to ibid., 295 (this press release came from the Information Department, not from Priština. Another, undated release was more detailed and dealt polemically with Walker’s statements, claiming at the same time that the police had acted “proportionally

statements on the events were much more outspoken. ''With a series of lies and fabrications he[589] accused our State authorities in an obvious attempt do divert the attention from terrorists, murderers, and kidnapers and to one again protect them the way he has been protecting them long ago. Ever since he came, he turned a blind eye to the crimes of the terrorists", Serb president Milan Milutinović declared in Belgrade.[590] In their later testimonies in the Milošević trial, high officers of the Serbian Ministry of the Interior claimed that at the time of the incident in Račak, the village had been empty and the only casualties of the fighting had been KLA fighters.[591]

Media Frames

The Yugoslav authorities were quite isolated in attempting to present the events in Račak as a justified and appropriate police intervention which had been triggered by terrorist attacks. The first doubts about Walker's Manichean vision of the events emerged several days after the Yugoslav authorities had already taken position and Western governments had blamed them for the alleged killing of innocent civilians. A reporter of France's Le Monde was among the first to enter the village and conduct his own research. He found the village inhabitants' versions of the events of January 15 "difficult to explain", and cast doubts on the interpretation, according to which a massacre had been perpetrated "in cold blood against disarmed victims."[592] Other reporters followed, like Berliner Zeitung's Bo Adam, who went there a year later and encountered various contradictions between the official versions of Western governments and the evidence he found on the ground. In 2005, Milošević called him as a defence witness.[593]

---

and in accordance with the international agreements between Yugoslavia and the OSCE." The press release specifically rejected Walker's statement about 45 casualties.

589 "He" refers to William Walker.

590 AFP 1/17/1999; Tanjug 1/17/1999.

591 Transcript Milošević Trial, police colones in Urosevac, Bogoljub Janicijevic, 30.09.2005. http://www.icty.org/x/cases/slobodan_Milošević/trans/en/050930IT.htm

592 "La version rapportée par les habitants albanais de ce village du Kosovo comporte des éléments difficilement explicables, rapporte notre envoyé spécial, et oblige à s'interroger sur un massacre qui aurait été perpétré froidement contre des victimes désarmées", Le Monde 21.1.1999.

593 Anna Uzelac: "Witness disputes Račak findings." IWPR TRI issue 391, 17 Nov 2005.

The Frames of the US Government

The Serb version stood in strong contrast to the version human rights organisations and Western governments promoted during the days following January 15. The US government issued several very emotional and accusatory statements, directly blaming the Serb government for the alleged killings. These statements were phrased in a style which was quite unusual for official declarations made on behalf of governments and considerably went beyond the language of diplomacy, denouncing the events as a "massacre", as "murders", "brutal murders", and "barbaric killings". Already on January 16, the Press Office of the White House distributed a statement by president Bill Clinton, which condemned "in the strongest possible terms the massacre of civilians by Serb security forces that took place last night in the village of Račak in Kosovo. This was a deliberate and indiscriminate act of murder designed to sow fear among the people of Kosovo. It is a clear violation of the commitments Serbian authorities have made to NATO. There can he no justification for it."[594] Even when compared to the White House's and the State Department's comments on Rwanda in April, these statements were quite emotional.

Already the following day, several members of the House of Representatives introduced a draft resolution, which was submitted to the Committee of International Relations and which requested NATO to implement its activation order from October 12, 1998, in order to compel the Serb government to comply with the respective UNSC resolutions. The draft resolution contained a section dealing with the events in Račak: "There have been numerous reports of atrocities committed by the military forces and police of Serbia-Montenegro since the Holbrooke-Milošević agreement, including the brutal murders of at least 45 ethnic Albanians in Račak, Kosovo, in January 1999."[595]

In retrospect, the events in Račak were a turning point in the history of the Kosovo conflict, and contributed to the hardening of the Western states' position toward Serbia. It is difficult to say whether they actually triggered the NATO bombing campaign, which started in March 1999, but they were often and extensively used as a justification for military intervention. In April, when the bombing campaign was already underway, Albright told the Foreign Relations Committee of the Senate: "By opposing Slobodan Milošević's murderous

594 The White House, Office of the Press Secretary. Statement by the President on the Massacre of civilians in Račak. Washington, DC, 16.01.1999. http://1997-2001.state.gov/www/policy_remarks/1999/990118_pres_Račak.html

595 The House of Representatives, 106th Congress, 1st Session, H. CON. RES. 13, 19.01.1999. http://www.gpo.gov/fdsys/pkg/BILLS-106hconres13ih/html/BILLS-106hconres13ih.htm

rampage, NATO is playing its rightful role as a defender of freedom and security within the Euro-Atlantic region. Because our cause is just, we are united. And because we are united, we are confident that in this confrontation between barbaric killing and necessary force; between vicious intolerance and respect for human rights; between tyranny and democracy; we will prevail."[596] At a meeting at Brookings Institution in Washington D.C., she explained her interpretation of the conflict: "It was Milošević a decade ago who stripped the Kosovo Albanians of the autonomy to which they were entitled; who launched last Spring a campaign of brutal repression; who violated the ceasefire negotiated last October; whose security forces committed acts of barbarism such as the massacre at Račak earlier this year; and who refused to join the leaders of Kosovo in signing the balanced and just settlement negotiated at Rambouillet."[597]

The Frames of the French Government

Given the ideological differences and the conflicts of interest, which had often come to the fore between the US and France and the initially pro-Serbian attitude of the French governments during the breakdown of Yugoslavia, one could have expected the position of Paris to differ from the frames used by leading politicians in Washington. That was not the case; the events in Račak were strongly condemned. They were labelled as "massacre", "act of barbarity", "horror", "atrocities" and "crimes". Pierre Moscovici, Minister of European Affairs, spoke during a debate in the National Assembly several days after the events: "These atrocities were unanimously condemned by the international community. France expressed her protest and disgust, and the Prime Minister has qualified them as a 'barbarous act'. Like him, I think there are no words for characterizing the horror: Protest and disgust overwhelm us at the sight of those old men and children, who were assassinated. Those responsible for these barbarous acts must know that they will not be able to escape from justice and will have to answer for their crimes."[598] Just as in the US, Račak later became

596 Secretary of State Madeleine K. Albright Statement before the Senate Foreign Relations Committee Washington, D.C., 20.04.1999 "U.S. and NATO Policy Toward the Crisis in Kosovo":http://1997-2001.state.gov/www/statements/1999/990420.html

597 The Brookings Institution, National Issues Forum: "A New NATO for a New Century Washington", D.C., 06.04.1999 As released by the Office of the Spokesman U.S. Department of State.
http://1997-2001.state.gov/www/statements/1999/990406.html

598 "Ces atrocités ont été unanimement condamnées par la communauté internationale. La France a exprimé sa révolte et son dégoût et le Premier ministre a dénoncé «un acte de

the main cornerstone of explaining why NATO had launched an attack on Serbia and why France had participated in the bombing. Lionel Jospin stated in the National Assembly on March 26: "On January 15 last year, a new level of horror has been reached with the massacre of 45 Albanians at Račak. [...] We are not fighting a war against the Serb people. We remember its heroic past during the fight against Nazi oppression. We are not enemies of the Serb nation, which has the legitimate right to be offered a future in a democratic Europe. But we have to state that today the Serb authorities bear a heavy responsibility for the current crisis. It is not a people which is targeted, but a military and repressive apparatus. Not a nation is banned, but a regime, obstinately rejecting the rules of the international community.[599]

The Frames of The New York Times

For The New York Times, the case was initially not that clear. The day after the alleged massacre, The New York Times covered the events with a report claiming that 15 people had been killed in clashes between Serb police forces and the KLA and that a KVM member had been injured elsewhere in Kosovo.[600] The article mostly concentrated on the injured observer. It was only on January 17 that the daily started to discuss the implications of the events for the Clinton administration and possible NATO airstrikes against Serbia. Guilt and blame were not evident elements of the story and the question whether a massacre had actually taken place was not at issue. Several NATO officials and sources from

---

barbarie». Comme lui, je pense qu'il n'y a pas de mots pour qualifier l'horreur: la révolte et le dégoût nous saisissent à la vue de ces vieillards et de ces enfants assassinés. Les responsables de ces actes de barbarie doivent savoir qu'ils ne peuvent échapper à la justice et qu'ils devront répondre de leurs crimes." Pierre Moscovici, Minister of European Affairs during a debate in the National Assembly, 20.01.1999 http://questions.assemblee-nationale.fr/q11/11-1036QG.htm

599 « Le 15 janvier dernier, à Račak, avec le massacre de 45 Albanais, un nouveau degré était atteint dans l'horreur.(...) Nous ne faisons pas la guerre au peuple serbe. Nous gardons en mémoire son passé héroïque dans la lutte contre l'oppression nazie. Nous ne sommes pas les ennemis de la nation serbe, qui a le droit légitime de se voir offrir un avenir dans une Europe démocratique. Mais nous devons constater qu'aujourd'hui, ce sont les autorités de Belgrade qui portent seules la lourde responsabilité de la crise actuelle. Ce n'est pas un peuple qui est visé, mais un appareil militaire et répressif. Ce n'est pas une nation qui est mise au ban, mais un régime récusant avec obstination les règles de la communauté internationale." Lionel Jospin, Declaration of the government on the situation in Kosovo in the National Assembly, 26.03.1999, http://www.assemblee-nationale.fr/11/cra/1998-1999/99032611.asp

600 The New York Times, 16.1.1999.

the administration were quoted, among them Walker, who blamed the Serbian side for the escalation, but in general the report was more moderate and balanced than any of the official government statements preceding it.[601] The same day, The New York Times published a more emotional article, which exposed some of the gruesome details of the alleged massacre.[602] Now the unnamed author of the article called the events "a carnage", and the overall tendency of the article made it clear who was to blame, despite quotes summarizing the version of the Yugoslav authorities. "Many had been shot at close range, and residents of Račak village said Serbian forces had rounded up the men, driven them up the hill and shot them. Twenty-eight bodies lay heaped together at the bottom of a muddy hillside gully. All the victims were dressed in civilian clothing, despite the insistence of the Serbian police that most of the 'terrorists' wore uniforms of the rebel Kosovo Liberation Army."[603] Days later, the newspaper printed an abbreviated version of a KVM report about the events, which made it clear that at least some of the victims there had been shot "at extremely close range", among them a 12-year-old boy who had been shot in the neck.[604]

The Frames of Le Monde

Le Monde coverage of the events was not less emotional or colourful, but more space was dedicated to the dilemma of intervention versus non-intervention, which had gained salience after Račak. Le Monde titles often stipulated moral implications for Europe in the case of non-intervention, calling Račak "a shame for Europe" and comparing the reluctance of Europeans to intervene in the conflict to Western countries' failure to prevent the fall of Vukovar and Srebrenica.[605] On January 20, the French national daily published a large story by its Yugoslav correspondent, Christophe Chatelot, in which he cast serious doubts on the interpretation according to which Serb policemen and soldiers had carried out a cold-blooded massacre on unarmed civilians in Račak.[606] The newspaper printed a follow-up the next day, asking overtly whether the dead of Račak had really been massacred in cold blood.[607] The author, Christophe

601 Jane Perlez: "US weighs its reaction to massacre in Kosovo." The New York Times 17.1.1999.

602 "Mutilated Kosovo bodies found after Serb attack." The New York Times 17.1.1999.

603 Op. cit.

604 "Charting a massacre. The Monitors' report." The New York Times, 22.1.1999.

605 Jean Cot: Honte a l'Europe. Le Monde 20.1.1999.

606 Christophe Chatelot: Rien ne va plus depuis la mort du Maréchal. Le Monde 20.1.1999.

607 Christophe Chatelot: Les morts de Račak ont-ils vraiment été massacrés froidement? Le Monde 21.1.1999.

Chatelot, relied heavily on the film which the AP team had shot after entering Račak together with the Serb forces. He suggested that the Serb forces had actually entered an empty village, whose population had been hiding in the surrounding hills and forests, and had returned to the settlement after the Serb police had left shortly before sunset. Chatelot claimed that the corpses in the row had been discovered the next day, when KVM officers entered the town, "guided by KLA members" ("guidés par l'UCK").

At the end of the month, the "massacre frame" was strongly boosted by an article in The Washington Post, which revealed the content of telephone conversations between Serbian Interior Minister General Sreten Lukić and Yugoslav Deputy Prime Minister Nikola Šainović, indicating that government forces had obtained orders for "going in heavy" in Račak. The paper claimed that "the calls show that the assault on Račak was monitored closely at the highest levels of the Yugoslav government and controlled by the senior Serbian military commander in Kosovo."[608] The paper had already decided long before who was ultimately to blame for Račak. It was, according to an Editorial from January 18, "Mr. Milošević's Massacre". Slobodan Milošević, named "the despot of Serbia", had been "waging war against the people of Kosovo". In this respect, The Washington Post's frames were much more congruent with the ones used by Human Rights Watch, than with The New York Times' way of presenting things. A day after the Post's leak of the telephone intercepts, Human Rights Watch distributed a short and blunt press release which solved the problem of guilt. Human Rights Watch categorically rejected Yugoslav government claims that the victims of the January 15 attack on Račak were either Kosovo Liberation Army soldiers killed in combat, or civilians caught in crossfire.

The Frames of Human Rights Watch

After a detailed investigation, the organisation accused Serbian special police forces and the Yugoslav army of indiscriminately attacking civilians, torturing detainees, and committing summary executions. "The evidence suggests that government forces had direct orders to kill village inhabitants over the age of fifteen." The release ended with an appeal to the Yugoslav authorities to allow investigations on the ground, and to the international community "to take resolute action against Yugoslav President Slobodan Milošević and his government for brazenly violating international humanitarian law." Given the on-going debate about NATO intervention, the press release provided a strong

608 R. Jeffrey Smith: "Serbs Tried To Cover Up Massacre; Kosovo Reprisal Plot Bared by Phone Taps." Washington Post 28.1.1999.

argument for military action, although it did not specify how such action should be carried out.[609] On February 1, the organisation published another report entitled "A Week of Terror in Drenica" which, together with additional information about other sites with casualties, repeated the version about Račak from two days earlier.[610] After the start of the Rambouillet talks, the organisation strongly campaigned for a settlement which should exclude impunity for perpetrators of violence in Kosovo.[611] Despite framing the conflict as a Serb government attack on unarmed civilians, HRW had, on different occasions, also blamed the KLA for violating human rights and called on it to respect the Geneva Conventions. This, however, had only occupied a marginal part of its publications.

The Frames of the Kosovo Liberation Army

Since the purpose of this subchapter is to to find out which of the putative actors interested in the outcome of ICTY decisions exercised the strongest influence on the prosecution and the trial chamber, one organisation – which neither fulfils the criteria of a government, nor of a human rights organisation, nor of a media outlet – cannot be omitted: the Kosovo Liberation Army. In the course of the Račak events, the KLA was already a strong, organized movement with a centralized command structure and considerable firepower as well as unofficial representatives in Kosovo and abroad (who took part in the Rambouillet talks). These elements were later crucial criteria for the trial chambers dealing with atrocities in Kosovo in applying the Geneva Conventions to the conflict and treating the KLA as an armed force according to international criminal law. KLA's press releases, speeches of their political and military leaders, publications distributed on behalf of the KLA, and actions undertaken by its followers are therefore not unlikely to directly or indirectly have influenced media coverage, reports of non-governmental and intergovernmental organisations (like the KVM, the OSCE, the UN, the EU or even NATO) and they are not unlikely to have been channelled, in whatever way, into proceedings of the ICTY. It does therefore make sense to include the KLA version of the Račak events in this analysis.

The KLA consequently described the Račak events as a "massacre", "slaughter" and as "murders". Some KLA statements refer to a "massacre and

609 Human Rights Watch press release, 29.1.1999: "Human Rights Watch investigation finds: Yugoslav Forces Guilty of War Crimes in Račak, Kosovo."

610 Human Rights Watch: "A week of terror in Drenica." 1.2.1999.

611 Human Rights Watch: "No Kosovo Settlement Without Accountability for War Crimes. New Report Documents Yugoslav Government Atrocities." February 6.2.1999.

terrible atrocities". These accusations followed a twofold strategy directed at blaming the Yugoslav government and undermining its credibility in the world, and at the same time mobilizing support among Kosovo Albanians in Kosovo and abroad by presenting a common enemy. It must be kept in mind that the KLA was far from representing the entire political spectre of Kosovo, competing with other, more moderate strands of the autonomy movement there. After Račak, the KLA accused the Yugoslav government of having launched an experiment of "mass destruction of Kosovo Albanians'' and of losing its mind and committing a new massacre against the Albanian civilian population. In a political declaration, the KLA stated that the massacre in Račak should be a last warning to the Albanians to unite and join the Kosovo Liberation Army.[612] The language of these declarations reveals the usage of ethnic, national and cultural criteria in attributing guilt to the Serbian state, the Yugoslav government, president Milošević and Serbian forces, but also regional criteria by holding Serb volunteers responsible. In the first statements following January 15, all victims were described as unarmed civilians, including a "young woman and a 12-year-old boy". Later on, while testifying before the ICTY, KLA commander Shukri Buja admitted that nine members of the KLA were killed in fighting and eight were wounded by the Serbian police.[613] Contradicting its own claim that the government in Belgrade had "lost its mind", the KLA provided a relatively detailed explanation for the massacre, claiming that the massacre in Račak had been committed by the Serbian police in revenge for the killing of three Serbian policemen near the village Stimlje on January 8. The others were massacred because the KLA had pushed back a force of 500 Serbian policemen and soldiers from Račak.[614] In both cases, the alleged massacre was

612 Quote according to Croatian Daily Vjesnik, 18.1.1999.

613 Mirko Klarin: "The Case of the Missing Witnesses. Why are key US officials involved in the international bid to solve the Kosovo crisis absent from the witness list in the Milošević trial?" *IWPR BCR* Issue 342, 12.6.2002. According to the testimony of Shukri Buja, the KLA commander in Račak, who testified during the Milošević Trial, the KLA had 47 soldiers in Račak and on January 15, 1999 they opened fire on the Serbian police who were entering the village. See: Transcript from Milošević Trial, Shukri Buja, former KLA commander in Račak, 06.06.2002. http://www.icty.org/x/cases/slobodan_Milošević/trans/en/020606IT.htm

Buja also told the court during cross-examination by Milošević that on January 15, 8 of his KLA soldiers had been killed and eight others had been wounded. He admitted that two men aged 60 had reluctantly been admitted as soldiers and had to be regarded as combatants rather than civilians.

614 Local KLA commander Shukri Buja told this to a reporter of the British daily The independent a few days after the events. Ryamond Whitacker: "A fearful return home." The Independent 24.1.1999.
http://www.independent.co.uk/life-style/a-fearful-return-home-1076022.html

therefore explained by revenge. The president of the FRY Slobodan Milošević was held responsible for the massacre. In later statements, guilt was extended to the whole government of Serbia and, in part, to the international community for not reacting.[615]

Table 2: Frames concerning the events in Račak during spring 1999

Content of the frame	Yugoslav /Serbian gover-nment	US gover-nment	French gover-nment	The New York Times	Human Rights Watch	Le Mon-de	The Washin-gton Post	Kosovo Libera-tion Army
Serbia attacks, KLA defends		X	X	X	X	X	X	X
Casualties in Račak were all civilians		X	X		X		X	X
Casualties in Račak were all combatants	X							
Armed fighters were present in Račak				X		X		
Račak was a "massacre"		X	X	X	X	X	X	X
Račak was staged by KLA ("hoax frame")	X							
Serbian and Yugoslav autho-rities are blamed		X	X	X	X	X	X	X
KLA is blamed	X							
Both sides are blamed								
Serb forces acted on orders		X	X	X	X		X	

615 We are grateful to Irena Ristić for many of the Yugoslav and Serbian sources about Račak. References for the KLA frames can also be found in the following sources: Transcript from *the pros. vs. Limaj et al*, IT-03-66, http://www.icty.org/case/limaj/4. During the prosecution's case, a KLA book called "Fallen Heroes" was tendered. This book, although incomplete, lists the names of KLA members who were killed during the war. The quote concerning guilt of the Serbian government and of the international community stems from Vjesnik, ibid.

Serb forces acted on own account								X
Milošević is personally responsible		X			X		X	X
KLA is solely responsible	X							
KLA are "rebels"				X				
KLA are "terrorists"	X							
KLA are legiti-mate fighters					X			
Serb attack was proportional	X							
Serb attack was exaggerated		X	X	X	X	X	X	X
Summary executions took place in Račak					X			
Fighting was an "internal armed conflict" in legal terms					X			
Fighting was police action	X							
Conflict emerged from Serb oppression against Kosovo Albanian population		X			X			X
Conflict is a result of Serb oppression by Kosovo Albanians								
Conflict falls under ICTY jurisdiction		X	X		X			

The table conclusively shows the isolated position of the Yugoslav authorities – whatever frame they used for describing the events in Račak, no other actor would agree with them, whereas the US government could be sure that its frames would collide with practically all other frames, except for the Yugoslav and Serbian ones. Only with respect to Milošević being personally responsible for Račak, the US was a little isolated. The French government supported this claim. ICTY jurisdiction for Račak was supported explicitly by Human Rights Watch and the government of France and the US; though none of the other actors rejected the idea of charging the ICTY with the case. Strikingly enough, Serb action in Kosovo was condemned most strongly not by a government or even by the KLA: Human Rights Watch surpassed all other actors included in the table by claiming that summary executions had been carried out in Račak and an order had been given to kill all Albanians in the village over the age of 15. This claim was not even substantiated by the quotes the organisation mentioned in its press release. No other actor, including the KLA itself, mentioned a similar accusation. The human rights organisation also maintained that all victims in the village had been civilians. At the same time, HRW regarded the KLA as legitimate fighters, which fell under (and had to respect) the Geneva Conventions. Opposite to many other actors involved, it looked upon the conflict as an internal armed conflict, to which the Geneva conventions could be applied (an interpretation which differed considerably from William Walker's concept of a "crime against humanity.") Only HRW, the US government (Secretary Albright, to be precise) and the KLA shared the belief that it had been the Serb oppression of Albanians in Kosovo which had led to the conflict.

Both the US and the French government appealed to the Yugoslav authorities to let the ICTY investigate the events in Račak. They condemned the police and military action, but left open whether they blamed local commanders, the military leadership, the Serb (or Yugoslav) government, or Milošević personally for the alleged massacre. ICTY chief prosecutor Louise Arbour had immediately travelled to the region and attempted to enter Kosovo from the Macedonian border, in order to inspect the crime site in Račak. Yugoslav border guards refused access. After his unequivocal comments about the events, William Walker was declared persona non grata by the Yugoslav government and asked to leave the country within 48 hours.[616] In May of the same year, during NATO's bombing campaign, Arbour submitted the first indictment against Milošević for war crimes and crimes against humanity allegedly committed in Kosovo. She accused him together with several other prominent

616 BBC: "Yugoslavia denounces OSCE claims." 18.1.1999.

politicians and military leaders of Serbia, Milan Milutinović, Nikola Šainović, Dragoljub Ojdanić and Vlajko Stojiljković.[617]

Human Rights Watch played an important role in securing evidence for the indictments concerning Kosovo. HRW researchers had travelled to Albania and interviewed refugees in provisional camps. Transcripts were given to investigators of the OTP. Before the Milošević trial started, Human Rights Watch distributed to journalists and tribunal observers a large volume, which contained many of these testimonies, an analysis of the command structure of the Yugoslav Army and the Serbian police, and a legal assessment of the crimes described in the book. The book concentrated almost entirely on atrocities committed after the NATO bombing had started (when these atrocities actually had dramatically increased, leading to waves of forced migration into Albania and Montenegro). The events in Račak were dealt with only in a cursory way. HRW no longer claimed that only civilians had been killed in Račak; the report now spoke only about "ethnic Albanians". HRW sustained the claim that summary executions had been carried out in the village, quoting, as a reference, its own reports from early 1999.[618]

By 2001, the juridical reckoning with the events in Račak in 1999 had led to several verdicts in Kosovo courts (some of which had been issued by trial chambers comprising international judges) against 3 Serb policemen and the former mayor of Orahovac. As Human Rights Watch' *Under Orders* mentioned, these trials were strongly criticized by human rights organisations for bias and lack of procedural fairness. The verdicts oscillated between 5 and 20 years of imprisonment.[619]

The Prosecution Frames About the Events in Račak

In early 2002, after Slobodan Milošević had been ousted from office in Belgrade and transferred to the ICTY in 2001, the trial against him – based on the Kosovo indictment drafted by Louise Arbour – began under the auspices of the new OTP chief, Carla Del Ponte. In this indictment (which would later be merged into one with indictments concerning Bosnia and Croatia) the counts relating to Račak were the first cases of alleged mass murder presented against Slobodan Milošević and the only crime at the time attributed to Milošević before NATO had launched its air strikes. They remained in the

617 *The pros. vs. Milošević et al.* IT-99-37.

618 Human Rights Watch: Under Orders. War Crimes in Kosovo. New York, Washington, London, Brussels 2001, 56-57, 80, 103, 112, 157, 483.

619 Human Rights Watch: Under Orders, 483.

indictment after the Milošević trial had started, and became a major issue of controversy during the prosecution case.

The prosecution framed the events in Račak in the following way: "Although scores of OSCE verifiers were deployed throughout Kosovo, hostilities continued. During this period, a number of killings of Kosovo Albanians were documented by the international verifiers and human rights organisations. In one such incident, on 15 January 1999, 45 unarmed Kosovo Albanians were murdered in the village of Račak in the municipality of Stimlje/Shtime." Further, the indictment claims, that "beginning on or about 1 January 1999 and continuing until the date of this indictment, forces of the FRY and Serbia, acting at the direction, with the encouragement, or with the support of Slobodan Milošević, Milan Miluntinović, Nikola Šainović, Dragoljub Ojdanić and Vlajko Stojiliković, have murdered hundreds of Kosovo Albanian civilians. These killings have occurred in a widespread or systematic manner throughout the province of Kosovo and have resulted in the deaths of numerous men, women, and children. Included among the incidents of mass killings are the following." Here the indictment specifically deals with the situation in Račak in January 1999. "On or about 15 January 1999, in the early morning hours, the village of Račak (Stimlje/Shtime municipality) was attacked by forces of the FRY and Serbia. After shelling by the VJ units, the Serb police entered the village later in the morning and began conducting house-to-house searches. Villagers, who attempted to flee from the Serb police, were shot throughout the village. A group of approximately 25 men attempted to hide in a building, but were discovered by the Serb police. They were beaten and then were removed to a nearby hill, where the policemen shot and killed them. Altogether, the forces of the FRY and Serbia killed approximately 45 Kosovo Albanians in and around Račak."[620]

At the end of June 2001, the OTP submitted an amended indictment for Kosovo. In October of the same year, the indictment was altered again. But none of the changes affected the framing of the Račak case and the wording of the relevant parts of the indictment remained unchanged.[621] On September 5, 2002, the trial chamber separated the Milošević case from the cases against the remaining accused. Since then, Milošević was accused on the basis of a single

620 The initial Milošević indictment is *the pros. vs. Slobodan Milošević, Milan Milutinović, Nikola Šainović, Drgoljub Ojdanić, Vlajko Stojiljković* IT-99-37.

621 The first amended Milošević indictment is *the pros. vs. Slobodan Milošević, Milan Milutinović, Nikola Šainović, Drgoljub Ojdanić, Vlajko Stojiljković* IT-99-37-I, and the second amended Milošević Indictment (concerning Kosovo) is *the pros. vs. Slobodan Milošević, Milan Milutinović, Nikola Šainović, Drgoljub Ojdanić, Vlajko Stojiljković* IT-99-37-PT.

indictment, directed only against him.[622] The charges relating to Račak remained in this single indictment. The other accused were indicted separately, but their indictment had to be amended a third time, because the name and charges relating to Vlajko Stojiljković, the former Serb Minister of the Interior and Head of the Police under Milošević had to be removed – he had shot himself in the head on the stairs leading to the Yugoslav parliament, hours after the parliament had voted on a bill which facilitated the surrender of suspects to the ICTY.[623]

The third indictment of *the pros. vs. Milutinović et al.* (IT-99-37-PT) comprised an altered version of the original fragment about Račak that had been in the Milošević indictment. Several details had of the earlier version had been changed. Apart from purely technical changes, the prosecution now no longer claimed that the army had shelled the village before the police had entered it. Now the indictment avoided any specification concerning the perpetrators of the shelling, mentioning only that it had been shelled, and subsequently overrun by FRY forces. In this part of the frame, the police no longer played a role. The fragment about the execution of 25 people from the village had also been altered. In the prior version, these "approximately 25 people" had tried to hide, but had allegedly been discovered by the Serb police. In the third amended indictment, it was now "the forces of the FRY and Serbia" that had discovered them. Then, according to the prosecution's version, these people had been beaten, removed to a nearby hill, and shot. Once again, the wording does not reveal, who exactly abused, removed and shot them, though it emerges clearly from the context that the prosecution regarded the "forces of FRY and Serbia" as guilty of these crimes. The prosecution had also added the formula "and others known and unknown" into the enumeration of the accused.

But the Račak case had not yet finished its odyssey through the OTP's indictments and trials. In April 2005, General Nebojša Pavković arrived in The Hague and the OTP applied for a joinder of his case with the case of the other high-ranking militaries and politicians who had been indicted for crimes in Kosovo. The motion was granted by the trial chamber, and an amended joinder indictment was drafted. However, since Vlastimir Djordjević was still the only one of the accused who remained at large (he was finally transferred to the Hague in 2007), his case was separated from the joint cases of Milutinović et al. and Pavković, and he was later tried on the basis of an indictment of his own.[624]

622 After the joinder decision (which merged the indictment for Croatia, Bosnia and Kosovo into one joint indictment) the trial against Milošević was conducted under the case number *the pros. vs. Milošević* IT-02-54.

623 BBC: "Top Serb suspect dies." 14.4.2002.

624 *The pros. vs. Djordjević* IT-05-87/1.

In the subsequent amended indictments of *the pros. vs. Milutinović et al.*, the Račak case was dealt with in exactly the same way as in IT-99-37-PT.

Members of the OTP had suspected Djordjević to be living in Russia. However, in June 2007, he was arrested in Montenegro, where he had been hiding in the seaside town of Budva under a false name. He was transferred to The Hague.[625] His trial started in January 2009.[626] However, the OTP decided to withdraw all elements referring to Račak from his indictment and to charge him only with crimes committed during and after March 1999. [627]

Prosecution frames about Račak can therefore only be found in two cases: in *the pros. vs. Milutinović et al.* (IT-99-37-PT) and in the Milošević indictment (IT-02-54). Only in these two cases can we expect the judges to give their version of the events in Račak in a judgment. Due to the death of the defendant, the trial chamber in the Milošević case never issued a verdict, neither on the indictment as such, nor specifically on the Račak case. When in April 2003, after the Prosecution had rested its case, the *amici curiae* in the Milošević case filed a motion for judgment of acquittal arguing that the Geneva Conventions could not be applied to the situation in Kosovo in 1999 prior to NATO bombing – since the armed conflict had not been widespread and the KLA could not be regarded as an organisation with respect to which the Conventions could be applied – the trial chamber dismissed the majority of the *amici* arguments, sustaining the indictment. In numerous cases, the *amici* brief's arguments were accepted by the judges, but they did not enter into a deeper discussion of the events in Račak and stated only that the conflict in Kosovo in early 1999 fulfilled the criteria for an armed conflict, and that the KLA had to be regarded as an organized armed group with a unified command and considerable control over large parts of the territory.[628] For these reasons, the judges of the Milošević trial never made a decision about their own version of the events in Račak and how to classify them in legal terms. But Račak remained an issue in the subsequent indictments concerning the group of high-ranking suspects around Milutinović, until it was removed for procedural reasons. This occurred after the prosecution had filed a motion seeking to join the cases against Milutinović et

625 Sense Agency: "Vlastimir Djordjević arrested." 17.6.2007. http://www.sense-agency.com/icty/vlastimir-Djordjević-arrested.29.html?cat_id=1&news_id=10355 B-92: "Hague indictee Vlastimir Djordjević arrested in Montenegro. 17.6.2007 http://www6.b92.net/eng/news/crimes-article.php?yyyy=2007&mm=06&dd=17&nav_id=41862

626 *The pros. vs. Djordjević* IT-05-87-1. It was once amended, but the changes were minor and not connected to the events in Račak.

627 *The pros. vs. Djordjević* IT-05-87/1-PT (operative indictment from 9.7.2008)

628 Decision on motion of acquittal, 16.6.2004. *The pros. vs. Milošević* IT-02-54.

al. and Pavković, and, with the motion granted, the Trial Chamber ordered the Prosecution to file an amended joinder indictment. The redacted indictement was accepted as the operative indictment against six accused, assigning a new case, now titled *the pros. vs. Šainović et al.*[629] in July 2006, before the start of the trial of *the pros. vs. Šainović et al.*[630] On July 7, the Chamber conducted a pre-trial conference and after an oral hearing, on July 11, 2006, the Chamber issued its 'Decision on Application of rule 73' in which it made the following order: ''Pending further order by the Chamber, the Prosecution may present evidence in relation to all crime sites and incidents listed in paragraph 72, and 75, except subparagraphs which set forth the charges in respect of Račak, Padalište and Dubrava.''[631] This way the Chamber "refused to allow evidence to be presented in relation to (among others) Račak on the ground that what allegedly occurred there was not, unlike other killing sites, associated with locations from which persons were allegedly forcibly displaced, and thus did not fall within the 'nature or theme' of the prosecution case."[632] In the very extensive judgment of *the pros. vs. Šainović et al.*, Račak was no longer mentioned and the judges avoided any assessment concerning the character of the events there in 1999. This should not be understood as a decision indicating that Račak (and the other sites) had not been crime sites, or that no crime had occured there in early 1999, since the Rule 73' bis decision was made only in order to expedite the trial and because the prosecution and the chamber agreed that Račak and the other two sites had not been linked to deportation and the forcible transfer of persons. The question whether killings falling under the jurisdiction of the tribunal had occured in Račak was left unanswered for purely procedural reasons.[633]

It was, however, another trial chamber which decided to give its interpretation of the Račak events. As already set out above, the OTP had decided to remove the initial murder charges against the accused[634] pertaining to Račak. But the events in Račak became an issue during the trial anyway, for two reasons. First, the defence called witnesses in order to prove that Račak had not

---

629 *The Prosecutor of the Tribunal against Milan Milutinović, Nikola Šainović, Dragoljub Ojdanić, Nebojsa Pavković, Vladimir Lazarevći, Sreten Lukić*, Third Joint Indictment IT-05-87. http://www.icty.org/x/cases/milutinović/tjug/en/jud090226-e1of4.pdf

630 Op. cit., paragraph 75.

631 Op. cit. paragraph 16.

632 Ibid.

633 The chamber acted in reaction to a motion of the Ojdanić defence and after consultation with the prosecution. See: *the pros. vs. Milutinović et al.* IT-05-87-T, decision on application of Rule 73' bis, 12.7.2006

634 They had been regarded as murder, as a crime against humanity, and a violation of the laws or customs of war.

been a crime against humanity, but an armed clash between, on the one hand, the Army and the police, and, on the other hand, an armed unit of the KLA.[635] The second reason is more opaque. Although the accused was never charged with crimes linked to the Račak events, the trial chamber decided to include the events in the judgment and thoroughly analysed the evidence from the trial in its extensive assessment. Paradoxically, the trial chambers dealing with defendants who were accused of crimes linked to the Račak events never dealt with them in their verdicts, either because they never issued one (in the Milošević trial), or they ordered Račak evidence to be withdrawn from the trial (as in *the pros. vs. Šainović et al.*). The only trial chamber which actually conducted an in-depth analysis (in a judgment whose size amounts to nearly a thousand pages!), was a trial chamber dealing with an accused who had not been charged of crimes linked to Račak.[636]

From a legal standpoint, it would be an abuse to compare the charges against one group of accused (*the pros. vs. Šainović et al.*) with the judgment of another accused in another trial (*the pros. vs. Djordjević*). From the perspective of framing analysis, it makes perfect sense to do so, since it makes it possible to find out how far prosecution frames of the Račak events permeated into the frames used by judges, and how far the prosecution's and the judges' frames were from the ones used in public before the trial in the media, by governments, and by the KLA and non-governmental organisations. The latter comparison allows drawing conclusions about to what extent external actors framed the prosecutors' and judges' understanding of the Račak events as set out in their documents.

As mentioned at the beginning of this subchapter, international media, NGOs and Western governments were almost unanimous in their interpretation of the Račak events, which was largely congruent with the accusatory statements William Walker had given in Priština the day after the events. It was generally accepted that the events had constituted another element in the persecutions of Albanians in Kosovo by the Serb state; it was accepted that Serb forces had attacked the village, and the KLA had defended it. These "Western" frames only

635 Sense Agency: "Defense 'expands' indictment against General Djordjević." 17.3.2010. Given the tight schedule, which the trial chamber tried to enforce during the trial, it already comes as a surprise that the defence was allowed to proceed in this way, especially because a positive outcome for the defence would still have exposed the accused to a charge of (multiple) murder as a war crime, instead of murder as a crime against humanity.

636 See: Public judgment with confidential annex in the case of *the pros. vs. Djordjević*. IT-05-87/1-T (together with the confidential annex, the judgment considerably exceeds a thousand pages).

differed with respect to the character of the victims, whether all or only some victims had been civilians and whether armed fighters (KLA rebels) had been present in the village. From the outset, the "massacre frame" also included blame of the Yugoslav and Serb authorities, however, the different actors using the frame differed with respect to the question who exactly was to blame, whether the alleged massacre had been ordered from above, whether it had been a revenge action of lower ranks in Kosovo, and whether Milošević was personally responsible or not. The notion of "summary executions", carried out by Serb and Yugoslav forces against civilians in Račak, had been put forward only by Human Rights Watch.

The prosecution frame in both *the pros. vs. Šainović et al.* and the Djordjević indictment repeated this "massacre frame", and entirely rejected the "hoax frame" supported by the Yugoslav and Serb authorities and a part of public opinion in the former Yugoslavia and in Western Europe in 1999 and later. It took over the claim concerning "mass executions" from Human Rights Watch, adding the notion of "house-to-house searches" carried out prior to these executions. As time went by, the prosecution drafted the fragments concerning the involvement of the Yugoslav Army in subsequent indictments more prudently, altering the claim about the Army having shelled the village into one which left open who had actually shelled it and which role the Army had played in the events. This was probably due to new evidence which had become available to the OTP and which suggested that the higher levels of command in the Army had not had knowledge of Army involvement in Račak. The prosecution also claimed that Army and police members had entered the village after the shelling, and incriminated both with the physical abuse and execution of "approximately 25 men".

It is worth mentioning that despite the schedules with victims' names, which the prosecution added to the various indictments involving Račak (except *the pros. vs. Djordjević*), there was never any precise quantification of victim numbers, neither concerning the overall number of victims in Račak on January 15, nor of the alleged executions. Only approximate figures are given in the indictments and in the Djordjević judgment, and the name schedules do not specify who was killed during the execution and who was killed before or after it.

In the early prosecution frames about Račak, the police was blamed for the execution and no reference was made to the Army. In the updated frame of *the pros. vs. Šainović et al.*, the prosecution refrained from blaming a specific institution and claimed only that the "approximately 25 men" had been shot and killed on a nearby hill. In the subsequent sentence, the indictment claims that "altogether, the forces of the FRY and Serbia killed approximately 45 Kosovo Albanians in and around Račak," leaving it open whether the Army or the police were to be held responsible for the execution. The question would have probably been important from a legal perspective if Djordjević were indicted of murder in Račak as the superior of the police, because it would have been difficult to hold him accountable for the executions, had Army members committed them.

A comparison between the core elements of the "massacre frame" and the indictment of *the pros. vs. Šainović et al.* reveals several major omissions. For example, the prosecution avoided assessing the character of the victims (by using words such as "villagers" and "Albanians" instead of "civilians", "rebels" or "KLA members", which had been frequently used in the "massacre frames" of 1999), it did not decide whether the village had hosted KLA-fighters at all during the events and whether the police and Army action had evoked any armed response, and whether such a response had inflicted casualties on the other side.[637] The Human Rights Watch report from January 29 had hypothesized that KLA members could have attempted to defend the village. The prosecution frame adopted the belief that the events had been caused by a Serb attack on the village, but it refrained from stating whether the village had also been defended by someone. It now added some elements to the pre-existing "massacre frame": the intruders had shot at "villagers" in order to prevent them from fleeing and the some 25 men who had gathered in one building (and then were allegedly beaten and executed) had done so in order to "hide".

The vagueness of these allegations made it difficult to assess whether the whole incident qualified as a war crime (if Račak was regarded as part of an internal armed conflict and in case the victims had been combatants killed after being captured or having surrendered), or as part of a crime against humanity (if there was no armed conflict and Serb forces had solely shelled a civilian target, killing unarmed villagers). The prosecution frame also failed to explain the motives of the perpetrators. Had they acted in the way alleged by the prosecution on the grounds of revenge (for the prior killings of Serb policemen by KLA members), because of orders from above, and what was the alleged purpose of the whole action: punishment, ethnic cleansing, the expulsion of the villagers, intimidation?

The Frames of the Trial Chamber in *the Pros. vs. Djordjević*

The picture drawn by the judges in *the pros. vs. Djordjević* was much more precise and detailed than any of the previous prosecution frames from *the pros. vs. Milutinović et al.*, *the pros. vs. Šainović et al.* and *the pros. vs. Pavković*

637 The trial chamber in *the pros. vs. Djordjević* found in its judgment that one person on the Serb side had suffered non-fatal injuries during the events.

cases. The judges put the events into a broader framework, meticulously examined the evidence (including evidence from other trials), compared crime-based and expert testimonies, and then created their own "hoax frame", which ran opposite to the well-known "hoax frame" of the Serbian and Yugoslav government from 1999, and was built on elements of the "massacre frame", supplemented with elements from the indictments of *the pros. vs. Milutinović et al.* and *the pros. vs. Šainović et al.* It also lacked consistence in some parts and refrained from a legal assessment of the events, but it was much more coherent than any of the prior frames.

The judges found that the attack on the village had been a reaction to the previous murder of Serb policemen in a nearby village in early January but had many more reasons and objectives. "While there are suggestions in the evidence that the aim of this operation may have included arresting the persons responsible for the killing of the Serbian police officers a few days earlier, in the view of the Chamber, the extensive Serbian forces engaged, the size and force of the weapons used, the number and equipment of the forces involved and the casualties caused, especially the very high number of Kosovo Albanians killed, establish that the actual aim of this operation was not to carry out arrests but to retaliate against the earlier killing of police by the KLA, to punish the potential perpetrators and perceived supporters for the killing of the Serbian police officers, and to terrorize and punish the population in a village that was regarded as a KLA stronghold."

According to the judges, on January 15, units of the Army and the police had planned a joint action in Račak in order to arrest the murderers of these policemen. In preparation for the assult, tanks and heavy weaponry had fired onto the village, "thus preventing the civilians from leaving the village safely." Then armoured vehicles and infantry had entered the village and conducted "house–to–house searches" (here the judges used exactly the same wording as the prosecution in all previous indictments). According to the judges, the KLA had been present in the village before the attack, but had not fired back. During the action, high-ranking members of the OSCE's Kosovo Verification Mission (KVM) had warned the local commanders of the Army, that the "firing of anti-aircraft weapons into a village in which there were women and children could not be accepted as a police operation. General Drewienkiewicz[638] requested that this action be ceased."

The chamber, which had previously in the indictment lauded the testimonies given by "international observers" as honest and trustworthy, shared

638 General John Drewienkiewicz, a British officer, had been military advisor to the High Representative for Bosnia and Herzegovina. In January 1999, he was the second in command under William Walker at the KVM.

Drewienkiewicz's assessment of January 1999: "Even if it were accepted that the operation in Ra~ak [sic]/Račak had a legitimate military or anti-terrorist purpose, in view of the type of weapons used by the VJ and the MUP[639] in this operation, the lack of any suggestion in the evidence about any outgoing fire from Račak, the high number of Kosovo Albanian casualties and the virtual absence of casualties on the side of the VJ and the MUP, suggest that the use of force in Račak was grossly disproportionate to any such military or anti-terrorist objective."

The judges completely rejected the defence claims, according to which the Army had not been involved in the events, as "false". The evidence pointing to a lack of knowledge of higher levels of Army command about the events in Račak were dismissed as attempts to cover up the killings there and to keep the Army's image untainted. The judges conceded that one non-fatal injury had occurred on the Serb side during the action, but failed to explain how this could have happened if the KLA had not fired on the intruders, as had been earlier established in the judgment. The judges also concluded that the KLA had still been present in the village the next day (despite the house searches, the huge presence of soldiers and policemen, and the executions) and had fired on Serb investigators, who had attempted to enter the village. When these investigators finally could enter the village on January 17, they found a crime scene which differed considerably from the one observed by KVM members and journalists two days earlier. The judges did not dismiss the findings of the Serb investigators, but explained the difference between the two crime scenes by alleging that the crime scene had been "staged" and "set up by the police, designed to give "a false impression of the true events" [sic]. Later in the judgment, the chamber found, that "not less than 45 Kosovo Albanians were killed in Račak on 15 January 1999, including a woman and a child. At least one victim had been decapitated. Most of those killed were over 50 years of age. Many had been shot in the head apparently at close range. Those killed were wearing civilian clothes when killed." From the further argument of the judgment, it becomes clear that the judges also regarded the events as planned and instigated from high above the level of local commanders. "Vlastimir Djordjević was the most senior MUP official involved in the operation. As such he had full information about the events in Račak and exercised control, or was in a position to exercise control, over the forces conducting the operation and those charged with conducting the operation. The Chamber must conclude from the known circumstances that as

639 MUP is the Serb abbreviation for Ministarstvo unutarnjich poslova or Ministry of Internal Affairs.

the most senior MUP official involved, and his two conversations with the Deputy Prime Minister of the FRY responsible for Kosovo, Vlastimir Djordjević was able to inform the senior political leadership of the FRY of the progress of the operation in Račak and took an organising role regarding the actions of the police on the ground."

It comes as a complete surprise that despite these findings, the chamber did not convict Djordjević for any crime connected to the events in Račak. After having meticulously reconstructed the events in Račak, having reached the conclusion that the action had been disproportionate and the evidence pointing in other directions fabricated; after having established that the accused was responsible for these actions, the trial chamber stopped short of convicting him, refrained from a legal categorisation of these deeds, and sentenced Djordjević to 27 years of imprisonment for other crimes, committed elsewhere, but not in Račak. This might have been due to the fact that he had no longer been indicted for the Račak events – but why then did the judges dedicate so much space in the judgment to findings, which could not have any impact on the legal outcome of the trial? The trial chamber never explained its approach and even the sentencing hearing on February 23, 2011 did not disclose anything which could have elucidated the judges' reasoning. As one of the trial judges of *the pros. vs. Djordjević* explained during an interview, the trial chamber decided to include a large paragraph about Račak, because "the events were prior to the events, which were part of the indictment." He declined to elaborate further on the issue, pointing to the principle of confidentiality of the chamber's deliberations judges are bound by. However, according to other sources – who requested anonymity – we were able to establish that the perceived causal link between the Račak events and subsequent actions of NATO and Serb and Yugoslav forces in Kosovo in early 1999 was at least partly the result of the trial chamber's preconceptions about the conflict, which had been shaped by contacts with journalists. The chamber had decided to include the events in Račak, because they regarded them – in accordance with most of the external frames about the topic – as the trigger of the Rambouillet negotiations and the bombing of Serbia in 1999.

It is beyond the scope of this chapter to investigate the motives which might have guided the judges. It is the purpose of this chapter, however, to assess in how far external factors influenced the framing of the Račak events by the judges. First, they explicitely and wholly rejected the "hoax frame". They incorporated important elements of the HRW version of the "massacre frame", but without the claim about an order "to kill village inhabitants over the age of fifteen", as stipulated in the HRW report from the end of January 1999. Their frame fits perfectly into the generally accepted, overarching narrative behind the "massacre frame", according to which Račak was another element in the assault of Serbia against the Kosovo Albanian population. The "Serbs attack, Albanians defend" was a very popular frame used in many indictments and the underlying argument in the construction of the JCEs which, according to the OTP, consisted in terrorizing the Albanian population in Kosovo (and, beginning March 1999, in the ethnic cleansing of Kosovo) in order to strengthen and expand the rule of Serbia over Kosovo. This frame, which is not limited to the indictments linked to Račak, is consistent with the dominant media frame (and the frames used by Western governments in 1998-99) and constitutes part of a comprehensive narrative, which describes the conflict in Kosovo as a Serb struggle for power, rather than as a Kosovo Albanian struggle for independence.

Establishing the Level of Congruence between Judges' and External Actors' Frames

The trial chamber in the Krstić trial issued its verdict on August 2, 2001, whereas the trial chamber's judgment was dated April 19, 2004. The events, which can be expected to be framed by both chambers, had taken place between July 13 and July 19, 1995 in and around Srebrenica. Only frames created by external actors or the prosecution between July 13, 1995 and August 2, 2001 can be reasonably expected to have influenced the trial chamber, and only frames which emerged between July 13, 1995 and April 19, 2004 to have influenced the appeals chamber.

The same logic must apply to the other cases. In the case of Račak, frames may have had an influence on the trial chamber in *the pros. vs. Djordjević* only between January 15, 1999 (when the events in Račak took place) and the trial chamber's judgment on February 23, 2011. At the time of writing, the appeal in *the pros. vs. Djordjević* is still pending. In *the pros. vs. Bagosora et al.*, events took place between April 6, 1994 and the end of 1994, whereas the trial judgment was issued on December 18, 2008. In *the pros. vs. Akayesu*, frames may have influenced the judges between April 7, 1994 and September 2, 1998, when the trial chamber's verdict was issued (or, respectively, until October 2, 1998, when they issued the sentence). Akayesu's appeal was rejected in June 2001.

In the preceding chapters of this part, we have tried to demonstrate which frames were created by external actors and prosecutors, and which could have influenced the trial chambers and, where relevant, the appeals chambers. In this concluding chapter, we now invert our perspective, identify the frames which show up in the judgments and ask which external actor had previously used such a frame in public. In cases where the judges' frames considerably differ from all earlier frames and where no preceding frame, in which a chamber's frames could be rooted, can be identified, we assume that the chamber used the utmost of its autonomy in interpreting the events it examined during the proceedings. It should be clear, though, that congruence between external actors' frames and frames of a chamber is likely to reveal influence, but is in itself no proof for such an influence, since it also can be the result of influences which were beyond the scope of our research. Only in case of identical frames might it be possible to deduce influence rather than autonomy.

Tab. 3: Time schedule for the evaluation of frame congruence

Starting date of event, which is being framed	Date of indictment's confirmation	Initial appearance of accused in court	Trial chamber judgment	Appeals chamber judgment
Killing of peacekeepers 6.4.1994	*The pros. vs. Ntuyahaga*: 29.91998	13.11.1998	(case was finally judged in Belgium)	
	The pros. vs. Bagosora et al.: 12.8.1999	30.8.2001[640]	18.12.2008	14.12.2011
Events in Taba (7.4.1994)	13.2.1996	30.5.1996	2.9.1998	1.6.2001
Dutchbat in Srebrenica (13.-19.7.1995)	2.11.1998	7.12.1998	2.8.2001	19.4.2004
Račak (15.1.1999)	Kosovo indictment the pros vs. Milošević: 24.5.1999	3.7.2001	None	None
	The pros. vs. Djordjević: 2.10.2002	19.6.2007	23.2.2011	(pending)

Since the appeals chamber did not construct any new frames about the events we are analysing, we limit our consideration to the interpretation the trial chamber in *the pros. vs. Bagosora et al.* developed in its judgment. There are several distinct and original frames which can be identified in this document. First, the judges were sceptical about the intentionalist version of the genocide. They doubted whether the available evidence had actually proven the existence of a plot or conspiracy to carry out the genocide against a large part of Rwanda's civilian population and suggested that the large-scale massacres that followed the airplane crash also could have been an unintended escalation of a power

640 This was the time period for which Bagosora's initial appearance was scheduled. In fact, he refused to show up and the status conference was held without him.

struggle, which went beyond the plans of those who had instigated the massacres in Kigali. They also rejected two very popular frames about the death of Belgian peacekeepers, which had been put forward by external actors before and during the trial. Both frames relied on the assumption of conspiracy, which dated back years. According to the "obstacle frame", which comes from Gourevitch's book, the peacekeepers had to die because they were regarded as an obstacle to the genocide by Hutu Power politicians, who were aware that the Belgians were the best-equipped and best-trained part of UNAMIR. According to the other frame, which we label the "withdrawal frame", the Belgians were killed in order to scare off the countries, which had contributed to UNAMIR of deployment, to cause the immediate withdrawal of all blue helmets, and leave Rwanda without foreign witnesses to the genocide. This version was favoured by Human Rights Watch, and with particularly elaborately by Alison Des Forges. The prosecution had taken over that view from Des Forges and introduced it into the indictment. The OTP also relied on the evidence Dallaire had revealed in his book about earlier plans to provoke and attack the Belgian part of UNAMIR. The judges in *the pros. vs. Bagosora et al.* significantly deviated from these assumptions and declared the evidence to be insufficient for proving a conspiracy against the Belgians. They largely supported the "mutiny frame", which was contained in the Belgian parliament's report. By doing so, they proved unimpressed by the strong normative frames issued by Human Rights Watch and Alison Des Forges. Since the judges avoided to frame the genocide again, and instead invoked it as an adjudicated fact, it is impossible to assess how much they were influenced by Alison Des Forges' interpretation of the genocide as a means of carrying out the political power struggle of a regional elite against groups it had defined as enemies. However, it is important to stress that the judges did not follow the line of Des Forges, the OAU report or the RPF version of the recent past, according to which a conspiracy to genocide or the genocide itself (as presented in the Rwandan Senate's report) had started years before 1994.

This constitutes a strong contrast to the behaviour of the trial chamber in the *pros. vs. Akayesu*, which proved deeply impressed by the campaigns launched by Human Rights Watch and the *Coalition*, which in turn were reinforced by The New York Times' coverage of the rape issue. In the latter case, the trial chamber and the appeals chamber appear to be entrapped in a highly asymmetrical principal-agent relation with interest congruence and hardly any information deficit. It is difficult to explain why this happened, but it is equally tricky to understand why the judges' behaviour differed so significantly in these two cases.

In *the pros vs. Akayesu*, which was the first case before the ICTR, the trial chamber comprised two men and one woman, Navanethem Pillar, a judge and former anti-apartheid activist from South Africa with a strong inclination for women's rights. The two men on the bench were the Swedish lawyer Lennart Aspegren and the presiding judge Laity Kama from Dakar.

In *the pros. vs. Bagosora et al.*, the chamber consisted of the Norwegian Erik Møse; Jai Ram Reddy, a former politican from the Fiji Islands; and the Russian judge Sergei Alekseevich Egorov.[641] This trial chamber did not comprise members from Africa; two of the judges came from Europe.

While the trial chamber in *the pros. vs. Akayesu* provided a striking example of how a court can successfully be influenced by a precisely targeted campaign of international NGOs, the trial and the appeals chamber in *the pros. vs. Krstić* delivered proof of judicial independence.

In their verdicts, the ICTY judges demonstrated a considerable margin of independence from strong external frames, which, in the case of the frames pertaining to "Serb" or "Bosnian Serb" guilt and genocide, even fulfilled Entman's criterion of "repetition". However, none of the ICTY trial chambers went so strongly against the mainstream of public opinion as the trial chamber in *the pros. vs. Bagosora et al.* This stance was supported by the appeals chamber, which sustained the trial chamber's finding with respect to the narrow genocide frame and the rejection of a conspiracy, and even reinforced it by lowering the main accused's prison sentence.

Contrary to almost all other producers of frames – from HRW to subsequent Dutch governments – the judges in *the pros. vs. Krstić* totally refrained from assessing the role of Dutchbat, despite the appearences of Dutchbat soldiers and officers as prosecution witnesses in court. Only in the trial chamber's verdict, the helpless bystander-frame was used. The judges neither followed the OTP's concept of a specific "Bosnian Serb propensity for ethnic cleansing", nor Human Rights Watch's claim according to which "Bosnian Serb hatred and omnipotence" had triggered the massacres. They also excluded revenge or overreaction as causes for the massacre. They followed a line which could be described as shaped by rational choice theory: The town had fallen and the massacre taken place because the Bosnian Serb Army had won a conflict over territory and feared that its military victory could be turned into a political defeat once the huge population of the town had returned after a peace settlement, driving a wedge between the Serbian part of Bosnia and the Republic of Serbia. This, however, was a claim put forward by Halilović and remained unconfirmed

641 Names are written according to their spelling in official ICTR and ICTY documents, even when they deviate from the appropriate scientific transcription.

by evidence from the Bosnian Serb side. Despite the strong words both chambers used when condemning the massacres, the judges did not put any blame on "the Serbs" or the "Bosnian Serbs" for the events that had preceded the fall of the town in July 1995. Instead, they kept the same kind of equidistance as the Dutch government back in 1995 and the authors of the UN report. For them, it was the Bosnian Serb leadership which was to blame, and its instrument, the Drina Corps. Guilt was not extended further; not the whole Serb Bosnian Army was to blame. The perpetrators were described in ethnic and functional terms (sometimes as "Bosnian Serb Army" or VRS, but more often as "Drina Corps"), and the victims in religious ones, which was consistent with almost all other frames – except the ones from the UN report and the Dutch governments interpretation of 1995. Consequently, the defenders of the town were also labeled as "Muslims". In their discussion of the character of the column, which had left the town to reach Bosniac-held territory, the judges again took an equidistant stance, estimating that about one third of the column consisted of soldiers, of whom many were unarmed. The trial chamber's and appeals chamber's verdicts – taken together as one source of frames – were close to, but not identical with all other frames. The most striking differences consist in the judges' reticence to assess the events which led to July 1995, their determination to focus on the Drina Corps (instead of blaming any larger group of perpetrators), and their refusal to decide whether the column leaving Srebrenica after its fall had been clearly "military" or "civilian". The most important differences between the judges on the one hand, and the Dutch government and Human Rights Watch on the other hand, was the trial chamber's and the appeals chamber's ambition to explain the massacres in exclusively rational terms as the result of strategic and political considerations. It may be less surprising but nevertheless worth mentioning that the judges did not deviate from the generally uncontested rule, according to which the perpetrators of the atrocities in Bosnia are usually described in ethnic terms and the victims are portrayed in religious categories. This has become so common that any other kind of frame now needs justification, although it is far from evident why one would regard perpetrators under orders from Pale or Banja Luka as "Serbs" (or Bosnian Serbs) rather than "Orthodox Christians" and (mostly non-religious) fighters for the Sarajevo government as "Muslims" rather than "Bosniacs".[642]

642 It is worth mentioning that a small part of Bosnian Muslims defied the orders of the government in Sarajevo and sided with the Bosnian Serb entity of Bosnia and Herzegovina. This happened in a part of Western Bosnia under the leadership of Fikret Abdić, who in 1993 declared the territory controlled by his units the "autonomous land

The trial chamber in *the pros. vs. Djordjević* had been exposed to a strong and hardly ever disputed "massacre frame", which had been generally accepted in the West European and North American public, and had been put forward by NATO countries against Yugoslavia in 1999. The judges' frames about the events in Račak showed a strong congruence with this powerful frame about a "Serb massacre of unarmed civilians in Račak". However, this should not overshadow the fact that prosecutors and judges in some cases also deviated from the pre-existing frames used by governments, the media and human rights campaigners. By avoiding phrasing their assessment in legal terms, they hesitated to decide whether the events in Račak had been "a crime against humanity" (as claimed by William Walker) or rather a "war crime" as stipulated by Human Rights Watch. They only rejected the Yugoslav version of a "legitimate police action against terrorists". Finally, they refrained from assessing who actually bore criminal responsibility for the events and thus left the question unanswered whether the police command, the Army hierarchy, the political leadership, or Slobodan Milošević personally were responsible. They only excluded (by blaming, but not by convicting Djordjević) one possible frame (which no one actually invoked), according to which the killings had been a police action, which had got out of control and had been carried out by local commanders seeking revenge, or had overreacted without the approval of their superiors. At the end of the day, the judges' frames were very close to, but not congruent with the prevailing "massacre frame" shaped in the early days of 1999. They were close to the KLA frame (but neither endorsed the claims of "Serb overreaction", nor "Milošević being personally responsible", nor did they agree with the later disproved KLA version that all casualties had been civilians). In this case, the influence of HRW's frame is much more difficult to

---

of Western Bosnia" (Autonomna Pokrajina Zapadna Bosna). See: Goldstein: Hrvatska 1918-2008, 737-738.

The notion of "Muslim" for the non-Serb and non-Croat population of Bosnia stems from the concept of a "Muslim Nation" in socialist Yugoslavia, which had, at the time when it was created, rather national or citizenship-related implications than religious ones. Nevertheless, in the context of the war in Bosnia, it has also been used in many other languages (like French or English), which lack such a national context and treat the word "Muslim" purely as a religious denomination. Calling a person from Bosnia a "Muslim" might not have included a religious context in the Yugoslavia of 1970, and it even might not have had a predominantly religious meaning in the 1990s (which may be the reason why more derogatory and ethnically exclusionist labels for the Bosniac population were created, like, for example "Turks"), but it certainly had such a meaning when used by, for example, secular French, German or British media or politicians. Calling Bosniacs "Muslims" instead of chosing another label amounts to a choice and this choice contributes to the emergence of a frame.

assess than the impact of NGO frames on the prosecution and trial chamber dealing with the Taba rapes, mainly because the HRW frame can be less easily disentangled from the frames used by governments and the media, which all endorsed very similar and emotional versions of the "massacre frame". Opposite to what happened in the Akayesu trial, there was no direct attempt by NGOs to influence the prosecuting or sentencing policy at the tribunal in order to create specific outcomes. Despite the enormous attention which the Račak events had attracted in January 1999, they became a rather minor element in both *the Šainović et al.* and *the pros vs. Djordjević*. More space and time were dedicated to them in the Milošević trial, but even then they did not trigger any legal activism comparable to the Coalition's campaign to judge Akayesu for rape as a crime of genocide. [643]

Explaining Judicial Behaviour at the ICTY and the ICTR

Our four case studies provide a very diverse picture of judicial behaviour at both tribunals. On one side, we have the extreme case of *the pros. vs. Akayesu*, where the prosecution and the trial chamber acted like an institutional extension of international human rights organisations and international media. As the Bagosora trial shows, this cannot be explained by the lower efficiency or the institutional and financial weaknesses and shortcomings which are generally attributed to the ICTR, since the trial chamber in *the pros. vs. Bagosora et al.* used its discretion and autonomy in a way even the ICTY trial chambers did not dare to. The difference may be explained by the targeted approach of Human Rights Watch and the *Coalition* in *the pros. vs. Akayesu.* In all other cases examined in this part of the book, external pressure had been vague and directly targeted at the prosecution and the trial chamber. It is worth mentioning that the theories of judicial behaviour, which are summarized at the beginning of this part of the book, do not make any claims about how the character of an advocacy campaign may affect judicial behaviour. Such claims rather stem from theories on lobbying.

In the theoretical chapters of this part, several hypotheses that make claims about the impact of different factors on judges' decisions were presented. Due to the specific incentive structures which influence the work of international judges, we expected to see a relatively stronger external influence of actors who

643 In both cases, *the pros. vs. Milošević* and *the pros. vs. Djordjević* HRW expert Fred Abrahams appeared as a witness for the prosecution. See:
Sense Agency: Police without the internet. 06.05.2009 and Sense Agency: Witness: Serbian authorities knew about crimes. 05.05.2009. See also: Fred Abrahams: Face to face with Milošević. The New York Times Magazine 21.o7.2002. http://www.hrw.org/en/news/2002/07/20/face-face-Milošević

are not part of the judicial hierarchy. This assumption has been confirmed in *the pros. vs. Akayesu,* but it does not explain judicial behaviour in the other cases, maybe with a minor exception of *the pros. vs. Djordjević,* where the judges adopted the "massacre frame" and the concept of Serb guilt, which had been dominant in Western European and US public discourse, and had only been challenged by the Serb and Yugoslav authorities. The relatively wider autonomy of international judges as compared to municipal ones became apparent in *the pros. vs. Bagosora et al.,* where the judges risked arousing the anger of an important external stakeholder (the government of Rwanda) and went against the interpretations of Human Rights Watch, which was an influential ally of the court in the public realm. One possible argument for this huge difference between *the pros. vs. Akayesu* and *the pros. vs. Bagosora et al.* may consist in the lower level of institutional interest at stake in the second case. When the judges in *the pros. vs. Akayesu* issued their verdict, the ICTY was still in the initial stage of its existence and very much dependent on good relations with other countries, which it wanted to extradite suspects at large.[644] When the verdict in *the pros. vs. Bagosora et al.* was due, the ICTR already had a considerable number of suspects in its detention facility, and the completion strategy was being implemented. The potential consequences of retaliation from Rwanda were therefore more acceptable than in the initial years, when the ICTR was weak, depended on state cooperation, and was on the hunt for extraditions.

Another important factor potentially affecting judicial behaviour is derived from Nancy Combs' hypotheses. She claims international judges to be more inclined to believe Western expert witnesses than local ones. Combs did not test this assumption against evidence from the ICTY, because she assumed cultural and linguistic differences and institutional shortcomings to be smaller than in the case of the ICTR and the other courts which she examined. All four trial chambers heard expert witnesses and there was considerable variance across the trials with regard to the impact which their testimonies had on the judges' frames in the verdicts. Due to the fact that many judges are no longer available for interviews, because they have either left the tribunal or, in some cases, even passed away in the meantime[645], the only method available for measuring the

644 Due to the ICTR statute, these countries were obliged to give priority to extradition demands from the ICTR when faced with a competitive demand from Rwanda, but since there was hardly any efficient enforcement mechanism at the ICTR's disposal (other than blaming non-complying states before the UNSC), it was usually the quality of mutual relations between a country and Rwanda which decided whether a suspect would be sent to Arusha or to Kigali.

645 Some judges rejected requests for interviews or did not answer them (or these answers were not forwarded to us by the press office). This happened with two judges who were

impact of witness statements was to look at the judgments and see how the judges assessed expert testimony ex post. The most surprising example is probably the Djordjević trial chamber judgment, because it very frequently quotes four expert witnesses in extenso, three of whom come from the former Yugoslavia (and are, for the purpose of this research, not treated as "Western expert witnesses" in Nancy Combs' sense) and were called by the defence. However, throughout the judgment, only Eric Baccard, a forensic expert from the University of Toronto, was able to garner the trust of the judges. All the other expert witnesses were quoted by the judges with the sole aim of rejecting their testimony. While in the Djordjević trial forensic evidence was paramount and all expert witnesses came from this field, the Srebrenica trial was dominated by expertise from military analysts. Also in this case, experts were called by the prosecution and the defence; however, only the prosecution witnesses were regarded as credible in the judgment. Richard Butler, military expert and member of the prosecution team, appeared as the most credible expert witness in the judgment.

Also in the Bagosora trial judgment, the defence called more expert witnesses than the prosecution did. However, not all were given the same credit by the judges. Throughout the document, two experts on Rwandan history were quoted by the trial chamber in a constant and affirmative manner: Alison Des Forges and the Belgian political scientist Filip Reyntjens, both of whom had been summoned by the OTP. The defence had called French archeologist and historian Bernard Lugan and Peter Caddick-Adams from the United Kingdom Defence Academy as a military expert. Both sides also called a number of linguistic and demographic experts and presented reports from experts who had appeared in other trials and were not called in person. Despite the fact that an alleged death list, first published by historian André Guichaoua in one of his books,[646] played a crucial role in the trial, the sociologist was not called as a witness.[647] The judgment gives the impression that the judges mostly relied on

about to leave the ICTY and had already been appointed at the ICC (Judge Claude Jorda and Judge Christine van den Wyngaert). It must be emphasized that conducting interviews with judges about *in camera* deliberations does not make sense, because they are bound by confidentiality. *In camera* discussions are not protocolled, and even the notes of the trial chamber members are destroyed after the closure of the session. It will therefore also not be possible to reconstruct the motives of judges for judging and sentencing at a later stage.

646 Guichaoua, André: Les Crises Politiques au Burundi et au Rwanda. Lille: Diffusion Karthala 1995.

647 Guichaoua's relations with prosecutor Carla Del Ponte and the ICTR soured after 2002 as a consequence of the Rusatira case (*the pros. vs. Rusatira* ICTR-02-80). Léonidas

Des Forges' and Reyntjens' intepretations of Rwanda's recent past, including the chronology of the genocide. Des Forges' famous book was accepted as a prosecution exhibit.

During the Akayesu Trial, the one-sided reliance of the trial chamber on Western expert witnesses was even more apparent. Several expert witnesses were called by both sides, but only one, Alison Des Forges, was quoted extensively in the judgment with regard to Rwanda's history and the chronology of events in April 1994. Mathias Ruzindana, a linguistic expert from the University of Rwanda, was only heard in order to provide explanations about the meaning of problematic terms used in propaganda and by crime-based witnesses. When the judges drew conclusions about Rwandan history, they derived them from Alison Des Forges. Therefore the judgment in many fragments reads like a summary of her testimony.

The tendency of trial chambers, either to rely only on Western expert witnesses, or, when experts from the conflict region are available, to trust the Western experts more, both confirm Natalie Comb's findings. A further assumption is also corroborated: Judges tend to trust prosecution expert witnesses more than experts who are called by the defence. This is consistent with Comb's hypothesis concerning the "culture of conviction". However, since there is not much variance in the trial chambers' attitudes toward expert witnesses, the huge difference between the Bagosora trial (almost completely independent judges) and the Akayesu trial (judes who follow external influence) remains unexplained by the expert witness factor.

When it comes to potential pressure from public opinion, there is a substantial variance across the cases. Whereas the Bagosora trial was highly controversial and

---

Rusatira was a former FAR general, who had been taken over by the RPF in 1994 as a consequence of his brave behaviour during the massacres. He fled Rwanda in 1995 and began to criticize the Rwandan government, which retaliated by delivering evidence against him to the ICTR, and Carla Del Ponte decided to indict him. However, several of his friends carried out their own investigations and convinced the Belgian minister of Justice to block his extradition to Arusha. They also presented exculpatory evidence and indications pointing to other perpetrators of the crimes which he was charged with by the OTP. Several furious encounters between Carla Del Ponte, lawyers from the Belgian Ministry of Justice and Guichaoua (who was one of those who had conducted investigations on their own) followed, and the OTP finally withdrew the accusations against the general. Interview with André Guichaoua in May 2012 in Paris. The episode is also described in T. Cruvellier, Le tribunal des vaincus, 223-228; and Reyntjens, Ruling under a Volcano, chapter "The ICTR". See also The International Justice Tribune: "Shocking arrest of Rusatira", 21.06.2001, http://www.rnw.nl/international-justice/article/shocking-arrest-rusatira

After that, Guichaoua refused to testify in any further military trials at the ICTR.

intensively observed by the Rwandan public and the government in Kigali, and the Krstić trial was regarded as a milestone of the ICTY, much less public attention was directed at the Djordjević trial and the Akayesu trial. There is a certain asymmetry, which has to be taken into account when we contemplate the potential links between public awareness of the trial and the impact this awareness may have had on judges' inclination to endorse frames from the public into their judgments. This asymmetry concerns the role of the conflict region for the functioning of the two tribunals. The ICTY was able to work without cooperation from the successor states of the former Yugoslavia, since the international organisations which supported the ICTY, had direct leverage over these republics. The UN, the EU, and NATO had enough capabilities and potential for political, diplomatic, and even military pressure to coerce local authorities into compliance with the ICTY's mandate; the first part of this book provides exhaustive evidence for that. There was no such leverage for the ICTR with respect to Rwanda. Without access to Rwandan territory, to Rwandan documents and witnesses, the ICTR had no chance of fulfilling its mandate, and the ICTR organs were well aware of that. No regional or international organisation and no external power had enough capabilities in Rwanda to coerce the RPF government into compliance with the ICTR. Therefore, public opinion in and governmental pressure from Rwanda provided a much stronger influence on the ICTR than public opinion and state pressure could cause in the case of the ICTY. There is a broad consensus in the literature that NATO pressure prevented the OTP from prosecuting several incidents during the bombing of Serbia in 1999, but it would be difficult to detect NATO or EU pressure pushing the ICTY towards a specific prosecution or sentencing outcome. The ICTR did not enjoy such a broad autonomy, and was frequently pressurized by the Rwandan government in order to create specific outcomes. For these reasons, the Barayagwiza appeals judgment was reversed and Carla Del Ponte's special investigations into RPF atrocities were halted. We can therefore assume public pressure and institutional interest to play a bigger role for ICTR judges than for ICTY judges. By taking advantage of the EU's conditionality and US pressure, the ICTY was able to coerce states into compliance. The ICTR never had such a chance. Actually, both factors played a relatively big role in *the pros. vs. Bagosora et al.* and *the pros. vs. Akayesu.* Akayesu was the first suspect ever to be tried by the ICTR, and the pressure not only to convict him but also to sentence him to a high prison term must have been much stronger than in the case of the ICTY's first accused, Dusko Tadić. The same is true for the Bagosora trial, whose main defendant was regarded a national enemy and the mastermind behind the genocide by a large part of the public, the media and human rights organisations. In other words – had the judges acquitted Akayesu or Bagosora, the future of the ICTR would have been at stake. In the case of an acquittal for Krstić and Djordjević, the

ICTY would have risked public outrage and protests from politicians, but the proper functioning or the very existence of the whole tribunal would not have been put on the line. *The pros. vs. Dordjević* is even an extreme example for the opposite – when his verdict was due, there was no media interest at all. As Nerma Jelačić recalls, a purely technical hearing in *the pros. vs. Haradinaj et al.*[648] was more interesting for Kosovo state television, than the judgment of a defendant who was regarded as one of the architects of ethnic cleansing in Kosovo.[649]

Tab. 4: Incentive structure and external factors affecting judicial behavior at the ICTR and the ICTY

	Bagosora Trial	Akayesu Trial	Krstić Trial	Djordjević Trial
Mode of lobbying (“voice” versus “noise”) before and during the trial	noise	voice	noise	none
Did institutional interest reinforce “culture of conviction”? (yes/no)	no	yes	no	no
Existence of overarching frame before the trial?	“Genocide”	“Genocide”	“Genocide” (launched by the ICTY itself)	no
Existence of a dominant specific frame before the trial?	No	No	no	“Serb massacre against Albanian civilians”
Was the trial chamber more confident toward Western expert witnesses than other ones?	Yes	yes	yes	Yes
Was the trial chamber more confident toward OTP expert witnesses than defence experts?	yes	yes	yes	yes
Readiness to endorse external frames by the trial chamber	low	very high	average	high
External actors whose frames were adopted by the trial chamber	-	HRW, *Coalition*	-	-
Level of independence (distance of the trial chamber to pre-existing frames)	Very high	Very low	high	high

648 IT-04-84.

649 Interview with ICTY press spokeswoman Nerma Jelačić in The Hague in May 2012.

As can be seen from the above table, in general, the autonomy of trial chambers (and, where relevant, the appeals chambers) was quite high at both tribunals, and the Akayesu trial remains the exception to the rule. When strong, largely accepted narratives exist in the public before a trial, the judges are likely to adopt them, but they also tend to amend them in their judgments. The judges in all four trials adopted the prevalent genocide frames for Rwanda and Srebrenica, but then altered them, narrowing the time frame, rejecting conspiracy theories, or even (in the appeals judgment about Krstić) acquitting the accused of the genocide count. In the Djordjević trial, the trial chamber endorsed the massacre frame, which put the blame on Serb forces and had prevailed for a long time outside Serbia, but then rejected most of the one-sided and strongly normative claims put forward by Western politicians, governments, human rights organisations, and the media. The final version was closer to the prudent investigations of Le Monde than to the emotional frames launched by the French or US government. Except for the Račak case, there was no dominant, generally accepted specific frame. Before the trials, the public had been divided about how to assess the behaviour of Dutchbat in Srebrenica (opportunism, cowardice, helplessness, victimhood), the reasons for the death of the Belgian paracommando (premeditated conspiracy, mutiny), and the intentions of the perpetrators (get rid of witnesses, remove obstacle to genocide, scare off foreigners, punishment for the president's death). Also in the Akayesu case, the powerful frames of HRW and the *Coalition* had been developed shortly before the trial started. In all other cases, the judges showed considerable ambition to add their own interpretations to the ones coexistent in the public.

The question remains: what was so different in *the pros. vs. Akayesu* that it inclined the judges to deviate from the behaviour one could have expected? First, the campaign of Human Rights Watch and the *Coalition* was targeted directly at the prosecution and the trial chamber, whereas in the other trials, frames had been created in a manner of "noise" rather than "voice" – without specific aims or targets. Second, there is reason to assume that the composition of the OTP and the trial chamber had something to do with the readiness to endorse the "rape as genocide" frame: Louise Arbour had become head of the OTP and had the reputation of being a gender-sensitive person. Navanethem Pillay, a member of the trial chamber also had a strong record as an activist for women's rights.[650] Lennart Aspregren, the Swedish judge, had a better record in

650 In an interview for Nerma Jelačić's documentary "Sexual Violence and the Triumph of Justice", Pillay claims the initiative to ask the prosecution to amend the indictment had been caused by the testimony of a witness, who had mentioned her 6-year-old daughter being raped. http://www.youtube.com/watch?v=zD1t6fB5sisn

administrative and labor law than in criminal proceedings, but had been socialized in a very gender-sensitive society. The HRW and *Coalition* campaign offered them an opportunity to write legal history and secure the institutional interest of the ICTR, whose image had been shattered by allegations of corruption and lack of sensivity for rape victims.

There is strong circumstancial evidence indicating that the personal factor played a decisive role in the choices of prosecutors and judges to follow the line of the *Coalition*'s and HRW's campaign. Much later, in 1999, the OTP was offered evidence about mass rapes in Cyangugu.[651] In order to prosecute them, the OTP had to file a motion for leave to amend the indictment against three accused, which had already been confirmed by a judge, but did not yet contain rape charges. The situation was almost identical to *the pros. vs. Akayesu*. But after a meeting with judges, the chief prosecutor decided to drop the charges. But by then, the chief prosecutor was Carla Del Ponte, not Louise Arbour. And the trial chamber consisted of three men, Lloyd Williams from Jamaica as presiding judge, Yakov Ostrovsky (Russia), and Pavel Dolenc (Slovenia).[652] During the trial, the judges ordered the prosecution not to address the rape issue, even when witnesses raised it in their testimony, and to erase the relevant passages from the protocol, arguing that rape was no count of the indictment. When the *Coalition* addressed the trial chamber in an *amicus curiae* brief asking the chamber to demand a revision of the indictment, the judges turned the *Coalition* down.[653] This time, the *Coalition* had acted alone (without HRW and media support), in a case in which public pressure was low and institutional interest weak, and it had met the resistance of the OTP and the trial chamber, both dominated by persons with a low level of sensivity for gendered violence.

---

651 *The pros. vs. Ntagerura, Bagambiki and Imanishimwe*. ICTR-99-46-A. All defendants were acquitted by the trial chamber and on appeal.

652 Nawrojee, Binaifer: Your Justice is too slow. Will the ICTR fail Rwanda's rape victims? United Nations Research Institute for Social Development working paper 10, Nov. 2005. Retrieved from: http://www.womensrightscoalition.org/site/pdf/binaifer_paper.pdf

653 *The pros. vs. André Ntagerura, Emmanuel Bagambiki, Samuel Imanishimwe*, ICTR-99-46-T.
Here: Decision on defence motion to exclude evidence. 25.3.2002, and *the pros. vs. André Ntagerura, Emmanuel Bagambiki, Samuel Imanishimwe*, ICTR-99-46-T.Decisionon the Coalition for Women's Human Rights in Conflict Situation's motion for reconsideration of the decision on application to file an *amicus curiae* brief. 24.9.2001.
http://www.unictr.org/Portals/0/Case%5CEnglish%5CBagambiki%5Cdecisions%5C240901.pdf

In *the pros. vs. Akayesu*, the Prosecution as well as the trial chamber were anxious to reject such allegations in their public statements. This was probably due to the fact that the defence and the accused claimed the indictment had been amended as a result of the NGO campaign and denounced this as an example of external interference and bias of the court. Pierre Richard Prosper, the leading prosecutor in court, said: "I would like to say to this Chamber right now and make it perfectly clear that the *amicus curiae* is not motivating us today. It is not motivating us today and, in fact, it can only be considered as a factor. And I say this as a factor because what it does is it reminds us of the importance of the issue of sexual violence."[654] The prosecution claimed that the rape issue had come to its attention because one of the protected crime-based witnesses, witness J, had mentioned that she and her six-year-old daughter had been raped. Before that, allegations about rape in the prosecution records had been too vague to be directly linked to the accused. The trial chamber was also anxious about refuting suspicions of being influenced by the NGO campaign. The trial judgment contains the following fragment:

> "The Chamber notes that the Defence in its closing statement questioned whether the Indictment was amended in response to public pressure concerning the prosecution of sexual violence. The Chamber understands that the amendment of the Indictment resulted from the spontaneous testimony of sexual violence by Witness J and Witness H during the course of this trial and the subsequent investigation of the Prosecution, rather than from public pressure. Nevertheless, the Chamber takes note of the interest shown in this issue by non-governmental organisations, which it considers as indicative of public concern over the historical exclusion of rape and other forms of sexual violence from the investigation and prosecution of war crimes. The investigation and presentation of evidence relating to sexual violence is in the interest of justice."[655]

Later, individual members of the trial chamber tried to present their decision in the same way. During an interview for Nerma Jelačić's documentary "Sexual Violence and the Triumph of Justice", Pillay claimed that the initiative of asking the prosecution to amend the indictment had been triggered by the testimony of witness J. The court records show a different picture, though. Witness J had testified in court at the beginning of January. As usual in the adversarial system, which the ICTY had adopted, the leading questions were asked by a prosecutor. The rape issue was also revealed during the prosecutor's questioning. Only at the end did the presiding judge intervene, asking the additional question of whether witness J knew the men who had raped her and

---

654 Van Schaack, Engendering, 11.

655 *The pros. vs Akayesu*. Trial Judgment, also quoted in Van Schaack, Engendering, 10 (footnote 19).

her daughter. Later, judge Aspegren wanted to know whether there had been other cases of rape in Taba. The witness answered that she only had heard about, but not directly witnessed other cases. For months after the testimony, nothing happened. In March, the *Coalition* sent its brief to Arbour and in June, the prosecution sought leave to amend the indictment. According to Van Schaack, who refers to a message from the OTP, "various amended indictments were drafted between April and May" – hence long after the testimony of witness J, but soon after the *Coalition* brief.[656]

All in all, *the pros. vs. Akayesu* remains the exception to the rule, which is best explained by two factors: the mode of lobbying which HRW and the *Coalition* applied for their advocacy campaign, and the unique combination of a gender-sensitive prosecutor and a gender-sensitive trial chamber. Most of the hypotheses, which we derived from Comb's book, are also corroborated at the ICTY, but they fail to account for the variance in the frames created by the trial chambers (and, in *the pros. vs. Krstić*, the appeals chamber).

656 Van Schaack, Engendering, 8 (footnote 14). It should be mentioned that this could also be due to the testimony of the last prosecution witness, protected witness H, who had linked rapes at the bureau communal to the accused. Witness H testified in March, stating that Akayesu had been present in the bureau while others were raping women and girls there.

Part III
Politicizing Tribunals? Reconciliation in Sentencing and Judging at the ICTR and the ICT

In the first part of this book, we examined how much initiative and agenda setting power the ICTY enjoyed in its relationship with the European Union, Serbia, and Croatia. The second part concentrated on the independence and autonomy of judges vis-à-vis external actors, such as governments, non-governmental organisations, international media, and other stakeholders with an interest in a specific result of a trial. In the following part, we scrutinize whether, and eventually how, the judges at the ICTY and the ICTR have attempted to carry out the UNSC and General Assembly's task to foster reconciliation in the respective region by including this non-legal and therefore political rather than juridical concept into their judgments. How have the judges, trial chambers, and appeals chambers tried to translate this specific, and – for municipal courts – quite unusual task into their concrete decisions? What were their understandings of the reconciliation concept? Were references to "reconciliation" more likely to increase a sentence or to diminish it? What situations, what kind of dilemmas inclined judges to apply the concept? What were the consequences for the conduct of the trial, the judgment, and the sentence?

In order to answer these questions, we first review scientific literature on reconciliation and propose an analytical toolkit to disentangle the meanings with which the concept has been operationalized in the context of transitional justice. Subsequently, we present the results of our scrutiny of the ICTY's and ICTR's judgments and sentences, respectively, in order to establish the ways in which the tribunals or trial chambers have taken up the reconciliation concept, and how they have translated their understanding thereof into specific judgment policies.

As will be shown, "reconciliation" does not have a unified meaning and therefore provides room for differences in interpretation and some flexibility, but also for debate and contestation. The concept is mobilized by several strategic logics which affect the Tribunals' judgments and sentences in various ways. In this way, as an epistemic vantage point, the concept of reconciliation serves to shed light on various logics that underlie the judging and sentencing practices of the international justice institutions.

From a more general point of view, it has to be stressed that it is only indirectly our aim to contribute to the already existing interpretations of whether the ICTR has actually contributed to reconciliation in Rwanda or not.[657] The objective is rather to provide more insight into the operational validity of the concept of reconciliation in the international criminal tribunals.

---

657 See Kamatali, Jean-Marie: "The Challenge of Linking International Criminal Justice to National Reconciliation: the Case of the ICTR." *Leiden Journal of International Law*, 16 (2003), 115-133; and Paradelle, Murielle; Dumont, Hélène; Boisvert, Anne-Marie: Quelle justice pour quelle réconciliation? Le tribunal pénal international pour le Rwanda et le jugement du génocide. *McGill Law Journal* 50 (2005), 359-413.

When the International Criminal Tribunal for Rwanda (ICTR) was initiated in November 1994, the Security Council was convinced that "the prosecution of persons responsible of such acts and violations [...] would contribute to the process of national reconciliation and to the restoration and maintenance of peace."[658] The judges of the Tribunal seemed to have taken this objective seriously when they wrote that "[r]econciliation amongst Rwandans, towards which the processes of the Tribunal should contribute, must also weigh heavily in the Chamber's mind when passing sentence."[659]

In contrast to its resolutions concerning the ICTR, the UNSC never placed such a duty on the ICTY. Resolution 827, which established the ICTY legally only determines: "to establish an international tribunal for the sole purpose of prosecuting persons responsible for serious violations of international humanitarian law committed in the territory of the former Yugoslavia between 1 January 1991 and a date to be determined by the Security Council upon the restoration of peace and to this end to adopt the Statute of the International Tribunal annexed to the above-mentioned report."[660]

Among all the UNSC resolutions which defined the statute of the ICTY (and, in many cases, also the ICTR's) over the years, only resolution 1534 from 2004 mentions the notion of reconciliation with regard to the ICTY. Surprisingly, resolution 1534 is one of those dealing with the so-called completion strategy, a complicated plan which aimed at scaling down the ICTY's activities. The relevant fragment of resolution 1534 states:

"(...) the important work of both tribunals in contributing to lasting peace and security and national reconciliation and the progress made since their inception, commending them on their efforts so far to give effect to the Completion Strategies and calling on them to ensure effective and efficient use of their budgets, with accountability (…).[661]"

Since the UNSC used to refer to reconciliation only in the context of the ICTR, and since the quote above deals with both tribunals and does not specify to which tribunal the qualifications apply, one can assume, that when mentioning reconciliation in resolution 1534, the UNSC had in mind rather the ICTR than the ICTY. This, however, means that the UNSC never formally imposed the task of reconciliation onto the ICTY. Even in resolution 808, which charged the Secretary General with a report about the possibilities of creating an international tribunal for

658 UN document S/RE/955 of 8 November 1994.

659 *The pros. vs. Kamuhanda* ICTR-99-54, Judgment, 22.01.04., 208.

660 Security Council Resolution nr. 827 S/RES/827 (1993), 25.5.1993.

661 UNSC Resolution 1534 (2004). Adopted by the Security Council at its 4935th meeting, on 26 March 2004. S/RES/1534 (2004) 26 March 2004.

Yugoslavia, the UNSC only mentions in its introductory remarks that such a tribunal would "contribute to the restoration and maintenance of peace." Reconciliation is not mentioned among the tasks of the tribunal, which the UNSC intended to establish. Nevertheless, judges and prosecutors many times emphasized reconciliation as one of the main tasks of the tribunal. In some of these cases they argued that reconciliation was to be seen as an implicit goal of the ICTY which arose from the explicit task of contributing to the "restoration of peace."[662] From such a perspective, enhancing reconciliation thus became a means of overcoming violent conflict, and an element of peace. This perspective was not consensus among the judges. In the majority of judgments, the notion of reconciliation is not even mentioned, and there are ICTY judges who frankly reject it as a concept of justice applicable in the ICTY context. When asked about his understanding of reconciliation, Judge Flügge pointed to UNSC resolution 827, which established the ICTY "for the sole purpose of prosecuting persons responsible for serious violations of international humanitarian law committed in the territory of the former Yugoslavia," emphasizing the phrase "for the sole purpose." "We are not supposed to provide reconciliation, we are supposed to prosecute, judge, and punish," he said. "Trying to further reconciliation is something which would considerably overstretch the possibilities of the tribunal." He added that the ICTY could make a contribution for future generations by inclining them to accept "historical facts and to decide to live together peacefully with other ethnic groups."[663] In this context, reconciliation appears as a vision or a concept for a rather distant future.

In contrast to the rather prominent use of the notion of reconciliation in the official documents at least of the ICTR, academics have so far not produced a unified definition of the term. Its meaning remains ambiguous, while its widespread use – especially since the South African *Truth and Reconciliation Commission* – might qualify it as fashionable. The present book section aims at clarifying and reflecting upon two issues: the above quote suggests that the idea of reconciliation is intended to impact rather fundamentally on the quality of sentences produced by the international criminal tribunals *ad hoc*. To do this, however, it seems indispensable for the tribunals to have a shared idea about what is meant when using the term.

---

662 The trial chambers which constructed such a link between the maintenance of peace and reconciliation could (and sometimes did) refer to various resolutions of the UN General Assembly. The trial chamber in *the pros. vs. Babić* did so with respect to a UNGA resolution of 1996, which, in reality, had been voted on in 1997. *The pros. vs. Babić*. Sentencing judgment. IT-03-72-S. See: U.N. General Assembly resolution A/RES/51/203 88th plenary meeting 17 December 1996.

663 Interview with Judge Christoph Flügge in May 2012 at the ICTY.

A first question this chapter tries to answer therefore is whether the tribunals' members speak with one voice, or whether they ascribe different meanings to the notion. If the latter is the case, which are these meanings and what does this mean for the importance of reconciliation as a guideline for sentencing? Linked to this is our intention to investigate whether it is possible to deduce from an analysis of the judgments and sentences to what extent the idea of reconciliation has affected the sentences that were passed, and in which way.

Secondly, we intend to examine the discursive power of the language spoken by the tribunals, i.e. whether or not their reconciliation discourse has actually been able to fashion a popular mindset of reconciliation, as it has been the case in South Africa.

A first section gives an introduction to the theoretical discussion of the concept of reconciliation from an academic point of view and builds up a theoretical framework for our analysis. The two subsequent sections present the results of our analysis that has applied this theoretical framework to the empirical data.

The empirical data consist of two kinds of documents: Firstly, the official documents of the UN Security Council concerning the foundation and implementation of the ICTR and the ICTY. These documents are important because they set the tone for both Tribunals' missions to contribute to national reconciliation. The second set of documents are the transcripts of the judgments and sentences which the ICTR and the ICTY have pronounced until the day of writing. The first chapter starts off by summarizing the state of the art of reconciliation theory, thus presenting reconciliation as a theoretical tool, and then moves on to explain its underlying logics: the intended (re)configurations of social, legal, and memory space. Insight will also be provided into the discursive nature of the concept, which, given its illocutionary power, has the ability to impact upon the social process of reality construction. The latter aspect is inspired by Annelies Verdoolaege's doctoral thesis on the Reconciliation Discourse of the South African Truth and Reconciliation Commission.[664] An attempted open definition of the concept of reconciliation is being given to solidify our theoretical framework. The chapter continues by focusing more specifically on the potential contributions of retributive justice to reconciliation. With a view to sharpening our analytical lens, we have attempted to establish a typology of the ways in which the academic literature presents justice as a contributor to reconciliation. Together with the open definition, this classification constitutes the conceptual toolbox which will help us to explore the use of reconciliation in the ICTR and the ICTY judgments and sentences, respectively.

---

664 Verdoolaege, Annelies: Reconciliation Discourse. The Case of the Truth and Reconciliation Commission, Amsterdam-Philadelphia, 2008 (Discourse Approaches to Politics, Society and Culture – DAPSAC, 27).

Concepts of Reconciliation

Reconciliation in Theory

When, with the end of the Cold War, "[t]he maps of states and the maps of warfare no longer fit an older, realist geography,"[665] the International Community became aware of its growing responsibility to prevent and react to conflicts.[666] With the report "An Agenda for Peace", former Secretary General Boutros Boutros-Ghali openly manifested this awareness by stressing that the challenges of the international community exceeded the emission of peacekeepers. Published in 1992, the Agenda for Peace advocated a more integrative engagement including political rebuilding (i.e. democratic institutions) and economic restructuring as well as social and humanitarian issues.

One of the biggest challenges to any post-conflict situation is the question of how to face a violent past with a view to ensuring a peaceful future on the long run. Depending on the nature and the root causes of the conflict, this respectively involves the relationship between at least two social entities, i.e. one or more individual(s), group(s) and/or government(s). These two elements, temporal and social, find themselves combined in the notion of reconciliation. In other words, and on a very general level, reconciliation both affects, and is affected by, the kind of relationship that exists between two formerly conflicting social entities, with a view to arranging a relational setting so as to insulate it against future violence. In a climate of intra-state violence, which has been on the increase since the early 1990s, the often ethnically framed conflicts are responsible for the growing importance of reconciliation. Seen in this way, reconciliation is not a state of mind or an attitude, but rather a process involving a variable set of mechanisms aiming at structurally instigating a "culture"[667] of non-violence and non-violent conflict resolution by ideally using intentions and agency from the grassroots level of society.

If today the general awareness has risen that there is no one-size-fits-all answer to the question of how to face the past for the future[668], "the virtually

665 Appadurai, Arjun: Fear of small numbers. An Essay on the Geography of Anger. Duke University Press 2006, 10.

666 See the "*The rule of law and transitional justice in conflict and post-conflict societies.* Report of the Secretary-General", 23August 2004, available on http://www.unhcr.org/4506bc494.html.

667 Rigby, Andrew: Justice and Reconciliation after the Violence, Boulder-London, 2001, 183-192 talks about a "Culture of Reconciliation".

668 See the above-mentioned report of the Secretary General "*The rule of law and transitional justice in conflict and post-conflict societies*" of 23 August 2004.

simultaneous creation of the South African Truth and Reconciliation Commission and the International Criminal Tribunal for the former Yugoslavia became emblematic of the heated debate in the mid-1990s between the advocates for a policy of forgiveness and those in favour of a policy of punishment."[669] Given the rather acknowledged success of the South African TRC, reconciliation as a programme for a specific set of actions has become a fashionable stake in many post-conflict environments. Yet, as we will see, the notion is ambivalent, and its uses in academic literature very often contrast with the general presumption that reconciliation is about restoring social harmony and friendship.

For many, the term reconciliation evokes religious associations. This is particularly obvious in Germanic languages where the German "Versöhnung" and "Aussöhnung",[670] or the Swedish "försoning" directly refer to the Christian tradition of the broken relationship between God and Man. The latter was cast out of paradise into terrestrial materiality as a result of the original sin. But as Paul explains: "God was reconciling the world to himself in Christ, not counting men's sins against them. And he has committed to us the message of reconciliation."[671] Thus, through his death, Jesus the son becomes the ultimate mediator for mankind in order for man to reconcile himself with God.

From its Christian roots arises the question of the universal applicability of the notion, and some direct criticism like "reconciliation, a nonsense Christian term we should get rid of"[672] is sometimes uttered in this regard. However, as language is the result of a deep cultural construction of meaning and codification, and thus profoundly culture-bound, it is understanding that a globalizing spread of concepts and notions in our information age[673] produces a heterogeneous field of representations. This is all the more striking since English seems to be advancing towards a universal lingua franca in an increasingly interconnected world. However, we must remind ourselves that the transfer of

669 Hazan, Pierre: "Measuring the impact of punishment and forgiveness: a framework for evaluating transitional justice". *The International Review of the Red Cross*, 88, 861, March 2006, 20.

670 See Feldman, Lily Gardner: "The Principle and Practice of 'Reconciliation' in German Foreign Policy: Relations with France, Israel, Poland and the Greek Republic," *International Affairs*, vol. 75, no. 2, 1999, pp. 333–355.

671 *The Bible*, 2 Cor., 5.19.

672 Quote from a presentation on the panel "Beyond National History and Memory Politics. Transnational Genocide Studies" on the *Second European Congress of World and Global History*, 3-5 July 2008 in Dresden, Germany.

673 Castells, Manuel 1996-1998: The Information Age: Economy, Society, and Culture, 3 vols, Blackwell Publishers (Oxford, and Malden, MA).

words, a globalisation of semiotic forms, does not automatically include the transfer of their cultural origins and semantic connotations. A common 'language of communication' such as English is tending to become it in the present world, ought not to be confused with a 'language of culture' and of culturally generative power. Reconciliation, therefore, must be understood as a semiotic mask, a verbal format for a semantic field. Given that any semiotic form travels lightly, i.e. without the heavy semantic baggage of its local origination (which is generally lost, or at least altered and exchanged in the transcultural transit zones of the de- and reproduction of meaning), also reconciliation is prone to lose its Christian overtones if a categorically local perspective is applied. This, however, can only be investigated locally and "in the field." Hence we limit ourselves here to these sensitizing remarks.[674]

More concretely, criticism concerning the questionable relevance of reconciliation has been uttered for situations in which most victims have been killed and thus cannot participate themselves in any such an activity, process or work.[675] In the Rwandan case, this argument appears to be of particular relevance.

A far as its conceptual siblings are concerned, reconciliation mostly appears next to notions such as peace, peacemaking, peacebuilding, truth, apology, forgiveness, amnesty, healing, rehabilitation, harmony, reconstruction, relationship building, reconstitution, restoration, peaceful coexistence, and also justice. Generally speaking, we can resume that reconciliation signifies neither and all of them. None of these notions is univocal to reconciliation, but none carries a totally antagonistic meaning, either. Though some efforts of conceptual clarification have been attempted, a common sense of understanding is far from being reached. In order to understand the variety of meanings that are generally associated with reconciliation, an overview of different definitions that have been suggested may be helpful.

Louis Kriesberg considers reconciliation to be a set of "processes by which parties that have experienced an oppressive relationship or destructive conflict with each other move to attain or to restore a relationship that they believe to be minimally acceptable."[676] He stresses the variability of forms of coexistence that

674 Clearly, the ideal solution to prevent confusion over universal vocabulary from arising would be to shape new words from scratch, concepts that are designed and fitter for cross-cultural mobility than reconciliation tends to be.

675 See Lambourne, Wendy: "Justice and Reconciliation. Postconflict Peacebuilding in Cambodia and Rwanda", in: Mohammed Abu-Nimer (ed.):Reconciliation, Justice, and Coexistence: Theory and Practice, Maryland, 2001, 332, note 9.

676 Kriesberg, Louis: "Changing forms of coexistence", in: Abu-Nimer, Mohammed (ed.): Reconciliation, Justice, and Coexistence: Theory and Practice, Maryland 2001, 47-64.

two or more groups of people can have and that reconciliation affects the quality of the relationship between these groups as the defining factor for the form of coexistence. The theme of relationship configuration returns in Hamber and Kelly's attempt to elaborate a working definition: As a substantial component of peacebuilding, reconciliation is seen as "the reestablishment or mending of damaged interpersonal and social relations", i.e. "the process of addressing conflicting and fractured relationships and this includes a range of different activities."[677]

It seems to be common sense that these group relationships can mainly be affected through socio-psychological mechanisms. Accordingly, Daniel Bar-Tal conceives of reconciliation as "a psychological process for the formation of lasting peace." i.e. the "transformation of beliefs, attitudes and emotions regarding one's own group, the others and the relationship between them."[678] The theme of socio-emotional transformation has been synthetically addressed by Nadler and Shnabel who define intergroup reconciliation as "the process of removing conflict-related emotional barriers that block the way to ending intergroup conflict."[679] This primarily works through the rehabilitation of the identities of victims and perpetrators, a theme that is echoed in the definition given by Hugo van der Merwe. He calls reconciliation "all initiatives which bring together, or engage, both sides in a pursuit of changing identity, values regarding interaction, attitudes and patterns of interaction that move them to a more cooperative relationship."[680]

The belief in emotions rather than rational choice incentives as the basis for reconciliation is also the basis of Long and Brecke's book on reconciliation events. In their view, reconciliation, in the sense of individual and, later on, collective forgiveness, is an evolutionarily constructed conflict-solving

677 Hamber, Brandon; Kelly, Gráinne: "A Working Definition of Reconciliation". *Democratic Dialogue*, September 2004, 1-11. http://cain.ulst.ac.uk/dd/papers/dd04recondef.pdf

678 Daniel Bar-Tal, personal communication with Karen Brounéus at Tel-Aviv University, see: Brounéus, Karen: Rethinking reconciliation: Concepts, methods, and an empirical study of truth telling and psychological health in Rwanda (PhD). Uppsala University, Uppsala, Sweden, 15.

679 Nadler, Arie, Shnabel, Nurit: "Instrumental and Socio-Emotional Paths to Intergroup Reconciliation and the Need-Based Model of Socio-Emotional Reconciliation." In: Nadler, Arie; Malloy, T.; Fisher, J. D. (eds.): The Social Psychology of Intergroup Reconciliation, New York: Oxford University Press, 2006.

680 Van der Merwe, Hugo: The Truth and Reconciliation Commission and Community Reconciliation: An Analysis of Competing Strategies and Conceptualisations (Diss. George Madison University 1999), available at http://www.csvr.org.za/wits/papers/paphd2.htm.

mechanism that has evolved because of the human necessity to maintain relations despite aggression and violence. On this ground, reconciliation is defined as "mutually conciliatory accommodation between former antagonists" and the "process integral to mitigating future violence and maintaining societal relationships after violent conflict."[681]

Johan Galtung stresses that it is a "process of healing the traumas of both victims and perpetrators after the violence, providing a closure of the bad relation. The process prepares the parties for relations with justice and peace."[682] Even though the 'bad' relationship remains the central preoccupation, Galtung thinks that reconciliation precedes justice and peace, whereas many other thinkers look at justice and peace as elements of reconciliation.[683] Taking into account Galtung's concept of positive peace, which includes the absence of any form of structural violence, it becomes clear that he conceives of reconciliation as an element of peace. This way of looking at it returns in Hamber and Kelly's working definition, where reconciliation equals one of several elements of the process of peace building.

As a first conclusion, we can note that the definitions mentioned so far chiefly focus on the modification of social relationships. Reconciliation, in this sense, is a fundamentally social process.

An important and very much related question is whether reconciliation is an individual phenomenon or rather a collective one. Priscilla Hayner distinguishes between reconciliation on the collective (national and political) scale on the one hand, and reconciliation on the personal or individual scale involving the processes of healing and forgiveness on the other. In her work on truth commissions, she stresses that by speaking openly about a violent or conflicting past, truth commissions help establishing a common truth about the past and thus can enhance reconciliation on a collective scale. Whether or not these still politically induced attempts to foster reconciliation through truth commissions may actually reach down to the individual levels of people's everyday lives is however not guaranteed.[684]

Facing, recounting, and absorbing the past in order to elaborate a common truth and a shared vision of the future is an always-recurring theme in the

---

681 Long, William J.; Brecke, Peter: War and Reconciliation: Reason and Emotion in Conflict Resolution, Cambridge, Mass., 2003.

682 Galtung, John: "After Violence, Reconstruction, Reconciliation, and Resolution: Coping with Visible and Invisible Effects." In: Abu-Nimer, Mohammed (ed.): Reconciliation, Justice, and Coexistence: Theory and Practice, Maryland 2001.

683 As we will see, this confusion stems rather from a different understanding of *justice* and not of *reconciliation*.

684 Hayner, Unspeakable Truths, 155.

academic literature. Andrew Rigby distinguishes between forgiveness, which is oriented towards the past, and reconciliation, which mainly addresses the common future ahead.[685] *The Handbook of Reconciliation* issued by the International IDEA think tank equally stresses this important aspect of memory politics in their definition of reconciliation: It is "a process through which a society moves from a divided past to a shared future."[686] Some emphasize that archival truth and accessible documentation about past atrocities is more essential to assure long term reconciliation, which Priscilla Hayner calls "building or rebuilding relationships today that are not haunted by the conflicts and hatreds of yesterday."[687] Hayner stresses the importance of the past, i.e. the collec(tiva)tion of "truth" about past discord and violence that have to be shared and communalized in order to achieve reconciliation. An equal accent is put on the action of generating truth itself through ritualized apology and forgiveness cycles. In this way, Karen Brounéus defines reconciliation as "a societal process that involves mutual acknowledgement of past suffering and the changing of destructive attitudes and behaviour into constructive relationships toward sustainable peace."[688] John Paul Lederach similarly contends that reconciliation as the "space for the acknowledging of the past and envisioning of the future[,] is the necessary ingredient for reframing the present."[689] Hizkias Assefa considers reconciliation to be one conflict-handling mechanism among others, which gains particularity from its methodology: "The essence of reconciliation is the voluntary initiative of the conflict parties to acknowledge their responsibility and guilt [...] [T]he parties are not only meant to communicate one's grievances against the actions of the adversary, but also [to] engage in self-reflection about one's own role and behaviour in the dynamic of the conflict."[690]

As a second intermediary conclusion, we note that reconciliation is deeply linked with generating truth about the past, with a view to collectively facing it and addressing it. Reconciliation thus has a strong connotation of temporality.

The reconciliation literature appears to be surprisingly unreceptive to anthropological sensitivities. At least as important as the purely theoretical debates should be the understanding of the notion by the people it is meant to

685 Rigby, Andrew: Justice and Reconciliation after the Violence, London, 2001, 12.

686 Bloomfield, Reconciliation: an Introduction, 12.

687 Hayner, Unspeakable Truths, 161.

688 Bounéus, Rethinking Reconciliation, 3.

689 Lederach, John Paul: Building Peace: Sustainable Reconciliation in Divided Societies, Washington D.C.: United State Institute of Peace, 1997, 27.

690 Assefa, Hizkias: "Reconciliation." In: Reychler, Luc; Thania Paffenholz, Thania: Peace-Building: A Field Guide. Columbia: Boulder 2001, 341.

reach at the grassroots level. By applying the notion to the specific case of Rwanda, Wendy Lambourne remarks that *bwiyunge* (Kinyarwanda for reconciliation) implies a personal, two-way process. She quotes a survivor: "Reconciliation should be between the victim and the person responsible – a new beginning, because the relationship is broken and [one] should start anew and rebuild the relationship."[691] The reference here to temporality – a new start – invites a comparison of indigenous notions of time, social remembering and forgetting with Western models of memory and memory politics. It is not difficult to grasp the fundamental nuances in the longevity and texture of public consciousness and modes of remembering, as they are conditioned by the biases of oral and written cultures, for instance, or the questionable divide between the public and private domains of information in African urban settings.[692] It should suffice here to urge caution when universalizing the validity of memory models such as theories by Maurice Halbwachs, Pierre Nora, and Jan and Aleida Assmann, for instance.

Two general themes are recurrent in the definitions: first, the psychological transformations of the individual and/or collective self-awareness (or identity) which member of a social space continuously generate in order to mutually affect their relationships and bridge societal dissent. Second, many authors orient their interpretation of reconciliation towards the politics of memory, mainly by focussing on the establishment and en-actment of truth, in order to bridge the discontinuities of trauma between past and present.

Beyond the didactic purpose of terming phenomena and processes of social and psychological nature, it is evident that both ideas are mutually dependent. Facing past atrocities through apologies by former state decision-makers, for instance, simultaneously helps reshape the collective identity of victims. These two categorical lines of understanding, which we have elaborated out of the definitions above, are thus inextricably linked and mutually interdependent.

The complexity is not facilitated by the fact that different instruments of action for achieving these objectives have to be added to the picture. The main instruments are presented as healing, justice, truth telling, and reparation, which in the meantime have to be considered along with the process of in-depth democratisation.[693] Due to the multifariousness of potential ingredients that give

691 Lambourne, Justice and Reconciliation, 315.

692 See Ellis, Stephen: "Tuning in to Pavement Radio", in *African Affairs* 88 (352), 1989, 321-330.

693 Bloomfield, Barnes, Huyse: Reconciliation After Violent Conflict. A Handbook (International Idea: Handbook Series).

meaning to the notion of reconciliation, different attempts have been made to organize the polysemic field, some of which can be summarized as follows:

Applying a prismatic view, Karen Brounéus slices the theme of reconciliation into seven aspects that she deems important for development workers to consider: The religious aspect reminds the reader of the cultural relativity of forgiveness and revenge. In Cambodia, for instance, Buddhism predisposes all people to rely on the principle of Karma which will retribute by socially discriminating a perpetrator in his next life. Forgiveness thus becomes either pointless or very easy. This contrasts with the dogma of Christianity where, in Orthodox belief, sin ruptures the relationship between God and Man, while in the Protestant and Catholic dogma; it refers to a more legal rupture with canonical law. People on earth must therefore forgive in order to live with and in their sinful world because ultimate punishment cannot be imposed before the last judgment after death. Besides a socio-cultural aspect, which stresses that culture is generally more or less prone to forgiveness and reconciliation (cf. "Ubuntu" in the South African context), Brounéus further stresses the importance of economic security as an indispensable basis for reconciliation. The political aspect consists of the institutionalisation of democracy as an ongoing mechanism of peaceful conflict resolution. Formally ritualized political reconciliation events can also contribute to this process. The psychological aspect deals with the importance of healing individual trauma and the potential danger of re-traumatisation. Finally, the juridical aspect discusses the tension between retributive justice and stability or peace, the role amnesty can play, and the contribution of truth commissions. Surprisingly, Brounéus does not enter the debates about the reconfiguration of collective identities as a chief factor in reshaping relationships between groups of people.[694]

William J. Long and Peter Brecke show in their book about reason and emotion in conflict resolution that formal reconciliation events have had decisive influence upon the ability of people to forgive. The authors assert that, although a rational choice approach to understanding the motives for such reconciliation events might still suit formal inter-state reconciliation, it no longer holds any relevance for intra-state or civil conflict in general. A perspective of evolutionary psychology is proposed in order to understand what drives people to actually reconcile and forgive each other. The authors assimilate their understanding of reconciliation with the meaning of forgiveness and consequently contend that forgiveness consists of the following factors or elements: acknowledgement, identity transformation or reframing, overcoming

694 Brounéus, Rethinking reconciliation, 21-31.

the feeling of revenge (= breaking the cycle of injury and counter-injury), and a reconciliation event as a political incentive.[695]

In their attempt to elaborate a working definition of reconciliation, Brandon Hamber and Gráinne Kelly show that, as part of the larger framework of peace building, reconciliation consists of five elements: 1. Developing a shared vision of an interdependent and fair society; 2. acknowledging and dealing with the past; 3. building positive relationships; 4. significant cultural and attitudinal change; and 5. substantial social, economic, and political change.[696]

The Truth and Reconciliation Commission of South Africa has triggered a lot of scholarly debates and literature about the meaning of reconciliation and the main tendencies in its discursive usage.[697] As an example, Hamber and van der Merwe have applied five chief lines of understanding: Reconciliation can follow 1. a non-racial ideology (to transcend racial identity); 2. a religious ideology (by stressing forgiveness); 3. a political ideology to promote and secure the human rights regime (by regulating and preventing violations through democracy and the rule of law); 4. an ideology for ending conflicts between communities; or 5. an ideology that aims at ending conflicts inside communities.[698] The two latter categories appear distinct merely through their either individual or collective perspective. According to Annelies Verdoolaege, the religious-redemptive discourse of reconciliation was the most important approach in post-apartheid South Africa.[699]

The panoply of conceptual organigrams that scholars have designed to organize the complex elements and meaning of reconciliation is vast. A last important example that should not be discarded is Jean-Paul Lederach's approach. In his view, reconciliation is the process and social space where truth, forgiveness (mercy), justice, and peace come together: "Truth is the longing for acknowledgement of wrong and the validation of painful loss and experience, but it is coupled with Mercy, which articulates the need for acceptance, letting go, and the new beginning. Justice represents the search for individual and group rights, for social restructuring and for restitution, but is linked with Peace, which underscores the need for interdependence, well-being and security."[700]

---

695 Long, Brecke, war and reconciliation,passim.

696 Hamber, Brandon; Kelly, Gráinne: "A Working Definition for Reconciliation." *Democratic Dialogue (*Belfast), September 2004, 4.

697 For an overview, see Verdoolaege, Reconciliation Discourse, 26-27.

698 Hamber, Brandon; van der Merwe, Hugo: "What Is This Thing Called Reconciliation?", paper presented at the Goedgedacht Forum, Cape Town, 1998, quoted in Brounéus, Rethinking Reconciliation, 15-16.

699 Verdoolaege, Rethinking Reconciliation, 27.

700 Lederach, Building Peace, 29.

Depending on the perspective one applies to reconciliation, its meaning may shift from a collective to a rather individual process or from a change in social psychological to a transformation of political psychology (in-depth democratisation, see below). In view of the multiple forms in which reconciliation can be understood, it undeniably runs the risk of being turned into or understood as a morally loaded concept,[701] which, depending on the ideological tendency of the author, can contain different semantic elements. The normative orientation thus conveyed can put either more or less stress on one or another of the elements invoked, the most important of which – as has become apparent from the definitions examined above – are the (socio-) psychological or intercommunal approach which emphasizes the reorganisation of collective identities in order to bridge their divides, and the memory approach, focusing on truth generation and truth digestion as a means of overcoming the past.

Reconciliation Within Social Space

According to Pierre Bourdieu, the social world can be represented as a space with several dimensions in which strength and power are conferred on "agents and groups of agents (…) defined by their relative position within that space."[702] Each group holds power in the form of economic, cultural, social and/or symbolic capital, "commonly called prestige, reputation, renown, etc."[703] The kinds of capital define the chances of profit in a given field ("like the aces in a game of cards").[704]

The fact that an objectively valid representation of a social space configuration is impossible to be drawn is an inherent attribute of the concept. This is due to the fact that "the most objectivist theory has to integrate the agents' representation of the social world,"[705] and these representations differ. They are always the result of the respective self-representation of a group or an agent who subjectively relates to any perceived "other". Given the importance of subjective representations, power relations are mainly present in people's minds, and "the form of the categories of perception of these relations" thus becomes an argumentative stake in the sociological configuration of social space.[706]

---

701 Hamber, Kelly, A working definition, 5.

702 Bourdieu, Pierre: "The social space and the genesis of groups", in: *Theory and Society* 14, 6 (1985), 723.

703 Op. cit. 724.

704 Ibid.

705 Op. cit. 727

706 Op. cit. 729.

Consequently, the ability to shape these categories of perception is highly desirable, and Bourdieu stresses the discursively constructive power of knowledge: "Knowledge of the social world, and, more precisely, the categories that make it possible, are the stakes, par excellence, of political struggle, the inextricably theoretical and practical struggle for the power to conserve or transform the social world by conserving or transforming the categories through which it is perceived."[707]

Although arguing from a more psychological point of view (perception is also caused by emotions), the assumption that the social world can be transformed through altering mutual perceptions is also underlying Nadler and Shnabel's concept of socio-emotional reconciliation. Referring to Kelman, reconciliation is compared to "the removal of the negation of the other as an element in one's own identity."[708] This identity change is driven by the psychological need for restoring the identity of former victims and perpetrators as powerful actors and moral actors, respectively. Nadler and Shnabel claim that this form of socio-emotional reconciliation can only prevent the unilateral outcomes of revenge and denial (each of which only serve the interests of one group) if interaction takes place in the form of an apology and forgiveness cycle. By apologizing, the former perpetrator burdens himself with debt[709] of which he can only be released by the forgiveness of the former victim.[710] This cycle inverts the role of victim and perpetrator. Now, in order to reintegrate with the community, whose rules he has violated, the perpetrator needs the forgiveness of the victim, which returns agency to the victim and opens the way for the perpetrator back into society. In contrast to revenge, which also gives back agency to the victims and inverts the perpetrator-victim relationship, such an apology-forgiveness cycle does not entail the risk of a socially damaging feud. The cycle stops after the victim has accepted the apology. In order to function, such a cycle unfortunately needs a general agreement within the relevant community about who is a victim and who is a perpetrator. Without such an agreement, which is difficult to achieve in international or inter-group conflicts, it remains open, which of the parties in the conflict should start the cycle and apologize.[711]

---

707 Ibid.

708 Ibid.

709 In German, the words *debt* and *guilt* are equivocally combined in the word *Schuld.*

710 See Arie Nadler, Arie; Nurit Shnabel, Nurit: "Instrumental and Socio-Emotional Paths to Intergroup Reconciliation and the Need-Based Model of Socio-Emotional Reconciliation." In: A. Nadler, T. Malloy, J.D. Fisher (eds.): Social Psychology of Intergroup Reconciliation, New York: Oxford University Press, 2006.

711 Bachmann, Klaus: "Measuring reconciliation after violent ethnic conflicts." *The Review of International Affairs,* vol. LIX, No 1130-1131, April – September 2008, 5-15.

Public acknowledgement contributes to the restitution of victim's identity as powerful actors. In this regard, Bourdieu mentions different mechanisms of identity politics: "The capacity to make entities exist in the explicit state, to publish, make public (i.e. to render objectified, visible, and even official) what had not previously attained objective and collective existence and had therefore remained in the state of individual or serial existence – people's malaise, anxiety, disquiet, expectations – represents a formidable social power, the power to make groups by making the common sense, the explicit consensus, of the whole group."[712] This political steering or governing of the configuration inside the social space by means of diverse instruments of identity politics is what we might call structural enhancement of socio-psychological reconciliation.

This public acknowledgement affecting group relationships inside a social space occurs by manipulating the "work of categorisation, i.e. of making explicit and of classification" of the different societal entities. [713]Though Bourdieu maintains that this "is performed incessantly, at every moment of ordinary existence, in the struggles in which agents clash over the meaning of the social world and over their position within it, the meaning of social identity", he stresses that it chiefly happens "through all the forms of benediction or malediction, eulogy, praise, congratulations, compliments, or insults, reproaches, criticisms, accusations, slanders, etc." Therefore, "[i]t is no accident that the verb kategoresthai, which gives us 'categories' and 'categoremes' means to accuse publicly."[714] Accordingly, the extend of power conferred by the right to simply name people and parts inside the social space becomes apparent, which cannot find a better exemplification than by the denomination politics of ethnic belonging in pre- and post-genocide Rwanda: while in the post-colonial era before 1994 the ethnic belonging to either Hutu, Tutsi or Twa, inherited from Belgian colonial rule, had been inscribed on all Rwandan identity cards, Rwanda's post-genocide regime has prohibited all formal denominations of any such category since the aftermath of genocide in late 1994. It has been argued, however, that such an attempt to create a generalized identity of "Rwandanness" may be counterproductive, as it denies the possibility for difference and the uttering of legitimate grievances[715] which may require more time.

Bourdieu's concept of social space with its inherent assumptions about reciprocally perceived otherness and the governing mechanisms of identity

712 Bourdieu, The Social Space , 729.

713 Op. cit. 729-731.

714 Op. cit. 730.

715 Buckley-Zistel, Susanne: "Dividing and Uniting: The Use of Citizenship Discourses in Conflict and Reconciliation in Rwanda", in: *Global Society*, Vol. 20, No. 1, January, 2006.

politics show great similarities with recent versions of socio-psychological reconciliation models.

Reconciliation as Truth Production and Memory Work

Aleida Assmann argues that memory has a spatially integrating effect in that "memory spaces" evolve through the partial illumination of the past, i.e. by the ways in which an individual or a group uses the past in order to construct a sense of the present, to ground its (collective) identity, to orient its life and to justify its actions.[716] While every individual has a personal memory space which can be seen as a reservoir of elements of putative past actions, encounters, feelings and phenomena to fulfill the tasks of ongoing identification and individuation, collective social entities also have a memory space in which they construct their common here and now through consciously resurfacing their collectively imagined there and then.

Memory is basically inseparable from its individual and/or collective bearer. It is consequently highly relative, relational and always perspectivist in nature. A slice of the past is being lit up from a particular point of view in the present, in order for it to open a certain horizon of action in the future. If something is selected to be remembered, it meanwhile enhances the forgetting of something else. In a spatially adequate metaphor, Assmann quotes Francis Bacon: "When you carry the light into one corner, you darken the rest."[717] This space of perpetual remembering and forgetting, a process steered by the ongoing *panta rhei* of the here and now, is decisive for the projection of the future, even more so in traumatic post-conflict situations, and because this process is often collectively shaped and enhanced, it is a substantial element of the concept of reconciliation.

"Truth", as it is established by historians and tribunals, is an important stake here in that it constitutes a factual framework that has crossed the margins of doubt to become the unquestionable frame for the range of interpretations that can be made about the how-it-really-was. As social relations are mainly driven (and governed) by the representations that individual and collective entities have of themselves and reciprocally of one another, the control of the putative historical truth, one of the constitutive elements of our human imaginary and

716 "Zum einen entstehen Erinnerungsräume durch jene partielle Ausleuchtung der Vergangenheit, wie sie ein Individuum oder eine Gruppe zur Konstruktion von Sinn, zur Fundierung ihrer Identität, zur Orientierung ihres Lebens, zur Motivierung ihres Handelns brauchen." Assmann, Alaida: Erinnerungsräume. Formen und Wandlungen des kulturellen Gedächtnisses, 3d ed., Munich: C.H. Beck, 2006, 408.

717 Op. cit. 408.

thus a building block in the process of identification, is of high relevance to the process of socio-emotional reconciliation.

Nonetheless, scholars tend to agree today that it is not so much the absolute or ultimate truth which is of paramount importance, but that much depends on the truth resulting from a spontaneous social and collective truth generation process which follows various epistemic regimes and processes.[718] The Rankean credo of positivist historiography, "wie es eigentlich gewesen," has lost much of its paradigmatic status since the 19th century. Historians have become increasingly aware that hermeneutics are just as important as critical source work in the construction process of historical narratives. The same criticism has been applied to the "truth" generated in tribunals. Rigby, for example, questions the validity of the truth generated through prosecution, because "truth" in this case is the result of a negotiation process: Trials "are combative encounters where defendant and prosecutor compete to get their version of the truth accepted as authoritative. In this process both sides are engaged in what we might term the manipulation of history, insofar as they each have an interest in concealing some aspects of the past and highlighting others."[719]

This takes us on to the social constructivist conception of truth and historical truth as the result of socially negotiated common sense, guided by the habits, invisible rules, and logics of the everyday. Henri Lefebvre "never ceased to remind us that the problem of truth was not located within the vagaries of knowledge or consciousness as Cartesian thought has it, but lay in social life and its practices."[720] Truth, according to Lefebvre, does not so much depend on the epistemological quality of human perception and reason. It rather depends on the relational arrangements of a social space and the production processes that lie within.

These elements of the profoundly cultural nature of truth and its fundamental dependence on the social practices that bring it about are central if we are to think reconciliation from the perspectives of manifold cultural contexts. Michel Foucault has emphasized how in the Western world the entire ontological attitude towards the rule of law as well as towards knowledge in general is fundamentally based on, and driven by, the desire for absolute

718 See among others Luckmann, Thomas; Berger, Peter: The Social Construction of Reality: A Treatise in the Sociology of Knowledge. New York: Ancor 1966; Fleck, Ludwig: Zur Entstehung einer wissenschaftlichen Tatsache. Einführung in die Lehre vom Denkstil und Denkkollektiv, Frankfurt am Main: 1989 (1935); Kuhn, Thomas: The Structure of Scientific Revolutions, Chicago 1962.

719 Rigby, Justice and Reconciliation, 6.

720 Aronowitz, Stanley: "The Ignored Philosopher and Social Theorist. The Work of Henri Lefebvre." *Situations*, vol. 2, 1, 139.

veracity and ultimate doubtlessness (which for Foucault, however, remains but a discourse). With regards to the Western culture of law, Foucault remarks: "I am thinking, again, of the manner in which such prescriptive ensembles as the Penal Code have sought their basis or justifications. For example, the Penal Code started out as a theory of Right; then, from the time of the 19th century, people looked for its validation in sociological, psychological, medical and psychiatric knowledge. It is as though the very words of the law had no authority in our society, except insofar as they are derived from true discourse."[721]

The legal space which the rule of law has come to occupy in Western statehood is a result of historical zeitgeist, especially of the modern period, with its importance increasing during the XIXth century, and with its predilection for absolute, knowable "truth" as a perfect representation of ontological reality. The focus of the legal system on truth and veracity, its conviction to be able to find out the factual grounds for punishment by state authority can thus be considered the result of a particular cultural history.

In line with this, the better truth, according to Galtung, is the one negotiated at the grassroots level, a bottom-up truth constructed by the population in truth commissions or civil society gatherings, round tables, and public debates. The top-down approach of the official version risks jeopardizing people's adherence to it.[722] Invoking the example of the Opsahl commission in Northern Ireland, the author promotes the idea of producing a local record of people's histories in the form of a big book: "[R]ather than the Truth lawyers and historians think they can establish, that book will accommodate thousands of truths. [...] [T]he citizens would themselves establish their truths."[723] It is the psychological purpose of the collective social practice of truth production that is more important than the putative ultimacy of its content, because truth building is about externalizing the conflict.[724] Galtung emphasizes the performative effects of communicative practice: "Let ten thousand dialogues blossom."[725]

Another critique has been put forward against the Western conception that "One does not forget and forgive. One remembers and forgives."[726] Talking and rationalizing about past traumatic experiences has for a long time been deemed conducive to the overall healing process. Galtung challenges the idea that "tout

721 Foucault, Michel: "The Discourse on Language." In: Adams, Hazard and Searle, Leroy (eds.): Critical Theory Since 1965, Tallahassee: University Press of Florida, 1986, 148-162.

722 Galtung, After Violence, 12.

723 Op cit. 12-13.

724 Op. cit. 13

725 Ibid.

726 Long, Brecke, War and Reconciliation, 29.

comprendre, c'est tout pardonner" by stressing that "truth alone is merely descriptive, not spiritual."[727] Andrew Rigby shares his opinion, stressing that, in some circumstances, it is more conducive to forget than to remember.[728]

On the other hand, one might argue that storing and remembering past traumatic events is the only way to really be able to forget them, in the sense of Derrida, who thought that we have to focus on the truth, in order to archive and forget it: "When I handwrite something on a piece of paper, I put it in my pocket or in a safe, it's just in order to forget it, to know that I can find it again while in the meantime having forgotten it."[729]

No matter whether memory serves to remember or forget the past, it is undoubtedly an important element in the process of reconciliation. In this way, the contribution of tribunals to foster the process of truth generation, though not too participatory in its approach, may help to constitute documentary material that may serve the (re-) construction of collective identities.

Reconciliation and Legal Space

Besides the social and temporal dimensions of reconciliation which we have discussed so far, reconciliation is often attributed a political dimension as well, in that it contains a certain normative direction in which to steer the political activity that might surround, support, or frame it. In the understanding of the International Idea think tank, mainly concerned with democratisation on a global scale, reconciliation is unthinkable without being paralleled by efforts to democratize. The handbook on Reconciliation After Violent Conflict[730] starts off with Churchill's quote that "Democracy is the worst form of government except all those other forms that have been tried from time to time."[731] The underlying idea of strengthening democracy in no matter what cultural context is the theoretical conviction that a democratic system is inherently able to assure ongoing conflict resolution, thus preempting the recurrence of violence.

The reader may rightfully ask about the link between the structural institutionalisation of democracy and the process of reconciliation. The answer is not difficult, but still complex: democracy is more than institutions. David Bloomfield, the chief editor of International Idea's handbook, clearly distinguishes between the structural set-up of democratic institutions and the

727 Galtung, After Violence 12.
728 Rigby, Justice and Reconciliation, 12.
729 Derrida, Jacques as quoted in Verdoolaege, Reconciliation Discourse, 32.
730 Bloomfield, Barnes, Huyse, Reconciliation After Violent Conflict, passim.
731 Bloomfield, Reconciliation: an Introduction, 10.

importance of constructive working relations between the people who are thought to activate, actualize, and enact the democratic system. Once again, social relations are invoked. Yet, it is not so much the collective identities and their mutual intergroup understanding that is meant here, as the normative framework of action in which these relations take place. This framework of action is the rule of law, which in the long run is thought to affect and condition people's ways of relating to each other – collectively in groups, but also individually.

We must not think, however, that the gradual introduction of the rule of law into the lives of people and their everyday habits, feelings and thoughts – no doubt a Herculean task – would lead to a singularly uniform outcome. This would mean falling prey to positivist thinking. Legal culture is not systemic and should rather be understood as "a product of social forces, and itself a conduit of those same forces."[732] In this way, law becomes a guideline for action that penetrates people's imagination to an extent that it becomes naturalized, self-perpetuating, and self-sustaining evidence. In this way, the rule of law becomes part of a "complex totality in which it constitutes as well as is constituted, shapes as well as is shaped,"[733] according to the moving and morphing underground of perceiving and conceiving of the world through habits of sensation, socialisation, and interpretation.

From this perspective, reconciliation may be served by entrenching the rule of law and human rights into the imaginary that governs the working relationships of people. This spread and penetration of the principle of positive state law into the personal and individual spheres of people is what we have called (extending) legal space, which is the space of encounter between the rule of positive state law and people's social everyday.

Reconciliation as a Discoursive Device

A study of the concept of reconciliation in use at the ICTs of Yugoslavia and Rwanda would run short of substance were it to focus exclusively on the semantic archeology of the notion. Rather, we intend to integrate the performativity of a notion like reconciliation in the context of its production and usage within the ICTR. Looking at the role of the medium that both carries and shapes our object of investigation – written and oral speech – and at the constitutive power that speech exerts over the popular outlining of the world,

732 Silbey, S. S.: "Legal Culture and Legal Consciousness", in: International Encyclopaedia for the Social and Behavioural Sciences, 8623-8629.

733 Ibid.

actually promises to substantially complement our analytical focus, by pointing to new important questions.

It has become a commonplace of constructivist theory and cultural studies that language is considered not merely a representation of the "ontic",[734] but that as a discourse that identifies and classifies the world it meanwhile constitutes reality. Language or the linguistic act, in this sense, is the performative and socially interactive arena in which meaning is negotiated and produced. Pre-existing knowledge, rational and embodied, curbs and conditions our perception, and it is in this context that our understanding 'indigenizes' or 'appropriates' phenomena that hitherto we were not familiar with. The latter are ultimately reactions resulting from the depths of doubt, in the vicinity of which they remain until they are actualized and shared in the moment of expression through a social act of speech. It is through this performative act of speaking, of calling and naming things, that reality is construed. But not only has the a priori order that seems to govern our individual mind preconditioned the linguistic act. It is also "controlled, selected, organized and channelled by procedures inside a social setting,"[735] and hence the act of speaking has both a social and a political element to it, in that it is socially produced, and in that it purveys in its own very semantic arrangement a model to (normatively) order the world. This hints at the meaning of what Michel Foucault has called discourse.

Critical Discourse Analysis (CDA) contends that "discourse is both socially constitutive as well as socially conditioned, which means that a discursive event is shaped by situations, institutions and social structures, but it also shapes them. Therefore CDA stresses the relevance of investigating language use in institutional settings [...]."[736]

From this methodological perspective, Annelies Verdoolaege has examined the "reconciliation discourse" of the Human Rights Violations Committee, which was one of the main components of South Africa's Truth and Reconciliation Commission (TRC). Her findings show that the TRC did not actually achieve or create reconciliation, but that it started the process of reconciliation by deliberately shaping a constitutive discourse and a "culture of open debate and open discussion." As a result, in 2004, it has been acknowledged that the general attitude towards reconciliation and forgiveness in

---

734 The notion of ontic reality refers to the opening article by Ernst von Glaserfeld in: von Förster, Heinz; von Glaserfeld, Ernst and Hejl, Peter M. (eds.): Einführung in den Konstruktivismus, 10th ed., Munich 2008. The adjective *putative* has been added to emphasize the belief of radical constructivists that even the ontic is a result of our perception rather than a preordained absolute reality.

735 Foucault, Michel: Die Ordnung des Diskurses, 10-11. Emphasis by Peter Lambertz.

736 Verdoolaege, Reconciliation Discourse, 43.

South Africa was favorable, which allows to retrospectively praise the TRC as "an important symbolic instrument to enhance reconciliation."[737]

Verdoolaege has tried to identify the different structural elements or "ideological layers" that have ordered the discourse about reconciliation in the hearings of the TRC's Human Right Violations Committee (HRVC). Through meticulous analysis of a well-balanced sample of hearings, she discovered ten structural features that were framed by the categories of ideology, history, and identity.[738] Overall, they indicated a very broad conceptualisation of the term at the HRVC hearings.[739]

Verdoolaege summarizes her findings by stating that, "as a result of the reconciliation discourse constructed at the HRV hearings, a reconciliation-oriented reality was established in South Africa. This reality was multifaceted, since the concept of reconciliation could be interpreted in manifold ways [...]. Ultimately, the TRC's institutional power was extremely influential in South Africa."[740] This was mainly due to the large publicity that was accorded to the different hearings through large-scale media coverage: "Everybody talked, discussed and read about the Commission."[741] In addition, the TRC enjoyed a high level of authority through its deeply grounded institutional legitimacy[742] to which gradually growing output legitimacy can undoubtedly be added. In this way, the concept of reconciliation "became firmly rooted in South African public life, which might have influenced people's perspective on society,"[743] and thus has discursively enhanced the population's sensitivity for reconciliation as a fact.

Reconciliation and the Everyday

At the same time the contribution of discourse to the generation of (social) reality is highly dependent upon its outreach into people's everyday life and habits, its governmental penetration into the soil of living culture.

---

737 Op. cit. 17-18 and 61-61.

738 Op. cit. 54-128. The ten features are respectively: Ideology: 1. Introducing reconciliation; 2. Stressing national unity / community spirit; 3. Respecting testifiers; 4. Emphasizing emotional discourse; History: 5. Appartheid-talk; 6. Continuity between the past and the present; 7. Audience as actor; Identity: 8. Struggling with an Afrikaner/white identity; 9. Victim-perpetrator identity; 10. Pro-con ANC identity.

739 Op. cit. 154.

740 Op. cit. 182-183.

741 Op. cit. 182.

742 Op. cit. 169

743 Op. cit. 188.

Henri Lefebvre has shown and advocated that social change, if introduced in a top-down process, has to be ingrained in and embraced by the social, imaginary and working practices of the everyday. His thinking is inherently driven by the urge to rehabilitate the harmony between nature and mankind, which, in his view, has increasingly been strained by the accelerating technological momentum of "modernity". His apprehension of the small things and situations out of which people weave their habits are valuable for our concerns, because reconciliation appears at large to be nothing but a certain form of social change, a transformation in social space, from a formerly conflicting relationship to a mutually constructive one. In the words of Stanley Aronowitz: "If the forms of social life are not changed, the old order will reappear. If the state and the economy attempt to dominate and to assert their primacy over social life, this domination is only the form of appearance of social relations. If the old regime remains in force at the level of the family, personal relations, especially sexuality, and the structure of authority at the workplace, if the routines of repetitive everyday existence are preserved, if life is bereft of pleasure and desire is relegated to the dream work but is denied in the everyday, nothing much has actually changed."[744]

Also Andrew Rigby talks about everyday life. Advocating a "Culture of Reconciliation", Rigby claims that "the only sound basis for that is the development of a new and resilient culture of respect for human rights and for human difference, a culture that is embodied in the everyday routines of life within the family, the school, the neighbourhood, and the wider community."[745] It is here that the dividing line between the theoretical intentions and the actual effects of reconciliatory attempts may be located.

Discourse, seen as a first intruder into the realm of micro-social realities, can help to bridge this gap. Given the necessary mechanisms for public impetus, its reliance on the most ordinary and ever-present form of communicational scapes – language –, the South African case has proved its instrumental efficiency for the promotion of reconciliation on the grassroots level by discursively seeding it into public awareness. Bearing this in mind we will be able to evaluate whether the same can be said for the discursive power of the "reconciliation discourse" at the ICTR and the ICTY. It is clear by now that this will depend on the tribunal's capacities of outreach into the people's everyday.

---

744 Aronowitz, The Ignored Philosopher, 136.

745 Rigby, Justice and Reconciliation, 180.

Result: An Open Definition

From this follows that reconciliation can be seen as a (more or less structurally induced or triggered) self-modification of a variable set of connecting and overlapping areas of influence that relate to one another in any unique post-conflict situation in a specific configuration. These areas are social space, legal space, and memory and truth production. The relevant weight that each of them bears in the configuration of each individual post-conflict situation can gradually shift from one space to another over time and over geographical space.

As will be shown, with regards to justice, the transformation of social space tends to be rather enhanced by a restorative approach to justice, while legal space is rather affected by a retributive understanding of justice. Truth and memory work apply to both restorative and retributive practices of justice. The former is better served by negotiated truth while the latter encourages an absolute understanding of truth (see below).

What's more, as a discursive phenomenon, reconciliation can affect (or resonate from) the social processes of reality construction by entering people's habits of self- and world production in their local everyday routines.

How Justice Contributes to Reconciliation: A Typology

After these general theoretical remarks on reconciliation, it is time to continue our systematizing reflection by focusing more particularly on the relationship of reconciliation and justice. After a reminder of the historical and cultural context in which justice has become a stake for reconciliation, the upcoming section discusses the different functions by means of which justice is supposed to contribute to reconciliation. The conceptual organisation follows the above outline of social space, memory and truth production, and legal space, and is meant to provide us with a typology of six logics or perspectives (aspects) which reveal the different meanings that reconciliation may acquire when relating to justice.

Sublating Vengeance

Retributive justice intends to sublate the victim's urge for revenge, which can be considered a form of transcending or outsourcing of vengeance. The sine qua non condition for this to succeed, however, is that the victim can identify with and does not feel alienated from the judicial body that takes over the task. Much depends therefore on the credibility and (output) legitimacy of the latter.

The notion of sublation refers to Hegel's idea of *Aufhebung* and has an equally double connotation of lifting (to raise, to transcend) and removing (to make disappear, to evaporate) as in the German original. While in Hegelian dialectics, the opposition between thesis and antithesis is eventually sublated by synthesis, it is the overarching legal institution, mostly and ideally the state as legitimate dispensator of law, that sublates or preempts intuitively generated feelings of vengeance and reprisal by taking care of adequate punishment of wrongdoers.

According to the perspective one takes regarding the nature of vengeance itself, opinions differ whether retributive justice should be motivated by vengeance. The perception of vengeance as a "natural and legitimate human desire"[746] provides for a different position than the idea that vengeance is the result of the personal agency power which an individual can or cannot develop

746 Jacoby, Susan: Wild Justice: The Evolution of Revenge, London, 1983, as quoted in Kaju Brandner, Anne: Justice & Reconciliation in Rwanda: An evaluation of judicial responses to genocide and mass atrocities, London, Ontario, 2003 (MA thesis: The University of Western Ontario), 6.

for the sake of personal satisfaction.[747] Invoking Foucault, Simon maintains that this question also follows historical trends. In modern times, the idea that punishment should serve as an instrument for private vengeance for the victims or as a catharsis for the public was clearly excluded from penal thought. In contemporary penal thought, though, 'populist punitiveness' has become a major feature.[748] It has been proposed that the satisfaction victims might encounter through acts of effective rectificatory justice directly affects their progress of healing in a positive manner.[749]

Long and Brecke support the idea of justice to prevent and remove feelings of revenge, in order to demonstrate its "willingness to break the cycle of injury and counter-injury."[750] This could be seen as a major contribution to the overall process of reconciliation. As long as the potential for spontaneous acts of reprisal and retaliation has not disappeared, the crimes of the past continue to "hang like Damocles' sword over every new generation."[751] Yet retribution should not be confused with revenge. Both emphasize the suffering of the offender and neglect the objective of reducing crime. But "while revenge highlights the individual right of the victim to carry out a reprisal, retribution highlights the moral values of society as a whole and views crime as an affront to these values."[752]

Beside this rather theoretical debate about whether or not retribution ought to pursue an objective of vengeance, there are very concrete reasons for the importance of sublating vengeance and its assumed contribution to the process of reconciliation. When taking over the victim's urge for vengeance, retribution also prevents spontaneous reprisals, or self-help justice,[753] which would undermine general security and the precious stability of a returning peace after a violent conflict. This would jeopardize the process of the intended democratic state rehabilitation, to which successful delivery of justice can be a crucially helpful instrument. Meanwhile, its success naturally entails trust in, and credibility of, the institutions of the state as being capable of bringing about justice.

---

747 Govier, Trudy: Forgiveness and Revenge, New York, 2002, as quoted in: Kaju Brandner, Justice & Reconciliation in Rwanda, 6.

748 Simon, J.: Punishment: "Social and Legal Aspects." In: International Encyclopaedia of the Social and Behavioural Sciences, 12606 – 12612.

749 Brounéus, Rethinking Reconciliation, 29.

750 Long, Brecke, War and Reconciliation, 30.

751 Arendt, Hanna: The Human Condition, 1958, 213, as quoted in: Rigby, Justice and Reconciliation, 12.

752 Simon, Punishment, 12606-12612.

753 Rigby, Justice and Reconciliation, 4.

Acknowledging Victims

Restorative justice is more victim-oriented than retributive justice. Yet, from the victim's point of view, formalized and ritualized retributive justice publicly displays who is right and who is wrong. In this way, it implicitly acknowledges victims and helps them rebuild a sense of political self-confidence and an awareness of their own capacity to act. We have already emphasized the importance of public acknowledgement for the rehabilitation of victim's collective identity as politically valuable actors. The mechanism at work here follows what Nadler and Shnabel have called "socio-emotional intergroup reconciliation", which aims at a reconfiguration in the self-identification of two formerly antagonistic parties through respectively transforming their own collective perception and representation. While victims are generally keen on regaining credence in political agency, of which they had been violently deprived, perpetrators are mostly interested in a moral rehabilitation of their collective self.

It is obvious that active and public acknowledgement of victims' suffering may impact more intensely upon this process of identity rehabilitation than the indirect and implicit attempts of enhancing the rule of law by displaying legally sanctioned justice. Publicity and contact with the affected population is of crucial importance, and the media can play an important role in the process, as the South African Truth and Reconciliation Commission has shown. Broadcasts of public hearings, such as those involving Desmond Tutu, were important events.

But there are different ways in which victims and their grief can be acknowledged. One of them is *reconciliation events*, which Long and Brecke have meticulously analyzed. They collected nineteen cases of civil and interstate violent conflict that clearly have become more peaceful after the occurrence of a reconciliation event, and investigated the conditions which were necessary for a conflict situation to positively react to a reconciliation event.[754] Good examples of political apologies include Willy Brandt's kneeling down in the former Warsaw ghetto in 1970, or the UN secretary general Kofi Annan's apology for the UN's failure to prevent the Rwandan genocide, in 2000, in order to enhance the apology and forgiveness cycle in Rwanda. Still other moments of the acknowledgement of victims and their suffering are ritualized moments like anniversaries and sites of commemoration.[755]

754 Long, Brecke, War and Reconciliation, 30. Problematic is that *reconciliation* is considered merely a reconciliation event. The concept, as the authors use it, does not include a more integral set of measures.

755 See Nora, Pierre: Les lieux de mémoire, Paris, 1997.

Nadler and Shnabel as well as Long and Brecke stress the importance of the apology-forgiveness cycle, as is the key mechanism behind socio-emotional reconciliation. If we look for elements of apology and forgiveness in the sessions of retributive justice, the only moment prone to acknowledging victims and their grief might stem from the guilty plea of a perpetrator, which might be interpreted, under certain circumstances, as a formalized act of apology. In many judicial traditions that are oriented towards the restoration of broken social relations because of excessive or deviant behaviour, the admission of guilt constitutes an efficient means of conflict resolution.[756] By admitting his crime, the accused reshapes his contact with the victim and its group. It signifies the respect of the social order and the readiness of the accused to restore this social order. Often, a guilty plea is accompanied by a request for forgiveness, which is often considered to be an inevitable condition for the process of reconciliation.[757] In view of this, the admission of guilt is often respected as a mitigating circumstance.

According to *Paradelle et al.*, the ICTR has missed many opportunities to publicly instrumentalize guilty pleas for the sake of reconciliation. It has been criticized, among others, by the Organisation of African Unity (OAU), especially for not using the guilty plea of former Prime Minister Jean Kambanda, who had admitted the meticulous planning of the genocide and revealed the stages and elements of its preparation.[758]

Given its primary focus on perpetrators, the acknowledgement of victims can generally be seen as the most indirect or implicit contribution that justice can make to the process of reconciliation. Yet, efficient marketing of guilty pleas may increase the chance for impact and might enhance the apology-forgiveness cycle.

Individualizing Guilt

If the aspect of sublating vengeance is driven by the wish to structurally enhance the restoration of the victim's political self-esteem, the individualisation of guilt aims at rehabilitating the moral identity of the perpetrators. By punishing the planners and those chiefly responsible for a crime against humanity, the message conveyed to all others who might be generally associated

756 Paradelle, Murielle; Dumont, Hélène; Boisvert, Anne-Marie: "Quelle justice pour quelle réconciliation? Le tribunal pénal international pour le Rwanda et le jugement du génocide. " *McGill Law Journal* 50 (2005), 375.

757 Op. cit. 375.

758 Paradelle, Dumont, Boisvert, Quelle justice, 378-380.

with the perpetrators' ethnic or other collectivity is clearly that they are not guilty as such only because they belong to the same social group.

This theoretical principle is highly dependent on the political neutrality of the judicial instance, or at least the public belief in this neutrality. The slightest hint or rumour of victor's justice or partiality may ruin the purpose of individualizing guilt, because members of the population that are generally associated with the perpetrators of the crimes might feel endangered instead of feeling protected and encouraged by the rule of law. In such a case, ethnic cleavages are strengthened instead of weakened. This is what happened to a large extent in Croatia, Serbia, and the Serb part of Bosnia with regard to the ICTY.

Article 6 §1 of the ICTR Statute states that "a person who planned, instigated, ordered, committed or otherwise aided and abetted in the planning, preparation or execution of a crime referred to in articles 2 to 4 of the present Statute, shall be individually responsible for the crime."[759] This is a good representation of the credo of modernist political philosophy, which since the enlightenment philosophers John Locke and Immanuel Kant has postulated that responsibility of action and thought is to be sought in the individual, which, as a subject, is seen as equal to all other subjects before the law.[760] The underlying model of personhood at work here is far from universal as it postulates the free will of the individual who acts according to rational, self-interested choices as an autonomous moral agent.[761]

Retributive justice in the sense of the ICTR claims to contribute to reconciliation chiefly by individualizing guilt. In this way, the blame is thought to be removed from the collective shoulders of an entire ethnic group (such as "Hutu" or "Interahamwe" in the Rwandan case), in order to enhance the reconfiguration of the collective identity of the respective group whose name is connoted with the guilt of mass atrocity. Once again the principle of collective identity rehabilitation through socio-emotional intergroup reconciliation (Nadler and Shnabel) is invoked: While in the latter mechanism, the victims were at the centre of attention, the individualisation of guilt strategy focuses on the rehabilitation of perpetrator identity.

---

759 ICTR – Statute of the Tribunal, available at http://www.un.org/ictr/statute.html (emphasis ours).

760 Anzenbacher, Arno: Einführung in die Philosophie, 8th ed., Freiburg-Basel-Vienna, 2002, 281.

761 Kamatali, Jean-Marie: "The Challenge of Linking International Criminal Justice to National Reconciliation: the Case of the ICTR." *Leiden Journal of International Law*, 16 (2003), 124.

Formal political immunity of state representatives, which is rejected in the Statute of the ICTR,[762] no longer appears to be an obstacle for indictment. The indictment of the Sudanese president Omar Hassan Ahmad Al-Bashir on July 14, 2008, by the International Criminal Court demonstrates this.

While the Nuremberg trials had still earned a lot of criticism for merely convicting some individuals for atrocities perpetrated by thousands, "the notion of individual responsibility for war and related crimes has become internationally accepted." [763] The practices of the ICTR and the ICTY are good examples here.

The issue of individual guilt remains highly controversial and intensely debated, mainly because of the broader patterns of group dynamics that underlie collective violence, especially in the case of genocide.[764] Consequently, the argument is being challenged on the multiple fronts of social psychology, cultural and genocide studies.

Social psychology, especially since Milgram's experiments on authority and obedience, has shown that the freedom of individual action is strongly conditioned and compromised by the perceived authoritative hierarchy in which the individual feels himself/herself to be situated. Individual morality can be compromised in the face of authority. Obedience and authority[765] condition our decisions[766] and make it accordingly hard for Kantian idealists to continue to claim that the human being is free to make use of inherent moral law.

If the ICTR affirms the individual responsibility of the accused and denounces obedience to an order as a means of defence (the latter can, in fact,

---

762 ICTR – Statute of the Tribunal, article 6, § 2: "The official position of any accused person, whether as Head of State or Government or as a responsible Government official, shall not relieve such person of criminal responsibility nor mitigate punishment." http://www.un.org/ictr/statute.html.

763 Huyse, Justice", *op.cit.*, 100.

764 Ibid., 105.

765 The ICTR Statute is explicit on these issues, as Article 6, § 3 demonstrates: "The fact that any of the acts referred to in articles 2 to 4 of the present Statute was committed by a subordinate does not relieve his or her superior of criminal responsibility if he or she knew or had reason to know that the subordinate was about to commit such acts or had done so and the superior failed to take the necessary and reasonable measures to prevent such acts or to punish the perpetrators thereof." - § 4:"The fact that an accused person acted pursuant to an order of a Government or of a superior shall not relieve him or her of criminal responsibility, but may be considered in mitigation of punishment if the International Tribunal for Rwanda determines that justice so requires." http://www.un.org/ictr/statute.html.

766 Welzer, Harald: Täter. Wie aus ganz normalen Menschen Massenmörder werden, Frankfurt am M., 2007.

have a mitigating effect on the sentence), there is nothing new about the affirmation of these principles. All of them had already been used by the International Military Tribunal of Nuremberg in 1945.

Concerning the issue of individual guilt in collective crimes, we might ask whether responsibility as such follows universal rules or rather the underlying logic of historical and cultural circumstances, i.e. the patterns of personhood that differ culturally. Ifi Amadiume writes about the Biafran war in which from 1960 to 1970 approximately three million people lost their lives, that "the evil is in the social system, in the guise of inequality and oppression. According to this African logic, guilt is collective; Africans turn to their own social mediators, healers and reclassifiers, such as diviners and prophets. It is a modern arrogance to assume that courts are instruments of healing."[767] Unfortunately, the culturally specific interpretations of the origins of evil cannot be discussed here. Suffice it to say that evil is linked to the cultural relative nature of personhood and agency.

Another question is whether a crime that is collective in its nature can be redressed by punishing individuals. Common law presupposes disobedience or deviance from the commonality as the ground for a criminal act. In case of genocide, we might ask whether it is not much more obedience rather than disobedience to the commonality of action which carries on this crime *hors du commun*. More bluntly put: Is genocide not rather a crime of conformity than a crime of deviance?[768]

Some reject these points of criticism and stick to the concept of individual guilt and responsibility as the basis of penology. Others have argued, on the contrary, that collective responsibility is necessary and even essential for the process of reconciliation.[769] Adopting a pragmatic point of view, Paradelle et al. maintain that, in the context of Rwanda, individual retribution of all criminals who participated in the Rwandan genocide is impossible to achieve. Consequently, reconciliation will not be reached unless collective justice is rendered. Still, they argue that retribution has to be part of the reconciliation process, and as the ICTR does not conceive of guilt in any collective way, they are radically critical of the institution.[770] The statute of the ICTR in fact affirms the principle of individual responsibility. This implies that neither the state, nor the military or other armed groups, nor the media (heavily involved in

767 Amadiume, Ifi: "The Politics of Memory: Biafra and Intellectual Responsibility." In: Idem-Abdullahi An-Na'im (eds.): The Politics of Memory: Truth, Healing and Social Justice, London: Zed Books, 2000, 38-55.

768 Paradelle, Dumont, Boisvert, Quelle Justice, 371-372.

769 McGregor, L.: "Individual accountability in South Africa: Cultural Optimum or Political Façade?", in: *American Journal of International Law* 95 (2001), 7.

770 Paradelle, Dumont, Boisvert, Quelle justice, 371-372.

catalyzing the genocide), nor any other group or moral person can be held accountable in its collectivity.[771]

Given the fact that theoretical debates often run the risk of being driven by the nature of their concepts rather than by the nature of the phenomena that justify their existence, we are strongly in favour of Kamatali's position that "blameworthiness and responsibility are issues that must integrate falsely dichotomizing tendencies such as seeing either the individual or society as being to blame. Shouldn't we replace either/or with both/and thinking?"[772]

The discussion about whether collective crime can or should be reprimanded individually or not is inherently linked to the question of the universality of human rights, because both ideas are based on the enlightenment principle of the subject who is both inherently worthy and, because of this worthiness, also 'responsible'. Retributive justice, as it is applied by the United Nations, is based on this very principle of individual responsibility.

Consolidating Democracy and the Rule of Law

Democratic consolidation is another factor through which justice is thought to contribute to the process of reconciliation. This means the strengthening of the rule of law and the state institutions that should protect it, which mainly works through (re-)building common trust and belief in the state as a neutral and overarching agent of the values it incorporates.

The relationship between democracy and reconciliation is complex. As mentioned above, David Bloomfield points out that the functioning of democracy chiefly depends on two major principles: working relationships and structures.[773] Functioning democratic structures can be seen as an ongoing non-violent conflict resolution mechanism. So (re-)habilitating democratic structures through constitutional and institutional reform is a way of ensuring that the reconciliation process is not jeopardized by newly arising violence. Structural democratisation, i.e. the formal set-up of a democratically organized political architecture, does not suffice, however, to affect social space or memory space at all. If justice claims to contribute to the building up of a democratic state, this cannot, as such, be understood to be a direct contribution to the process of reconciliation.

771 Kamatali, The Challenge, 124.

772 Norrie, A: Punishment, Responsibility and Justice: A Relational Critique, Oxford, 2000, 4, as quoted in Jean-Marie Kamatali, The Challenge, 126.

773 Bloomfield, Reconciliation: an Introduction, 10-18.

Bloomfield further contends that functioning working relations at the grassroots level are the real stake of democratic success, and meanwhile also its Achilles heel: without favourable relationships between the people who enact democracy and on whose shoulders it lies, structures and institutions are mere lip service to the theoretical poetry of political philosophy. Reconciliation, in this context, is thought to be the process that can lead formerly antagonistic groups of people to engage in a "democratic way of thinking of the other", i.e. in a non-violent way.[774] In this perspective, reconciliation means not only the building of trust and relationships, but also educating people to become democratic in their mind, in order to become supportive of and reliant on the democratic structures that are being set up in parallel.

We have seen above that the most fundamental condition for the effective extension of legal space, i.e. for both democratic structures and democratic culture to go beyond political rhetoric, is the undisputedness of the rule of law. Both structures and relationships cannot be truly democratic in nature as long as the rule of law has not penetrated the deeply rooted everyday habits of working, thinking, speaking, and feeling of all members of a common social space.

To cut a long story short, if justice is to contribute to reconciliation, from this perspective, it has to foster democratic "culture" rather than democratic structures, mainly through the promotion of the rule of law. As the symbolic executor of law, a tribunal of course has a privileged role in this regard, because it can prove the impartiality of law towards both victims and perpetrators, and hence generate a general atmosphere of honesty, transparency, and trust.

The theoretical aspirations of state (re-)habilitation and the reform and/or institution of democratic structures do not suffice to drive the process of reconciliation, which, as we have mentioned earlier, should be rooted in people's habits and customs of the everyday. Lederach supports this when he writes: "Peace building must be rooted in and responsive to the experiential and subjective realities shaping people's perspectives and needs." [775] Lederach believes that "this paradigmatic shift is articulated in the movement away from the concern with the resolution of issues and toward a frame of reference that focuses on the restoration and rebuilding of relationships. This calls for an approach that goes beyond a mechanical strategy. The framework must engage and address the relational aspects of reconciliation as the central component of peace building."[776]

774 Ibid.

775 Lederach, Building Peace, 24.

776 Ibid.

Ending Impunity

Impunity is the chief symptom of a lack of the rule of law. It is inherently counterproductive to the process of extending legal space. The understanding has risen that both war and peace tend to have a spiral dynamic, i.e. that they perpetuate themselves in ongoing cycles of repetition. The underlying objective of reconciliation through justice is accordingly to face the challenge of turning the cycle of conflict and impunity into a self-perpetuating dynamic of peace through assuring justice.[777] This can be achieved by deterrence, whose efficiency depends on the credibility of the judiciary system.

"Deterrence occurs when some would-be law breakers conclude that the price of crime is prohibitive."[778] As it is usually aimed at preventing crime or violence from happening, its contribution to the process of reconciliation is just as indirect as the set-up of a democratic institutional framework: both merely assure that the potential reconciliation process is not being jeopardized by the flaring up of new violence.

The theory of deterrence considers punishments as necessary "evils that can only be justified by their effect on the rational calculus of the free and responsible individuals."[779] Once again, we can discern the notion of the individual subject as a morally responsible agent who, moreover, follows the rational choices prompted by his/her individual aspirations. The aim of deterrence in this perspective is to threaten with just enough 'pain' or 'disutility' in response to the respectively forbidden act that a rational agent will consider the gain of a crime less valuable than the value he will lose by being punished. Despite considerable criticism of these presumptions – are humans really rational? – deterrence has proved to be one of the most enduring penal paradigms.[780]

Ending impunity as such does not contribute to reconciliation if we understand the latter as a reconfiguration of a social space setting with its dynamic imaginary of the past. It can be seen, however, as a powerful means for extending the rule of law and democratisation in general. It intervenes as an influential factor in what we have called the legal space, which interacts with social spaces.

---

777 Brounéus, Rethinking Reconciliation, 9.

778 Nagin, D. S.: "Deterrence: Legal aspects." In: The International Encyclopaedia of the Social and Behavioural Sciences, 3544-3550.

779 Simon, Punishment, 12608.

780 Ibid.

Generating Truth

While Luc Huyse does not mention truth generation as a tribunal mechanism conducive to reconciliation, the evidence assembled in the course of a criminal investigation undeniably contributes to a common archive of the past. It is not without reason that the archives of the ICTY and the ICTR will be maintained and preserved also after the Tribunals' closure in order to become constitutive of a growing global memory.[781]

The quality of truth that has been generated in tribunals is that of a negotiated truth. This has to be kept in mind when examining the potential contribution of this often pretended historical truth to the process of reconciliation. What's more, (historical) truth can only be considered as a potential contribution to reconciliation under the paradigm that the past has to be remembered. As we have seen, this is challenged by some who promote legitimate amnesia if the necessary circumstances for constructive remembering are not given.

As far as the ICTR is concerned, one of the biggest problems in generating truth is that the indictment of former RPF members for crimes committed in the early 1990s has not been possible. Rwanda has blocked any inquiry by the prosecutors of the ICTR, and Carla Del Ponte's removal from the office of chief prosecutor at the ICTR (and the splitting of the two posts in The Hague and Arusha) was a result of her intention to reopen the investigations of RPF killings in 1994.[782] However, the tribunal has made of the genocide a kind of public truth, declaring it a so-called *adjudicated fact*.[783]

Based on the conceptual architecture developed in the first chapter of this part, our typology has assembled and discussed a range of issues that have respectively been classified according to whether they impact on social space, memory and truth production, or on legal space. We argue that each time the concept of reconciliation is used in the context of post-conflict justice, its meaning integrates one or several of the semantic layers which have been classified in the typology. Naturally, a typology is heuristic in nature and cannot claim ultimacy concerning its set-up. Nevertheless, we hope it contributes to future analytic endeavors in that it assists in reducing the complexity of a fluid configuration of meaning like the concept of reconciliation.

---

781 Fondation Hirondelle: UN to construct new structure in Tanzania for ICTR archives. http://www.hirondellenews.com/ictr-rwanda/404-ictr-institutional-news/33226-240512-ictrtanzania-un-to-construct-new-structure-in-tanzania-for-ictr-archives.

782 Hazan, Justice, 30-31.

783 Ibid.

The Concept of Reconciliation at the ICTR

The present chapter discusses in which ways the actors of the ICTR conceived of the Tribunal's vocation to contribute to the national reconciliation of Rwanda. The empirical data we have analyzed comprise important documents, judgments, and sentences, as well as speeches that have been delivered by the high-ranking representatives of the ICTR. The aim is to gain insight into the argumentative logics with which the ICTR has shaped the linkage between justice and reconciliation, as well as to investigate to what extent the ICTR has managed to produce a "reconciliation discourse" as it has been analyzed for the South African TRC.[784]

Important documents

One of the first pieces of information one finds when browsing the ICTR website under "Generalities" is that the Tribunal was created for:

> "[t]he purpose of […] contribut[ing] to the process of national reconciliation in Rwanda and to the maintenance of peace in the region. The International Criminal Tribunal for Rwanda was established for the prosecution of persons responsible for genocide [...]."[785]

Although from the outset, reconciliation has featured prominently in the justification of the Tribunal's existence, no specification is given as to how the Tribunal intends to pursue this aim. The website also informs that:

> "[t]he ICTR mandate encompasses establishing the fundamental role of the rule of law, under which persons found guilty are held accountable for their offences, promoting national reconciliation, and restoring peace in the Great Lakes region of Africa."[786]

Also here, a common understanding of reconciliation is postulated. The co-appearance of the rule of law and the idea of individual accountability might be interpreted as a hint towards a rather legalistic understanding of reconciliation (aspects 4 and 5), but this cannot be confirmed with any certainty. The open use of the notion is representative of how reconciliation is mostly used in ICTR documents. Apart from some indirect hints through certain notions being mentioned next to each other, the reader is left alone to make sense of an uncertain concept. A main cause for the appearances of reconciliation in the ICTR documents is resolution 955 of the UN Security Council:

784 Verdoolaege, Reconciliation Discourse, 84.

785 See http://69.94.11.53/ENGLISH/geninfo/index.htm.

786 Op cit.

The ICTR was set up no later than six months after the end of the Rwandan Genocide, on the November 8, 1994. By creating this institution, the UN Security Council declared that it was

> "Determining that [the situation in Rwanda] continues to constitute a threat to international peace and security,
>
> Determined to put an end to such crimes and to take effective measures to bring to justice the persons who are responsible for them,
>
> Convinced that in the particular circumstances of Rwanda, the prosecution of persons responsible for serious violations of international humanitarian law would enable this aim to be achieved and would contribute to the process of national reconciliation and to the restoration and maintenance of peace,
>
> Believing that the establishment of an international tribunal for the prosecution of persons responsible for genocide and the other above-mentioned violations of international humanitarian law will contribute to ensuring that such violations are halted and effectively redressed […]"[787]

Except for the hint that the prosecution of those responsible for the crimes will lead to national reconciliation, nothing indicates how the tribunal intends to pursue this aim. The Statute of the ICTR, which is annexed to the resolution, does, surprisingly, not mention reconciliation at all. Paradelle et al. already wondered about this inconsistency, pointing to the fact that it is the statute which organizes the architecture and functioning of the tribunal by defining the crimes, pursuits, penal responsibilities, sanctions, the procedure of inquiries, and the rights of the convicted.[788] If reconciliation were an important and univocal focal point of action in the understanding of the Tribunal's tasks, would it not have to figure in the statute as well? This is in contrast to the report of South Africa's Truth and Reconciliation Commission, where it is clearly indicated how instructions were given to the commission concerning what had to be kept in mind in order to enhance reconciliation.[789] This is entirely missing in the Statute of the ICTR.

Prior to the adoption of UNSC Resolution 955, the Rwandan government had expressed its hope that the prosecution and sentencing of perpetrators of crimes of genocide and other violations of international humanitarian law would, in the short term, contribute to peace and reconciliation among the parties of the conflict.[790] The respective understanding of reconciliation is

---

787 UNSC resolution 955 (1994).

788 Paradelle, Dumont, Boisvert, Quelle Justice, 367.

789 See TRC Report, 1998, 1/5: 109, quoted in Verdoolaege, Reconciliation Discourse, 60.

790 Letter of August 6, 1994, addressed to the Secretary General from the Minister of Justice of Rwanda, Mr. Nkubito (unpublished), and Letter from the Permanent Representative of Rwanda to the President of the Security Council, September 28, 1994,

elucidated in the statement of Rwandan ambassador Manzi Bakuramutsa as part of the statements of all members that preceded the adoption of Resolution 955 in the 3453th session of the Security Council, where Rwanda itself held a temporary seat at the time:

> "[...] it is impossible to build a state of law and arrive at true national reconciliation if we do not eradicate the culture of impunity which has characterized our society since 1959. The Rwandese, who were taught that it was acceptable to kill as long as the victim was from a different ethnic group or from an opposition party, cannot arrive at national reconciliation unless they learn new values. The national reconciliation can be achieved only if equitable justice is established and if the survivors are assured that what has happened will never happen again."[791]

Peace, security, and democratic culture/the rule of law ("new values") are presented as preconditions for reconciliation. The Tribunal is expected to contribute to the establishment of these preconditions. The Rwandan statement also presented the country's objections towards the creation of the ICTR which were due to many dissatisfactions with the contents of the statute,[792] especially the lack of considering the causes of the conflict and of the preparations for genocide (critique of the *ratione temporis* of the mandate):

> "will not contribute to eradicating the culture of impunity or creating a climate conducive to national reconciliation. In this respect, there is contradiction between articles 6 and 7 of the statute."[793]

Besides this request for the production of truth about the historical causes, the RPF's understanding of the tribunal's contribution to national reconciliation obviously aimed at the ability of the tribunal to efficiently fight impunity in the short term and promote the rule of law as a new framework of values.

In the same session preceding the vote on Resolution 955, a number of statements by the respective members of the Security Council were made. Most of these statements concur with Rwanda's view of the mission of the Tribunal and account for the general understanding that the Tribunal's "contribution to

---

UN Doc. S/1994/1115 (1994), quoted in Shraga, Dahne; Zacklin, Ralph: "The International Criminal Tribunal For Rwanda." *European Journal of International Law* 7, 4 (1996), 501-518, available at http://www.ejil.org/journal/Vol7/No4/art3.html.

791 See Security Council, *The Establishment of an International Tribunal for the Prosecution of Persons Responsible for Serious Violations of International Humanitarian Law Committed in the Territory of Rwanda and Rwandan Citizens Responsible for Such Violations Committed in the Territory of Neighboring States, Provisional Verbatim Record*, 3453rd meeting, 8 Nov. 1994, S/PV.3453 (hereafter *Verbatim report 3453*).

792 Kamatali, The Challenge, 119-120.

793 Verbatim report, 3453.

the process of national reconciliation" lies in its help to reinstall the rule of law as an over-arching governing mechanism. In this spirit, Argentina's representative expressed that:

> "the Tribunal will contribute to the process of reconciliation in Rwanda since, on the one hand, it shows the people, both the victims and the responsible [sic], that justice exists, and, on the other hand, that justice will be applied with impartiality and independence."[794]

The stress here lies clearly on justice per se. In hindsight, however, the intended impartiality and objective justice is questionable, as the impossibility of the Tribunal to prosecute former RPF members for their revenge killings shows. Pakistan's ambassador Jamsheed Marker also stressed the importance of the rule of law for reconciliation, although he talks about "restoring confidence in all sections of the Rwandese polity."[795] Equally, Juan Antonio Yáñez-Barnuevo from Spain states that, "in addition to investigating the facts and punishing the guilty, the Tribunal will make its biggest contribution by helping to restore the rule of law in Rwanda and by serving the purposes of justice and reconciliation between all the Rwandese."[796]

Madeleine Albright, US Secretary of State, who was then presiding over the Security Council, equally mentioned the hope that the Tribunal would promote both justice and reconciliation, "lest the Rwandan people be unable to escape the memory of madness and barbarism they have just lived through."[797] This statement is unfortunately not very specific, but it clearly hints at the understanding that the Tribunal, in its task to promote justice for the sake of reconciliation, is a mechanism to come to terms with the violent past, i.e. an instrument of truth and memory politics.

Ambassador Karel Kovanda from the Czech Republic presented the only critical position towards the idea of reconciliation through justice:

> "Murder, let alone genocide, has to be punished for a sense of right, a sense of law and order, to be restored in a society that has seen all norms of life shattered. Justice is one thing; reconciliation, however, is another. The Tribunal might become a vehicle of justice, but it is hardly designed as a vehicle for reconciliation. Justice treats criminals whether or not they see the error of their ways; but reconciliation is much more complicated, and it is certainly until and unless the criminals repent and show remorse. Only then can they even beg their victims for forgiveness, and only then can reconciliation possibly be attained."[798]

---

794 Ibid.
795 Ibid.
796 Ibid.
797 Ibid.
798 Ibid.

This statement shows that the Czech position clearly distinguishes between the restoration of the rule of law and the process of reconciliation, which is understood rather as the socio-psychological process, i.e. a cycle of apology and forgiveness. In contrast to all other positions, the Czech Republic clearly considers justice and the rule of law a precondition for reconciliation, and not a contribution. Besides this proof of sound reflection, the Czech statement is the only one to urge the Security Council to also consider intervening into the problem of the perpetrators who are hiding in Congolese and Tanzanian refugee camps, outside Rwandan territory. This problem, which was fostered by the French *Opération Turquoise*, prepared the ground for much of the Rwandan involvement in the subsequent Congo Wars, the results of which are still being seen today in the regions of North and South Kivu in the eastern Democratic Republic of Congo.

The statements by the ambassadors from Russia and New Zealand explicitly mention the aim of national reconciliation, but they do not specify how the tribunal ought to contribute to it. Stressing the importance of punishing those responsible for the genocide, the representative of the Russian Federation, Sergiej Lavrov, merely stresses that:

> "by its activity the tribunal must promote the process of national reconciliation, the return of refugees, and the restoration and maintenance of peace in Rwanda."[799]

New Zealand's ambassador Keating also mentions the importance of returning refugees. He somehow implies the wish that the tribunal might restore some sense of national order and security. Given the circumstances of the chaotic situation in the Great Lakes Region generally, we understand that this is also what seems to be implied when Keating quite formally mentions the purpose of reconciliation at the end of his speech. His delegation

> "therefore urges Rwanda to take the opportunity to support this Tribunal, to investigate and punish these people and also as an instrument of national reconciliation."[800]

The use of reconciliation in both Russia's and New Zealand's statements appear to be rather rhetorical than action-specific.

Two things can be concluded so far: Firstly, in the creation phase of the ICTR, reconciliation was mostly used to signify the fight against impunity and the introduction of the rule of law. In this usage, the meaning of reconciliation is close to democratisation (cf. aspects 4 and 5). Generally speaking, its abundant use reveals everything but a unanimous understanding. Secondly, given the fact that nearly all members of the Security Council mention the Tribunal's contribution to

799 Ibid.

800 Ibid.

reconciliation in their statement, we conclude that despite its inherent conceptual ambiguity, reconciliation has served to legitimize the creation of the ICTR.

Sentences

In the majority of the ICTR's 74 cases in which judgments and sentences have been pronounced until the time of writing, reconciliation has not played any role. In most cases the concept of reconciliation is not even mentioned in the trial chambers' and appeals chamber's judgments, and if it appears, the concept is often mentioned in direct or indirect reference to the Tribunal's initial inaugurating statement in the abovementioned Security Council Resolution 955. In cases that mention the concept differently, however, it often appears alongside other expressions such as "justice", "truth", "forgiveness", "rehabilitation", or "peace". In some of these instances, the intended meaning of reconciliation is more explicitly stated than in others. Similar to Klaus Bachmann's findings about reconciliation in the ICTY (see below), pleading guilty has become an important mitigating circumstance (in at least 7 cases) and will therefore be given special attention. Besides the screenings of implicit and explicit understandings of the concept by the ICTR personnel, we attempt to show how the meaning of reconciliation has played the role of an argument in the negotiations about the weight of mitigating circumstances in the judgments or sentences. As will become clear, "reconciliation" has been interpreted restoratively in order to stress the mitigating effect of a guilty plea, as well as to refute the latter using a retributive logic.

Reconciliation Through Retribution?

The following excerpt from the tribunal's first sentence, in *the pros. vs. Akayesu,* mentions the equation between ending impunity and national reconciliation:

> "In resolution 955 of 8 November, 1994 which was passed by the Council in this connection clearly indicates that the aim of the establishment of the Tribunal was to prosecute and punish the perpetrators of the atrocities in Rwanda in such a way as to put an end to impunity and thereby to promote national reconciliation and the restoration of peace. It is therefore clear that the penalties imposed on accused persons found guilty by the Tribunal must be directed on the one hand [to the retribution of the] said accused who must see their crime punished and on the other hand as deterrence, namely dissuading for good those who will be tempted in future to perpetrate such atrocities by showing them that the international community was no longer ready to tolerate serious violations of International humanitarian law and human rights."[801]

801 *The pros. vs. Akayesu,* ICTR-96-4, Sentence, 02.10.1998.

The author of the sentence here clearly indicates that reconciliation can be realized merely through punishment and deterrence. Whether in this passage "punishment" refers to reconciliation while "deterrence" pairs with "peace", or vice-versa, remains ambiguous. What is clear is that the purpose of punishment and retribution appears to be an objective per se. The idea of deterrence clearly hints at the intention of ending impunity, which is closely linked with the consolidation of the rule of (international) law .[802]

Part of our research question was aimed at establishing in to how far the judgments and sentences have actually conformed to the project of contributing to national reconciliation. The objective that sentences should take the promotion of reconciliation into consideration appears explicitly, at several instances. For example:

> "[…] Reconciliation amongst Rwandans, towards which the processes of the Tribunal should contribute, must also weigh heavily in the Chamber's mind when passing sentence."[803]

It is, however, seldom elaborated how exactly the relationship of potential reconciliation and mitigation of sentences should be understood. This problem is rooted in the conceptual ambiguity of the concept and is not diminished by the fact that inherent meanings often appear alongside the ultimate aim of reconciliation, indicating that reconciliation may consequently mean something else. As an example:

> "Having found the Accused guilty, the Chamber now turns to the question of sentencing. The appropriate sentence serves to further the goals of retribution, deterrence, stigmatisation, rehabilitation, protection of society, and national reconciliation."[804]

---

802 Other passages equally invoke justice as such as a contribution to reconciliation. Unfortunately, they often lack any specification as to the linkage between the two concepts. E.g.: "Through justice this Tribunal seeks to contribute to reconciliation. As Justice Murphy of the United States Supreme Court explained nearly sixty years ago [...]."
The pros. vs. Bagambiki (ICTR-97-36), Judgment and Sentence, 25.02.04.
See also *The pros. vs. Ntagerura* (ICTR-96-10A): "This Tribunal was established to contribute to the process of reconciliation and to the restoration of peace and security in Rwanda. The Tribunal's contribution in this area is by conducting impartial criminal proceedings where the burden of proving the guilt of an individual accused is on the Prosecution." *The pros. vs. Rwamakuba* ICTR-98-44C-T, Judgment and Sentence, 20.09.06. And also *the pros. vs. Imanishimwe,* ICTR-97-36,25.02.04, Judgment and sentence: "I understand that the importance of a fair trial may appear pale in comparison to the gravity of the massive human rights abuses which occurred in Rwanda in 1994. However, it is only through a fair trial that we can achieve any lasting justice. Through justice this Tribunal seeks to contribute to reconciliation."

803 *The pros. vs. Kamuhanda,* ICTR-99-54, Judgment, 22.01.04.

804 *The pros. vs. Semanza* ICTR-97-20, 15.05.03: Judgment and Sentence. (can only be retrieved from http://www1.umn.edu/humanrts/instree/ICTR/SEMANZA_ICTR-97-

Does this mean that national reconciliation in its essence has to be understood as something different from retribution, deterrence, or rehabilitation? The notion too often appears alongside other such concepts. Without much hesitation we dare predict that, if we proceeded by comparing and contrasting reconciliation to all notions which accompany it, and if we then claimed that it ought to mean something different, the semantic remainder would very probably be nil and reconciliation accordingly nothing but an empty shell. However, all the examined passages cannot be part of our presentation here. They indicate that there has been no rule according to which reconciliation should be or shouldn't be used inside the ICTR.

Reconciliation and Plea Bargaining: A Restorative Understanding

Similar to Klaus Bachmann's findings and discussion of the ties between guilty pleas and reconciliation at the ICTY (see below), also within the judgments of the ICTR, explanations are given with regards to the reasons why a guilty plea constitutes a mitigating circumstance. As an example, we take the trial chamber judgment in *the pros. vs. Semanza.* Laurent Semanza had been a mayor of the Bicumbi municipality, but had been ousted in 1993 and become an activist of the MRND, the *Mouvement Républicain National pour la Démocratie et le Développement*, former president Habyrimana's party. He had been accused of violent anti-Tutsi propaganda and participation in killings in his municipality. During the trial, part of the indictment was rejected by the chamber due to imprecise accusations which infringed the defendant's possibility to refute them, for example by presenting an alibi. In the judgment, the trial chamber explained:

> "In the opinion of the Chamber, when an accused pleads guilty, he is taking an important step towards rehabilitation and reintegration. Such admission of guilt is likely to contribute to the search for the truth; it shows the resolve of an accused to accept responsibility vis-à-vis the injured party and society as a whole, which may contribute to reconciliation which is one of the goals pursued by the Tribunal."[805]

One of Semanza's colleagues and friend, Paul Bisengimana, the former mayor of the Gikoro, was also indicted by the OTP for similar crimes. The trial chamber judgment reads:

> "The Chamber notes that the jurisprudence of the Tribunal and the ICTY has identified several reasons why the guilty plea may have a mitigating effect: the

---

20/SEMANZA_ICTR-97-20-T_Sentencing.htm, since the ICTR website published only a summary and the table of contents of the judgment.)

805 Ibid.

> showing of remorse, repentance, the contribution to reconciliation, the establishment of the truth, the encouragement of other perpetrators to come forward. […] Paul Bisengimana's guilty plea will assist in the administration of justice and in the process of national reconciliation in Rwanda."[806]

The same clarifications return in other judgments.[807] Reconciliation is considered to be a separate reason for mitigation through pleading guilty, while showing of remorse and repentance as well as the establishment of truth are seen as equally important. Are these elements not rather logically part of reconciliation than different from it? The formulation suggests how ambiguous the concept is. Important, however, is that pleading guilty is considered to be conducive to reconciliation, a theme that recurs regularly in the judgments and sentences of the ICTR, following the precedence of the ICTY. In the judgment of *the pros. vs. Plavšić*, discussed in detail below, it is noted:

> "Two matters related to a plea of guilt concern expression of remorse and steps toward reconciliation. In this regard, the Prosecution notes that the accused has expressed her remorse 'fully and unconditionally' and the hope that her guilty plea will assist her people to reconcile with their neighbours. The Prosecution states that this expression of remorse is noteworthy since it is offered from a person who formerly held a leadership position, and that it 'merits judicial consideration.'"[808]

Here, a guilty plea is understood as a reconciliation event[809] because of its publicly apologetic character. The better known and influential the person, the better his or her chances of enhancing the cycle of apology and forgiveness at the grassroots level. This interpretation is supported by the idea that remorse, the acknowledgement of guilt, and the conviction of the importance of truth go hand-in-hand with the importance of apologies in the process of reconciliation,[810] which clearly refers to the beginning of the apology-forgiveness cycle.

---

806 *The pros. vs. Bisengimana* ICTR-00-60 *(pleaded guilty)*, Judgment and sentence, 13.04.06 http://unictr.org/Portals/0/Case%5CEnglish%5CBisengimana%5Cdecisions%5C060413.pdf

807 *The pros. vs. Nzabirinda* ICTR-01-77-I, 23 February 2007: Judgment and Sentence; *The pros. vs. Rugambarara* ICTR-00-59-I, 16 November 2007: Judgment and Sentence. *The pros. vs. Kambanda* ICTR-97-23) (pleaded guilty), Judgment, 04.09.98,

808 *The pros. vs. Plavšić* IT-00-39/40-1.

809 Long, Brecke, War and Reconciliation, 30.

810 *The pros. vs. Bisengimana* ICTR-00-60 *(Pleaded guilty)*, Judgment and sentence, 13.04.06: "The Prosecution refers to the Plea Agreement in which Paul Bisengimana has shown some degree of remorse for the crimes he is charged with, acknowledges full responsibility for his actions and omissions, and is convinced that it is only the full truth that can restore national unity and foster reconciliation in Rwanda. The Accused has also indicated his deep and genuine desire to tell the whole truth and expressed his

In *the pros. vs. Plavšić*, which constituted the precedence for the argument that pleading guilty contributes to reconciliation, the Tribunal's logic is thus restorative in the sense that it helps to sublate vengeance, to acknowledge victims, and to individualize guilt while rehabilitating the moral identity of the perpetrator. However, as we will see, the Tribunal has not consistently applied this understanding of the concept.

That reconciliation can play a role in the bargaining over the sentence appears in the context of several cases and throughout the Tribunal's history.[811] In the judgment of Rwanda's former Prime Minister Jean Kambanda, it reads:

> "[…] The Defence Counsel in his submissions emphasised that Jean Kambanda was only a puppet controlled by certain military authorities and that his power was consequently limited. He thus submitted that the Tribunal, taking into account the guilty plea, Jean Kambanda's cooperation and willingness to continue cooperating with the Prosecutor, and the role Jean Kambanda could play in the process of national reconciliation in Rwanda, sentence him for a term of imprisonment not exceeding two years."[812]

Without mentioning it directly, the defence counsel obviously hinted at Kambanda's notoriety and the public impact that his guilty plea had. This brings us back to what we said about pleading guilty being a reconciliation event in Long and Brecke's sense. As the tribunal acknowledges, pleading guilty as a contribution to reconciliation can become a tool in the negotiations about mitigation and punishment.

The judgment and sentence of *the pros. vs. Bisengimana* of 2006 demonstrates well how guilty pleas have a mitigating effect on the sentence passed. Bisengimana, another former *bourgmestre* from Gikoro, who was accused of inciting the local population to kill Tutsis, had, similar to Rutaganira, pleaded guilty. In his sentence, the trial chamber stressed the accused's conviction that

> "only the full truth (…) can restore national unity and foster reconciliation in Rwanda."[813]

This direct reference to the generation of truth had already appeared in the judgment of Rwanda's former Prime Minister Jean Kambanda in 1998. In his

---

profound and heartfelt apologies to all the direct and indirect victims of the offences he has been charged with."

811 *The pros. vs. Rugambarara* ICTR-00-59-I, 16 November 2007: Judgment and Sentence; *The pros. vs. Serushago* ICTR-98-39, 05.02.99: Appeal Chamber Decisions.

812 *The pros. vs. Kambanda* ICTR-97-23 (pleaded guilty), Judgment, 04.09.98,

813 *The pros. vs. Bisengimana* ICTR-00-60. (Pleaded guilty), Judgment and sentence, 13.04.06.

plea agreement, he had explained that his prime motivation for pleading guilty had been his profound desire to tell the truth, because

> "the truth was the only way to restoring national unity and reconciliation in Rwanda."[814]

The same reasoning was demonstrated by the former witness BRK, who had been charged with arson in Rwanda right after the genocide, and, after his release from prison, had been charged with additional and much more severe crimes. He became a prosecution witness in *the pros. vs. Nchamihigo.* In January 2007, BRK explained the motivation for his guilty plea before a Rwandan court:

"My position is that by telling the truth, I will be fostering reconciliation in Rwanda and that this might help in the reduction of my sentence."[815]

All three passages suggest that, from the perpetrator's point of view, the truth argument is decisively connoted with the idea of reconciliation. This is understandable insofar as the logic of a guilty plea is to reveal a formerly hidden truth which the notion of reconciliation allows to connect to the overall aims of the tribunal. On a more performative level, by pleading guilty the accused presents a sort of public declaration of remorse or asking for forgiveness, thus enhancing the apology-forgiveness cycle, which we classified under the aspect of acknowledging victims. The function of truth telling serves the socio-psychological mechanism of socio-emotional reconciliation, and might contribute to the historical archive as well.

While at this stage we reject the possibility that the use of reconciliation does not follow any semantic common sense among the members of the ICTR, the authors of the judgments often seem to take for granted the reader's knowledge of the complex theories behind the different meanings of reconciliation. In Jean Bosco Barayagwiza's judgment and sentence of 2003, the judges took time to refer to the historical construction of ethnicity in Rwanda and the responsibility of the former colonizers. They criticize the fatal instrumentalisation of ethnic cleavages by national politicians in order to revoke the all too common theme of a dominating structural past for the sake of the moral responsibility of individual political agency. In this way, the individualisation of guilt can also be understood in conjunction with reconciliation through the politics of historical memory.[816]

---

814 *The pros. vs. Kambanda* ICTR-97-23, (pleaded guilty), Judgment, 04.09.98.

815 *The pros. vs. Nchamihigo* (12 November 2008), Footnote 193.

816 *The pros. vs. Barayagwiza et al.*ICTR-97-19, Judgment and Sentence, 03.12.03

A passage reads:

> "The Chamber recalls that its fundamental purpose of holding individuals accountable for their conduct is intended to 'contribute to the process of national reconciliation and to the restoration and maintenance of peace.'"[817]

Depending on the perspective, "holding individuals accountable" can be placed in line with either the individualisation of guilt or the sublation of vengeance. On the one hand, by putting the blame on some individual culprits, the moral conscience of the Hutu collectivity might be (re-)habilitated. On the other hand, the survivors may feel satisfied by seeing the perpetrators individually punished. Thus the sentences do not contain clearly formulated information as to how justice is actually thought to contribute to reconciliation in Rwanda.

Strategic Signifying: Retributive Versus Restorative Interpretations of Reconciliation

In December 2003, the intended reconciliation mission of the ICTR became an argumentative tool for the accused Jean-Bosco Barayagwiza. Asking "who would face trial before the Tribunal after the RPF had executed all the *génocidaires*, [and] who would [consequently] be left for reconciliation,"[818] he frankly uttered suspicion that "[i]n reality, the United Nations was manipulated by powers sponsored by the RPF," thus suggesting that the idea of fostering national reconciliation through ICTR justice was, in fact, a smokescreen to cover the intention of actual victor's justice.[819] When going into appeal, Barayagwiza claimed that too much weight had been given to deterrence and retribution, while not enough had been put on the reconciliation aspect:

> "Appellant Barayagwiza argues that, in determining his sentence, the Trial Chamber placed too much emphasis on the objectives of retribution and deterrence, and not enough on those of national reconciliation and rehabilitation."

The appeals chamber replied that it was not convinced by this argument:

> "[...] First, the Appellant does not explain how the sentence imposed by the Trial Chamber would damage national reconciliation. Secondly, the Appeals Chamber is of the opinion that, in view of the gravity of the crimes in respect of which the Tribunal has jurisdiction, the two main purposes of sentencing are retribution and deterrence; the purpose of rehabilitation should not be given undue weight. In these

817 Ibid.

818 *The pros. vs. Barayagwiza et al.* ICTR-97-19, Judgment and Sentence, 03.12.03.

819 Ibid.

circumstances, and having regard to the crimes of which the Appellant has been convicted, the Appeals Chamber cannot find that the Trial Chamber committed an error by giving undue weight to the purposes of retribution and deterrence."[820]

While the accused perceives deterrence and retribution to be antagonistic to reconciliation, the judges merely answer that they think deterrence was not overemphasized. They fail, however, to clarify that the true meaning of reconciliation itself might lie inside the very ideas of deterrence and retribution for the sake of fighting impunity, as had been noted in many different instances. Here, the changes in meaning accorded to reconciliation obviously reach contradictory character. This not only indicates that, again, there is no clear and common understanding by the judges, but also that this conceptual ambiguity and lack of common understanding inside the ICTR has been, at least occasionally, an obstacle to the swift functioning of the Tribunal.

The idea of linking justice with reconciliation has not only been debated by scholars. The case of Clément Kayishema, whose appeal judgment was issued in 1999, reveals that inside the courtroom the debate was raised as well. Kayishema, a former prefect of the Kibuye province, accused the Tribunal of being a politicized arm of the United Nations whom he accused of partial responsibility for the Rwandan genocide. The idea of contributing to national reconciliation, he claimed, was a politically intended programme in which he saw himself as victim.[821]

The debate over the Tribunal's usage of its aim to contribute to reconciliation came also from within: when former Minister of Culture and Education Jean de Dieu Kamuhanda received his judgment in January 2004, one of the responsible judges, Judge Maqutu, did not agree with his fellow justices about the sentence of life imprisonment. He justified his decision with a

820 Ibid.

821 "Kayishema refers to the events that occurred in Rwanda in 1994 and to the United Nations reaction in the face of those events. He holds the United Nations partially responsible for the genocide that occurred in Rwanda and questions the independence and legitimacy of the Tribunal. In Kayishema's submission, the idea of the Tribunal administering justice to contribute "to the process of national reconciliation and to the restoration and maintenance of peace", runs counter to the concept of Justice as understood by States under the rule of law. Thus, he sees himself as a scapegoat since the Trial Chamber failed to address such observations, which, he also submits, amounts to a miscarriage of justice. [...] The Appeals Chamber is satisfied that the view expressed by the Security Council with regard to the process of national reconciliation and to the restoration and maintenance of peace is not prejudicial to the Tribunal's independence and impartiality, which the judges are required to exhibit in ruling on each case". *The pros. vs. Kayishema* ICTR-95-1; *The pros. vs. Ruzindana* ICTR-95-1; 2: ICTR-96-10), 21.05.99.

reference to the Rwandan Gacaca courts by stressing their importance in the process of national reconciliation:

> "The purpose of this Tribunal (in a traditional judicial fashion) is to firmly and robustly punish genocide and crimes against humanity with the object hopefully of helping Rwanda's reconciliation."

He then added that in the Gacaca procedure the alleged failures of the accused

> "have to be assessed by people who have been through the same pressures and who can empathise with him. It is before them that the accused has to show penance. Only then can an attempt at moral restitution be worked out. The International Tribunal has no system or guidelines of the nature that Gacaca courts have, to actually put into effect the reconciliation element. These belong to the indigenous Rwandan culture."[822]

In this passage a judge explicitly questions the court's relevance to reconciliation as part of a judgment or sentence. We can assume that he does this with a view to encouraging his fellow justices to reconsider their decision of life imprisonment by stressing the importance of reconciliation, which, as he explains, is considered of crucial importance inside the Rwandan territory. He informs us about his understanding of reconciliation through justice by stressing empathy and participation in the trials which render penance instrumental when it is publically displayed. Only under these circumstances, moral restitution can be achieved, which corresponds with what we have called moral rehabilitation as part of the aspect of acknowledging victims. This passage displays the most explicitly critical position of the ICTR's own contribution to reconciliation that has been publically uttered as part of the Tribunal's proceedings and appears to have given rise to internal tensions between ICTR judges. The notion mostly appears on documents for public display.

Sentenced to life imprisonment in January 2004, Kamuhanda had filed an appeal with some arguments at his disposal. In September 2005, his appeal was dismissed, i.e. his arguments turn out to have been unsuccessful. One of them lends itself extraordinarily to our purpose of showing how reconciliation was used inside the ICTR and whether it had a genuine impact on the quality of sentences. Encouraged by the standard passage in his first sentence that

> "[r]econciliation amongst Rwandans, towards which the processes of the Tribunal should contribute, must also weigh heavily in the Chamber's mind when passing sentence,"[823]

---

822 *The pros. vs. Kamuhanda* ICTR-99-54, Judge Maqutu's Dissent on the Sentence, 22.01.2004.

823 *The pros. vs. Kamuhanda* ICTR-99-54 Judgment, 22.01.04.

and given the fact that Judge Maqutu had formally disagreed with his life imprisonment, Kamuhanda had an obvious reason to stress his contribution to the process of national reconciliation as a mitigating circumstance. Judge Maqutu had also praised the efficiency of the Gacaca courts in the process of national reconciliation by indirectly discrediting the Tribunal's "facade of national reconciliation."[824] Consequently, Kamuhanda's defence claimed that "the Accused should not have been given the heaviest sentence, precisely because the wisdom derived from his severe experience could benefit the aim of national reconciliation." In his view, the Trial Chamber "ostentatiously first outlined the rules it purported to have applied. However, it did not apply those rules."[825]

This sharp attack against the Tribunal to use reconciliation as a mere smokescreen without respecting its own promises, is then supported by the question in what way his sentence would contribute to reconciliation at all:

> "In support of this assertion, the Appellant contends that the Trial Chamber "gave no explanation whatsoever as to what extent [...] the sentence it imposed would help restore peace and national reconciliation."[826]

The Prosecution rejected the criticism by responding that

> "[...] it is unclear from the Appellant's argument how the Trial Chamber failed to assess this subject properly, or how a reconsideration of it would lead to the sentences being reduced to the level the Appellant now seeks [...]." [827]

Kamuhanda's argument, based on the ambiguity of the notion of reconciliation, is countered by exactly the same ambiguity. Then some clarification is offered: the Appeals Chamber intervenes by explaining that national reconciliation and the restoration of peace are important goals, but that they are not the only goals. The response sounds somewhat like a justification attempt:

> "[...] Indeed, the Trial Chamber correctly referred to 'deterrence, justice, reconciliation, and the restoration and maintenance of peace' as being among the goals consistent with Security Council Resolution 955 of 8 November 1994 which set up the Tribunal. These goals cannot [however] be separated but are intertwined, and, in any case, nothing in Resolution 955 indicates that the Security Council intended that one should prevail over another. The Appellant contends that sentencing him to life imprisonment would deprive 'both his fellow Rwandans and

---

824 *The pros. vs. Kamuhanda* ICTR-99-54. Judge Maqutu's Separate and Concurring Opinion on the Verdict. This expression is actually used in the context of the Arusha peace agreement which had also followed a reconciliation-oriented etiquette.

825 *The pros. vs. Kamuhanda* ICTR-99-54, Appeal judgment, 19.09.05

826 Ibid.

827 Ibid.

> their country of what they could learn from him upon his release' and therefore not serve the goal of national reconciliation. The Appeals Chamber is not persuaded by this argument. The Trial Chamber was free to conclude that any advantage in terms of national reconciliation gained by the Appellant's eventual release was either minimal or was outweighed by the harms to both general deterrence and national reconciliation that would be created by a lenient sentence that was not perceived to reflect the gravity of the crimes committed."[828]

The passage indicates how bluntly the different understandings of reconciliation rival each other. If we do not apply different meanings to the term, the last argument by the Appeals Chamber is nearly cyclical in its logic: releasing the accused would either have been less or not at all favourable to national reconciliation as would have been deterrence through life imprisonment. If Kamuhanda had been released, reconciliation would have been favoured by what Rwanda "could learn from him."[829] Whatever this means, it would have been reconciliation in a restorative way, either by Kamuhanda publically apologizing, or by him publically revealing some important pieces of truth about what happened. From the Tribunal's retributivist point of view, on the other hand, reconciliation is seen as being better served by a fierce judgment and the accompanying effect of deterrence.

Anyhow, the Chamber has not allowed for this terminological debate to continue. Referring to its position of authority as mere executer of the rule of law, it stated:

> "[i]n any case, it is not a matter – as the Appellant contends – of 'the triumph of the law over the barbarous acts that were committed' or of whether or not 'sentencing [him] to life imprisonment [would] contribute, even momentarily, to the restoration of peace or national reconciliation, which is one of the Tribunal's goals'. It is settled case law before both the ICTR and the ICTY that the underlying principle is that Trial Chambers must tailor the penalty to fit the individual circumstances of the accused and the gravity of the crime. The Appellant has neither demonstrated that the Trial Chamber committed any error in its assessment of the goals behind the creation of the Tribunal, nor that the Trial Chamber improperly exercised its discretion in determining the appropriate sentence."[830]

Although reconciliation was exhibited from the beginning on as a guiding principle for the quality of sentencing, this intention has somehow fallen prey to its own inherent ambiguity. "Reconciliation" had been offered as a possibility for plea bargaining. However the notion's potential of being interpreted either

---

828 Ibid.

829 Unfortunately, we do not have any additional material available that would inform us about what Kamuhanda actually meant.

830 Ibid.

according to a restorative or a retributive logic has enabled the ICTR to eventually support their own retributive agenda.

Only one exception contrasts with these major finding: after Vincent Rutaganira's voluntary surrender in Tanzania and his guilty plea, he was sentenced to six years of imprisonment in March 2005. His sentence had apparently been reduced due to many personal individual circumstances, especially concerning his family life. His wife, mother of his nine children, had testified that she served in the government as deputy mayor in charge of women's development in her community. Consequently,

> "[t]he Chamber [was] of the view that such evidence augur[ed] well for the potential rehabilitation of the Accused into the local community and his joining the national reconciliation process."[831]

Reconciliation is seen here not as a state of peaceful coexistence with a tendency to social cooperation (socio-emotional reconciliation). Though the sentencing report does not contain any further details, the idea of reconciliation has affected the sentence passed. It is striking that it is an *a posteriori* establishment of achieved reconciliation as a well-established fact that served to influence the judgment, and not, as was initially intended, the *a priori* potential of a suspect to contribute to the process of national reconciliation. Here, reconciliation was a diagnosed indicator on the basis of which the accused could be sentenced; it was not a guiding principle or an intended ambition.

Findings

The notion of reconciliation appears most of the time without any specification as to how the Tribunal intends to impact on the Rwandan process of national reconciliation. Often it is invoked merely to justify the Tribunal's existence by quoting or referring to the Security Council Resolution 955, the foundational document of the ICTR. In those cases where we are informed more or less explicitly about how the Tribunal intends to contribute to reconciliation, nearly all logics of our typology have been applied in one or the other way. The retributive logic to expand legal space by strengthening the rule of law and by fighting impunity is being given slightly more weight, which is understandable given the retributive agenda of the ICTs.

However, the occurrences of reconciliation in the judgments and sentence are, generally speaking, few and far between. A deliberately intended rhetorical purpose aimed at discursively shaping a public opinion by means of a "reconciliation discourse," as has been the case in South Africa, can therefore not be diagnosed.

831 *The pros. vs. Rutaganira* (ICTR-95-1C-I), 14 March 2005: Judgment and Sentence.

When plea bargaining was introduced by referring to the Tribunal's contribution to reconciliation, a guilty plea initially appeared to be considered by the Tribunal as a small-scale reconciliation event. It was thought to enhance the apology-forgiveness cycle and contribute to the acknowledgement of victims. Thus, the precedence case of Plavšić (see below) had promised an understanding of reconciliation from the perspective of a restorative agenda. Here, the retributive agenda had been compromised; it seems, for reasons that are elucidated in more detail in Klaus Bachmann's discussion of reconciliation in the ICTY.

As far as the ICTR is concerned, by allowing for both restorative and retributive interpretations of reconciliation, the notion has at times become the locus of debate between the restorative intentions of a perpetrator pleading guilty and the agenda of the ICTR to punish him or her nonetheless.

Thus, the flexible meaning of reconciliation offered an open space for negotiation between defendants, prosecutors, and judges. On the one hand, the indeterminacy of its meaning has on several occasions led to unproductive debate and disagreement. On the other hand, however, the ambiguity which the concept carried from the outset has made it strategically useful for the ICTR's judges in that the restorative promise of plea bargaining could still be replied to by a retributive response.

Reconciliation at the ICTY

Similar to Peter Lambertz' findings concerning the ICTR, leading figures of the ICTY have on various occasions highlighted reconciliation as a task, or even an achievement of the tribunal, but they have very rarely indicated what exactly they mean by reconciliation.[832] In 2000, Claude Jorda, the president of the ICTY, addressed the UN General Assembly. During his speech he presented several ideas, the aim of which it was to extend the capabilities of the tribunal, where several high-level trials were expected for the near future. One of these ideas was the following: "For instance, we considered the possibility of holding some trials away from the Tribunal, that is, trials by the Member States including those in the Balkans. This solution has merit: it would bring the Tribunal closer to the local population and contribute to national reconciliation." [833] A year later, Jorda addressed the Security Council, responding to increasing criticism against the lack of expedience and the bureaucratic effort and high cost that the ICTY trials required. He did so by proposing to defer minor cases to the national courts in the former Yugoslavia. This would, he claimed, "make the trial of the cases referred before the national courts more transparent to the local population and so make a more effective contribution to reconciling the peoples of the Balkans."[834] Two years later, Jorda's successor as ICTY president, Theodore Meron, appeared in a documentary about the ICTY, rejecting claims about the high expense at which the tribunal had been functioning: "The expense of running the tribunal is not insignificant, but it is the best investment that the international community could make toward establishing peace and reconciliation in the Balkans consistent with notions of justice, and without justice that peace and reconciliation will not be achieved [sic]." [835]

All these statements link reconciliation directly to the administration of retributive justice, but they leave open what their authors actually expected to

---

832 Swart, Bert; Zahar, Alexander; Sluiter, Göran: The Legacy of the International Criminal Tribunal for the Former Yugoslavia. OUP 2011, 14.

833 Speech by his Excellency, Judge Claude Jorda, President of the International Criminal tribunal for the former Yugoslavia, to the UN General Assembly, 20.11.2000; ICTY Press Release, available at: www.icty.org/sid/7806/en

834 Address by his Excellency, Judge Claude Jorda, President of the International Criminal Tribunal for the former Yugoslavia, to the UN Security Council. The Hague, 27 November 2001
JD/P.I.S./641-e. http://www.icty.org/sid/7927/en

835 Theodore Meron interviewed in the 2003 documentary "Against all odds", retrieved from: http://www.sense-agency.com/documentaries.42.html

happen if reconciliation was to be achieved. Jorda's quote, for example, seemed to indicate, that reconciliation could be furthered by bringing the ICTY closer to the local communities affected by the crimes, whereas in Meron's statement, practising justice in the way the ICTY does was presented just as a precondition for peace and reconciliation. From the mere mentioning of the two notions peace and reconciliation we may deduce that Meron did not regard them as identical, but rather as different. It is, however, difficult to draw any conclusions about what it was meant to be, since Meron did not provide any definition of peace either.

Descriptions of reconciliation and peace uttered by judges and prosecutors were often woolly and cryptic. More surprising are some very down-to-earth definitions used by people whom one would hardly expect to bother about such abstract and lofty topics.

The documentary film "Against all odds", which describes the work of the ICTY, also contains a quote by Timothy McFadden, the detention unit commander, who describes how reconciliation has been achieved within the tiny and very specific community of ICTY detainees: "There is no apparent animosity between detainees of different ethnic backgrounds that are currently in the detention unit. They support one another in their daily lives. I think the reason for it is that one: they are all facing the same judicial process, so they have the same problem, albeit for different reasons. They share that information with one another. So, it's through those things that this reconciliation, or apparent reconciliation, takes place." This statement is commented by a narrator in the following way: "While in the courtrooms the horrors and trauma of the wars in the former Yugoslavia are being relived, in the UN Detention Unit the erstwhile enemies have achieved reconciliation." As if this was not enough to astonish the audience, the sequence is concluded by Goran Jelisić, the relatively young camp warden from Brčko, who had robbed, mistreated, and killed civilians and had been sentenced to 40 years in prison despite a partial guilty plea. Jelisić says: "There was a discussion about the fact that this institution, the Tribunal, should establish a lasting peace in Bosnia and Herzegovina through us. We sat down together later and realized that we have reached the lasting peace here, but what really worries us is how those guys down there in Bosnia will do it."[836]

From this perspective, reconciliation is no longer a process, but a state of coexistence and cooperation, devoid of any conflict and facilitated by external pressure (detention), which had inclined them to forget about their past

836 "Against all odds. The first ten years of the ICTY" 2003. The video and the transcript of the film can be retrieved from: http://www.sense-agency.com/documentaries.42.html

animosities and to accept each other. There are some strong indications of the validity of Jelisić's claim. When in 2005, Slavko Dokmanović, accused of killing civilians during and after the fights in Vukovar, hanged himself in his cell right before the sentencing hearing, all 27 inmates of the Scheveningen prison asked Dokmanović's lawyer to send a telegram to his family and to buy a wreath in their name with the inscirption: "To our Slavko, from all prisoners of The Hague." Among the 27 prisoners at that time were Bosniacs, Serbs and Croats.[837]

Reconciliation in ICTY Trials: Guilty Pleas and Plea Bargaining

The ICTY has managed to try many more defendants than was the case at the ICTR. But similar to Peter Lambertz above findings concerning the ICTR, also in the majority of the ICTY's cases reconciliation did not play any role; it was for the most part not even mentioned as a word in the trial chambers' and appeals chamber judgments. Only in 24 cases a trial judgment referred to the concept of reconciliation. 20 of them were cases in which a defendant had admitted guilt. Only in four cases (*the pros. vs. Blagojević*, *the pros. vs. Mucić et al.*, *the pros. vs. Stakić* and *the pros. vs. D. Tadić*) did judges mention reconciliation in their judgment without any prior guilty plea of the accused.

After December 13, 2001, the ICTY amended its statute and introduced a formal procedure which explicitly permitted the use of plea agreements and plea bargaining.[838] Already before, judges had had the possibility to take guilty pleas into account and lower sentences, although the application of formal plea agreements had been ruled out by the ICTY's first president, Antonio Cassese.[839] As Scharf points out, there is a considerable difference between entering a guilty plea in the hope of lowering a sentence and formal plea bargaining.[840] The first procedure does not change the charges against a

837 (Unnamed author): "Slavko Dokmanović's death." IWPR Tribunal Update 83 (29 June-4 July 1998). 4.5.2005. The unnamed author commented the story with the words: "the process of inter-ethnic reconciliation apparently works faster behind bars." *pros. vs. Blagojević* IT-02-35 and IT-98-33/1, *the pros. vs. Mučić* IT-96-21, *the pros. vs. Stakić* IT-97-24 and *the pros. vs. D. Tadić* IT-94-1.

838 Clark, Janine Natalya: "Plea Bargaining at the ICTY: Guilty Pleas and Reconciliation." *The European Journal of International Law* Vol. 20 no. 2, 417.

839 Ibid.

840 Scharf, Michael P.: "Trading Justice for Efficiency. Plea bargaining and International Tribunals." *The Journal of International Criminal Justice* 2 (4) 2004, 1070-1081.

defendant (which could only be dropped if the prosecution requested leave to amend the indictment or claimed not to possess any evidence about some charges), whereas formal plea bargaining, also called "charges bargaining" by Scharf, can, but need not include changes in the indictment. The latter procedure allows both the prosecution and the defence to agree on some charges (to which the defendant subsequently pleads guilty) and to erase others (usually the most severe ones) from the indictment. The trial chamber remains a veto player in both procedures, since it can grant or refuse leave to amend the indictment (in the guilty plea procedure) as well as accept or reject a plea agreement. Even when it accepts a plea agreement and the prosecution and the defence present a joint proposal for a sentence, the court may issue a verdict which deviates from that proposal. Plea agreements are often criticized as a shortcut to justice, which allows the court to issue verdicts with a minimum of effort, since, when a plea agreement is accepted, a formal trial is no longer necessary and judges, prosecutors, and the defendant only meet a few times for a so-called sentencing hearing, a debate about the gravity of the crimes, the aggravating and mitigating circumstances, and the sentence itself. Since this procedure makes analysing evidence and hearing witness testimony redundant, it also deprives the court and the public of the possibility to create their own truth about the events that led to the trial. The only truth that remains is the one presented by the defendant in the plea agreement, both in the factual basis and in his personal statement in court during a sentencing hearing. This version of the events cannot be tested against evidence. Trials which end with a plea agreement aim at establishing guilt rather than establishing a truth. They are therefore less likely to foster reconciliation in the sense of the production of truth and memory work.

From 2001 onwards, defendants at the ICTY could ask their legal counsel to negotiate a deal with the prosecution which would usually lead to lower charges (some counts of the indictment were dropped), to the admission of guilt by the defendant (and sometimes to his cooperation with the OTP as a prosecution witness in other cases), to no hearing of the evidence, and to a joint plea of the prosecution and the defence concerning sentencing.[841] Although some trial chambers rejected such pleas and handed down higher sentences than the joint plea had suggested, the likelihood of a relatively low sentence was much higher with such an agreement than without it. Such a strategy also dramatically

841 It is worth mentioning here, that according to our sources from the OTP and from defense counselors, plea agreement negotiations were usually initiated by the OTP and not by the defense.

increased the likelihood of reconciliation to be mentioned by the trial chamber in its judgment.

When it comes to appeals chambers, plea agreements and guilty pleas did not have any impact on the number of cases in which appeals chambers referred to reconciliation concepts. In four cases, appeals judges mentioned reconciliation in their judgments, but only one of the accused had previously pleaded guilty (*the pros. vs. Zelenović*). [842] Only in two cases the trial chamber sentenced the defendant to a long prison term despite a guilty plea. This was the case in *the pros. vs. Jelisić*. In this case, there was no formal agreement, but Jelisić pleaded guilty concerning all counts of the indictment except the genocide charge, which was dismissed by the trial chamber after the defence had submitted a request seeking an acquittal based on Rule 98bis. This procedure allows the defence to ask for an acquittal if the evidence presented by the prosecution does not in itself sustain a charge. In *the pros. vs. Jelisić*, the trial chamber agreed with the defence and acquitted Jelisić of genocide, arguing that no evidence had been produced during the prosecution's case which could support the claim that Jelisić had been driven by a genocidal intent. Jelisić pleaded guilty to the remaining charges and was sentenced to 40 years in prison by the trial chamber.[843]

The second case was *the pros. vs. Momir Nikolić*, who had been assistant commander of the Bratunac Brigade of the Bosnian Serb Army and therefore directly involved in the events which followed the fall of Srebrenica and led to the massacres in and outside the town. He had been arrested in April 2002 by SFOR and stood trial for genocide, crimes against humanity, and war crimes in a joint trial which also included the accused Vidoje Blagojević, Dragan Obrenović, and Dragan Jokić. Nikolić was an extraordinary case at the ICTY for several reasons: he was the first defendant who was indicted for Srebrenica and ready to confess; he was ready to cooperate with the prosecution against others and to deliver evidence against them. Biljana Plavšić, probably the most controversial case of a guilty plea, had been on trial before him, but she had not been charged with crimes connected to Srebrenica and had refused to cooperate with the prosecution after her trial. Nikolić was a mid-level perpetrator who had passed information from the ground to the commanders, and who had given

842 These cases were: *the pros. vs. Krstić* IT-98-33, *the pros. vs. Martić* IT-95-11, *the pros. vs. Blagojević* IT-98-33/1, IT-02-60 and *the pros. vs. Zelenović* IT-96-23/2. The trial chamber in *the pros. vs. Blagojević* also had used a notion of reconciliation in the judgment.

843 The sentence was sustained by the appeals chamber. *The pros. vs. Jelisić* IT-95-10.

orders and transmitted orders down to the army units which had carried out the killings after the fall of the town, later had reburied the corpses, and had tried to remove the traces left by the massacres. He could not only be used as a prosecution witness against his fellow defendants, but also against other suspects. The mere news of his cooperation with the prosecution could upset perpetrators who were still at large and could stir up informal networks of former army officers who had been relying on the discretion and secrecy of their former comrades. The full scale of these benefits was within the prosecution's reach when Nikolić signaled his readiness for a deal, but it could only be obtained if the deal was actually concluded and then accepted by the judges. Not only in his case could one observe a striking overlap of interests emerging between the defence and the prosecution. Both were now fighting like lions to get a mild sentence for the accused. First, they introduced a joint motion which suggested that Nikolić should be given a prison term of not more than 20 years. They even asked the court to delay judgment until Nikolić could prove his readiness to cooperate by appearing as a prosecution witness in the trial against his fellow defendants. Next, they both argued in court in favor of the plea agreement and the low sentence. In the agreement, the prosecution dropped the genocide and the war crime charges against him, whereas he pleaded guilty to the remaining counts of a crime against humanity, persecutions on political, racial, and religious grounds, and agreed to cooperate with the prosecution. Most probably, this was too much for the judges, who now saw a genocide trial being reduced to one count of persecution. They regarded his plea as a mitigating circumstance, since it would contribute to the "establishment of the truth", would "promote reconciliation" and make the appearance of Srebrenica survivors as witnesses in his trial obsolete. The judges had doubts, though, whether he would fully cooperate: "Trial Chamber takes into consideration numerous instances where the testimony of Momir Nikolić is evasive and finds this to be an indication that his willingness to cooperate does not translate into being fully forthcoming in relation to all the events, given his position and knowledge."[844] The latter statement proved prophetical. During the trial against his former co-accused and superiors, Dragan Jokić and Vidoje Blagojević, the latter's defence counsellor, Michael Karnavas, managed to get Nikolić to admit that he originally had lied to the prosecution about his involvement in some events in which he had not taken

844 Transcript of sentencing hearing of *the pros. vs. Momir Nikolić*, IT- 02-56, 2.12.2003, 1691-1694.
http://www.icty.org/x/cases/Nikolić/trans/en/031202IT.htm

part, and even had confessed crimes he never had committed. These statements had been kept secret by the prosecution and were never included into his plea agreement, but they had come to Karnavas' notice and were used by him to undermine Nikolić's credibility. Apparently, Nikolić had admitted what the prosecution had wanted him to admit. In order to get the agreement and a lower sentence, he had even confessed to having ordered the killing of about a thousand unarmed civilians in Kravica and Sandići.[845] Nevertheless, the prosecution and the defence continued to press for a lower sentence before the appeals chamber. During the hearing they argued that Nikolić's plea had driven Blagojević into a plea agreement and a confession of guilt. Despite the fact that Blagojević had been a superior to Nikolić, the trial chamber had sentenced him only to 17 years. Peter McCloskey, who had negotiated the Nikolić agreement for the prosecution, expressed serious doubts about whether the discrepancy between Nikolić's and Blagojević's sentence would be comprehensible to the outside world.[846] The appeals chamber reduced it to 20 years.

In all other cases of defendants pleading guilty, the trial chambers handed down mild or moderate sentences, sending a clear message to defendants that guilty pleas and plea agreements would strongly increase their chances for a more favourable verdict and an opportunity to leave prison alive. With the exception of *the pros. vs. Jelisić*, no case which involved a guilty plea led to a final verdict amounting to a *de facto* lifelong sentence.[847]

---

845 Stacy Sullivan: "Nikolić Testimony Under Scrutiny Again." IWPR Tribunal Update 355, 9.11.2005.

846 Janet Anderson: "Nikolić. Appeals chamber hears claims that jail term was excessive." IWPR tribunal update 433, 9.12.2005.

847 Even in Momir Nikolić's case, the final sentence was unlikely to keep him in prison until his death. Nikolić was born in 1955; he spent 5 years in the ICTY's detention facility and for this period his was given credit by the appeals chamber. When he was transferred to Finland in 2007, he had to serve only 15 years of his sentence, being 52 years old. Even if he served the whole sentence, he would be able to leave prison at the age of 67. Given the widespread practice of granting early release, for example after having served 2/3 of a prison term, Nikolić could hope to be free again at the age of 62. Jelisić, who was born in 1968 and transferred in 2003, may leave prison at age 70 if he serves his whole sentence of 40 years. (He was given credit for 5 years in the detention facility).

Tab. 5: Plea agreements at the ICTY

Defendant	Ethnic affiliation of defendant	Reconciliation mentioned in trial chamber judgment	Trial chamber sentence (in years of imprisonment)	Appeals Chamber sentence
Milan Babić	Croatian Serb	yes	13	13
Predrag Banović	Bosnian Serb	yes	8	no[848]
Miroslav Bralo	Bosnian Croat	yes	20	20
Ranko Banović	Bosnian Serb	yes	18	o
Miroslav Deronjić	Bosnian Serb	yes	10	10
Damir Došen[849]	Bosnian Serb	no	5	no
Duško Sikirica	Bosnian Serb	no	15	no
Dragan Došen	Bosnian Serb	no	3	no
Dražen Erdemovič[850]	Bosnian Serb	yes (I + II)	(10) 5	no
Goran Jelisić	Bosnian Serb	no	40	40
Miodrag Jokić	Bosnian Serb	yes	7	7
Darko Mrdja	Bosnian Serb	yes	17	no
Dragan Nikolić	Bosnian Serb	yes	23	20
Momir Nikolić	Bosnian Serb	yes	27	20
Dragan Obrenović	Bosnian Serb	yes	17	no
Biljana Plavšić	Bosnian Serb	yes	11	no
Ivica Rajić	Bosnian Croat	yes	12	no
Milan Simić[851]	Bosnian Serb	yes	5	no
Stevan Todorović	Bosnian Serb	yes	10	no
Dragan Zelenović	Bosnian Serb	yes	15	15

848 "No" means, that neither side lodged an appeal against the trial judgment or that for other reasons the appeals chamber did not issue any judgment in that case (e.g., because the defendant had died).

849 Kolundžija, Došen and Sikirica were tried in one trial.

850 Erdemović was first sentenced to 10 years, then the appeals chamber ordered a retrial and the trial chamber reduced the initial sentence to 5 years.

851 *The pros. vs. Simić* was quite specific, because when the trial started, the accused was severely handicapped and sat in a wheelchair, hardly able to follow the proceedings. The prosecution proposed a plea agreement to his defence lawyer, but then was not satisfied with the content to which the accused was ready to agree. The trial started, but, according to Simić's lawyer, Slobodan Zečević, turned into a "logistic nightmare", with the accused unable to be brought to court, following the proceedings on a screen in his cell and his lawyer communicating with him on telephone. After some time, the OTP came to the conclusion that even a plea agreement without any obligation to cooperate with the prosecution would be better than continuing the trial. It should be kept in mind that Simić was a minor perpetrator, accused of abusing prisoners in Bosanski Šamac, who had been indicted in 1995, during the start-up phase of the ICTY, when the OTP had no prospect of indicting important perpetrators with command responsibility. At a later stage, when the OTP was struggling with high-ranking military commanders and politicians as accused, it would most probably not have bothered to indict someone like Simić. Interview with Slobodan Zečević in Belgrade in June 2012. See also: "Simić and Avramović cases: Bribery and intimidation of witnesses." IWPR tribunal update 146, 9.10.1999. http://iwpr.net/report-news/simic-amp-avramovic-case-bribery-and-intimidation-witness

The table shows that reconciliation and guilty pleas became almost inextricably linked notions for the ICTY judges. Reconciliation as a rhetorical device shows up when a defendant pleads guilty or enters into a plea agreement with the prosecution. Otherwise it is very unlikely for the notion of reconciliation to play a role in judgment and sentencing.

In order to get the maximum benefit (a considerably lower sentence), an accused had to enter a guilty plea before the trial started, because then the administration of justice would be more expeditious and victims did not have to testify in court. Next, the defendant had to describe his crimes in detail (the so-called "factual basis" of his self-accusation) and he had to show remorse and cooperate with the prosecution.

Some defendants at the ICTY fulfilled this plan one hundred per cent; others only partly complied with these requirements.

In order to incline the judges to accept a guilty plea or plea agreement as mitigating circumstance that would lower the sentence (although it never was clear with respect to what threshold the judges would lower the sentence), the following conditions had to be fulfilled. First, the accused had to cooperate substantially with the prosecution; he also had to express sincere and convincing remorse; he had to admit his guilt; his plea had to be honest, incline other suspects to come forward, and should contribute to establishing the truth about the crime. Furthermore, a guilty plea had to save the tribunal's resources and to relieve witnesses of the stressful testimonies in court.

When confronted with the different aspects through which reconciliation can be understood, as set out by Peter Lambertz earlier in this book, several potential clashes become apparent. If, for instance, acknowledging victims and giving them a voice (in court) is regarded as an important step on the way to reconciliation, plea agreements become rather counterproductive to reconciliation understood in this way, since the guilty plea of the accused renders the appearance of victims redundant. However, it is exactly this consequence of plea agreements that is often emphasized by the judges as a contribution to reconciliation (and treated as a mitigating circumstance), because, as they frequently claim, it relieves witnesses of the stress of testifying in court. Individual, inter-subjective reconciliation is being put forward here as an argument, forgetting that for the socio-emotional rehabilitation of the victim's collectivity (their direct vengeance would be sublated), the victim's public appearance is of crucial importance. An argumentation as the one presented here is possible, however, because of the semantic ambiguity of the notion of reconciliation, which seems to be a convenient rhetorical tool for strategic argumentation.

The same is the case with respect to the reconciliatory element of individualizing guilt. By blaming precise and individual perpetrators for crimes which were carried out in a large social setting and supported by many, justice facilitates the externalisation of guilt of the relevant community – a mechanism, which may undermine the process of reconciliation in the region and which runs contrary to the goal of inclining other perpetrators to come forward. Ending impunity as an element of reconciliation has the aim of preventing victims from engaging in acts of vengeance and of deterring potential future perpetrators. Plea bargaining contradicts this aim because its key feature is the perspective of a shorter prison sentence for the defendant. Without this perspective, plea agreements cannot work, because they lack incentives for perpetrators. Sometimes, as in the South African Truth and Reconciliation Commission, the drive to get confessions (and access to the perpetrators' insider knowledge) is strong enough to diminish punishment to zero and grant amnesty to perpetrators even if they do not show remorse.[852] A guilty plea which includes substantial new information for the victims may well contribute to reconciliation insofar as it provides acknowledgement to the victims and reveals a hidden truth to them (for example about the fate and burial sites of their murdered relatives), but it is quite unlikely to uphold deterrence and the aim of ending impunity.

There are several cases which enable us to observe how the quite fuzzy concept of reconciliation changed and what content it implied in varying situations. These cases have in common a strong focus of the judges on reconciliation due to the specific role defendants played in the proceedings. These cases are *the pros. vs. Erdemović*, *the pros. vs. Plavšić* and *the pros. vs. Babić.*

Reconciliation in *the Pros. vs. Erdemović*

Dražen Erdemović, a Croatian who had deserted from the Bosnian Croat Army and had then enlisted in the Bosnian Serb Army, was a member of one of the execution units that was charged with the massacres on abandoned farm sites outside Srebrenica during the aftermath of the town's fall. According to his own confession later in court, he had refused to take part in the executions, but was threatened with death by a superior. Later on, shaken by his participation in such a horrendous crime, he contacted a journalist in

852 See: Du Bois-Pedain, Antje: Transitional Amnesty in South Africa. Cambridge University Press 2007.

Belgrade to whom he explained his willingness to confess and assist the ICTY in elucidating the events in and around Srebrenica. Erdemović was one of the first accused at the ICTY and one of the OTP's most valuable crime-based witnesses. He was completely repentant, broke down on several occasions during the trial, gave a confession which had apparently been drafted by himself (rather than by his lawyer), and was full of emotional self-accusations. In some moments, it seemed as if Erdemović was so strongly tormented by his own consciousness and feelings of guilt that he pushed aside his lawyer's legal arguments and decided to entrust himself to the judges completely.

He cooperated wholeheartedly with the prosecution, appearing in a number of trials and incriminating a whole range of officers of the Bosnian Serb Army linked to the events in Srebrenica 1995.

Given all these apparently mitigating circumstances, the trial chamber sentenced him to 10 years imprisonment, mainly because it did not find any evidence for his claim of the extreme duress under which he allegedly had committed his crimes. According to his version of the events around the Pilica Farm, his officers had made it clear that he could either shoot the prisoners who were waiting for their execution – or join them. But since none of them could testify and the officers could not be found, there was no corroboration for Erdemović's claim.

When responding to his guilty plea, the trial chamber reiterated that refraining from punishment in his case would be contrary to the intentions of the creators of the ICTY. The judges quoted the UNSC and the General Assembly in claiming that "the impunity of the guilty would only fuel the desire for vengeance in the former Yugoslavia, jeopardizing the return to the 'rule of law', 'reconciliation' and the restoration of 'true peace.'"[853] It was a clear indication that the judges regarded punishment and the ending of impunity as an indispensable element of reconciliation. More clarity was provided by another fragment of the judgment:

> "The International Tribunal's objectives as seen by the Security Council – i.e. general prevention (or deterrence), reprobation, retribution (or 'just deserts'), as well as collective reconciliation – fit into the Security Council's broader aim of maintaining peace and security in the former Yugoslavia. These purposes (...) may provide guidance in determining the punishment for a crime against humanity."[854]

853 *The pros. vs. Erdemović* IT-96-22-T, trial chamber judgement 29.11.1996.

854 Ibid.

In this context, the reference to reconciliation looks very much like a justification for a high sentence. The appeals chamber concluded that Erdemović's guilty plea had not been well informed. The judges argued that Erdemović should not have pleaded guilty if he wanted to put forward the "extreme necessity" argument.[855] If he wanted to do so, he should have pleaded not guilty in the sense that he committed the deeds he had been charged with in the indictment, but – because of the lack of any other option – without burdening himself with guilt.[856]

The case was important for the ICTY for several reasons. First, it triggered a debate at the tribunal about whether duress could exonerate a soldier of guilt with regard to the killing of innocent people.[857] Second, the verdict of the trial chamber ran contrary to the institutional interest of the ICTY at that stage, because it deterred rather than attracted low ranking perpetrators from coming forward to confess and implicate superiors. In October 1997, when the trial chamber passed judgment on Erdemović, the ICTY was still being sidelined by the international community, waiting for big fish to come and dealing only with low and mid-level perpetrators. Erdemović's case could signal that surrendering to the Tribunal would pay and drive a wedge into the omerta which linked low-level executioners to their former superiors. The message of a 10-year sentence would rather have the opposite effect: low-ranking perpetrators from the former Yugoslavia would feel discouraged by the risk of surrender and confession. These arguments were never uttered in public, but the documents show a strong inclination of the prosecution and the appeals chamber to accommodate Erdemović as much as possible.

---

855 Extreme necessity means the lack of a moral alternative. In this concrete case it means that Erdemović, if threatened with death, had no choice but to follow the execution order and therefore had to be regarded as innocent, since only the existence of an alternative to the crime creates a situation in which a person can become guilty.

856 Another controversial issue was the choice between pleading guilty to crimes against humanity and pleading guilty to war crimes. Erdemović had had this choice due to the drafting of the indictment in an alternative way by the prosecution. He had chosen to plead guilty to crimes against humanity, the more severe one, which, for the appeals chamber, was another argument for its assumption of an ill-informed guilty plea. The judges sent the case to another trial chamber, giving Erdemović the explicit choice between a guilty plea and a plea of not guilty in the first place, and – if he wanted to sustain his guilty plea – to reconsider, whether this should concern the charge of a crime against humanity or the war crimes charge. See: *The pros. vs. Erdemović* IT-96-22, appeals judgment summary.

857 See separate opinions of the judges Gabrielle Kirk McDonald and Lal C. Vohrah in op. cit.

Instead of once again simply pleading guilty, Erdemović's lawyer concluded an informal plea agreement,[858] according to which the prosecution would withdraw the crimes against humanity charge and Erdemović would plead guilty to murder as a war crime. Prosecution and defence recommended a sentence of 7 years of imprisonment. This time, the trial chamber had a sound grasp of what was expected of it. It finally sentenced Erdemović to 5 years in prison, giving him credit for the years spent in custody. He was transferred to Norway and granted early release in 1999, but frequently appeared as a prosecution witness in the trials against defendants linked to Srebrenica.[859]

There is a short reference to reconciliation in the judgment of the second trial chamber, which dealt with Erdemović. The judges claimed that the ICTY had a duty "to contribute to the settlement of the wider issues of accountability, reconciliation and establishing the truth behind the evils perpetrated in the former Yugoslavia."[860] By juxtaposing these three notions, the judges treated the establishment of the truth, accountability (which, in this context, must be understood as punishment of perpetrators), and reconciliation as different concepts. In the next sentence, however, they pointed to the connection between them, adding some rather flowery explanations of why "[d]iscovering the truth is a cornerstone of the rule of law and a fundamental step on the way to reconciliation: for it is the truth that cleanses the ethnic and religious hatreds and begins the healing process."[861] In this paragraph, the judges appear as unanimous supporters of a concept of reconciliation based on memory rather than forgetting. It obfuscated the obvious fact that the trial of *the pros. vs. Erdemović* which had led to this judgment was far from revealing a truth, since it had been based on a guilty plea and refrained from any examination of evidence. From an ontological point of view, it had only presented a negotiated version of truth, based on the version of the perpetrator and devoid of any element of the victims' perspective. It had, in other words, not given victims a voice.

---

858 It must be taken into account that the ICTY's rules of procedure and evidence did not yet regulate plea agreements at that time. Therefore Erdemović's lawyer entered a "Joint Motion for Consideration of Plea Agreement between the Office of the Prosecutor and Dražen Erdemović", which was kept confidential until the trial chamber in *the pros. vs. Milošević* made it public in 2003.

859 In May 2012, his name was on the prosecution's witness list in *the pros. vs. Mladić*. See: IT-09-92.

860 *The pros. vs. Erdemović* IT-96-22-T*bis*, 5.3.1998.

861 Ibid.

The judges seemed to be aware of this shortcoming. They emphasized, that "[T]he International Tribunal must demonstrate that those who have the honesty to confess are treated fairly as part of a process underpinned by principles of justice, fair trial and protection of the fundamental rights of the individual." In other words, they endorsed the accused's guilty plea not as a contribution to reconciliation but as an element of fair trial for a repentant perpetrator. This constituted the unambiguous confirmation that rewarding a guilty plea with a lower sentence was an element of fairness and a cornerstone of a rational trial management which aimed at creating incentives for perpetrators to surrender and admit guilt. From this perspective, a lenient sentence was no element of reconciliation. This argument ran contrary to most other trial chambers' justifications of shorter prison sentences for repentant defendants. Other trial chambers did not link milder sentences for repentant perpetrators to such pragmatic arguments.

Reconciliation as a Rhetorical Smokescreen – *the Pros. vs. Plavšić*

The case of Biljana Plavšić became a paradigmatic one for the ICTY. It evoked at lot of emotions and debates about the sense of plea agreements and guilty pleas, about the role of reconciliation and what that could or should mean for the work of the tribunal, about deterrence and retribution, and about the appropriateness of extensive and colourful sentencing hearings, whose main aim was to direct media attention to the case.

Biljana Plavšić had originally been indicted together with Momčilo Krajišnik. The OTP had accused her of genocide and incitement to commit genocide, persecutions, extermination, deportation, and murder as crimes against humanity and murder as a war crime. The indictment had been confirmed by a judge in April 2000, but had been kept under seal. Nevetheless, Plavšić had been aware of the indictment, contacted the ICTY, and surrendered voluntarily in January 2001.[862] During her first appearance in court on January 11, she pleaded not guilty, but later in the same year changed her plea to a guilty one. When she did, plea bargaining was not yet included in the rules of procedure and evidence, so formally she just entered a guilty plea. But due to negotiations between her lawyers and the OTP, and after talks with Carla Del Ponte in the detention facility,[863] the OTP decided

862 Del Ponte, Madame Prosecutor, 161.

863 Confidential information from the OTP, obtained in The Hague in October 2001 by Klaus Bachmann.

to drop all charges against her except for the count of racial, ethnic, and religious persecutions as a crime against humanity. For the large victims' community of non-Serbs in Bosnia and Herzegovina this meant that one of the leading members of the Bosnian Serb Republic, who had instigated ethnic cleansing and tolerated (amongst others) the siege and sniping of Sarajevo, the destruction of Srebrenica, and the siege of the other enclaves, was no longer accused of genocide. But the deal with Plavšić's lawyers cleared the way to some sort of cooperation between Plavšić and the OTP and delivered the OTP the first high-ranking, repentant perpetrator who would deliver an account of the atrocities committed under her rule. As prosecutors and judges would later emphasize, her guilty plea and the factual basis which her lawyers delivered to the court would render negationism about Srebrenica and other crime sites much more difficult for other perpetrators, for the public in Republika Srpska, and for the political leadership of the Serb entity in Bosnia and Herzegovina, which, at that stage, still rejected any accusations of genocide and large-scale crimes, pointing instead to the crimes of the other conflict parties and presenting the entity as a war victim.[864]

Carla Del Ponte tried to get Plavšić to agree to a much closer cooperation than just a plea deal; she wanted Plavšić to testify against Slobodan Milošević, who had been transferred from Belgrade in April of the same year and was now awaiting trial. During the initial talks between the two women, Plavšić seemed to agree to the role designed for her by Del Ponte.[865] However, there never was a formal agreement on that, and Plavšić later never appeared in the Milošević trial. As Del Ponte later admitted, Plavšić managed to mislead her by making her believe that she would fully cooperate. The case would incline the OTP to sign written agreements in the cases to follow, a move that was difficult in *the pros. vs. Plavšić*, since the rules of the tribunal did not yet foresee formal plea agreements.

The trial chamber agreed to the amendment of the indictment by the OTP and accepted the guilty plea. This meant that there would be no formal trial, no evidence or witnesses called, and no cross-examination. Defence counsellors, prosecutors, and judges only met in order to discuss the gravity of the offences to which Plavšić had pleaded guilty, the aggravating and mitigating circumstances, and the final sentence. *The pros. vs. Plavšić* became famous

864 Daniela Valenta: "Regional Report: Plavšić Denounced as Traitor." IWPR, TRI Issue 293, 29.04.2005.

865 Confidential information from OTP in October 2001, obtained by Klaus Bachmann. In her memoir, Del Ponte describes the talks differently, as a "nauseating speech about the superiority of the Serbian people", interrupted by Del Ponte. Del Ponte, Madame Prosecutor, 161.

because the way the tribunal approached these issues proved to be quite unique and, to some observers, even opaque. The sentencing hearings were dominated by several prominent intellectuals who appeared as expert witnesses for reconciliation, attracting considerable media attention.

For the purpose of the three-day hearing, Alex Boraine, the former co-president of the South African Truth and Reconciliation Commission, appeared as a joint witness of the prosecution and the defence, together with the former US Secretary of State Madeleine Albright and Nobel Prize winner and writer Elie Wiesel, a survivor of Auschwitz. Additionally, the prosecution called three representatives of what were considered the communities of victims of Biljana Plavšić's crimes: Mirsad Tokač, the secretary of the State Commission for War Crimes of Bosnia and Herzegovina, Adil Draganović, a former camp prisoner and representative of the Association of Camp Detainees of Bosnia and Herzegovina, and Taufika Ibrahimefendić, a psychotherapist from *Viva žene*, a victims organisation from Tuzla. At the end of the hearings, the prosecution would ask the trial chamber for a sentence between 15 and 25 years, which, in the eyes of the defence, would have amounted to a lifelong sentence. Plavšić's lawyers proposed a sentence of 8 years. Despite their differences regarding the severity of the sentence, prosecution and defence often seemed to work hand in hand while trying to convince the judges that Plavšić's guilty plea, the "factual basis" she had signed, and her expression of remorse would strongly contribute to reconciliation in the former Yugoslavia.

During the hearings the prosecution, the defence, and the judges all went along with about the idea that Plavšić's guilty plea was a contribution to the establishment of the truth and a relief for the victims, who now would not have to testify in court. The inherent contradiction of these opinions became partly apparent after Alex Boraine had explained the functioning of the South African TRC, whose contribution to truth seeking and in this sense to reconciliation was based on a restorative rather than retributive notion of accountability and on extensive truth-telling by victims in public.

As already mentioned above by Peter Lambertz, "Giving victims a voice" was a paramount element of the TRC, which had run an extensive outreach programme and had included compensation and reparations for victims as well as public acknowledgement during the TRC deliberations. If the sterile environment and the ritualized procedures of the ICTY could contribute at all to such a process of acknowledging victims, then the curtailing of the formal, adversarial truth-seeking procedures by Plavšić's guilty plea had eliminated any chance of such an understanding of reconciliation. After the plea had been accepted by the trial chamber, no truth-telling comparable to the TRC's hearings was possible any more, and the only truth that was left was the one described (in the dry language of the ICTY's legal documents) in the factual basis that Plavšić's lawyers had drafted and made her sign. This truth could be commented by the parties and the witnesses, but the only voice victims were given in court was the voice of their representatives from Bosnia.

The apparent contradiction from earlier trials with guilty pleas returned. While the ICTY time and again claimed that its procedures would "give victims a voice" and "establish the truth" about the atrocities committed in the former Yugoslavia, and while ICTY trial chambers regarded these elements as crucial for reconciliation, the judges rewarded guilty pleas with lower sentences, arguing that guilty pleas made stressful testimonies of victims redundant. Therefore, the only elements of our reconciliation typology which *the pros. vs. Plavšić* actually addressed implicitly was the one pertaining to the individualisation of guilt.

The Plavšić trial with its highly publicized sentencing hearing can hardly be regarded as a factor that could have generated a truth, apart from the fact that the first high-ranking perpetrator from the Serb community in Bosnia had admitted the commission of crimes against humanity. One could argue that *the pros. vs. Plavšić* also fulfilled the requirement of ending impunity as an intended element of reconciliation. There might have been such intentions, but reality was different. The trial chamber endorsed Plavšić's plea, her expression of remorse, and her factual basis and granted her several mitigating circumstances, which altogether led to a verdict of 11 years, a sentence which came very close to the defence's demand to spare her from *de facto* lifelong imprisonment. Plavšić, who had been allowed to await the sentencing hearing in home arrest in Belgrade (in contrast to her non-repentant fellow defendant Momčilo Krajišnik, who had to wait for his trail in the detention facility in Scheveningen),[866] was transferred to Sweden, where she was eligible (upon approval of the ICTY) for early release after serving 2/3 of her term. Additionally, she was allowed to spend a part of her detention time in home arrest in a small villa with numerous amenities.[867] In 2009, the ICTY agreed to her early release. By then, she had actually withdrawn her guilty plea in public, arguing that it had only been

866 Klarin, Mirko: "Biljana takes her Leave." IWPR Tribunal Update 233, 30.4.2005, (the file is wrongly dated and, contrary to the date in the IWPR electronic archive, was published in 2001)

867 Plavšić later complained about her detention conditions in Sweden, causing reactions ranging from amusement to outrage, when she grumbled about the air condition being too cold or about the birthday cake she had been given by her wardens being "too small". Edina Becirevic: "Bosnian Court Should Try Plavšić." IWPR Tribunal Update 560, 28.7.2008.

dictated by the wish to avoid a long trial.[868] When the OTP summoned her to testify in the Krajišnik trial, she first refused, and then, after being transferred to the ICTY from Sweden, renounced her guilty plea and claimed to be innocent.[869] Del Ponte tried to get the trial chamber to reverse her sentence but failed. Contrary to many expectations in the media and in the OTP, Plavšić never testified against Milošević. In her case, plea bargaining backfired against the OTP – Plavšić had managed to get the reward of a guilty plea without giving the ICTY its share of the cake in the form of cooperation, evidence against other accused persons, or even in the form of a spectacular moral event that would impact public opinion in Bosnia.

Actually, public opinion there remained rather unimpressed, no matter which side uttered a view on the trial. Bosniac victims' organisations complained about the counts that had been dropped by the prosecution and about the mild verdict, whereas representatives of Republika Srpska found the verdict too harsh. Both agreed about her guilty plea not being that sincere. As usual in such cases, comparisons were made in order to discredit the verdict. Milorad Dodik, leader of the Independent Social Democrats (the leading Serb party in Republika Srpska) found the sentence "unjustifiably harsh." He told reporters in Banja Luka: "Plavšić has been sentenced to 11 years in prison while Alija Izetbegović, who is responsible for war casualties in Bosnia-Hercegovina, is not held accountable."[870]

In early November 2009, when Plavšić was released from Sweden and went back to Belgrade, she was flown in with a government jet, and upon arrival at Nikola Tesla airport she was greeted by Dodik personally, who, in the meantime, had become Prime Minister of the Serb part of Bosnia. The angry reaction of the Bosniac public is easy to imagine. But also a few human rights organisations from Belgrade protested.[871]

It is difficult to imagine how the Plavšić case could have contributed to the establishment of a truth that could have tamed or prevented the denial of crimes committed during the conflict. The character of plea agreements, and the impossibility of reversing a verdict issued on the basis of an agreement,

---

868 Simon Jennings: "Plavšić Reportedly Withdraws Guilty Plea. Biljana Plavšić tells Swedish media she pleaded guilty so she could 'bargain for the other charges'". IWPR Tribunal Update 586, 31.1.2009.

869 Del Ponte, Madame Prosecutor, 161.

870 Amra Kebo: "Regional Report. Plavšić Sentence divides Bosnia." IWPR Tribunal Update 30 2.22.2.2005 (the electronic article is dated wrongly and was actually published in 2001).

871 Iva Martinović: "Outcry at Plavšić's Belgrade Welcome." IWPR Tribunal Update 622. 4.11.2009.

encourages perpetrators to pretend to repent – and then renounce. From today's perspective, it astonishes that only so few of the accused used such an exit strategy. Probably the fear of being excluded by their own milieu at home was a stronger impediment to pleading guilty than the perspective of a lower sentence was an incentive to it. The Plavšić case provides some hints in that direction. When she had entered her plea agreement, Plavšić was immediately accused of treason against the Bosnian Serbs by media in her home country. According to confidential information we obtained in Belgrade, this was one of the reasons why she decided to stay in Belgrade rather than return to Republika Srpska after her prison term. After her case, the OTP was eager to conclude only written plea agreements, which contained commitments to cooperate. The tribunal president, who had the right to approve early release, and the registrar, who was responsible for selecting host countries for detainees, would increasingly link the fulfilment of such commitments to the choice of a country and their approval for early release. As Slobodan Zečević, president of the Association of Defence Counsel Practising before the ICTY explained, defendants had strong incentives to fulfil their promises from plea agreements even after the sentences had been passed. If they did not, they faced transfer to one of the unpopular countries and risked their chances of early release. "For politicians, who were anxious about their image back home and who had not personally taken part in any atrocities, such plea agreements were unacceptable anyway. And some other defendants decided to stick to their commitments also, because they had arranged security for their families from the OTP. Such an arrangement could be at risk, if they did not cooperate."[872]

Were Biljana Plavšić's guilty plea and the lower sentence likely to thwart vengeance? It is rather improbable. Some representatives of the victims' community testified in court that her guilty plea could contribute to reconciliation, but hardly anyone from the victims' communities in Bosnia and Herzegovina had warm feelings about the eleven years of prison for someone who had initially been indicted for genocide. Here, another paradox became apparent. In a strongly antagonized and polarized community, a low sentence for a perpetrator is likely to be accepted by the community which sympathizes with him, but it is also likely to be rejected by the opposite camp. It is therefore rather unlikely for any kind of punishment to contribute to reconciliation, if the latter requires both sides to accept a verdict.

Alex Boraine from the South African TRC pointed this out during his testimony in court. The TRC's main purpose had been to foster reconciliation

---

872 Interview with Slobodan Zečević in Belgrade in June 2012.

and unity, and punishment had been only a minor element of the TRC's work, not an aim in itself. Perpetrators whose crimes had been approved by one of the conflict parties in apartheid South Africa were granted amnesty if they delivered all the information about the crimes that was available to them. There wasn't even a need to express remorse. The TRC's was not devoid of retributive elements, but the threat of punishment was only the element that forced perpetrators to come forward. Revealing their truth about the crimes of the past in itself was not expected to cause reconciliation. This was to be achieved through a process of identity transformation: through a public dialogue, through the public exposure of the perpetrators' and the victims' truths a new, unifying narrative was to be created, whose aim it was to overcome the cleavages and redefine the community, merging the former enemy camps into a new nation which, in the case of post-apartheid South Africa, was given the inclusive branding of "the rainbow nation". The TRC's proceedings actually were accompanied by many examples of public expiation, identity transformation of individuals, dramatic cases of victims forgiving their perpetrators and perpetrators apologizing for their deeds and, in some cases, even chastising themselves in public. The whole process was extensively debated in the media, and despite the fact that not all former conflict parties contributed to it, a lot of evidence from psychological, psychiatric, sociological, and anthropological studies confirmed cases of individual trauma healing, and the emergence of a new national identity based on diversity rather than on the racial exclusionism of the apartheid era.

At the time of the Plavšić hearings, no such elements were present in Bosnia. The different entities were still strongly antagonistic, no unifying narrative was present, and the ICTY proceedings were usually rejected by the public when they affected suspects of one's own ethnic group, and hailed when they were directed against an ethnic out-group. Identity transformation as in the TRC's South Africa was very unlikely to occur even in the case of a high-ranking perpetrator with a sincere apology. There were some examples of identity change: Erdemović was one, but it was a case of an individual which triggered no collective identity transformation.[873] The Croatian soldier crossed a line when he confessed and cooperated with the prosecution in numerous other cases. After having incriminated so many others, there was no doubt left that he had broken with his past and would – from the perspective of his co-perpetrators – always remain on the other side of the historical barricades. But his example did not trigger any larger shift among Bosnian Serbs. When later, in his own

873 The transformation of Erdemović's identity was even literal. After his release, he was given a new identity under a national witness protection program.

trial, Slobodan Milošević was confronted with Erdemović's testimony, he dismissed it as "the story of a mentally deranged Croat."[874]

But the lack of collective identity transformation was not only a result of the smouldering ethnic and political conflict in Bosnia and Herzegovina; it was to a large extent also a consequence of the strongly ritualized character of the ICTY's legal proceedings. Researchers of the TRC have often pointed out that the TRC had its own rituals, but there seems to be a considerable agreement among scholars that the religious environment and the Christian talk which dominated the TRC proceedings created a better condition for identity transformation than the sterile atmosphere of the ICTY with its aquarium-like courtrooms, the technocratic atmosphere, and the legal terminology, which proved much less accessible to outsiders, victims, or even curious observers. At the TRC, victims could tell their whole story, and very often they received immediate and emotional feedback (with co-president Desmond Tutu even crying or praying in public with them), whereas the cold atmosphere of the ICTY's courtrooms and the professional ethics of judges and prosecutors made victims' appearances a source of stress even when no defendant was eager to attack them personally during cross-examination. The adversarial system itself encourages the prosecution and the defence to cast doubt on the credibility of a witness, a tendency which runs totally contrary to the aim of acknowledging him and "giving him a voice". The TRC proceedings were not at all adversarial. Since there was no need for a perpetrator to defend himself, there also was no need to call a victim's statement into question. This is why victims often left the TRC with a feeling of dignity, respect, and appreciation, whereas victims often returned home bitter and disappointed after testimony for the ICTY.

Paradoxically, and contrary to the trial chambers' claims about a link between plea agreements and reconciliation, the latter was much less likely to occur as a consequence of a guilty plea than in cases of an extensive trial with testimonies and evidence, which could less easily be refuted than the strategic move of a guilty plea by a cold and calculating perpetrator. In *the pros. vs. Plavšić*, the trial chamber argued that the plea would contribute to trial economy, the establishment of truth, and reconciliation in the region, but, as it occurred subsequently, only the claim concerning trial economy proved valid.

As Peter Lambertz has shown above in his discussion of reconciliation at the ICTR, guilty pleas can be thought of as being conducive to reconciliation in that they publically contribute to the acknowledgement of victims. This happens only to a certain extent, however, given that the victims themselves do no longer

874 The quote comes from Mikro Klarin: "Plavšić Plea bolsters reconciliation." IWPR Tribunal Update 296, (wrongly dated 22.2.2005).

participate in the production of truth through witnessing in public. As mentioned earlier in this book, publicity is an important requirement tying together justice and reconciliation: the alleged truth which Plavšić's admission of guilt invoked was immediately rejected by the Bosnian Serb public, dismissed as a strategic calculation in Sarajevo, and finally even discredited by Plavšić herself.

Despite the differences pertaining to the severity of the sentence, prosecution and defence have seemed to work hand in hand in Plavšić's case in trying to convince the judges that Plavšić's guilty plea, the "factual basis" she had signed, and her expression of remorse would strongly contribute to "reconciliation" in the former Yugoslavia.

This was argued by means of linking reconciliation to the fact that victims would no longer have to publically appear to testify. As the example of South Africa's TRC shows, however, the latter is inevitable if the objective of acknowledging victims is to be achieved. In Plavšić's case, the notion of reconciliation served the purpose of a trial economy guided by the paradigm of fighting impunity. While in the context of informal and backstage trial economy, fighting impunity could not be stated as the underlying logic of the notion of reconciliation, the concept has still proved strategically useful in that it has helped to produce a justification with which to legitimize Plavšić's lower verdict.

Individual Identity Transformation with Fatal Consequences – *the Pros. vs. Babić*

The abovementioned Dražen Erdemović was not the only perpetrator who decided to come forward, apologize for his deeds, and show consistent and compelling remorse. One of the most spectacular cases of identity transformation at the ICTY took place during the trial against Milan Babić, who had briefly been the leader of the Croatian Serbs in the Autonomous Republic of Serbian Krajina, a Serb separatist entity that had been created after Croatia's declaration of independence and had been protected by the Federal Army. During the few months of Babić's holding the post of Prime Minister of the entity, numerous atrocities were committed against the non-Serb population in this territory. They led to the exodus of most Croats to territories controlled by the government in Zagreb. The Kraijna Republic collapsed in 1995 as a result of the Croatian operations "Flash" and "Storm".

In 2001, when the OTP issued the so-called Croatian indictment against Milošević, Babić learned that he was mentioned as a co-perpetrator of a Joint Criminal Enterprise comprising crimes against humanity and war crimes. At that time, no separate indictment against Babić existed. Babić contacted the OTP and agreed to testify against Milošević. During the trial, he first appeared as a protected witness. It was an open secret that he would testify, since the OTP's pre-trial brief had revealed enough details to make it clear that one of the three subsequent Krajina leaders would testify against Milošević. All three had been mentioned in Milošević's Croatia indictment and Babić, who was in conflict with Milošević, was the most likely one to testify.[875] When he realized that his protection had evaporated, Babić himself asked the court to lift the confidentiality and made his further statements in open session.

Babić was a unique case, because he had agreed to testify against Milošević knowing that he might be indicted himself. Testifying involved a high risk for him, which he seemed to accept. Two years after he had agreed to talk to the OTP, he was indicted for crimes against humanity and war crimes, committed during his short premiership in Krajina during the early 1990s. He concluded a plea agreement with the OTP, which provided for a reduction of the counts he was accused of and inclined him to plead guilty to the count of persecutions as a crime against humanity. Defence and prosecution were eager to convince the trial chamber to sentence him to a prison term not exceeding 11 years, but they failed. The trial chamber found that a sentence of 11 years would not have served the interest of "punishment and justice" and instead sent him to prison for 13 years. The sentence was sustained by the appeals chamber with one dissenting judge who found that the only ground of appeal which the appeals chamber had accepted (to regard Babić's later conduct as a mitigating circumstance) would qualify Babić to a lower sentence. The judges never explained why a sentence of two more years would better serve the interest of "justice and punishment" than an 11-year sentence, given the probability that Babić was given credit for almost one year in jail and could count on early release after 2/3 of his prison term. The sentence provided a stark contrast to the one issued in *the pros. vs. Plavšić*. Both had been leaders of their ethnic communities, and both were accused of crimes against humanity and war crimes, but Babić had never been indicted for genocide, his leadership term had been much shorter than Plavšić's, and he had been the only suspect who had come forward and had begun to cooperate with the OTP even before being indicted. Yet he received two years more than Plavšić.

Reconciliation played a prominent role in the sentencing hearings. The OTP regarded reconciliation as a direct effect of his cooperation and admission of guilt. The defence was even more outspoken and claimed that his plea would

---

875 Mirko Klarin: "Comment: Milošević Trial: Protected Witness Goes Public." IWPR Tribunal Update 292, 29.4.2005.

"contribute to rendering justice to the victims, to deterring others, to providing a basis for reconciliation, and to preclude revisionism. The timeliness of his guilty plea has rendered a contribution to the public advantage and the work of the Tribunal."[876] The latter referred to the fact that in cooperating, Babić had neglected his own legal interest to a certain extent, aware that by testifying against others he could incriminate himself.

The trial chamber went back to UNSC resolution 827 and its commitment to re-establishing peace and security in the former Yugoslavia, and the UNSC's claim, that "it is only the truth that can cleanse the ethnic and religious hatreds and begin the healing process." During the sentencing hearing, the OTP and the defence had called a joint expert on reconciliation, who had confirmed a potentially positive impact of Babić's guilty plea on victims and, as the judges claimed, "in general on the entire population in the former Yugoslavia, including the Serbs."[877] The trial chamber endorsed this argument, but when defining reconciliation, the judges only quoted the expert as saying that "[a]dmission of guilt and remorse alone cannot restore unity and friendship, but it helps victims overcome the greyness of their past" and "expresses the truth which so many victims have 'silently' been saying for all these years."[878] Without elaborating on what they regarded as reconciliation, the judges conceded that Babić had "significantly contributed to reconciliation."

Surprising enough, the severe prison sentence did not prevent Babić from further cooperation. Like Erdemović, he had crossed the line that now divided him from his former environment. During his testimony against Milošević, he withstood the accused's verbal attacks and denigrations with dignity and resolution. He testified as one of the most important and valuable insider witnesses of the OTP in *the pros. vs. Krajišnik* and *the pros. vs. Martić*. If this contributed to reconciliation, Babić himself had no benefit from it. In Serb nationalist circles, and among the refugee community of Krajina Serbs who had been driven out of Eastern Slavonia after the Croatian offensive in 1995, he was called the worst names, "traitor" and "coward" being among the most polite ones.[879] His family was threatened and he was subject to aggression in the detention unit, despite being separated from most other detainees. In March 2006, he was transferred once again to The Hague in order to testify in the trial against another Krajina Serb leader, Milan Martić, who was accused of war

876 *The pros. vs Babić*, IT-03-72, trial chamber judgment.
877 Ibid.
878 Ibid.
879 See, for example the article in Večernje Novosti 6.3.2006, retrieved from: http://www.srpskapolitika.com/Tekstovi/Komentari/2006/043.html

crimes and crimes against humanity and, amongst others, the desperate shelling of Zagreb in 1995 in retaliation for the Croatian offensive in Krajina.[880] According to a later account by his lawyer, Peter Michael Mueller, Babić felt completely isolated since his family had been in hiding and under protection, and his attitude had been rejected by a large part of the public in Serbia (for whom he was a traitor) and in Croatia (for whom he was a perpetrator), where a part of his family had come from. His possessions there had fallen victim to operation "Storm", and before he became an insider witness for the OTP, the former Krajina leader had grown mushrooms in Voivodina on the farm of a friend. During his last stay in Scheveningen, he asked to be put into the Dutch part of the detention facility to avoid contact with other detainees from the former Yugoslavia.[881] On March 7, he was found dead in his cell hanging from his leather belt, his head covered by a plastic bag. He had succumbed to a heart attack while hanging. Despite some doubts about details of the hanging, his death was declared a suicide. Inside his bible, a letter to his wife was discovered, asking her to find peace for herself and not to mourn him.[882] Like Erdemović, his case can definitely been regarded as an example of individual identity transformation and even as an attempt at symbolic reconciliation. Babić had been a former leader, a person of a certain authority, who, much more so than the simple soldier Erdemović, could be expected to have some influence on others and initiate an apology-forgiveness-cycle. This, however, remains theoretical, since at the time he did (and because he did) apologize to the Croatian public, he had already ceased to be recognized as an authority in both Serbia and Croatia. He did so when he presented his guilty plea in court: "I have asked help from God to make it easier for me to repent, and I am thankful to God for making it possible for me to express my repentance. I ask from my brothers, Croats, to forgive us, their brother Serbs, and I pray for the Serb people to turn to the future and to achieve the kind of compassion that will make it possible to forgive the crimes."[883] Babić's concept of mutual forgiveness was much more precise than the trial chamber's notion of reconciliation, and it was strongly based on collective identity transformation of the former enemy camps. As reactions to his guilty plea and his death showed, it did not trigger any

880 *The pros. vs. Martić*. IT-95-11, Case Information Sheet http://www.icty.org/x/cases/Martić/cis/en/cis_Martić_en.pdf

881 Helen Warrell: "Babić's death, unanswered questions." IWPR Tribunal Update445, 24.3.2006. Del Ponte, Madame Prosecutor, 331.

882 Janet Anderson: "Babić suicide report exonerates jail staff." IWPR Tribunal Update (no number) 9.6.2006.

883 ICTY case information sheet, Milan Babić, see: http://www.icty.org/x/cases/babic/cis/en/cis_babic_en.pdf

collective change, and the credibility of his testimony, which had not been blurred by compromises about punishment or material calculations, even increased the hate against him. What might have been his dream when he made the speech in court actually happened four years later, in November 2010, when Serb Prime Minister Boris Tadić took a ferry from the Serbian side of the river Danube to Vukovar, the town that had been almost totally destroyed by the first JNA operation against Croatia in 1991, met his counterpart Ivo Josipović, and apologized for the destruction of the town and the massacres against civilians and prisoners which had followed its fall.[884] Earlier the same year, in March, the Serbian parliament had passed a declaration on Srebrenica, blaming Serbia for not doing enough to prevent the genocide there. Tadić also attended the symbolic funeral in Srebrenica, which marked the 15th anniversary of the massacres.[885]

Reconciliation and Guilty Pleas of Low-Level Perpetrators

The numerous plea agreements concluded between the OTP and low-level perpetrators, who were mostly Bosnian Serbs, give rise to the assumption that it was rather the perpetrator's social status that decided about the likelihood of a guilty plea, than the perspective of a lower verdict. After *the pros. vs. Plavšić,* no leading politician, no army general agreed to a plea bargain with the OTP. Neither General Ante Gotovina[886] nor Slobodan Milošević,[887] neither the Bosnian generals,[888] Naser Orić,[889] the leadership cases from Serbia,[890] nor any other figure that was regarded as a "national hero" by his ethnic constituency ever made a guilty plea. As Mirko Klarin has pointed out, the publics in all post-Yugoslav republics tended to focus on heroes rather than victims when covering the ICTY trials.[891] It is this heroic perspective which provides a partial explanation why not more suspects decided to follow Plavšić's example, to plea

---

884 BBC: Serb leader Tadić apologizes for 1991 Vukovar massacre, 4.11.2010. http://www.bbc.co.uk/news/world-europe-11689153

885 BBC: Victims buried as Bosnia marks Srebrenica anniversary, 11.7.2010. http://www.bbc.co.uk/news/10589614

886 *The pros. vs. Gotovina*, IT-01-45.

887 *The pros. vs. Milošević* IT-02-54.

888 *The pros. vs. Haradinaj et al.* IT-04-84, for which a re-trial is taking place at the time of writing.

889 *The pros. vs. Orić* IT-03-68.

890 *The pros. vs.Šainović et al.* (IT-05-87); *the pros. vs. Pavković* IT-03-70.

891 Klarin, Mirko: "The Impact of the ICTY Trials on Public Opinion in the Former Yugoslavia." *Journal of International Criminal Justice* 2009, 89-96.

guilty, and cash in on a lower sentence and then withdraw their plea and refuse to cooperate with the OTP. The above-mentioned incentives from the registrar and the trial president to incline defendants to stick to obligations from plea agreements are only part of the picture. The OTP tried (but did not always manage) to get an accused to deliver additional evidence or testify against others before a plea agreement was submitted to a trial chamber. However, there is no single case of a plea agreement being reversed by a trial chamber or appeals chamber because of non-compliance of a convicted suspect. Suspects chose either to fight to the end, proclaiming their innocence, or to conclude plea agreements and stick to their commitment. They did so because they feared the reaction at home more than a higher sentence in court. This is not only confirmed by the lack of any high-ranking suspects among those who pleaded guilty (except perhaps for Babić, who was a short-term leading figure of a part of Croatia's Serb minority, but who can hardly be compared to Gotovina, Milošević, or even Šešelj). It is also confirmed by the fact that all suspects who decided to plead guilty were low-ranking perpetrators, executioners on the spot with limited social capital and a narrow ethnic constituency that was limited to a town or municipality, i.e. whose public image was not as crucial to their social identity as for high-ranking celebrities. In other words – they had much less to lose when pleading guilty than an army general, party leader, former president, or someone who, like Naser Orić, Ante Gotovina, or Ratko Mladić, was praised as hero by a large part (or even the totality) of his national constituency. According to the very understanding of what a hero is, he cannot repent without ceasing to be a hero (and becoming a traitor). On the other hand, such heroes are much more likely to initiate a apology-forgiveness-cycle and to contribute to reconciliation understood as a transformation of collective identities than low-ranking perpetrators, whose admittance of guilt and remorse for crimes which are often still doubted by their constituency may or may not reach out to their community, or may be rejected because of their weak moral authority.

It is therefore doubtful, whether the numerous guilty pleas of low-ranking perpetrators actually had a chance to contribute to initiating an apology-forgiveness-cycle on the ground. Sharing this doubt, some trial chambers justified lower sentences for the accused by assuming an impact of their guilty plea on their local community only. In some of these cases, victims and witnesses from these communities were heard during the sentencing hearings.[892] Miroslav Bralo, a member of the special forces of the Croatian Defence Council (HVO) who had been indicted for murder and rape in the Lašva River Valley of central Bosnia, had already engaged in community work and helped to establish

892 For example in *the pros. vs. Djeronić* IT-02-61; and *the pros. vs. Bralo* IT-95-17.

the fate of victims before his indictment had been made public. Shortly after he had surrendered to the ICTY, pleaded not guilty and then altered his plea as the result of an agreement with the OTP. Dragan Nikolić had also delivered evidence to the OTP before concluding his plea agreement.[893] The reasoning according to which a prior remorseful behaviour was regarded as a contribution to reconciliation can also be observed at the ICTR, as shown in Peter Lambertz' analysis of *the pros. vs. Rutaganira* above.

Usually trial chambers argued that guilty pleas contributed to the truth-finding mission of the ICTY and by doing so, made reconciliation more likely. The link between "establishing the truth" (by confirming the veracity of the indictment) and reconciliation appears in nearly all trial chamber judgments dealing with repentant suspects. This probably was overspill from the ICTR, where high-ranking defendants made guilty pleas relatively early on.

The second element shared by some chambers, was "relief for victims" who were spared the need to undergo the stress of testifying thanks to a guilty plea.[894] When it comes to sparing the resources of the tribunal, this argument was sometimes regarded as a mitigating circumstance, but never as a contribution to reconciliation. Some trial chambers even refrained from treating the resource argument as a mitigating circumstance and mentioned it only as a "side effect".[895]

There was no consistency in the trial chambers' approach to the "relief for victims" argument. Some regarded it as a potential direct cause of reconciliation (*the pros. vs. Češić*), others did not mention it at all as a possible contribution to reconciliation. Usually, it was treated as a mitigating circumstance. The same variation across cases occurred with respect to the potential impact of punishment on reconciliation and – in a few cases – the rehabilitation of the perpetrator. Most trial chambers clearly prioritized punishment and deterrence over any other goal of the tribunal, arguing (in some cases), that even a guilty plea should not lead to disproportionally low retribution, or in other cases, that low punishment would hamper rather than further the rehabilitation of the accused.[896]

One judge strongly disagreed with this stance, writing several dissenting opinions. In *the pros. vs. Djeronić*, judge Florence Ndepele Mwachande Mumba disagreed with the trial chamber on the issue of rehabilitation of the offender –

893 *The pros. vs. D. Nikolić* IT-94-2
894 *The pros. vs. Češić* IT-95-10/1
895 For example in *the pros. vs. Djeronić* IT-02-61
896 *The pros. vs. Bralo* IT-95-17, *the pros. vs. Mučić* IT-96-21, and *the pros. vs. D. Nikolić* IT-94-2.

an issue which had been only marginally dealt with by other trial chambers, if at all. “In addition to the objectives of prevention and deterrence, in imposing a sentence, another key consideration, is the rehabilitation of the convicted person. A guilty plea is accepted as a first step to rehabilitation of the offender and a positive factor towards reconciliation of the offended community,” she wrote in her opinion.[897] This is the only case of the ICTY in which a judge used a concept of reconciliation with a perpetrator-centred rather than a victim-focused approach. Mumba was the only one who examined not only the likelihood that victims would react positively to a guilty plea, but also asked herself (and her fellow judges) what should be done in order to facilitate the reintegration of the perpetrator. Whereas the trial chambers usually emphasized the need for retribution and punishment, which, in their mind, would incline victims to reconcile more easily with perpetrators, Mumba wrote a harsh reckoning with her colleagues’ tendency to favour deterrence over reintegration. In *the pros. vs. Bralo*, the trial chamber had reiterated that only punishment could have a “rehabilitating effect” – an argument that ran contrary to the defence’s claim that Bralo should not be punished too severely for the sake of reconciliation. This was a common conviction in many chambers, whose sole focus was on the victims’ side of a reconciliatory process.

Judge Mumba deeply disagreed with the dominating trend at the ICTY when she wrote in her dissenting opinion that

> “International justice in cases similar to these, in this Tribunal, is not about unfair retribution; if that were the case, humanity should forget about reconciliation and its off-shoot, peace. It is my humble view that this Tribunal is not about vengeance, using the pen as the firearm, much as the victims’ plight has been acknowledged; that would be erroneous, such a practice would amount to accepting the erroneous view that you can conquer hatred with hatred. This, in my view, does not work. Vengeance may be manifested in terms of a harsh sentence for an accused person who has pleaded guilty. In my humble opinion, rehabilitation, after turmoil, may serve to reduce the incidence of political instability and conflict.”

In Mumba’s view, a verdict did not necessarily contribute to reconciliation by reducing the probability of vengeance, but it became a kind of hidden, indirect, and socially applied vengeance if it did not take into account the sentence’s impact on the perpetrator. It must be mentioned that Mumba did not disagree with the sentence of ten years imprisonment for Djeronić, but she dissented with the justification for that sentence.[898]

---

897 Judgment in *the pros. vs. Djeronić* IT-02-61, separate opinion of Judge Mumba. 30.3.2004, 92.

898 Ibid.

Also in *the pros. vs. Blagojević,* the trial chamber attributed some importance to the rehabilitiation of the defendant, arguing that "[p]articularly in cases where the crime was committed on a discriminatory basis, like this case, this process of reflection – and hearing the victims testify – can inspire tolerance and understanding of 'the other', thereby reducing the risk of recidivism. Reconciliation and peace would thereby be promoted."[899] This paragraph in the judgment is also unique – it contradicts the dominating claim according to which guilty pleas, sparing victims the stress of testifying, were a contribution to truth and reconciliation exactly because they did not require the court to hear evidence. Now, the judges in *the pros. vs. Blagojević* argued that conducting a trial would contribute to reconciliation, since it exposed the perpetrator to the consequences of his actions (as reflected in victim's testimonies) and therefore prevent recidivism and foster reconciliation by facilitating his reintegration into society. In the last sentence of the paragraph, the trial chamber became aware of the potentially unexpected consequences of this argument's logic, and attempted to relativize the hypothesized impact of lower sentences on the rehabilitation of an accused: "However, the Trial Chamber notes that the rehabilitative purpose of sentencing will not be given undue prominence in determining the sentence."[900] Blagojević, who had been involved in the execution of the Srebrenica genocide, was sentenced to 18 years in prison, a sentence that was later reduced to 15 years by the appeals chamber.

Reconciliation Without a Guilty Plea

There were four cases in which a judgment mentioned reconciliation despite the lack of a guilty plea or plea agreement by the accused. These four cases can be used as a test showing how judges understood reconciliation when there was no apology, no admittance of guilt, and no sign of repentance from a perpetrator. These cases also may show us whether trial chambers understood reconciliation differently in cases with guilty pleas and in cases without such pleas. The four cases involve only minor perpetrators; none of the accused was a political or military leader, and none of them could claim to be a national hero of his community or ethnic group. The four cases were: *the pros. vs. Blagojević, the pros. vs. Mucić et al., the pros. vs. Stakić* and *the pros. vs. D. Tadić.*

In one of the first trials at the ICTY, the trial chamber applied a similar notion of perpetrator-focused reconciliation as judge Mumba in her dissenting

899 Sentencing judgment of *the pros. vs. Blagojević*, IT-02-60-T, 17.1.2005.
900 Ibid.

opinion cited above. In *the pros. vs. Mucić et al.*,[901] the trial chamber launched a polemic against "the theory of retribution, which is an inheritance of the primitive theory of revenge," arguing that this theory "urges the Trial Chamber to retaliate to appease the victim. The policy of the Security Council of the United Nations is directed towards reconciliation of the parties. This is the basis of the Dayton Peace Agreement by which all the parties to the conflict in Bosnia and Herzegovina have agreed to live together. A consideration of retribution as the only factor in sentencing is likely to be counterproductive and disruptive of the entire purpose of the Security Council, which is the restoration and maintenance of peace in the territory of the former Yugoslavia. Retributive punishment by itself does not bring justice." Suddenly, and only in this case, punishment for perpetrators became potentially counterproductive for reconciliation and accommodating the victims was equalized with revenge. This is even more astonishing because none of the accused pleaded guilty. At the end of the trial, the chamber meted out sentences ranging from one acquittal to prison terms of 9, 15, and 18 years, which were sustained in all subsequent proceedings.[902]

The ICTY's sentencing policy – or rather the absence of any consistent sentencing policy – is a separate topic. Miodrag Jokić, an officer of the JNA responsible for the bombing of Dubrovnik in 1991 who pleaded guilty, was sentenced to 7 years in prison. His attack had destroyed protected civilian buildings in the famous old town and caused the death of two inhabitants, injuring three others. At the time the JNA bombed Dubrovnik, a less famous town in Eastern Slavonia on the Serbian border was also shelled by JNA troops. The shelling destroyed the inner town completely, and after the fall of the town, the JNA ransacked the local hospital, abducted about 200 injured patients, and executed them on the premises of an empty farm in Ovčara. The three accused in the case were sentenced to 5 and 20 years; one was acquitted, another one (Slavko Dokmanović) died before his judgment was issued. The development of atrocities in Vukovar was similar to the fall of Srebrenica – a long fight (even fiercer than the siege of Srebrenica) was followed by the fall of the town, and

---

901 *The pros. vs. Mučić, Delić, Landžo and Delalić* IT-96-29.

902 All of the accused, except Zejnil Delalić, who was acquitted, filed appeals. The appeals chamber urged the trial chamber to retry the three accused. The trial chamber issued new, but very similar sentences, which were again attacked on appeal by the defence without success. Hazim Delić's defence filed a motion in order to review the proceedings and quash the sentences on three different counts, but the motion was dismissed by the trial chamber. For the impact of the trial (the first one implicating Bosnian government forces in war crimes before the ICTY) on public opinion in Bosnia see: Nettlefield, Courting democracy, 174-209.

then the victors carried out mass executions of defenders on empty farms.[903] Similar to the case of Srebrenica, the ICTY had even conducted Rule 61 hearings after the events. But what was regarded as genocide in Srebrenica was declared a mere war crime in the case of Vukovar. The sentences were so low that the appeals chamber felt compelled to increase it to 10 years. The five judges even found the verdict of 5 years for the accused Veselin Šljivančanin so misguided that it explicitly quashed the original sentence and replaced it by one of 17 years for charges of which the accused had been acquitted by the trial chamber.[904] The trial verdict induced Croatian newspapers to attack the trial chamber fiercely.[905]For different reasons (concerning the applicability of the International Covenant on Civil and Political Rights) the verdict was also controversially debated among judges and the epistemic community.[906] After the Plavšić case, many observers also pointed to the discrepancy between low sentences for high-ranking but repentant perpetrators, and low-ranking criminals who did not enter guilty pleas.

---

903 It must be taken into account that the organisational efforts behind the Srebrenica massacres were much bigger than the efforts the JNA (and the militias acting under its protection) had to undertake in order to kill the civilians in Vukovar. This bigger effort required the VRS to plan and order transport in advance, which provided the OTP with a relatively easy proof of the perpetrators' *mens rea* for genocidal intent. In the case of Vukovar, no such effort was necessary and therefore also the proof standard for genocidal intent would have been much more difficult to fulfil. We are grateful to Refik Hodžić from the International Center for Transitional Justice in New York for this argument.

904 *The pros. vs. Mrkšić et al.*IT-95-13/1.

905 Berislaw Jelinić: "Kevin Parker, the judge who freed the villains of Vukovar." Nacional 620, 2.10.2007.
http://www.nacional.hr/en/clanak/38490/kevin-parker-the-judge-who-freed-the-villains-of-vukovar
The Croatian Parliament even held a special debate about the case. Rejection turned into triumph in Croatia once the appeals chamber had increased the prison sentences again. The verdict was then praised in Croatia as a victory for the truth. Interview with Novak Lukić in June 2012 in Belgrade.

906 Simon Jennings: "Šljivančanin's Lawyers to Challenge Appeals Judgment." IWPR Tribunal Update 602, 22.5.2009. The problem is a general one in international tribunals, see : Bagarić, Mirko; Morss, John: "International Sentencing Law: In Search of a Justification and Coherent Framework." *International Criminal Law Review* 6 (2006), 191–255; Hola, Barbora; Smeulers, Alette; Bijleveld, Catrien: "Is ICTY Sentencing Predictable? An Empirical Analysis of ICTY Sentencing Practice." *Leiden Journal of International Law,* 22 (2009), 79–97 (with corrigendum in *Leiden Journal of International Law*, 22 (2009), 411.

One of these cases was the first trial at the ICTY, *the pros. vs. D. Tadić*. Dusko Tadić was a local leader of the Serb Democratic Party (SDS) in Kozarac who co-organized the takeover of the town of Prijedor by the JNA and then helped to orchestrate the ethnic cleansing of the town, which led to the confinement of many non-Serb inhabitants in the concentration camps of Keraterm, Omarska, and Trnopolje (which would later be the subject of many other trials against wardens and officers of these camps). The trial chamber first sentenced him to 20 years, a verdict that was sustained in the final appeal after a partial retrial by another trial chamber. In the second trial chamber's verdict, one can read the following reference to reconciliation, in which reconciliation is equated with deterrence, fighting impunity, and prevention: "It is the mandate and the duty of the International Tribunal, in contributing to reconciliation, to deter such crimes and to combat impunity. It is not only right that *punitur quia peccatur* (the individual must be punished because he broke the law) but also *punitur ne peccatur* (he must be punished so that he and others will no longer break the law). The Trial Chamber accepts that two important functions of the punishment are retribution and deterrence." [907]Differently to *the pros. vs. Mucić et al.* and in contrast to judge Mumba's dissenting opinion quoted earlier, the trial chamber found no contradiction in retribution and reconciliation. Reconciliation features once again with a lot of ambiguity; it could lead to weaker, but just as well to more severe punishment.

In a similarly cursory way, reconciliation was dealt with in *the pros. vs. Stakić*. Stakić could have been co-accused with Tadić, as he was the head of the Prijedor municipality and was accused of ordering ethnic cleansing and the creation of the above-mentioned concentration camps in the region. On trial, he was sentenced to lifelong imprisonment, which was changed by the appeals chamber to 40 years of imprisonment, one of the highest sentences ever meted out by the ICTY. Like Tadić, Stakić had pleaded not guilty. In their verdict, the judges argued that the "broader mandate of promoting peace and reconciliation in the former Yugoslavia is best served by providing a full and accurate record, on the basis of the evidence, of the individuals who became victims of the crimes committed in Prijedor in 1992."[908] But this was only a justification for including a list of missing persons into the evidence, based on a motion by the prosecution. The verdict does not make any link between reconciliation and truth finding, and it lacks any further explanation about the links between the two concepts.

---

907 *The pros. vs. Stakić* IT-97-24. Judgment.

908 Ibid.

It remains surprising that the only cases when judges applied a perpetrator-centred approach[909] of reconciliation, stressing the need for reintegrating perpetrators into society (and using the concept of reconciliation as an argument for lower sentences) were part of proceedings against non-repentant defendants. In trials against repentant defendants, the reconciliation argument could go both ways – as in *the pros. vs. Plavšić*, it could lead to a short prison sentence if the judges stressed the victims' relief argument and linked reconciliation to truth-telling (by the perpetrator), but it could also lead to a long prison sentence when the judges found that the gravity of the crimes did not entitle a defendant to a reduction of punishment and valued retribution and deterrence higher than potential reconciliatory effects.

The appeals chambers did not contribute much to clarify these inconsistencies. In *the pros. vs. Krstić* and *the pros. vs. Martić*, the appeals chamber only dismissed claims of the prosecution and the defence about potential contributions to reconciliation by the accused, but without any further explanation or elucidation of its understanding of the concept. There was more in the appeal verdicts of the remaining two cases, but this did not amount to a full description of the concept as understood by the appeals judges.

In *the pros. vs. Blagojević*, the defence had presented the defendant's participation in de-mining activities as a proof of his will to contribute to reconciliation, as an indirect apology which demonstrated his remorse. The prosecution had argued that remorse would have to be linked to an apology for his own criminal conduct and that a general altruistic attitude was not enough to prove remorse. The appeals chamber disagreed with the prosecution, reminding the OTP of the appeals chambers' verdicts in *the pros. vs. Plavšić* and *the pros. vs. Jokić*, where the judges had found that Plavšić's support for the implementation of the Dayton agreements and Jokić's political engagement after Dayton were enough to prove a commitment to reconciliation, and to entitle them to mitigating circumstances. These arguments can hardly be regarded as comprehensive guidance regarding reconciliation for trial chambers, but at least it made it clear that reconciliatory efforts by defendants needed not necessarily

909 We use the notion of "perpetrator-centred approach" of reconciliation as opposite to "victim-centred", in order to distinguish between concepts, which focus on the reintegration of a victim into the community (e.g., by acknowledging him or her, giving a voice, truth telling or by preventing revenge by ending impunity) and concepts, which focus on the reintegration of perpetrators (by lowering their sentences, taking into account their active repentance as mitigating circumstances etc.) Whereas the first concept asks how victims can further reconciliation, the latter asks how perpetrators can contribute to it.

concern a defendants' own crimes, but also could be more general in nature to entitle a suspect to mitigating circumstances.

In *the pros. vs. Zelenović*, the trial chamber based its findings on the usual approach of other trial chambers, according to which a guilty plea was considered mitigating due to the relief it was likely to bring to victims who otherwise would have to testify. However, Zelenović was a special case. Zelenović was one of several suspects who were accused of having carried out a campaign of organized rapes and tortures of Bosniac women in and around Foča. This campaign, during which Zelenović himself had raped several women and aided and abetted the rapes and mistreatment of numerous others, was qualified by the trial chamber as an element of crimes against humanity. This verdict attracted a lot of public attention and it was subsequently used by human rights organisations during *the pros. vs. Akayesu* at the ICTR, where it led to another case of legal innovation when the trial chamber declared the rapes in Taba an element of genocide. Had Zelenović not pleaded guilty, the prosecution would have had to call several of the rape victims as witnesses, which, given the patriarchal character of rural Bosnia, would have exposed them to much more stress than in any other case of a crime-based testimony. In *the pros. vs. Zelenović*, the victims' relief argument was likely to have a stronger impact as a mitigating circumstance than in other cases. The trial chamber actually agreed that "the guilty plea can be given considerable weight in mitigation."[910] It also used the argument that guilty pleas would contribute to reconciliation through their impact on truth finding. But the appeals chamber just quoted these findings without expanding on the content or correcting it. Although the appeals chamber provided guidance to trial chambers in many other ways, there was no such assistance with respect to the notion of reconciliation.

910 *The pros. vs. Zelenović*, IT-96-23-2-S, judgment on 4.4.2007.

Reconciliation at the ICTR and the ICTY: Findings

While the founding resolutions by the UN Security Council and the General Assembly prominently declared that the ICTR and the ICTY should contribute to "national reconciliation" in Rwanda and the former Yugoslavia, respectively, our analysis has shown that the actors within the ICTs did not have a shared understanding of how the Tribunals should live up to this claim. We even detected an apparent paradox: whereas the UNSC put the task of reconciliation directly and explicitly into the relevant resolutions establishing the ICTR and did not do so with the ICTY, it was actually the latter which more often (in absolute and relative numbers) referred to the notion of reconciliation in trial and appeals chamber judgments. Nevertheless, this reference was far from coherent. By analyzing the language of the Tribunals' documents, judgments, and sentences, we have demonstrated that the ways in which key members of the ICTR relate the idea of transitional justice to the concept of reconciliation differ widely.

The reasons given for justice to be conducive to reconciliation range from structural democratisation and the extension of legal space to the transformation process of individual and collective identity inside a social space. A third interpretation opens up a temporal way of understanding through truth generation about the past and collective memory enhancement.

On the level of appearance, the inherent ambiguity of the notion as a programmatic objective of the Tribunal's activity seems to have generated confusion over what might or might not be a judgment or sentence that contributes to reconciliation. Depending on the perspective applied by the tribunal's personnel, a guilty plea and the subsequent mitigation of a sentence, for instance, was seen as conducive to reconciliation in that it stages and displays the rehabilitation of the perpetrator and an acknowledgement of victims. At the same time, and contrary to this position, reconciliation has also been understood as the result of the democratizing effect of deterrence and severe punishment, as in *the pros. vs. Kamuhanda*.

However, on a deeper level of analysis, what appears to be a confusing, arbitrary, and contradictory understanding of the notion of reconciliation reveals that the conceptual ambiguity of the notion of reconciliation has provided for instrumental reasoning and usage. Especially in the case of pleading guilty and plea bargaining, this has become apparent. At the ICTY, plea bargaining was regarded as a means to speed up lengthy trials and influence public opinion in the former Yugoslavia, especially in cases where high-level perpetrators agreed to reveal details about their crimes and publicly admit and utter remorse about atrocities, which, at that stage, were still being negated by influential parts of their constituencies at home. This was a major motivation for the prosecution to offer Biljana Plavšić an informal plea agreement. In her case, fighting negationism was seen as a precondition of reconciliation. This, however, already reveals the internal contradiction of such a link between guilty pleas and reconciliation. Since guilty pleas from high-level perpetrators, which are more difficult to obtain (as the ICTY's statistics show), are expected to do more for reconciliation than those of middle- and low-ranking criminals, the prosecution should strive to obtain as many guilty pleas as possible – which would run contrary to its task of prosecuting and punishing. Actually, after Plavšić, the ICTY prosecutors did not initiate further negotiations with high-ranking defendants partly because it would have led to the paradoxical situation of big fish getting lower prison sentences than non-repentant small fish, partly because of the OTP's and the ICTY's institutional interest.[911]

Therefore, when thinking about the seeming contradiction between, on the one hand, the Tribunal's important claim to act in favour of reconciliation and, on the other hand, its conceptual ambiguity and at times its confusing argumentation with regards to the objective of reconciliation, we cannot but agree that, from our analytical point of view, the Tribunal's task to contribute to reconciliation has endowed it with a rhetorical instrument for strategic rather than for communicative action, to invoke Habermas' dichotomy.[912]

Our findings therefore tend to support the existing critical opinion that "the ICTR is doing more to assuage the guilt of the international community for the reluctance to intervene earlier to stop the genocide than it is to promote a sense of justice for Rwandan people."[913] They also support already existing criticism

911 Before the completion strategy, which forced the ICTY to scale down its activities and end new investigations, the ICTY had sometimes more defendants, than it could deal with. Under such conditions, plea bargaining was regarded as a means to speed up trials and spare tribunal resources. But after the completion strategy had been imposed by the UNSC, the tribunal had no longer an interest in speedy trials and plea bargaining, since now its institutional interests was concentrated on extending the time of its existence (also in order to get additional time for apprehending and judging Karadžić and Mladić). Under the reign of Serge Brammertz, the OTP did not engage in new plea negotiations, as one member of the OTP told us, requesting anonymity, "because it would now no longer be in our interest."

912 Habermas, Jürgen: Theorie des kommunikativen Handelns. Frankfurt am Main, 1981.

913 Lambourne, Justice and Reconciliation, 326. This opinion is shared by Jean-Pierre Kamatali: Given that the ICTR is more accountable to the UN than to Rwanda, some have seen it as an international instrument of relief "for the benefit of the spectators of the 1994 genocide whose conscience needed to be eased and whose credentials as

of the ICTR's engagement with the objective of reconciliation by *Paradelle et al.*, who claim that the reconciliation discourse was mere rhetoric and that the penal philosophy of individual guilt was counterproductive to national reconciliation.[914]

It should not be forgotten, however, that language, even if inconsistent in its argumentation, is a powerful resource that through its performative nature, its active utterances of speech orders, categorizes, shapes, and thus also makes reality. In the section on the constitutive power of language, we have seen that language not only has a representative capacity, but, when mediated, can also have a powerfully constitutive one. Annelies Verdoolaege has shown that in South Africa the construction of a reconciliation discourse within the Truth and Reconciliation Commission has established a reconciliation-oriented reality in South Africa's public opinion: "This reality was multifaceted, since the concept of reconciliation could be interpreted in manifold ways and because the reconciliation discourse was inclusive and multidimensional."[915] The strength of South Africa's reconciliation discourse clearly lay in its being heavily mediated through public outreach mechanisms (media, participation, Desmond Tutu, etc.). It thus impacted on people's categorisation of the world and penetrated their everyday worlds. As convincing as this argument may be in the context of the South African TRC, it is more than unlikely to be relevant for the ICTR, given the hesitation and late initiative of the ICTR to publicize its work in the Rwandan public sphere and thus discursively fashion everyday routines of

---

'civilized nations' needed to be reaffirmed by the creation of such a tribunal." Jean-Pierre Kamatali, *op.cit.*, 199. See especially Akhavan, P.: "Justice and Reconciliation in the Great Lakes Region of Africa: The Contribution of the ICTR." *Duke Journal of Comparative and International Law*, 325, 7 (1997), 327.

Prominent criticism also from Andrew Rigby: "[...] [T]here are strong grounds for believing that the establishment of the two tribunals was a political ploy by the UN Security Council members to deflect criticisms that they were not doing enough to curb the atrocities in Bosnia and Rwanda. The tribunals were, if you like, originally conceived for display and show, public symbols to indicate that the international community of sovereign states represented in the UN really did care about the crimes and would not let them go unpunished." Andrew Rigby, Justice and Reconciliation, 176.

And, more generally, also Philip Gourévitch who quotes a refugee: "[L]es gens viennent au Rwanda, parlent de réconciliation. C'est insultant, affirmait un rescapé. Vous imaginez parler aux Juifs de réconciliation en 1946? Peut-être dans longtemps, mais c'est une affaire privée." Gourévitch, We would like to inform you, 333.

914 Murielle Paradelle: "[Il y a] antinomie entre la poursuite d'une fin – la contribution à la réconciliation – et un moyen pour l'atteindre – la seule sanction d'un nombre limité de responsables." Paradelle, Dumont, Boisvert, Quelle Justice, 365.

915 Verdoolaege, Rethinking Reconciliation, 182-183.

interpretation. The ICTR started its own outreach program in 2005 and with fewer resources than the ICTY, sometimes supported by European governments and the EU.[916]

The same is true for the ICTY, with some additional arguments. At both tribunals, outreach was established late and rather as a reaction to negative reactions of the public than in order to create a positive image from the beginning. The ICTR outreach started in 2000, while the ICTY outreach was established in 1999 under president Gabrielle Kirk McDonald and became operational in 2000. But under subsequent tribunal presidents, it ceased to be a priority in the case of the ICTY, which acted like an NGO, raising funds for short-term projects.[917] Thus, even if the semantic indeterminacy of the reconciliation concept might have favoured the generation of a reconciliation-oriented reality, as in the case of the South-African TRC, in both the cases of the ICTY and the ICTR it did not succeed.

It could not succeed in a strongly divisive environment with strictly separated ethnic communities like Bosnia and Herzegovina. Replacing antagonistic talk about "them", the blacks, whites, coloured and Indian by an integrative and inclusive "we, the rainbow nation" through discoursive action such as that undertaken by the South African TRC was no option in the former Yugoslavia, since all incentives from outside and from other communities supported exclusive notions of identity. The ICTY alone, even with the best outreach programme one could imagine, would have failed here.

But the trial and appeals chambers of both tribunals also never tried to impose any compelling concept of reconciliation or even harmonize their understanding of what reconciliation was and what it should include. For the

---

916 Klaus Bachmann's interview with Innocence Kamenzi, head of the ICTR's outreach program in Rwanda. The interview took place in Kigali in July 2012. Before 2005, the ICTR had occassionally sent journalists and human rights activists from Rwanda to Arusha in order to acquaint them with the ICTR proceedings.

917 This is the assessment of Refik Hodžić, who was responsible for outreach under Kirk McDonald. According to him, the launch of the outreach program was a reaction to deeply entrenched negationism in his home region, Prijedor, where the local population would flatly deny the existence of any camps during the conflict. When reporters who had been there confronted Kirk McDonald with their findings, she asked her *chef de cabinet* David Tolbert to set up a programme. Hodžić's opinion about the marginal role of outreach and the lack of understanding at the ICTY "that our constituency is there, not in the Netherlands" are largely consistent with Sara Nettlefields findings on the ground in her book "Courting Democracy in Bosnia and Herzegovina: The Hague Tribunal's Impact in a Postwar State" (Cambridge Studies in Law and Society), Cambridge University Press 2010. Interview with Refik Hodžić at the International Center for Transitional Justice in New York in April 2012.

overwhelming majority of trial and appeals chambers, it did not play any role at all. Among those who used it as an empty signifier, which would justify milder or tougher verdicts, the overwhelming majority regarded reconciliation as a goal that had to recede before more important ones, like retribution, punishment, satisfying victims, and furthering general deterrence.

Against the background of the South African TRC and the general prominence of *Ubuntu* (inclusion and reconciliation) in Southern Africa, it may not be surprising that the use of reconciliation was invoked for justifying lower sentences by trial chambers dominated by judges from non-European countries. In the Celebići case (*the pros. vs. Mucić et al.*), the trial chamber meted out (and the appeals chamber accepted) a mild verdict in the name of reconciliation even without a guilty plea. The trial chamber consisted of Judge Richard May from Britain as the presiding judge, Patrick Robinson from Jamaica, and Mohammed El Habib Fassi Fihri from Marocco.[918] This may have been pure coincidence. But it may be due to the fact that the two dissenting opinions, which emphasized a perpetrator-centred approach to reconciliation and questioned the dominant trend to retribution in both tribunals, came from judge Mumba from Zambia (in *the pros. vs. Djeronić*) and from Winston Churchill Matanzima Maqutu from Lesotho (in *the pros. vs. Kamuhanda*). Both are countries in which the South African transition was observed by the public with great interest.

918 The composition of the appeals chamber was: Judge David Hunt (Australia, presiding), Judge Fouad Riad (Egypt), Judge Rafael Nieto-Navia (Columbia), Judge Mohamed Bennouna (Marocco), Judge Fausto Pocar (Italy).

Conclusion: Actorness and Autonomy of the ICTY and the ICTR

Ad hoc international criminal tribunals are special institutions. They seek justice and judge perpetrators, so in that sense they are like any other criminal court. But at the same time, they are created by and dependent on states, alliances of states, and international organisations. They are subject to power politics and international bargaining not only during the process of their establishment, but also during their proceedings. This book examines precisely those political influences – both external and internal – to try and answer a set of questions that are at the very basis of the academic debate about the sense, efficiency, and legitimacy of international criminal tribunals and their ability to serve justice. These two questions are crucial in the debate: have the tribunals been independent in their decision-making process from the states that created them? What factors have constrained their capacity to function as actors?

To answer those questions, we divided this monograph into three sections and used three different approaches and methods for measuring their autonomy and independence from external influences.

The first part of the book set out to analyse the role of the ICTY in the ongoing accession process of Serbia and Croatia to the European Union. It explained the tribunal's decision-making dynamics by examining a series of specific EU policy shifts towards Belgrade's and Zagreb's obligation to cooperate with the ICTY as a precondition to entering the EU. By using a principal-agent approach and a simple process-tracing model, it showed that the ICTY managed to trigger EU action towards Croatia and Serbia whenever there was no considerable danger of a nationalist backlash in one of the two Balkan countries. The ICTY was most efficient in using EU conditionality for its own purpose when it could rely on the support of an internal EU veto player – a country able and willing to block the negotiation process for whatever reason while linking it to the issue of "full cooperation with the ICTY". This was the case with the Netherlands. The country used veto power, conferring it de facto to the ICTY chief prosecutor, in order to coerce Serbia into surrendering Mladić and Hadzić. This must be regarded as an outstanding case of a state transferring part of its sovereign rights to an external actor whom it cannot entirely control. Although the risk of deceit or surprise was relatively low, even traditional theories of delegation and supranational decision-making do not explain this case, since the ICTY prosecutor cannot be regarded as a supranational institution, and there was no collective delegation that could have helped the

Netherlands to use Serge Brammertz to prevent other member states from free-riding. The free-riding issue does not occur here, and the same affect could have been achieved by the Netherlands if the government had used its veto power without delegation.[919]All in all, the combination of conditionality and support from EU institutions and specific member states empowered the ICTY in an extraordinary way, enabling it to apprehend all the suspects on its list. From the perspective of the task which the ICTY had been given by the UNSC and from the point of view of the tribunal's own objectives, this must be regarded as a success. The ICTY managed to get hold of all the living fugitives who had been indicted. It managed to judge the overwhelming majority of them. When in May 2012, almost 17 years after the Srebrenica massacres, the trial of Ratko Mladić started, the ICTY press office proudly put up a double poster on the walls of its lobby: on the first half, it showed a large list of fugitives, while the second half was empty except for a seal claiming that there were "no more fugitives" to be apprehended. For the ICTY and the EU, the conditionality game was to a large extend a win-win game, since it also allowed the EU to lower transaction costs in negotiations with Serbia and Croatia, giving it an additional bargaining chip which it could use in order to force concessions from the accession countries. Given the asymmetry between the block of 25 or, after 2007, 27 member states and the small and rather poor Balkan candidates, and given the strategic advantage of the EU's regatta strategy and the additional asset of the ICTY, the outcome of the accession negotiations with the Western Balkans can be expected to be much more asymmetrical than in the case of the 2004 and 2007

919 Some theorists of international organisations reduce the impact of supranational organisations to the enforcement of collectively taken decisions by states. According to this concept, such organisations do not shape or alter states' preferences, but only enforce their collective will by preventing potential defectors of an agreement from free-riding (using a collective good – like a common market – without sharing the cost of it). The ICTY could be regarded as a supranational organisation for Serbia and Croatia, but not with respect to the EU. It had no comparable leverage over EU members, because they had not delegated powers to the ICTY which could be used in order to prevent them from free-riding. The only exception is the case of the Netherlands, but even here, this was no collective delegation and there was no public good of several or all member states involved which the ICTY could have guarded. This is another reason why we use the principal-agent approach in the first part of the book, instead of regarding the ICTY as a supranational body like the European Commission or the European Court of Justice. See also: Moravcsik, Andrew: "A New Statecraft? Supranational Entrepreneurs and International Cooperation." *International Organization* 53 (2), 1999, 267–306. Young, Oran P.: "Political Leadership and Regime Formation: On the Development of Institutions in International Society." *International Organization* 45 (3), 1991, 281–308.

enlargements. It is far beyond the scope of our research to underpin this claim empirically, but it should be kept in mind by students of Europeanisation and the next EU enlargement. For institutionalists and supranationalists, it also may be quite striking to observe how the ICTY became an autonomous player between the EU (and NATO) and its member states on the one and Serbia and Croatia on the other hand without having any attributes of supranationality. From the perspective of International Relations theory, the ICTY quickly became an actor. Its actions were sometimes more, sometimes less successful, but that does not distinguish it from other actors in International Relations.

The second part of the book investigated the potential influence of external actors on the ICTY's and ICTR's judgments. In particular, we analysed four highly political, salient, and controversial cases, two connected to each tribunal. These case studies employ "frame analysis", a method based on a specific form of content analysis drawn from media and public opinion research. Its goal is to compare the frames used by certain external actors – mainly governments, non-governmental organisations, and influential media outlets – to the frames used by judges in their judgments and sentencing, and during sentencing hearings. The comparison showed enormous differences from case to case and from trial chamber to trial chamber. The most extraordinary case is *the pros. vs. Akayesu,* during which the prosecution amended its initial indictment according to the request of a number of international non-governmental organisations that used the trial for strategic litigation. Supported by the New York Times, they triggered far-reaching legal activism by the prosecutor as well as by the trial chamber, which allowed the amendment of the indictment and finally sentenced the accused among others for counts that had not been part of the initial indictment but where congruent with the requests of the NGOs. Due to its institutional weakness and the absence of any conditionality game, the ICTR was potentially much more exposed to strategic litigation and the influences of external actors. However, our second case study concerning the fate of the Belgian peacekeepers and the frames created in *the pros. vs. Bagosora et al.* clearly showed that this could, but needed not, limit a trial chamber's independence. In *the pros. vs. Bogosora et al.*, the judges showed an astonishing level of autonomy, using a genocide frame that ran counter to the mainstream in historiography, media interpretation, and the Rwandan government's official version of the past. In the case of the events in Račak in early 1999 and the events in Srebrenica four years earlier, the trial chambers restricted themselves to the creation of frames that remained within the scope of the mainstream interpretation of NGOs, media, and Western governments.

The comparison between *the pros. vs. Akayesu* and *The pros. vs. Ntagerura, Bagambiki and Imanishimwe* revealed that the composition of a trial chamber and the interplay between NGOs, prosecution, and trial chamber were more relevant for the success of legal intervention by external actors than the institutional embedding of the tribunal. It also must be mentioned here that the campaign in *the pros. vs. Akayesu* was precisely targeted and orchestrated by international NGOs with the support of well-respected international media, whereas in all other cases attempts to influence trial outcomes lacked focus and precision and were rather directed at the general public than at the prosecution and the judges. The cases of Račak and Srebrenica showed that in the absence of such a targeted campaign, judges tend to remain within the scope of mainstream frames, especially in cases in which a broad public consensus concerning the interpretation of the events under scrutiny has been established beforehand, as was the case with the genocide frame for Srebrenica and the massacre frame for Račak.

It has often been argued that *ad hoc* international criminal tribunals are at odds with the usual principles of carrying out justice in municipal settings because of the explicit and inherent political tasks conferred on them by the UNSC and the states which support them logistically and financially. One of these explicit tasks is the one pertaining to "reconciliation". Both tribunals were, to a different degree, assigned to contribute to the maintenance of peace and stability (in the former Yugoslavia) and explicitly to reconciliation (in Rwanda). Our books' third part tested whether this has influenced the sentencing policy of trial chambers and appeals chambers, and whether it has even led to a politicisation of judgments. We set out to answer how the judges, trial chambers, and appeals chambers translated this task into concrete decisions, and whether references to reconciliation were more likely to make a sentence harsher or milder. A review of the scientific literature on reconciliation served as an initial base to discover several ways in which this concept could be operationalized in judgments. Subsequently, various judgments were reviewed as a means of establishing whether tribunals or trial chambers resorted to coherent concepts of reconciliation, and whether they translated these concepts coherently into specific judgments. This served to answer the overarching question of this section: how the imposition of a political rather than legal task by the UN contributed to the politicisation of the ICTY and the ICTR.

The chapters about the ICTY's and the ICTR's interpretations of reconciliation showed that there never was a consistent approach about what this goal should mean for trial and appeals chambers. Reconciliation was consequently marginalized as an objective of justice and dominated by punishment and retribution. Reconciliation was highlighted in judgments concerning repentant defendants, and in connection with guilty pleas and plea agreements. In those cases, it was mostly (but not without exception) invoked in order to lower the final sentence. Pleading guilty was regarded by most judges as a way of furthering reconciliation, with reconciliation conceptualized as a task for the perpetrator, not the victim. Only very few exceptions pointing to other notions of reconciliation could be found – victim-oriented ones or concepts arguing that a guilty plea should not lead to lower punishment because this would endanger, rather than further, reconciliation. Counter to our expectations, by introducing reconciliation as an additional, political rather than legal goal for the ICTY and the ICTR, the UNSC and the General Assembly did not politicize these tribunals, since the judges largely ignored this task, conceiving retribution, punishment, and carrying out justice as their main objective, no matter what the consequence for reconciliation. Both tribunals have become strongly politicized, though, and there is a large amount of literature on their politics and the policies that the OTP and the tribunals as whole applied in order to achieve their goals. Yet politicisation was not the result of charging the tribunals with the objective of restoring and maintaining peace or contributing to reconciliation. In part because the chambers applied such different and often internally contradictory concepts of reconciliation, this political task did not leave a consistent imprint on the judgments in which it was applied.

When speaking of the mission of the tribunals, judges usually mentioned reconciliation in a context which indicated that they had in mind the aim of foreclosing vengeance and ending impunity, although they hardly ever mentioned vengeance explicitly. But whenever we find reconciliation mentioned in the judgment of a case in which a plea agreement was reached and endorsed by the trial chamber, it has more to do with the acknowledgment of victims who are spared the inconvenience and stress of testifying in court, with truth-telling, understood as setting a good example for other perpetrators, and with speeding up the administration of justice. In other words, reconciliation as a concept changed its content depending on the circumstances in which it was used.

Most trial chambers which based their arguments on reconciliation had a retributive, deterrence- and victims-centred concept in mind. There were only a few exceptions of judges using perpetrator-centred concepts, stressing the need to reintegrate not only victims, but also perpetrators into their community (and therefore opting for milder sentences). Paradoxically, these took place when the defendants had not pleaded guilty beforehand. It is likely, but beyond the scope of our research and empirically very difficult to establish, that these arguments stemmed from a deeper reservation of these judges against the dominant retributive mainstream at both tribunals. In general, judges saw it as their main task to strengthen deterrence by severely punishing those defendants who had been found guilty. Confronted with a dilemma in which severe punishment (mostly described as "proportional to the gravity of the crimes") risked to damage other important interests (tribunal resources, trial expediency, or the potential harm done to victims) they referred to reconciliation in order to justify less severe punishment.

All in all, our study confirms that *ad hoc* international criminal tribunals are important actors in international relations and, although they cannot be regarded as supranational actors, they possess a number of attributes which are specific to supranational institutions. They can act independently from the preferences of the states and international organisations which brought them into being, they can, under favourable circumstances, change state preferences, and they interfere with the sovereign rights of the states for which they were created, which, in our case, means Rwanda and the successor states of the former Yugoslavia. There are also some important differences to supranational institutions. *Ad hoc* international criminal tribunals depend to a large extent on the infrastructure and cooperation of states, they are unable to control them (though they can successfully lure them into "rhetorical action" and "joint decision traps"), and they do not help them to overcome collective action dilemmas and delegation problems. Just like other international organisations, however, they tend to develop strong institutional interests that influence their policies, but may also prevent them from applying explicitly political tasks conferred on them by their founders. We demonstrated this reluctance in our analysis of the role of reconciliation in judging and sentencing. Due to their almost elite status, the lack of embeddedness and hierarchy (as compared to municipal courts), and the prestige emanating from the status of international judges, individual judges and trial chambers at *ad hoc* international criminal tribunals enjoy enormous autonomy. They can issue verdicts that run contrary to any conventional wisdom and to the mainstream in politics and media (as was shown in *the pros. vs. Bagosora et al.*), and they even can use their prestige and autonomy to influence public opinion by establishing precise and powerful frames in public discourse, like the ICTY did when conducting *Rule 61* hearings after the fall of Srebrenica. However, the lack of embeddedness also makes judges at international criminal courts more vulnerable to external influence and targeted lobbying by international stakeholders, who can circumvent costly and time-consuming access points at the national level and directly approach the judges, thus creating outcomes which they can use to further their goals on the national level. *The pros. vs. Akayesu* provides a stunning example of such top-down lobbying. However, when widely accepted frames are already pre-existent and no "voice" lobbying is present, judges tend to stay within the boundaries of the mainstream narratives and offer interpretations of past events which vary from, but do not challenge existing frames. We showed this in *the pros. vs.*

Krstić and *the pros. vs. Djordjević*. In a few summarizing words: *Ad hoc* international criminal tribunals are more than just instruments of justice; they are important players on the international scene, which inclines (and sometimes even forces) them to engage in power politics, political games, and bargaining with states, and politicized their external actions. At the same time, their judges enjoy much more leeway and autonomy than municipal judges could ever dream of, but this exposes them to specific external influences from which municipal judges are sheltered. International judges are therefore not more or less independent than municipal ones – they are independent in a different way, which creates specific dangers and challenges, but also opportunities for what they usually call "the interest of justice".

Literature, Sources, and Databases

Information about the interviews

Klaus Bachmann and Thomas Sparrow-Botero conducted a number of interviews, whose content is quoted in this book. All interviews were treated as primary historical sources, whose purpose it was to elucidate events which could not be sufficiently explained by documentary analysis. It was our aim to use the interviews as additional source material that would help us to understand better the written documents, to provide further insights, and to develop interpretations that were not obvious from the analysis of other sources. All interviews were used for qualitative rather than quantitative analysis and were therefore conducted by using oral history methods rather than social science methodology. Most of the interviews were carried out as semi-structured interviews, during which the interviewer uses a list of topics and questions which he allows (and inclines) the interviewee to elaborate on freely. No coding method was used; the content was either written down by the interviewer or recorded. Except in interviews conducted online (by using e-mail), all interviewees had the opportunity to authorize their quotes in the respective context. None authorized interview are marked with *. In some cases, respondents forgot to authorize their quotes or we lost contact with them. None of our interviewees at the ICTR in Arusha and none of our contacts in Kigali ever requested autorisation. These cases are also marked with *.

All interviews in 2011 were conducted by Thomas Sparrow-Botero, all interviews in 2012 were carried out by Klaus Bachmann. All were carried out in English, except the one with André Guichaua and with Jean-Pierre Dusingizemungu, which were conducted in French, and the ones with Judge Flügge and Serge Brammertz, which were conducted in German.

- Frederick Swinnen, Special Advisor to the ICTY Prosecutor, The Hague (interviewed face-to-face by Thomas Sparrow-Botero in 2011 and by Klaus Bachmann in May 2012, both times at the ICTY).
- Geraldine Mattioli-Zeltner, International Justice Advocacy Director at Human Rights Watch, Brussels (phone interview by Thomas Sparrow-Botero in April 2011).
- Aleksandar Fatić, Director of the Centre for Security Studies, Belgrade. (interviewed by e-mail by Thomas Sparrow-Botero in April 2011).
- Jelena Obradovic-Wochnik, author of Ethnic Conflict and War Crimes in the Balkans: the Narratives of Denial in Post-conflict Serbia (IB

Tauris, 2009), and lecturer at Aston University, Birmingham, UK (interviewed by e-mail by Thomas Sparrow-Botero in May 2011).

- Refik Hodzić, responsible for the ICTY outreach program in Bosnia and Herzegovina, now at the ICTJ in New York (interviewed face-to-face by Klaus Bachmann in April 2012 in New York).*
- Richard Dicker, International Justice Program of HRW in London during the Milošević Trial, now at HRW in New York (interviewed face-to-face in April 2012 by Klaus Bachmann in New York).*
- Filip Reyntjens, professor at the University of Antwerp, expert witness in (amongst others) the Bagosora Trial at the ICTR (interviewed face-to-face by Klaus Bachmann in Antwerp in April 2012).
- Judge Christoph Flügge, trial chamber judge at *the pros. vs. Tolimir*, *the pros. vs. Mladić*, *the pros. vs. Dordjević* (interviewed face-to-face in May 2012 by Klaus Bachmann in The Hague).
- Nerma Jelačić, spokeswoman for the ICTY (interviewed face-to-face by Klaus Bachmann in May 2012 in The Hague).
- Serge Brammertz, chief prosecutor of the ICTY (interviewed face-to-face by Klaus Bachmann in May 2012 in The Hague).
- André Guichaoua, sociologist, professor at Université Paris 1 and expert witness at the ICTY in *the pros. vs. Bagosora et al.* (interviewed face-to-face by Klaus Bachmann in May 2012 in Paris).
- Gabrielle Kirk McDonald, former president of the ICTY (interviewed via telephone by Klaus Bachmann in June 2012).
- Param-Preet Singh, International Justice Program of HRW in London during the Milošević Trial, now at HRW in New York (interviewed face-to-face in April 2012 by Klaus Bachmann in New York).
- Novak M. Lukić, defence counsellor in *the pros. vs. Mrkšić et al.* as Mr. Šljivančanin's lawyer (interviewed face-to-face in June 2012 by Klaus Bachmann in Belgrade)*
- Slobodan M. Zečević, president of the Association of Defence Counsel Practising Before the ICTY and defence counsellor for Miroslav Djeronić (*the pros. vs. Djeronić*), Milan Simić (*the pros. vs. M. Simić*), Milan Milutinović (*the pros. vs. Milutinović et al.*), and Jovica Stanišić (*the pros. vs. Stanišić and Simatović*) (interviewed face-to-face in June 2012 by Klaus Bachmann in Belgrade).*
- Confidential interview by Klaus Bachmann with one of Zoran Djidnjić's security advisors, Belgrade 2009. *
- Interview by Klaus Bachmann with Innocent Kamenzi, outreach officer, ICTR Kigali, in July 2012.*

- Interview by Klaus Bachmann with Jean-Pierre Dusingizemungu, president of *Ibuka* (genocide survivors' umbrella organisation), Kigali, July 2012.*
- Interview by Klaus Bachmann with Polycarpe Ntagwabira, *Ibuka* Kigali, May 2012.*
- Interview by Klaus Bachmann with Danford Mpumilwa, assistant information officer ICTR, Arusha, in July 2012.*
- Interview by Klaus Bachmann with Anees Ahmed, senior legal officer (chief of chambers), ICTR, Arusha, in July 2012.*
- Interview by Klaus Bachmann with Judge Vagn Joensen, ICTR president, ICTR, Arusha, in July 2012.*
- Interview by Klaus Bachmann with Hassan Bubacar Jallow, chief prosecutor of the ICTR, Arusha, in July 2012.*
- Interview by Klaus Bachmann with Claver Sindayigaya, defense counselor in *the pros. vs. Ngirabatware*, Arusha, in July 2012.*

Databases and Electronic Archives

- The New York Times (US) www.nytimes.com
- Le Monde (French) www.monde.fr
- Der Spiegel (German) www.spiegel.de
- El Pais (Spanish) www.elpais.com
- Vjesnik (Croatia) www.wjesnik.com
- Nacional (Croatia) www.nacional.com
- Oslobodjenje (Bosnia and Herzegovina) www.oslobodjenje.ba
- Danas (Serbia) www.danas.rs
- Politika (Serbia) www.politika.rs
- The Washington Post (US) www.washingtonpost.com
- Time Magazine (US) www.time.com
- The ICTY www.un.org/icty
- The ICTR www.ictr.org
- Human Rights Watch www.hrw.org
- Amnesty International www.ai.org
- Médecins Sans Frontières www.msf.org
- The Organisation for Security and Co-operation in Europe www.osce.org
- The African Union www.africa-union.org
- The United Nations www.un.org
- The European Union www.europa.eu
- The Guardian (UK) www.guardian.com
- EurActiv www.euractive.com

- The British Broadcasting Corporation www.bbc.com
- The Economist (UK) www.economist.com
- The Hague Justice Portal www.haguejusticeportal.n
- Hirondelle Agency, Switzerland www.hironedellenews.org
- The Independent (UK) www.independent.com
- De Morgen (Belgium) www.morgen.be
- Le Soir (Belgium) www.lesoir.be
- The New Times (Rwanda) www.newtimes.co.rw
- Gazeta Wyborcza (Poland) www.gazeta.pl
- The Sense Agency (The Netherlands) www.sense-agency.com
- Foundation Hirondelle (Tanzania) www.hirondelle.org
- Trial Watch (Switzerland) www.trial-ch.org

Bibliography

Abramovsky, Abraham: Juror Safety: The Presumption of Innocence and Meaningful Voir Dire in Federal Criminal Prosecutions – Are They Endangered Species? *Fordham Law Review* vol 50 issue 1 (1981). http://ir.lawnet.fordham.edu/cgi/viewcontent.cgi?article=2501&context=flr&sei-redir=1#search=%22media%20presumption%20innocence%22

Akhavan, P: Justice and Reconciliation in the Great Lakes Region of Africa: The Contribution of the ICTR, in: *Duke Journal of Comparative and International Law*, 325, 7 (1997).

Álvarez, Michael and Hall, Thad. Controlling Democracy: The Principal-Agent Problems in Election Administration. *The Policy Studies Journal*, Vol. 34, No. 4., 2006.

Anzenbacher, Arno: Einführung in die Philosophie, 8th ed., Freiburg-Basel-Vienna, 2002.

Appadurai, Arjun: Fear of small numbers. An Essay on the Geography of Anger. Duke University Press 2006.

Arbour, Louise: The Chief Prosecutor's dual role. *Journal of International Criminal Justice* 2 (2004).

Arendt, Hanna: The Human Condition, 1958 (re-edited in 1998 by University of Chicago Press).

Aronowitz, Stanley: The Ignored Philosopher and Social Theorist. The Work of Henri Lefebvre. In: *Situations*, vol. 2, 1, 2007.

Assmann, Alaida: Erinnerungsräume. Formen und Wandlungen des kulturellen Gedächtnisses, 3d ed., Munich: C.H. Beck, 2006.

Bachmann, Klaus: Frontex and transborder governance in the EU. *The Review of International Affairs*, vol. LIX, No 1132, October – December 2008 Belgrade.

Bachmann, Klaus: Measuring reconciliation after violent ethnic conflicts. *The Review of International Affairs,* vol. LIX, No 1130-1131, April – September 2008.

Bagarić, Mirko; Morss, John: International Sentencing Law: In Search of a Justification and Coherent Framework. *International Criminal Law Review* 6, 2006.

Baldwin, David Allen: Neorealizm and neoliberalizm. The contemporary debate. Columbia University Press 1993.

Bass, Gary Jonathan: Stay the Hand of Vengeance. The Politics of War Crimes Tribunals. Princeton and Oxford 2002.

Batt, Judy; Obradović-Wochnik, Jelena (eds): War Crimes, Conditionality and EU Integration in the Western Balkans. Paris: Institute for Security Studies, June 2009.

Bauer, M.; Knill, C.; Pitschel, D.: Differential Europeanisation in Eastern Europe: The Impact of Diverse EU Regulatory Governance Patterns. *Journal of European Integration* 29, 2007.

Bellamy, Alex J.: The Formation of Croatian National Identity. A Centuries Old Dream. Manchester University Press 2003.

Bendor, Jonathan; Glazer, Andrew and Hammond, Theodore: Theories of Delegation. *Annual Review of Political Science*. Vol. 4 (2001).

Beyers, Jan: Voice and Access. Political Practices of European Interest Associations. *European Union Politics*, June 2004 vol. 5 no. 2.

Bloomfield, David; Barnes, Teresa; Huyse, Luc: Reconciliation After Violent Conflict. A Handbook (International Idea: Handbook Series) 2003.

Börzel, Tanja and Risse, Thomas: When Europe Hits Home: Europeanisation and Domestic Change. *European Integration Online Papers*. Vol.4, Nr. 15. (2000). http://eiop.or.at/eiop/texte/2000-015a.htm.

Bourdieu, Pierre: The social space and the genesis of groups, in: *Theory and Society* 14, 6 (1985), 723.

Brounéus, Karen: *Rethinking reconciliation: Concepts, methods, and an empirical study of truth telling and psychological health in Rwanda* (PhD). Uppsala University, Uppsala, Sweden.

Buckley-Zistel, Susanne: Dividing and Uniting: The Use of Citizenship Discourses in Conflict and Reconciliation in Rwanda, in: *Global Society*, Vol. 20, No. 1, January, 2006.

Cerone, John: Dynamic Equilibrium. The Evolution of US Attitudes Toward International Criminal Courts and Tribunals. *The European Journal of International Law*. Vol. 18, Nr. 2, (2007). http://ejil.oxfordjournals.org/content/18/2/277.full.pdf+html.

Clark, Janine Natalya: Plea Bargaining at the ICTY: Guilty Pleas and Reconciliation. *The European Journal of International Law* Vol. 20 no. 2.

Clark, Phil; Kaufman, Zachary D. (eds): After Genocide. Transitional Justice, Post-Conflict Reconstruction and Reconciliation in Rwanda and Beyond. London: Hurst & Co. 2008.

Combs, Nancy Armoury: Fact-finding without facts. The Uncertain Evidentiary Foundations of International Criminal Convictions, Cambridge University Press 2010.

Coppieters, Bruno; Emerson, Michael; Huysseune, Michel; Kovziridze, Tamara; Noutcheva, Gergana; Tocci, Nathalie and Vahl, Marius: Europeanisation and Conflict Resolution: Case Studies from the European Periphery. Special Issue of the *Journal of Ethnopolitics and Minority Issues in Europe* 1/2004.

Crocker, Chester A.: The Lessons of Somalia: Not Everything Went Wrong. *Foreign Affairs* May/June 1995.

Daalder, Ivo H.; O'Hanlon, Michael O.: Winning ugly. NATO's War to Save Kosovo. Washington D. C.: Brookings Institution 2000.

Dallaire, R. A.: Shake Hands With The Devil: The Failure of Humanity in Rwanda, London, Arrow Books, 2004.

De Bardeleben, J. (ed): The Boundaries of EU Enlargement. Finding a place for neighbors, Houndsmill, Basingstoke: Palgrave MacMillan 2008.

Del Ponte, Carla: Madame Prosecutor. Confrontations with Humanity's Worst Criminals and the Culture of Impunity. Milan: Feltrinelli 2008.

Des Forges, Alison: Kein Zeuge darf überleben. Der Genozid in Ruanda. Hamburg 2002.

Dimitrova, A. and Dragneva, R.: Constraining external governance: interdependence with Russia and the CIS as limits to the EU's rule transfer in the Ukraine. *Journal of European Public Policy,* 16(6) 2007.

Donohue, William R.; Rogan, Randall G.; Kaufman, Sandra (eds): Framing matters. Perspectives on Negotiation Research and Practice in Communication. New York, Washington, Baltimore, Bern, Frankfurt, Berlin Brussels, Vienna Oxford 2011.

Donsbach, Wolfgang; Traugott, Michael W. (ed): The Sage Handbook of Public Opinion Research 2008.

Du Bois-Pedain, Antje: Transitional Amnesty in South Africa. Cambridge University Press 2007.

Ellis, Stephen: Tuning in to Pavement Radio. *African Affairs* 88 (352), 1989.

Elster, Jon: Deliberative Democracy. New York: Cambridge University Press 1998.

Emerson M., Noutcheva G.: Europeanisation as a Gravity Model of Democratisation, *CEPS Working Document* N 214, November 2004.

Engle, Karen: Feminism and Its (Dis)contents: Criminalizing Wartime Rape in Bosnia and Herzegovina, *The American Journal of International Law,* Vol. 99, No. 4. (Oct., 2005).

Entman, R. M.: Cascading Activation. Contesting the White House's frame after 9/11. *Political Communication*, 20, 2003.

Feinberg, Gary: The International Criminal Tribunal for the Former Yugoslavia: The Establishment and Evaluation of a Unique Concept in International Justice Administration. War Crimes, Genocide & Crimes against Humanity. Volume 2 (2006).

Feldman, Lily Gardner: The Principle and Practice of 'Reconciliation' in German Foreign Policy: Relations with France, Israel, Poland and the Greek Republic. *International Affairs*, vol. 75, no. 2, 1999.

Fitzsimmons, Daniel: Following The Leader: The Impact of the Mass Media on American Foreign Policy in Somalia, Rwanda, and Kosovo.*Conference Papers -- International Studies Association*, 2007 Annual Meeting.

Foucault, Michel: Die Ordnung des Diskurses 1970. http://archive.org/stream/FoucaultDieOrdnungDesDiskurses#page/n0/mode/2up

von Förster, Heinz; von Glaserfeld, Ernst and Hejl, Peter M. (eds.): Einführung in den Konstruktivismus, 10th ed., Munich 2008.

Galtung, John: After Violence, Reconstruction, Reconciliation, and Resolution: Coping with Visible and Invisible Effects. In: Abu-Nimer, Mohammed (ed.): Reconciliation, Justice, and Coexistence: Theory and Practice, Maryland 2001.

Gourevitch, Philip: We wish to inform you that tomorrow we will be killed with our families. Stories from Rwanda. London, Basingstoke and Oxford 2000.

Gow, James: The Serbian Project and Its Adversaries. A Strategy of War Crimes. London: Hurst and Company 2003.

Gstöhl, S.: A Neighbourhood Economic Community: Finalité Économique for the ENP? *EU Diplomacy Papers,* no. 3. 2008.

Guichaoua, André: Les Crises Politiques au Burundi et au Rwanda. Lille: Diffusion Karthala 1995.

Guichaoua, André: Rwanda 1994: les politiques du génocide à Butare. Paris: Karthala 2005.

Guild, E., Khasson, V. and Mir, M.: State of the Art. The Nexus between European Neighbourhood Policy and Justice and Home Affairs, *CASE Reports* No. 73/2007.

Gwiazda, Anna: Europeanisation in Candidate Countries from Central and Eastern Europe. Paper prepared for the EPIC workshop in Florence, EUI, 19-22 September 2002.http://aei.pitt.edu/737/.

Habermas, Jürgen: Strukturwandel der Öffentlichkeit. Frankfurt/Main 1961.

Habermas, Jürgen: Theorie des kommunikativen Handelns. Frankfurt am Main 1981.

Hagan, John: The Political Economy of Genocide Intervention: Structural Conditionality, Collective Command Responsibility, and The Former Yugoslavia. *3rd Annual Conference on Empirical Legal Studies Papers* May 2008. http://ssrn.com/abstract=1132583.

Hagan, John: Justice in the Balkans. Prosecuting War Crimes in The Hague Tribunal. University of Chicago Press. 2003.

Hamber, Brandon; Kelly, Gráinne: A Working Definition of Reconciliation, *Democratic Dialogue*, September 2004, 1-11. http://cain.ulst.ac.uk/dd/papers/dd04recondef.pdf

Hamber, Brandon; van der Merwe, Hugo: What Is This Thing Called Reconciliation?, Paper presented at the Goedgedacht Forum, Cape Town, 1998.

Haukkala, H.: A Hole in the Wall? Dimensionalism and the EU's New Neighbourhood Policy. *UPI Working Papers*: 41, 2003.

Hayes, Peter; Diefendorf, Jeffry M.: Lessons and Legacies: New currents in Holocaust research. Northwestern University Press 2004.

Hayner, Priscilla: Unspeakable Truth: Confronting State Terror and Atrocity. New York: Routledge 2001 (and 2011 for the second edition)

Hazan, Pierre: Justice in a Time of War. The True Story Behind the International Criminal Tribunal for the Former Yugoslavia. Texas A&M University Press 2004.

Hazan, Pierre: Measuring the impact of punishment and forgiveness: a framework for evaluating transitional justice. *International Review of the Red Cross*, 88, 861, March 2006.

Hola, Barbora; Smeulers, Alette; Bijleveld, Catrien: Is ICTY Sentencing Predictable? An Empirical Analysis of ICTY Sentencing Practice. *Leiden Journal of International Law,* 22 (2009).

Howell K.: Developing Conceptualisations of Europeanisation: Synthesising Methodological Approaches, *Queen's Paper on Europeanisation*, nr 3/2004.

Howell, Kerry: Developing Conceptualisations of Europeanisation and European Integration: Mixing Methodologies. http://aei.pitt.edu/1720/.

Human Rights Watch: Under Orders. War Crimes in Kosovo. New York, Washington, London, Brussels 2001.

Huntington, Samuel: The Third Wave of Democratisation in the late Twentieth Century. University of Oklahoma Press 1992.

Idem-Abdullahi An-Na'im (ed.): The Politics of Memory: Truth, Healing and Social Justice, London: Zed Books, 2000.

Ivanković, Nenad: Što smo mu učinili. Zagreb 2011.

Jacoby, Susan: Wild Justice: The Evolution of Revenge, London, 1983.

Joksimovich, Vojin: Kosovo Crisis. A Study in Foreign Policy Mismanagement. Los Angeles: Graphics Management Press 1999.

Jovanović, Igor: Promising Mladić. *Center for South Eastern Studies Country Analyses* 4/2006 http://www.csees.net/?page=country_analyses&country_id=9&ca_id=3078.

Kaju Brandner, Anne: Justice & Reconciliation in Rwanda: An evaluation of judicial responses to genocide and mass atrocities, London, Ontario, 2003 (MA thesis: *The University of Western Ontario*).

Kamatali, Jean-Marie: The Challenge of Linking International Criminal Justice to National Reconciliation: the Case of the ICTR. *Leiden Journal of International Law*, 16 (2003).

Kavalski, Emilian: Extending the European Security Community. Constructing Peace in the Balkans. London: Tauris Academic Studies 2008.

Kelley, J.G.: New Wine in Old Wine Skins: Policy Adaptation in the European Neighbourhood Policy. *Journal of Common Market Studies, 44(1) 2006*,29-55.

Keren, Gideon (ed): Perspectives on Framing. New York and Hove 2011.

Kirk MacDonald, Gabrielle: Problems, obstacles and achievements of the ICTY. *Journal of International Criminal Justice* 2 (2004).

Knill, C. and Tosun, J.: Hierarchy, networks, or markets: how does the EU shape environmental policy adoptions within and beyond its borders? *Journal of European Public Policy*, 16, 2009.

Lapid, Yosef: The third debate. On the prospects of International Theory in a post-positivist era. *International Studies Quarterly* 1989, vol. 33.

Laughland, John: Travesty. The Trial of Slobodan Milosevi Milošević and the Corruption of International Justice. London, Ann Arbour: Pluto Press 2007.

Lederach, John Paul: Building Peace: Sustainable Reconciliation in Divided Societies, Washington D.C.: United State Institute of Peace, 1997.

Lefèvre, Patrick and Jean-Noël: Les militaires belges et le Ruanda 1916-2006. Tielt: Lannoo Uitgeverij 2006.

Long, William J.; Brecke, Peter: War and Reconciliation: Reason and Emotion in Conflict Resolution, Cambridge, Mass., 2003.

Mackenzie, Ruth; Malleson, Kate; Martin, Penny and Sands, Philippe: Selecting International Judges. Principles, Process, and Politics. Oxford University Press 2010.

Maskin, Eric; Tirole, Jean: The Principal-Agent Relationship with an Informed Principal: The Case of Private Values. *Econometrica*, Vol. 58, No. 2, 1990.

Mendell, Margarite: Empowerment. From Noise to Voice. *Universitas Forum*, Vol. 2, No. 1, September 2010. http://www.universitasforum.org/index.php/ojs/article/view/50/194

Merritt, Anna and Richard (eds): Public Opinion in occupied Germany. The OMGUS surveys 1945-49. Urbana, Chicago, London 1970.

Merritt, Anna and Richard (eds): Public Opinion In semi-sovereign Germany. The HICOG surveys 1949-1955. Urbana, Chicago, London 1980.

Moghalu, K. C.: Rwanda's Genocide: The Politics of Global Justice, New York, Palgrave Macmillan, 2005.

Mohammed Abu-Nimer (ed.): Reconciliation, Justice, and Coexistence: Theory and Practice, Maryland, 2001.

Moravcsik, Andrew: The Origins of Human Rights Regimes: Democratic Delegation in Postwar Europe *International Organization*, Vol. 54, No. 2 (Spring, 2000).

Moravcsik, Andrew: A New Statecraft? Supranational Entrepreneurs and International Cooperation. *International Organization* 53 (2), 1999.

Nadler, Arie; Malloy, T.; Fisher, J. D. (eds.): The Social Psychology of Intergroup Reconciliation, New York: Oxford University Press, 2006.

Nagin, D. S.: Deterrence: Legal aspects, in: *International Encyclopaedia of the Social and Behavioural Sciences*, 3544-3550.

Nalepa, Monika: Skeletons in the Closet. Transitional Justice in Post-Communist Europe. Cambridge University Press 2010.

Nettlefield, Sara: Courting Democracy in Bosnia and Herzegovina: The Hague Tribunal's Impact in a Postwar State (Cambridge Studies in Law and Society), Cambridge University Press 2010.

Noelle-Neumann, Elisabeth: Die Schweigespirale. Öffentliche Meinung – unsere soziale Haut. Langen Müller, München 1980.

Noelle, Elisabeth; Neumann, Erich Peter: Jahrbuch der öffentlichen Meinung 1947–1955. Allensbach 1956.

Nora, Pierre: Les lieux de mémoire, Paris M Gallimard 1997 (3 vol.).

Norrie, A: Punishment, Responsibility and Justice: A Relational Critique, Oxford, 2000.

Olsen, Johan P.: The many faces of Europeanisation. Journal of Common Market Studies Journal of Common Market Studies, december 2002, vol. 40, issue 5, 921–952. http://onlinelibrary.wiley.com/doi/10.1111/1468-5965.00403/pdf

Pantev, Plamen: The 'Europeanisation' of National Foreign, Security and Defense Policy. *Institute for Security and International Studies Research Reports*. (Sofia, November 2005). http://www.isis-bg.org/Publications/research_reports/RR18.pdf.

Paradelle, Murielle; Dumont, Hélène; Boisvert, Anne-Marie: Quelle justice pour quelle réconciliation? Le tribunal pénal international pour le Rwanda et le jugement du génocide. *McGill Law Journal* 50 (2005).

Peskin, Victor: International Justice in Rwanda and the Balkans. Virtual Trials and the Struggle for State Cooperation. Cambridge University Press 2008.

Peterson, Shannon: Stories and past lessons: Understanding United States decisions of armed humanitarian intervention and non-intervention in the post-cold war era (Somalia, Rwanda, Bosnia and Herzegovina. [Dissertation]. Ohio State University 2003. http://etd.ohiolink.edu/send-pdf.cgi?osu1047933325.

Pond, Elisabeth: Endgame in the Balkans: Regime Change European Style. Washington, D. C.: Brookings Institution, 2006.

Posner, Richard A.: How Judges think. First Havard University Press 2008.

Power, Samantha: A Problem from Hell. America and the Age of Genocide. London, New York, Toronto, Sidney 2003.

Radaelli, Claudio M.: Whither Europeanisation? Concept Stretching and Substantive Change. *European Integration Online Papers*. Vol. 4, Nr. 8, (2000). http://eiop.or.at/eiop/texte/2000-008a.htm.

Reychler, Luc; Paffenholz, Thania: Peace-Building: A Field Guide. Columbia: Boulder 2001.

Reyntjens, Filip: Ruling under a volcano. Political governance in post-genocide Rwanda (upcoming).

Rigby, Andrew: Justice and Reconciliation after the Violence, Boulder-London, 2001.

Robinson, Piers: The CNN effect. The Myth of News, Foreign Policy and Intervention. Routledge 2002.

Sachs, A.: Truth and Reconciliation, in: McGregor, L.: Individual accountability in South Africa: Cultural Optimum or Political Façade? *American Journal of International Law* 95 (2001).

Scharf, Michael P.: "Trading Justice for Efficiency. Plea bargaining and International Tribunals." *The Journal of International Criminal Justice* 2 (4) 2004.

Schimmelpfennig, Frank: The Community Trap: Liberal Norms, Rhetorical Action, and theEastern Enlargement of the European Union. *International Organization* 55, 1, 2001.

Silber, Laura; Little, Allen: The Death of Yugoslavia. London: BBC Books and Penguin 1996, 353-363 and Goldstein, Ivo: Hrvatska 1918-2008. Zagreb: Liber 2008.

Silbey, S. S.: Legal Culture and Legal Consciousness, in: International Encyclopaedia for the Social and Behavioural Sciences, 8623-8629.

Simić, Ilija: Istina o Račku, Beograd 2006.

Simon, J.: Punishment: Social and Legal Aspects, in: International Encyclopaedia of the Social and Behavioural Sciences, 12606 – 12612.

Smith, Karen E.: Genocide and the Europeans. Cambridge University Press 2010, 128-129.

Srebrenica, rapport sur un massacre. Tom 1, rapport et annexes, Tom 2: Auditions. Les documents d'information de l'Assemblée Nationale N3413 2001.

Subotić, Jelena: Explaining Difficult States. The Problems of Europeanisation in Serbia. *East European Politics and Societies*. May 11, vol. 4, 2010, 595-616.

Subotić, Jelena: Hijacked Justice. Dealing With the Past in the Balkans. Cornell University Press. 2009, 94.

Swart, Bert; Zahar, Alexander; Sluiter, Göran: The Legacy of the International Criminal Tribunal for the Former Yugoslavia. OUP 2011.

Tsebelis, George: Veto players. How political institutions work. Princeton University Press, New Jersey 2002.

Van den Berg, Dion: Rekindling the National Debate: How Public and Private Recognition Can Shift the Dutch Discourse on Srebrenica. Opening address at the "Transforming Images of the Enemy" seminar in Utrecht, theNetherlands on Oct. 8.9.2009, p. 2. It can be retrieved from http://www.scribd.com/doc/57273277/Rekindling-the-National-Debate

Van der Merwe: The Truth and Reconciliation Commission and Community Reconciliation: An Analysis of Competing Strategies and Conceptualisations (Diss. George Madison University 1999), available at http://www.csvr.org.za/wits/papers/paphd2.htm.

Van Schaack, Beth:_Engendering Genocide: The *Akayesu* Case Before the International Criminal Tribunal for Rwanda. *Santa Clara University School of Law Legal Studies Research Papers Series. Working Paper* No. 08-55, July 2008 (Revised 9.11.2008), 9-11. http://papers.ssrn.com/sol3/papers.cfm?abstract_id=1154259

Verdirame, Guclielmo: The Genocide Definition in the Jurisprudence of the *ad hoc* tribunals. *International and Comparative Law Quarterly*, vol. 49, July 2000.

Verdoolaege, Annelies: Reconciliation Discourse. The case of the Truth and Reconciliation Commission, Amsterdam-Philadelphia, 2008 (Discourse Approaches to Politics, Society and Culture – DAPSAC, 27).

Verfuss, Thomas: Trying Poor Countries' Crimes in a Rich City. The Problems of the Press from the Former Yugoslavia, *Journal of International Criminal Justice* 2004.

Waterman, Richard and Meier, Kenneth: Principal-Agent Models: An Expansion? *Journal of Public Administration Research and Theory*. vol. 8, no. 2, 1998.

Waters, Timothy (ed): The Milošević Trial. An Autopsy. Oxford University Press (upcoming) 2013.

Welzer, Harald: Täter. Wie aus ganz normalen Menschen Massenmörder werden, Frankfurt am M., 2007.

Wendt, Alexander: On constitution and causation in International Relations. *Review of International Studies*, 24 (1998).

Wilcoxson, Andy: No evidence for "Srebrenica Genocide" Verdict. The Balkan Monitor 12.4.2011. http://www.balkanstudies.org/articles/no-evidence-srebrenica-genocide-verdict.

Wilson, Richard Ashby: Writing History in International Criminal Trials. Cambridge University Press 2011.

Wolfgram, Mark A.: Democracy and Propaganda: NATO's War in Kosovo. *European Journal of Communication*, June 2008 vol. 23 no. 2.

Young, Oran P.: Political Leadership and Regime Formation: On the Development of Institutions in International Society. *International Organization* 45 (3), 1991.

List of Abbreviations

AI	Amnesty International
ARBiH	Army of the Republic of Bosnia and Herzegovina (*Armija Republike Bosne i Hercegovine*)
BBC	British Broadcasting Corporation
BiH	Bosnia and Herzegovina
CDA	Critical Discourse Analysis
CIA	Central Intelligence Agency
CNN	Cable News Network
CWHRCS	Coalition for Women's Human Rights in Conflict Situations
DPA	Dayton Peace Agreement
DS	Democratic Party (*Demokratska Stranka*)
DSS	Democratic Party of Serbia
EC	European Commission
EIOP	European Integration Online Papers
EMGS	European Masters in Global Studies
ENP	European Neighborhood Policy
EU	European Union
EUI	European Union Institute
EULEX	European Union Rule of Law Mission, Kosovo
FAR	Rwandan Armed Forces (*Forces Armées du Rwanda*)
FPR	(see: RPF)
FRY	Federal Republic of Yugoslavia
HDZ	Croatian Democratic Union (*Hrvatska Demokratska Zajednica)*
HRW	Human Rights Watch
HSLS	Croatian Social Liberal Party (*Hrvatska Socijalno-Liberalna Stranka*)
HRVC	Human Rights Violations Committee (of the South African Truth and Reconciliation Commission)
HVO	Croatian Defence Council (*Hrvatsko vijeće obrane*)
ICJ	International Court of Justice
KLA	Kosovo Liberation Army (*Ushtria Çilimtare e Kosovës*, UÇK)
KVM	Kosovo Verification Mission
JCE	Joint Criminal Enterprise
ICC	International Criminal Court
ICJ	International Court of Justice
IDEA	Institute for Democracy and Electoral Assistance
IDP	Internally displaced person
ICTY	International Criminal Tribunal for the Former Yugoslavia
ICTR	International Criminal Tribunal for Rwanda
IWPR	Institute for War and Peace Reporting
JNA	Yugoslav People's Army (*Jugoslavenska Narodna Armija)*
KVM	Kosovo Verification Mission
LDP	Liberal Democratic Party (*Liberalno Demokratska Partija)*

MRND	*National Republican Movement for Democracy and Development (Mouvement RépublicainNational pour laDémocratie* et le *Développement*)
NATO	North Atlantic Treaty Organisation
NGO	Non-governmental organisation
NIOD	Nederlands Instituut for Oorlogsdocumentatie
OAU	Organisation of African Unity
OSCE	Organisation of Security and Cooperation in Europe
OTP	Office of the Prosecutor
RPF	Rwandan Patriotic Front
SAA	Stabilisation and Association Agreement
SACEUR	Supreme Allied Commander Europe
SAP	Stabilisation and Association Process
SDS	Serbian Democratic Party *(Srpska Demokratska Stranka)*
SFOR	Stabilisation Force in Bosnia and Herzegovina
TRC	Truth and Reconciliation Commission
UÇK	Army for the Liberation of Kosovo (*Ushtria Çlirimtare e Kosovës*)
UK	United Kingdom
UN	United Nations
UNAMIR	United Nations Assistance Mission for Rwanda
UNPROFOR	United Nations Protection Force
UNSC	United Nations Security Council
US	United States
USA	United States of America
VJ	Army of Yugoslavia *(Vojska Yugoslavije)*
VRS	Bosnian Serb military *(Vojska Republike Srpske)*

Index of Names

(Includes only names, which show up in the main text, excluding case labels)

Studies in Political Transition

Herausgegeben von Klaus Bachmann

Band 1 Klaus Bachmann: Vergeltung, Strafe Amnestie. Eine vergleichende Studie zu Kollaboration und ihrer Aufarbeitung in Belgien, Polen und den Niederlanden. 2011.

Band 2 Klaus Bachmann / Thomas Sparrow-Botero / Peter Lambertz: When Justice Meets Politics. Independence and Autonomy of *Ad Hoc* International Criminal Tribunals. 2013.

www.peterlang.de

www.ingramcontent.com/pod-product-compliance
Ingram Content Group UK Ltd.
Pitfield, Milton Keynes, MK11 3LW, UK
UKHW021830100926
8556IPUK00004B/264

9 783631 633564